TEMPLAR SANCTUARIES IN NORTH AMERICA

"In this meticulously researched book William Mann demonstrates how that most peculiar and fascinating medieval institution, the Knights Templar, transported treasures from the Old World to the safety of North America. *Templar Sanctuaries in North America* is not only fascinating and illuminating, but typical of William Mann, it is also a thumping good read. As long as I continue to delve into the secret history of the United States, this book will never be far from my hand."

ALAN BUTLER, COAUTHOR *AMERICA: NATION OF THE GODDESS*

"If you would like to know the shocking truth about the long suppressed history of North America, read *Templar Sanctuaries in North America*. You will read that the truth is far more fantastic than fiction, as Mann convincingly relates how the medieval Templars brought their precious relics, scrolls, and treasure for safe keeping to this continent and intermarried with the Native Americans, thus strengthening the bloodline and ensuring the continuation of its guardians. Is now the time, when humanity is at a great crossroad both politically and in our treatment of Mother Earth, to reveal the repository to the world with all its truths and wisdom of the Ages?"

JANET WOLTER, COAUTHOR OF *AMERICA: NATION OF THE GODDESS*

TEMPLAR SANCTUARIES IN NORTH AMERICA

Sacred Bloodlines and Secret Treasures

WILLIAM F. MANN

Destiny Books
Rochester, Vermont • Toronto, Canada

Destiny Books
One Park Street
Rochester, Vermont 05767
www.DestinyBooks.com

Text stock is SFI certified

Destiny Books is a division of Inner Traditions International

Library of Congress Cataloging-in-Publication Data

Names: Mann, William F., 1954-

Title: Templar sanctuaries in North America : sacred bloodlines and secret treasures / William F. Mann.

Description: Rochester, Vermont : Destiny Books, 2016. | Includes bibliographical references and index.

Identifiers: LCCN 2015040885 (print) | LCCN 2016005184 (e-book) | ISBN 9781620555279 (paperback) | ISBN 9781620555286 (e-book) |

Subjects: LCSH: Templars—North America—History. | Templars—Genealogy. | Indians of North America—History. | Sacred space—North America—History. | Monuments—North America—History. | Treasure trove—North America—History. | Sinclair, Henry, Sir, 1345-approximately 1400—Travel—North America. | North America—Antiquities. | BISAC: BODY, MIND & SPIRIT / Mythical Civilizations. | SOCIAL SCIENCE / Freemasonry. | HISTORY / North America.

Classification: LCC CR4755.N7 M36 2016 (print) | LCC CR4755.N7 (e-book) | DDC 255/.7913097—dc23

LC record available at http://lccn.loc.gov/2015040885

Printed and bound in the United States by Lake Book Manufacturing, Inc.
The text stock is SFI certified. The Sustainable Forestry Initiative® program promotes sustainable forest management.

10 9 8 7 6 5 4 3 2 1

Text design and layout by Debbie Glogover

This book was typeset in Garamond Premier Pro with Mason, Gill Sans MT Pro, ITC Franklin Gothic, and Shelley Script for display fonts

To send correspondence to the author of this book, mail a first-class letter to the author c/o Inner Traditions • Bear & Company, One Park Street, Rochester, VT 05767, and we will forward the communication, or contact the author directly at **www.templarsnewworld.com**.

To my sons, William and Thomas:
The apple doesn't fall far from the tree.

Contents

Appendices of Outline Descendant Reports

Foreword

Scott F. Wolter

Finally! The true history of what really happened in North America prior to the "accepted" version of European contact in the fifteenth century is finally coming out. Currently people are becoming aware of the overwhelming evidence of multiple cultures coming to North America prior to Columbus—not only from Europe but from other continents as well. Yes, the world officially knows about the Norse arriving at L'Anse Aux Meadows in Newfoundland circa 1000 CE, but for a long time scholars didn't believe that the Norse also came to North America—until the factual evidence could no longer be ignored.

In 1960, Helge and Anne Stine Ingstad proved that the Norse had made it to North America prior to Columbus. With this discovery, however, academia continued to want the world to believe that after that *nobody else* arrived on the North American continent until Columbus. The truth is, however, that Columbus didn't actually step foot on these shores. Instead, there is speculation that Columbus was a double agent on behalf of the Portugeuse Knights of Christ and deliberately led the Spanish away from North America. It has now come to light that Columbus's wife was of Drummond-Sinclair descent, and, as such, it is believed that she provided her husband with valuable information concerning her ancestor, Prince Henry Sinclair's earlier voyage to the New World.

Think about how unlikely it is that after the Norse set up at least one confirmed long-term settlement with multiple dwellings, no one else arrived on the North American shores for nearly five hundred years. It doesn't pass the smell test, yet this was the official scholarly position. It's a position that's extremely close-minded and has been proved to be patently false. Admittedly, the evidence refuting it has been slow to come forward, but, with the increasing sophistication of technology and the enhanced information sharing that it entails, come forward it has. Many new and exciting theories have been proposed about others who may have come to this continent during this five-hundred-year period.

The truth is now ready to be told about what can only be described as one of the most important and previously unknown chapters in world history. It's the story of the operations of the Knights Templar in North America before, during, and after their put-down by the king of France and the Roman Catholic Church in 1307. What may be the most interesting aspect of this history is virtually unknown and has never before been considered by scholars: the critical role that Native Americans played for centuries in the successful operations of their "blood brothers" on this continent.

In Minnesota in 1898 a large slab of a stone inscribed with strange characters was found by a farmer by the name of Olof Ohman. Dubbed the Kensington Runestone, it is said to be a Scandinavian record from the fourteenth century. However, since its initial discovery its authenticity has been debated. More than a decade ago I performed geological relative-age weathering studies on the stone and realized that it was a genuine medieval artifact. I then began to consider who the party was that, in 1362, had carved and buried it as a marker attesting to a land claim. My five trips to Sweden between 2003 and 2005, investigating various aspects of the language, runes, dialect, and the grammar of the inscriptions, led to the conclusion that the carver had been a Cistercian monk from the southern Baltic region of Scandinavia.

This prompted me to learn all I could about the White Monks (the Cistercians), including their unprecedented successful growth and accumulation of wealth and influence in the early to mid-twelfth century. Initially I had no idea who they were. It was only through the extensive research presented in books written by people like Alan Butler that I came to understand the hows and whys of their success and the success of their military arm: the Knights Templar.

It didn't take long for evidence to lead me from the Kensington Runestone and its inscriptions directly to the Templars. It never made sense that the Vikings had come to Minnesota at this time, given that the Viking Age ended in 1066 CE. And there is no way that any European party could have *fought* its way to what is now Kensington, Minnesota.

So if not the Vikings—who had the knowledge, the motivation, and the means to undertake this long expedition in the middle of the fourteenth century—who was this party in Minnesota associated with the Kensington Runestone? Both Bill Mann and I came to the proper conclusion years ago; there was only one candidate.

Upon delving into the Templars' history it became pretty clear that, given their massive fleet of ships and long-range navigational abilities, they were the only logical candidates in 1362 to have sailed across the Atlantic and traversed the North American continent to what is now greater Minnesota. It also occurred to me that if ideological descendants of the suppressed Templar/Cistercian order had carved and buried the Kensington Runestone as a land claim, then they must have interacted with Native Americans. It thus made sense that some Native American tribes might know something about the Templars, as well as other cultures that had come to North America long before 1492. It turns out they most certainly do!

One of the reasons we know so little about these matters from the Native American point of view, however, is because of the genocide committed against indigenous people before and after European contact was made. Oral traditions of the Ojibwa/Algonquin in Canada tell of nearly half their population dying from disease brought by "white men" in the 1300s. After contact, we brought more diseases and used every excuse imaginable to break our treaties with the indigenous people, to commit atrocities against them, and to steal their land. It's no wonder they don't trust the white man, and it is perfectly understandable why the current generation of Native Americans don't care about the pre-Columbian history of Europeans on this continent. In academic publications there have been, from time to time, tidbits of information on this topic, presented by Native Americans who still retain much knowledge about their land's prehistory. This is true even given the drastic reduction in their numbers and the deliberate attempts by the American and Canadian governments to eradicate their culture through forced assimilation during the expansion days of both countries and beyond.

As I was writing my previous book a few years ago, I reached out to Bill for help with the research I was conducting. This research entailed comparing the rituals of the Mide'win secret society (the Grand Medicine Society) of the Ojibwa with the rituals of the Masonic Knights Templar. I knew Bill came from a family rich in Masonic history and that he also had extensive knowledge of the Mide'win, given that his mother was a full-blooded Algonquin. After answering my first few questions, Bill interjected, "How about if I fly to Minnesota and we spend a few days going through this?"

Bill's visit to Minnesota in January of 2012 was truly eye-opening and resulted in our learning that the parallels between the two groups weren't just similar, they were *identical*. The Mide'win rituals had been documented by agents of the Smithsonian Institution in the 1880s, and, when I shared my source, Bill was surprised that these sacred rituals had been documented at all, let alone in such detail. The knowledge of the Mide'win culture's rituals is divided into degrees of initiation that one must undergo in order to practice in the Mide'win tradition. Bill commented that even though it was surprising how much the institution had documented the first four degrees of Mide'win, whoever had shared this information back then hadn't said anything about the last four degrees, and I found this most interesting. When I asked if the number eight (the total number of degrees in the Mide'win culture's ritual scale) was significant, Bill smiled and replied, "The number eight is as sacred to Native Americans as the eight points of the Templar cross is to medieval Templars and modern Freemasons."

My education about Mide'win rituals was greatly advanced in the fall of 2014 when my wife, Janet, and I traveled with Bill and his wife, Sharon Marie, to Peterborough, Ontario, Canada, where I participated in a Mide'win sweat with an Ojibwa medicine man and his wife, who was a "keeper of the prophecies" in their tribe. We spent roughly two hours in the "bear's den" sweat lodge, which was enlightening beyond my expectations and helped me better understand how Native Americans keep track of their history with such vivid detail and accuracy. I learned that the Templars were considered brothers by the Mide'win, given that they shared a similar ideology of balance and respect for the Great Spirit and all things of the Earth, including the rocks. At one point I asked this lovely Indian couple why they were willing to share such sacred information and the secrets of their people with me, and they answered, "Because it is now time to share what we know."

Only a few years ago I would have scoffed at such a statement, but I now understand what they mean. Bill also knows why it is time to share what he reveals in this book, including the location of the repository of ancient artifacts brought to this continent centuries ago, which is still being guarded by the elders of the local indigenous tribe. The information Bill presents comes from the knowledge gained from his life experience as a native Algonquin and as a high-ranking member of the Masonic Knights Templar of Canada. Bill's book confirms not only that the medieval Knights Templar formed strategic alliances through intermarriages and like-minded ideologies but also warned their native brethren prior to contact about the dangers coming via persecution by Roman Christianity. Thus, although Native Americans all across the continent knew the persecution was coming, sadly, in the end, there was nothing they could do to stop it.

Bill Mann shares so much new historical knowledge about the true history of North America that it boggles the mind. For me, the information rings true and answers many questions I've had, including how the Kensington party could have traveled across half a continent to place their now famous land-claim stone. They didn't fight Native Americans to get there, they *traveled* with them. I also have every reason to believe the Scandinavian Templars didn't place the land claim in the ground behind the backs of their native blood brothers. Instead, they did it with the hope that the preemptive claim of land would protect their brethren from the genocide that they themselves had already experienced just a half century earlier in 1307.

I am proud to stand alongside Bill Mann as he reveals many long-kept secrets of the secret societies of both the Native Americans and the Knights Templar. He does this not for personal gain or recognition but instead so that it may enlighten the world and hopefully be a step in the right direction for all people to better understand and respect each other and our planet, for generations to come.

Scott Wolter is the host of *America Unearthed.* While working his day job as a world-renowned forensic geologist and the president of the Minnesota-based American Petrographic Services, Scott Wolter began developing a new science called archaeopetrography—a scientific process used to date and understand the origins of mysterious stone artifacts and sites. The first artifact Scott studied using this new science was the Kensington Runestone, which he believes is an authentic, pre-Columbian land claim carved in America by none other than the Knights Templar. The Kensington Runestone was the subject of a documentary special called *Holy Grail in America* that aired on History in 2009. Now, in *America Unearthed* on H2, Scott has the chance to use forensic geology and archaeopetrography to explore many other untold stories in American history, changing everything we think we know about the past.

Acknowledgments

In 2011, thinking that I would be the next Dan Brown, I wrote my first novel, *The 13th Pillar,* which was based on the extensive knowledge that I had gained while researching and writing *The Knights Templar in the New World* and *The Templar Meridians.* Believing that I was being extremely clever, I wrote the novel in an overly complex manner, layering the plot with several different levels of esoteric knowledge.

Unfortunately once the novel had been edited the basic premise and time line became muddled, and it unraveled. The direct result was that *The 13th Pillar* failed to gain a foothold in the mainstream paperback market. Having witnessed my well-earned lesson, a number of my closest friends and colleagues suggested that I direct my energy toward the final installment of a Templar-themed trilogy. In this, they suggested that I follow up my first two books on the secret exploration and settlement of the New World by the medieval Knights Templar with a book to be named, appropriately enough, *Templar Sanctuaries in North America.*

They convinced me that it was time to reveal the secrets behind my bloodline.

Heeding their advice, *Templar Sanctuaries in North America* brings me back to what I now know I do best: produce complex yet compelling nonfiction works that logically show a progression of thought and understanding relating to the hidden history of pre-Columbian North America. Thanks, therefore, must go out to those friends who encouraged me to continue on the hidden path that I discovered so many years ago. Only time will tell whether what I have discovered and now reveal is truly startling and a game changer in the field of American history.

These good friends are Niven Sinclair and Steve St. Clair (the administrator of the St. Clair Sinclair DNA Project); Scott Wolter (the host of *America Unearthed*) and his wife, Janet Wolter; British author Alan Butler; my lifelong best friend, the Honorable Dave Levac (presently Speaker of the Legislature of Ontario); Gordon H. Stuart and F. Douglas Draker (past supreme grand masters of the Knights Templar of Canada); the late Honorable John Ross Matheson (the man behind the design of the present-day Canadian flag); the late George Karski (a sorely missed friend with whom I shared my innermost secrets on many occasions); my two dear sisters, Vicki and Cheryl (who, as elders of the Algonquins of Greater Golden Lake, are currently participating in the Algonquins of Ontario Land Claim with the province of Ontario and government of Canada); Mark and Wendy Philips; and last but not least, renowned Cree traditional teacher Michael Thrasher (the man who, alongside Mark and Wendy Philips, taught me to open my eyes to my native background and bloodline). And, finally, to my friend and mentor among the Old Mide'win—the Grand Medicine Society of the Anishinabe/Algonquin Nation—who first asked not to be acknowledged at all but then relented if he remained anonymous, *Chi-Miigwich*!

No mention of the traditional native teachings revival of the 1970s in Canada would be complete without mention of Michael, who has spent the past thirty-plus years dedicated to the cultural survival and revitalization of Native American culture. An eloquent spokesman for traditional ecological knowledge, he was instrumental in establishing Trent University's Elders Conference and continues to be an adjunct professor of native studies. Just recently Michael most deservedly received an honorary doctorate of laws from Trent University in Peterborough, Ontario, Canada, for his lifetime of work maintaining traditional native teachings.

To be able to consider all of these extremely accomplished individuals as my friends is an honor unto itself.

It must be noted that on June 6, 2015, Chief Justice Murray Sinclair released the results of the Truth and Reconciliation Commission (TRC) relating to Indian residential schools in Canada. The commission was a requirement of the Indian Residential Schools Settlement Agreement reached in 2007, the largest class action settlement in Canadian history. In its report the TRC writes about the ongoing effects of colonialism, the "policies of cultural genocide and assimilation," and the huge rift this has caused between aboriginal and non-aboriginal people. Over six years the TRC collected 6,740 statements from witnesses and recorded 1,355 hours of testimony. This all culminated in ninety-four recommendations being presented in Ottawa amid four days of events and ceremonies attended by thousands of aboriginals and non-aboriginals. My hope is that all ninety-four recommendations are acted upon and that North America's indigenous people will finally be accepted as the true stewards of the land and treated respectfully as such.

Of course, I would be remiss not to acknowledge the far-reaching love and encouragement of my wife, Sharon Marie, and my two sons, William and Thomas. My sons' patience and kindness toward their father when he becomes entrenched in his writings is certainly telling, especially when he wanders the house at 4:00 in the morning, more often than not disturbing their sleep. Sharon Marie has acted as my critic and editor throughout the entire span of my writings, which are nearing the twenty-year mark. Many a time I would have given up on my ideas and thoughts if not for her encouragement and gentle questioning, which more than once has taken me down the right path in this labyrinth of hidden sanctuaries. She also has doggedly accepted the lingering smell of sweat and sweet grass/native tobacco smoke that pervades the entire house for days whenever I return from one of my many native ceremonies or explorations.

The relationship of my wife and sons to this story is left to the logical conclusions of the individual reader. I apologize in advance to Sharon Marie and the boys if I have inadvertently involved them in a lifelong enigma, but I hope that they accept their newfound status with dignity and pride. This is not to say that they possess any greater uniqueness than anyone else in the world. I only hope that my two sons are able to one day pass on their increased awareness of their ancestral background to their own children, specifically about their shared ancestor Prince Henry Sinclair. It will certainly give them all something to talk about.

Thanks must also go to the many institutions and museums around the world that have provided valuable resources at one time or another for my research. These great art galleries and museums have acted as sanctuaries of another kind to me throughout a lifetime of learning. Among others they include the British Museum, the Louvre, the National Gallery of Scotland, the Staatliche Museum of Berlin, the Royal Ontario Museum, the Cloisters Museum, the Cluny Museum, the Ashmolean Museum, and the Metropolitan Museum of Art. I wish to thank them specifically for their generous and gracious use of copyrighted material and pictures.

Acknowledgment and thanks must also go to the staff at Inner Traditions • Bear & Company. The enthusiasm and professionalism with which they lovingly accepted and massaged my three manuscripts is very much appreciated. Included in this are publisher Ehud Sperling, a true visionary and supporter of hidden traditions and spirituality around the world; acquisitions editor Jon Graham; managing editor Jeanie Levitan; cover designer/art director the late Peri Swan; contracts and royalties administrator Kelly Bowen; author liaison Nicki Champion; and, last but not least of all, editor Mindy Branstetter. Without Mindy's patience and assistance I would never have been able to consolidate my ever-growing sphere of what at times appears to be unrelated knowledge into a concise and readable format.

Finally, sincere acknowledgment must go to those who already believe in what is about to be revealed. However, if any true believer has a desire to run right out and dig up the "treasure," the only caution I can offer is that you first think long and hard about what's involved. From my own experience, it's extremely difficult to come back from that other world, to complete the labyrinth of the Grail once you've initially passed through that door! The continuing enigma of Oak Island in Nova Scotia is a perfect example of this. For more than 250 years, various generations of treasure hunters have been searching for the island's elusive treasure, with the only result to date being six deaths and countless wasted lives.

INTRODUCTION

A Timely Trilogy

It was in the pages of *The Knights Templar in the New World: How Prince Henry Sinclair Brought the Grail to Acadia* (Inner Traditions, March 2004) that I first presented the fascinating story of the medieval Scottish Prince Henry Sinclair. It was Prince Henry who arrived in the New World in 1398 CE, almost one hundred years before Columbus, having sailed to what is today mainland Nova Scotia from the Orkney Islands.[1] In his 1954 *Prince Henry Sinclair: His Expedition to the New World in 1398,* Frederick Pohl was the first author to make a connection between the Algonquin/Mi'kmaq legend of Glooscap and the purported arrival of Prince Henry Sinclair and his fellow knights to the shoreline of Nova Scotia in 1398. Then in 1996, in *Holy Grail Across the Atlantic,* author Michael Bradley built upon Pohl's work in various ways, including attempting to return King Arthur to his proper place in history as a descendant of the purported Holy Bloodline. Bradley also emphasized the North American segment of Prince Henry's voyage, which has been largely ignored by Europeans, even to this day.

Prior to writing the first book in this trilogy, I determined that together with approximately five hundred of his most trusted fellow knights, their families, and a number of Cistercian monks, it was at a suitably named community called Green Oaks in Nova Scotia that Sinclair had established a secret Rose Line settlement. This was done with the support and assistance of the local natives, the Mi'kmaq. This settlement would be the first of many New World sanctuaries to provide refuge to the inner circle of the Knights Templar and their related Grail family members fleeing persecution by the Roman Catholic Church and its armies and agents.

It bears repeating that in large part *The Knights Templar in the New World* is a personal story, because my late great-uncle, Frederic George Mann, was supreme grand master of the Knights Templar of Canada in the 1950s. And it was from him when I was just a child that I first received the "secret" geometric key that would eventually allow me to rediscover the site of the first Templar settlement established by Sinclair and his followers in what they considered at the time to be the new Arcadia.*[2] *The Knights Templar in the New World* became much more of a unique personal story when I later realized that my mother was descended from the Anishinabe/Algonquin, specifically the Kichespirini (people of the Ottawa River), and that my parents' union mirrored that of the much earlier strategic intermarriages between the Templars and the native Algonquin that had occurred more than four hundred years ago.

---

*In *Holy Grail Across the Atlantic,* Michael Bradley paid particular attention to various maps of the New World that had appeared in Europe during the sixteenth and seventeenth centuries. One such map is the Gastaldi map, which first appeared in the Venice Ptolemy of 1548, three years after the Vopell map, but may have been drawn as early as 1539. Of interest on this map is the key—p = refuge—and the place-names Larcadia, Angouleme, Flora, and Le Paradis. Bradley logically put the progression of these names together to form the message "The Flower of Angouleme has found a refuge in the Paradise of Arcadia." Of special note is the map's reference to "Norumbega" (New France), which calls the region of Nova Scotia "Terra de Norumbega" (land of Norumbega). It continues to become obvious that the land of Arcadia/Norumbega plays an important part not only in the discovery of a New Jerusalem by the medieval Knights Templar but also in the reasoning that Prince Henry Sinclair was following in his Norman ancestors' footsteps.

Much of Bradley's general information concerning portolan charts relies heavily on *Maps of the Ancient Sea Kings* by Professor Charles Hapgood. Professor Hapgood arrived at his conclusions after an exhaustive search through hundreds of early maps and a re-plotting of the important ones on a modern projection. According to Hapgood, these portolan maps are definitive proof that a highly advanced race preceded all others some ten thousand years ago and that they had circumnavigated and mapped the globe.

THE MEROVINGIAN CONNECTION

A key tenet of this book and the theories it contains is that the lineage known as the Merovingian dynasty is comprised of the descendants of Jesus and Mary Magdalene. Ruling over the Franks for approximately three hundred years from the fifth century until the eighth, the Merovingian dynasty was founded by Childeric, son of Merovech. Childeric lived from 457 until 481. The dynasty ruled over the area that was known in antiquity as Gaul after Childeric's son Clovis had united the territory.

It was in Arcadia (later known as Acadia) that Prince Henry Sinclair and his followers sought to find a lasting refuge for the "Grail"—the Holy Grail Bloodline connecting the House of David and the House of Bethany to the Merovingian dynasty. This goal of finding a lasting refuge for the Grail was achieved through the establishment of a series of hidden sanctuaries across North America. Support for this story was originally found in a rare historical document called the Zeno Narrative, which was written in 1555 by an Antonio Zeno, the great-nephew of the Venetian Templar admirals Nicolo and Antonio, who accompanied Sinclair on his journey to the New World.

Through the actions of many double agents such as Columbus and Champlain, all was kept relatively secret until the British persecuted and finally exiled the Acadians, many of whom were descendants of the bloodline, to Louisiana in 1755.[3] On the surface, the British claimed that the Acadians failed to swear allegiance to the British crown. The reality was that the Acadians resisted all attempts by the British to discover the secret locations of the hidden Grail settlements.

It was through authors Michael Baigent, Richard Leigh, and Henry Lincoln and their now famous book *Holy Blood, Holy Grail** that the idea that Jesus and Mary Magdalene were married first surfaced in the modern era. Although earlier decipherments and allegations appeared in many books devoted to the mystery of Rennes-le-Château, including *L'Or de Rennes* by Gérard de Sède, *Holy Blood, Holy Grail* was the

*[Published in the United Kingdom as *The Holy Blood and the Holy Grail.* —*Ed.*]

first to present, in English, a summary of the French research into the mystery of the Holy Bloodline. Indeed, a great deal of the material in *Holy Blood, Holy Grail* concerned the life of the French priest Bérenger Saunière and the mystery of Rennes-le-Château, originally derived from Gérard de Sède's *L'Or de Rennes.*

Of course, this monumental theory of the Holy Bloodline took on worldwide dimensions when presented in Dan Brown's fictional work *The Da Vinci Code.* Many readers will recognize the common threads between *Holy Blood, Holy Grail* and *The Da Vinci Code* as evidenced by the lawsuit for plagiarism brought against Brown by the three English authors. Regardless of the lawsuit having been dismissed as unfounded, with the publishing of *Holy Blood, Holy Grail* in 1982 it can generally be said that the stage had been set for *The Da Vinci Code.*

When *Holy Blood, Holy Grail* was first published the very idea that there were direct descendants of a union between Jesus and Mary Magdalene was met with ridicule and even threats of death from the faithful. However, with the advent of the Internet and the second millennium it appears that the time is now ripe for the general acceptance of an alternative world history.

Any reader of *Holy Blood, Holy Grail* will certainly have recognized that certain periods or dates (from medieval times to the present) have signaled an increase in discovery or investigation into the mysteries of the Knights Templar, Rennes-le-Château, the Holy Bloodline, and the mysterious "treasure island" located along the south shore of Nova Scotia; namely, Oak Island. The early 1950s appear to be one of the latest of these periods when new information surfaced concerning the mystery of Rennes-le-Château—as a result of the hidden material found deposited in the famed Bibliothèque Nationale, and through the discovery of Oak Island's stone triangle—which relates to the infamous Money Pit. The Money Pit is so named because its location on Oak Island became the focus for treasure hunters when a series of nine oak platforms within a vertical pit was first discovered back in 1795 by three local youths. The conjecture from this time forward was that an immense treasure of historical proportions lay at the bottom of the pit, just waiting to be recovered by anyone who dares to accept the challenge.

It may be pure coincidence, but it was between 1950 and 1954 that my great-uncle Frederic George Mann assumed the ultimate position of supreme grand master of the Knights Templar of Canada. Significantly, my great-uncle's immediate predecessor within the Knights Templar of Canada was a Halifax lawyer, Reginald Vanderbilt Harris, who not only represented the consortium that owned the island at that time but who also wrote one of the first books about the island and its mysteries.

PRINCE HENRY SINCLAIR AND HIS RELATIONSHIP TO THE HOLY BLOODLINE

One of the most fascinating aspects about Prince Henry Sinclair was that at the time of his voyage in 1398 he was hereditary grand master of the Scottish Knights Templar, as well as an earl and vassal of Margaret, Queen of Norway (and Denmark), due to Norway's control over the Orkney Islands. This meant that Prince Henry Sinclair and his followers were the most feared enemies of the Hanseatic League. This organization controlled most of the Baltic trade and looked to expand its seagoing empire out into the northern Atlantic from one of their home ports in Bergen, Norway.[4]

Author Andrew Sinclair, in *The Sword and the Grail,* was one of the first to present a logical explanation linking Prince Henry Sinclair to Norway and that country's battle for Baltic and Scandinavian seafaring supremacy in and around the fourteenth century. The Hanseatic League from northern Germany controlled most northern seas during the fourteenth and fifteenth centuries due to the Danish and Norwegian kings being deeply in debt to Hanseatic merchants. The newly crowned Queen Margaret of Norway and Denmark sought to develop a Northern Commonwealth to compete with the league and entered into a secret agreement with the Venetian trading ships that were venturing into Baltic waters. To cement the newly formed alliance between Prince Henry and Queen Margaret, the queen granted the earldom of Orkney to Sinclair.

What Andrew Sinclair also provided in *The Sword and the Grail* is the most wonderful description of Rosslyn, Scotland, the ancestral home of Prince Henry Sinclair, as well as other workings of Rosslyn Chapel and how sacred geometry and symbolism were applied during their late medieval construction. What he also confirmed, again perhaps unknowingly, is that if Rosslyn provided a resting place for the Holy Grail treasure then it only served as a temporary depository due to its relative accessibility to English invasion around the turn of the thirteenth century. The Queen's granting the earldom of Orkney to Sinclair provided him with the necessary resources and hidden knowledge to make his secret voyage to the New World, possibly transporting the Holy Grail treasure to what at that time was considered a safe haven and sanctuary.

With all of this in mind, let's just speculate for the moment that it was a combination of all of these factors that explains the Templars' meteoric rise in power. Then, just as suddenly, came their fall from grace, resulting in their demise on that fateful night of Friday, October 13, 1307, when Philippe the Fair, King of France, in conjunction with Pope Clement V, ordered the arrest and destruction of the French Templars.

THE APPETITE FOR THE GRAIL AND THE ONGOING SEARCH FOR IT

Prince Henry Sinclair was himself a direct descendant of the Holy Grail Bloodline.[5] This meant that he was and still is considered to be the ultimate guardian of the Templar treasure, which many researchers and authors have speculated is either a real booty of gold, silver, and jewels; a historical genealogical record of the Grail family; or a first-hand account of their life written by either Jesus or the Magdalene herself. On another level the treasure could be said to be the ancient secret information that allowed Sinclair and those earlier seagoing Norse—the Vikings who had sailed before him—to navigate the treacherous North Atlantic.[6]

In *The Sword and the Grail,* Andrew Sinclair traced the St. Clair name back to the More family of Viking and Norman ancestry. According to Sinclair, on the Epte River in the north of France, Rolf

Rognvald of the powerful More family concluded the Treaty of St. Clair in 911, when King Charles the Simple married his daughter and was converted to Christianity, taking the name of St. Clair, which means "holy light." The Epte River is in what was once the duchy of Normandy, which also included the southern states of the Lowlands. It is an area that was at one time part of the Merovingian dynasty, a dynasty that claims as offshoots the Byzantine emperors and empresses of the eastern Roman Empire, which traces its roots back to the union of Jesus and Mary Magdalene.

The sagas of the Viking explorers can be found in many books. It is generally said that Erik the Red died shortly after the return of the first Vinland expedition at the turn of the eleventh century and that Lief, his son, took his place as leader of the clan. At that time the Greenland settlement included several hundred farmers, hunters, fishermen, and traders. A Christian church, built to the order of Thorhild, Erik's consort, thrived until the settlers reverted to their pagan roots. The island population reached about four thousand at its peak, but many of its number eventually returned to their homeland.

It is recorded that Thorvald, the second son, borrowed Lief's knorr and sailed for Vinland in 1004 with a crew of thirty. The saga mentions no incident on the journey to the Liefsbodarna, Lief's wintering place. The saga says that Thorvald sent parties to first explore "the land to the west" and then he "followed the coast to the northward." After three years in Vinland, during which a long coastline (perhaps a thousand miles) was thoroughly explored (and mapped?), the settlement broke up and returned to Greenland. One version has it that the men fell to quarreling over the favors of the few women, but most references blame the relentless hostility of the natives.

The treasure may also consist of associated relics that can ultimately be tested against the DNA of known members of the Holy Grail Bloodline. (As such, in the pages of this book, I will reveal the startling results of my own DNA and its associated revelations, along with my direct descendancy from Prince Henry Sinclair and beyond.)

In terms of where the treasure might lie, many people believe its final resting place is the enigmatic Oak Island, located on the south shore of Nova Scotia. Of the numerous books and articles written about Oak Island and the Money Pit, three of them are prominent because of their in-depth background to the story and the theories as to the nature of the group of men responsible for the construction of such an impregnable defense. In *The Oak Island Mystery* author D'Arcy O'Connor concentrated on Captain William Kidd as the legendary depositor of the immense treasure. W. S. Crooker, in *Oak Island Mystery,* attributed the mystery surrounding the building of the Money Pit to be on the same level as the mysteries of Easter Island, the Nazca Plain, and the Great Pyramid of Egypt. To Crooker, Oak Island can only be compared with the many strange works found in various parts of the world that apparently originated long before recorded history. But, per Crooker, Oak Island is different in one way. Unlike the other great mysteries of the world, its artifacts or workings cannot be physically viewed and examined, because everything is underground. In Crooker's mind, Oak Island is an inverted Easter Island or Great Pyramid with its labyrinth of shafts and tunnels.

The book that I feel most comfortable with is *The Money Pit Mystery,* by author Rupert Furneaux, because of its more logical reasoning from an engineering viewpoint as to the identity of the mysterious Mr. X who constructed the Money Pit, and why. The conclusion that Furneaux comes to is that the intricate tunnel and vault system was engineered by the British military just prior to the American Revolution to safeguard British monies swept away from the colonies.

Following many attempts to decipher the ancient Templar code of sacred geometry, it's now been determined by several other researchers that Oak Island is *not* the final resting place of this treasure. Constantly being pursued by their enemies, the descendants of the Holy Bloodline moved farther westward across the vast wilderness of North America, all the while continuing to intermarry into the native population. Having thus been moved over several generations from one Templar sanctuary to another, all signs, seals, and tokens now point to the fact that the Templar treasure still remains an elusive talisman.

Yet still, this compelling story (when coupled with current events across Europe and the Middle East) has captured the public's imagination over the past decade and has caused an insatiable quest for anything and everything Grail related. With the explosive release of Dan Brown's novel *The Da Vinci Code,* this appetite hit an all-time high. As well, two recent movies, *National Treasure* and *National Treasure II: Book of Secrets,* presented (for the first time in a mainstream format) the idea that the founding of the United States was based on Masonic principles as well as the feminine Grail veneration. This line of thinking also posits that the founding of America was potentially financed through a small portion of the Templar treasure that was secretly provided to George Washington and Thomas Jefferson for that very purpose.

THE ROLE OF THE VENUS FAMILIES

Two good friends of mine, Scott and Janet Wolter, have been very much involved in ideas of this nature. Scott currently hosts the widely popular series *America Unearthed* found on the History 2 Channel, and he has authored books pertaining to the Kensington Runestone and the symbolism behind the mysterious Hooked X (a cryptic symbol found on the Kensington Runestone). His wife, Janet, has just recently coauthored *America: Nation of the Goddess* with a mutual friend of ours, Alan Butler.[7]

In *America: Nation of the Goddess* the authors reveal how a secret cabal of influential "Venus" families with a lineage tracing back to the Eleusinian Mysteries has shaped the history of the United States since its founding. The evidence for such incredible assertions comes from American institutions such as the National Grange Order of Husbandry and from the man-made landscape of the United States where massive structures and whole cities conform to an agenda designed to elevate the feminine in religion and society.

The authors explain how the Venus families, working through the Freemasons and later the Grange, planned the American Revolution and the creation of the United States. It was this group who set the stage for the founding fathers to create Washington, D.C., according to the principles of sacred geometry and with an eye toward establishing a New Jerusalem. The authors explore the sacred design of the Washington

Monument, revealing its occult purpose and connections to the heavens. They reveal how the obelisks in New York City depict the stars of Orion's Belt, just like the Giza pyramids do, and how the site of one of the obelisks, Manhattan's Saint Paul's Chapel, is the American counterpart to Rosslyn Chapel in Scotland.

Exposing the strong esoteric influences behind the establishment of the Grange in the United States, they connect this apparently conservative order of farmers to the Venus families and trace its lineage back to the Cistercians, who as we know were a major voice in the promotion of the Crusades and the establishment of the Knights Templar. The logical connection therefore is that these families are some of the remaining descendants of Prince Henry Sinclair's Holy Bloodline voyage of 1398—families whose lineage and intermarriage have been controlled by a guiding force over a number of centuries.

In their books the authors speak of the union of Jesus and Mary Magdalene producing the "Rose," "Star," "Grail," or "Venus family"—it goes by many different names. Others talk about the Dragon Bloodline, the Holy Grail Bloodline, the Rose Line, or the Grail refugees. No matter what the label, the substance is the same: this controversial yet sacred union has produced a unique family lineage that still exists to this day.

Of course not everyone is ready for such a dramatic shift in religious direction relating to the acceptance of the Holy Bloodline. The Vatican still clings to the basic tenets of the Bible, and the religious right in the United States is strengthening its evangelical beliefs through an ever-increasing influence on mainstream politics. Presently in Europe, within the context of a European Union, the long-established royal houses and even pretenders all appear to be vying for the ultimate "divine" position. At the same time and therefore no mere coincidence, the House of Windsor is constantly bombarded by stories of intrigue and possibly even murder. One such result is that following her tragic death Princess Diana's direct connection to the Merovingian bloodline through the Spencer family (originally De Spenser) was finally revealed and, along with it, a veneration of Diana that reached almost mythic proportions exploded upon the world.

In an attempt to counter this Goddess veneration and make

the House of Windsor even more legitimate and stronger, the union of Prince William and Kate Middleton, the Duke and Duchess of Cambridge, has recently given birth to a "rightful" and therefore "divine" heir, namely Prince George, who's now third in line to the throne. It is in this tiny baby boy that we now find the age-old notion of the royal male heir becoming the representative head of a new golden era. And, just to provide a little insurance and security, Kate has more recently given birth to Charlotte, a "spare to the heir." Indeed, this mass-marketing strategy appears to be working, with the British royals pulling out all of the stops, as the 2014 vote against Scottish independence has proved.

In an opposite vein, almost designed to counter the popularity of *The Da Vinci Code* and its Goddess/Magdalene-oriented story, recent dramatic productions such as *Noah* and *Risen* have stirred the inner soul of both the Christian believer and nonbeliever alike. Even Pope Francis currently appears to be championing the cause by introducing a more moderate position of the church. Francis has indicated that he chose his formal name in honor of Saint Francis of Assisi, which is quite interesting considering he is a Jesuit. His stated reason for choosing Francis of Assisi is that Francis was a man of poverty, a man of peace, a man who loved and protected Creation.

But even this relatively liberal stance has tended to polarize the views and opinions of several religious groups to the point where common ground relating to the true spirit of Jesus may again never be achieved—common ground that at one time had been established between the medieval Knights Templar and their supposed enemies, the Muslims, as well as the Jews, both during and following the Crusades, close to a thousand years ago.

THE ANTIENT GRIDLINES AND THE CELTIC *ELL*

All of this provides an appropriate background to my second book in the trilogy, *The Templar Meridians: The Secret Mapping of the New World* (Inner Traditions, 2008). Through an ever-expanding understanding and knowledge of what continues to be the true secret behind the Templar knowledge, within the pages of *The Templar Meridians* I deciphered an antient longitudinal/latitudinal grid pattern across North America based on maps and other related documents that had been discovered by the original nine Templars under the site of the Temple of Solomon.

This secret knowledge, among other things, provided the medieval Knights Templar with the ability to establish accurate latitudinal and longitudinal positions long before it became an acceptable practice in the eighteenth century. Through continuous archaeoastronomical observations of the sun, moon, and stars and their relative positions recorded through the numerous stone, earth, and native medicine circles established around the world, certain ancient secret societies were, in essence, able to map the world. They did this through the travels and settlements of those intrepid men who came to be known as the ancient mariners or the native shamans who traveled farther than anyone might imagine.

Thus it is now easy to understand the ever-increasing volume of evidence of pre-Christian exploration and trade throughout the New World by diverse groups such as the Celts, Carthaginians, Phoenicians, and Egyptians—and the rediscovery and application of this antient grid pattern across America by some of the earliest Knights Templar before Prince Henry and his followers ultimately established their last refuge at what I refer to as the Prime Templar Meridian. Indeed, there is a little-known document labeled the Cremona Document, which has caused speculation that the first Templar voyage to the New World occurred sometime in the late eleventh or early twelfth century.

This secret knowledge also provided those who were "in on the secret" with the ability to enjoy a limitless supply of precious metals and other earthly materials and medicines. In addition to the much sought after copper and gold, it has now come to light that the Templars also enjoyed an unlimited source of rare earth minerals including titanium, manganese, iridium, and chromite. This most likely explains their overwhelming military strength due to superior weaponry during the First (1096–1099) and Second Crusades (1145–1149).

In addition, this secret knowledge allowed for friendship and trade with the indigenous people of the New World and enabled Prince Henry Sinclair and his Knights Templar to reestablish a series of secret Rose Line settlements across North America, thus securing the Grail refugees' ongoing protection until they could be fully assimilated into the native population. It also allowed them to circumnavigate the world and to verify those ancient maps in their possession. These maps were so accurate that the Templars were confident that buried boundary markers, artifacts, manuscripts, and/or relics could easily be retrieved centuries later by future initiates of the sacred knowledge—by New World agents such as Jacques Cartier, Samuel de Champlain, Pierre de La Vérendrye, Louis Hennepin, Robert de La Salle, Duluth (Samuel Greysolon, Sieur du Lhut), and Louis Joliet, among others.

This understanding of antient wisdom certainly explains why esoteric visionaries such as George Washington and Thomas Jefferson sought to tap in to this pattern of concealed energy through their respective designs of Washington, D.C., and Monticello. English author and historian Alan Butler has done an admirable job of uncovering these aspects in his book *City of the Goddess,* which examines the use of the ancient Celtic ell measurement in the layout of America's capital city. This understanding also provides for a fascinating, underlying reasoning for Jefferson's sponsorship of the Lewis and Clark expedition in that the expedition's secret purpose was to search out the final resting place of the grand initiate who "reactivated" the meridians across North America—the same Prince Henry Sinclair.

Even Joseph Smith and his immediate successor, Brigham Young, of the Church of Jesus Christ of Latter-Day Saints (LDS), play into the notion that snippets of the secret antient knowledge surrounding the application of the rose line meridians across North America led not only to safe refuge and treasure but also to the establishment of a New Jerusalem. Many readers will be amazed at how the establishment of the meridian and base marker at the southeast corner of Temple Square in Salt Lake City, Utah, corresponds rather nicely to the most important north–south prime meridian in this overall story.

It now most certainly appears that this strategic navigational advantage over the established church and state, rather than their claim of being the guardians of the Holy Bloodline, led to the ultimate downfall of the Templars. For in the absence of a confirmed DNA match (which might be obtained from samples of blood, hair, or bone), a direct descendancy resulting from a union of Jesus and Mary Magdalene could continue to be discredited by the church and its propaganda machine, much as it had been doing for the past two thousand years.

The so-called New World represented not only unlimited wealth but also an opportunity to establish a "New World Order" free from the oppressive control of both the European church and state. Of course, both the Roman Catholic Church and church-acclaimed Holy Roman emperors could not allow these upstarts to undermine close to two thousand years of world dominance, so they unleashed their most trusted agents and spies and ruthless armies to hunt down and destroy what was left of the Knights Templar and the Holy Bloodline.

Again, it is this understanding that also explains the many aspects of the compelling, late-nineteenth-century French story of Rennes-le-Château and the priest Bérenger Saunière, for Saunière had obviously stumbled across the secret knowledge of the antient rose lines. Bits of this Goddess-related knowledge had also been deciphered earlier by the founders of Montreal, led by followers of the Order of Saint Vincent—the Sulpicians.

Both the Sulpicians and their inherent rivals, the Jesuits, had inklings of the clues that lay in two of the most masterful Renaissance paintings ever completed in the seventeenth century: *The Shepherds of Arcadia* (*Et in Arcadia Ego . . .*) by Nicolas Poussin, and *St. Anthony and St. Paul Fed by Ravens* by David Teniers the Younger. The reader will be amazed, I believe, by my discovery of how similar hidden levels of the two paintings come together to display one big treasure map across North America and the final resting place of the Templar treasure.

If only everybody had the eyes to see what has been in plain sight all along!

All in all, the third and final book in this timely trilogy, *Templar Sanctuaries in North America: Sacred Bloodlines and Secret Treasures,* is a fascinating consolidation and lasting revelation of the knowledge, understanding, and wisdom of the medieval Templar warrior/monks and their concept of a New World—starting with a New Jerusalem—located in New Scotland (Nova Scotia). It ends with a dramatic unveiling of the ultimate New World secret sought by so many factions over at least the past four hundred years—the location of the last Knights Templar refuge in the New World where the major portion of the lost treasure of the Templars remains to this day!

As we know, this treasure is assumed to be the same treasure taken from caverns below the site of the destroyed second Temple of Solomon. This treasure is required to sanctify the building of a proposed third temple in Jerusalem. The present-day political and religious ramifications of a discovery of this nature are limitless. It could result in Jerusalem once again being deemed the center of the world. Or the artifacts and relics could be used to sanctify a New Jerusalem, perhaps even in North America.

Conversely, if the treasure was to fall into the wrong hands, then the world's greatest religions could be held for ransom, or even worse.

MY PERTINENT FAMILY HISTORY

Finally, *Templar Sanctuaries* reveals that its author is one of the last remaining, modern-day, native Indian/Templar blood guardians left to stand guard over this secret knowledge. The time is now for the truth behind the Holy Grail, in accordance with the four-hundred-year-old Anishinabe/Algonquin prophecies, to be unveiled!

I find myself continually going back to the question of how my family could have become privy to certain information developed by a band of medieval Scottish Knights Templar. Why me? What is it about the Mann family's background that allows me such familial access to this seemingly unsolvable mystery? Luckily, Michael Baigent and Richard Leigh provided me with the solution to this piece of the riddle through their book, *The Temple and the Lodge,* in their explanation about the ties between the east coast of medieval Scotland and the countries of England and Flanders and Normandy.

The Mann family is of strong Flemish/Norman descent.

According to the British authors, following the Battle of Hastings in 1066 and the victory of William the Conqueror up to and during the reigns of Scottish kings David I (1124–1153) and Malcolm IV (1153–1165), there was a systematic policy of settling Flemish and Norman people along the east coasts of Scotland and England. As a result, early Scottish and English people and Scottish and English towns assumed certain distinctly Flemish/Norman characteristics. Other elements of Scotland's ancient Celtic heritage found their way back to Flanders and Normandy. Therefore, it's not that hard to imagine that old loyalties remained with the class of tradesmen and merchants, many of Flemish and Norman origin, who settled throughout the new towns of England and Scotland. Indeed, it was these "middle class" tradesmen and merchants who became the administrators and financiers of the newfound royalty and Templar network of holdings and who maintained regular shipping and trading between the larger urban centers of Europe. These old loyalties continued throughout the centuries through fraternities such as the Freemasons.

For years the Mann family of Norwich, England, made annual pilgrimages to the Chapel of Saint Sophia located in Glendaruel, Argyll, Scotland. Baigent and Leigh noted in *The Temple and the Lodge*[8] that in Argyll, Scotland, there appears to be a unique concentration of Masonic graves and anonymous military gravestones.

Indeed, in *The Temple and the Lodge,* Baigent and Leigh presented a great deal of background material concerning the centralization of English Freemasonry in support of the theory that in the United Grand Lodge there was an inner core of other Freemasonic bodies, which originated in Jacobite Freemasonry. Because of this the English Freemasonry of Grand Lodge was said to have an important role in both the French and the American Revolutions. (For more in-depth information concerning the influence of Freemasonry on eighteenth- and nineteenth-century societies, *The Temple and the Lodge* is a must read.)

The only advice that I can provide at this point to the reader is to open your mind to the possibility that there is an alternative history—or at least a previously unknown underlying reason—for all of the major world events that have transpired over the past two thousand years. The key is to be able to peel back the many veils of secrecy that have been laid layer upon layer. In a majority of cases the trails can and have led to a dead end, much like the classic labyrinth of legends and myths.

I apologize now to those readers who find what's presented here more akin to a roller-coaster ride than an immense revelation. The historical background can be rather boring at times but is necessary in order to understand the multilayered, multigenerational manipulations that have taken place over the past five thousand years. Please trust me when I say that this material is necessary to the story. My only advice is to skim through those sections that may be less than absorbing and then go back and reread the book again. I guarantee that every time you read it you will gain a new perspective on history the way it's been presented to us over time.

Do readers need to read the first two books in this timely trilogy to understand this third one? It's not absolutely necessary, given that I have selectively reconfirmed the necessary portions of the puzzle, unless the reader wants to explore in-depth the full background and knowledge of what led me to the final resting place of the Templar treasure. *Templar Sanctuaries in North America* is written in such a way that it stands on its own, building on the same foundations established in the first two books. One of the main themes of this book is that past societies have, for their own purposes, assumed the very foundations of those that went before them. As to who rightfully owns the treasure, readers will have to decide for themselves. Just remember one thing: Let he who has the understanding use it with wisdom.

1
D'ARTT OF THE ANTIENTS

Fig. 1.1. Jesus Christ depicted as the Great Architect of the Universe

FROM BRUNET TO BOURGET

In the fall of 2011, I received what first appeared to be a simple envelope from a fellow modern-day knight, whom I had last met during a visit to Montreal while attending a business conference. The envelope contained nothing more than an 8½ x 11-inch color photo of a single-page document with the original showing damage by fire and water. Thankfully the writing was still discernible. The document appeared to have been written on a parchment-thin, light-brown animal skin of some kind and bore the mark of the St. Sulpician Archives of Montreal.

Fig. 1.2. Map demonstrating range of St. Sulpician missions across eastern Canada in 1845, extending across most of what is now the Canadian Maritimes, the provinces of Québec and Ontario, coinciding with the eastern portion of the larger Algonquin Nation

The original, dated June 23, 1845, had been written in Old French script and was a letter report to Monsignor Bourget, then bishop of Montreal, from Father Brunet, a traveling priest or missionary of sorts. It was Brunet's stated task to travel the rivers and trails of the extensive archdiocese of Montreal to the various missions that the St. Sulpicians had established among the larger Algonquin Nation. Brunet was no common lay brother though. He was a direct descendant of one of those lesser French nobility families who had suffered immensely during the French Revolution. Luckily he had been able to escape Paris as a young novice, with the assistance of his St. Sulpician superiors, to the relative obscurity of New France.

Curiously, Brunet's report referred to a direct ancestor of mine on my mother's side, a Thomas Lagarde dit St. Jean, who had been the main subject of a conversation that I'd had with my friend from Montreal during my prior visit. Following a wonderful dinner, we talked about many things relating to the early beginnings of New France and the establishment of Montreal, in part because of two earlier books that I had written in relation to what I consider to be the hidden history behind the "discovery" and settlement of the Americas. The first book was *The Knights Templar in the New World,* and the second was titled *The Templar Meridians: The Secret Mapping of the New World.*

The fraternal bond that we shared during this conversation led to a most interesting fact: we both had European ancestors who had been involved in the very early development of the fur trade in New France in the early 1600s and had married into the Algonquin Nation. This was a trend at the time, done purposely to secure trade with the natives and to enable the traders to travel inland along the Ottawa River and Great Lakes into the hinterland of beaver and deer. In my friend's case, his particular ancestor had been of Scots origin, whereas mine was of the lesser French nobility who had come to New France with Champlain. Both obviously looked to find their fortunes in the Canadian wilderness.

It certainly appeared to be more than mere coincidence that our two families would individually determine it to be more than strategic to intermarry into what at that time, from a formal European perspective, would have been considered to be an inferior race. But there was something more to the report provided by the common priest Brunet to the then powerful Bishop of Montreal. It spoke of an intrigue of sorts, as the following translation of Brunet's letter illustrates.

> *Msg. Bourget,*
> *The twenty-third of June, 1845, you [directed or chose] [me] a community priest to evangelize in the distant regions of the North West from the immense diocese of Saint Sulpice. I happened upon the little mission at Allumette Island in the fall the twenty-second of September. With two young [Iroquois] Indians from Lake of Two Mountains, I [stayed] [secretly] with a*

voyager Thomas Lagarde dit St. Jean, [who is] a member of the Masons and also descended from Algonquins. He is a fugitive and has been condemned to death under the authority of the English at Montréal. He is to return in secret to Montréal with the voyager Urquet St. Jean of St. Francis of Templeton, and then retire among the Nipigon. We have the benefit of certain matters which I can discuss with you in depth soon.

Brunet

After reading the letter for the first time I was simply stunned at the notion that a direct ancestor of mine, more than a hundred and fifty years ago, was a hunted man and condemned to death by the British. The Brits militarily controlled Upper and Lower Canada ever since the French had been defeated on the Plains of Abraham in 1759. There was also the interesting reference to Allumette Island, a location in the midst of the Ottawa River that has tremendous spiritual and ancestral significance to the Algonquin. And it seemed that Brunet had deemed it of some importance to note that Lagarde was both an Algonquin and a Freemason, and I was intrigued by this as well.

The official story is that Freemasonry, including Templarism, had been introduced to British North America in the early eighteenth century by the many military officers who had been assigned to the various postings throughout eastern North America.[1] But I had come to realize through my own initiations that the higher degrees and Orders of both Scottish and York Rite Masonry (Knights Templar to be exact) were actually mirror images of some of the earliest ceremonies and rituals* practiced by a specific group of Native Americans (the Old Mide'win) long before the arrival of Champlain in 1604.

*For example, the notion of turning a "blind eye" to what may appear apparent to most can also be found in the Norse and Celtic myths of Woden and Lugh. Odin, the son of Woden, is blind in one eye, as is Cu Chulainn, the son of Lugh. This brings to mind the notion of an all-seeing third eye being present in everyone, but not everyone has the ability to see with it.

Was there some hidden Native American/Masonic connection to my family lineage?

Yet this is not what intrigued me the most when I read the letter for the first time. I couldn't help but think that I had read the same last sentence contained in Brunet's report—"We have the benefit of certain matters which I can discuss with you in depth soon"—somewhere before. The notion that Brunet had been told or shown something by Lagarde that could not be articulated in the letter and warranted a personal audience with the bishop suggested a unique "secret" in some manner. Perhaps the information related to the story behind Lagarde being wanted by the British, or perhaps the information related to something far more mysterious and invaluable.

And then there was the date: June 23, 1845. From my previous research I was very much aware that to the Knights Templar, June 24, Saint John the Baptist Day, was the most important day of the year. It was the day that the knights venerated the man who had baptized Jesus. (June 24 was also the date in 1314 when the Scottish Knights Templar purportedly rode to the rescue of Robert the Bruce and helped turn the tide at the Battle of Bannockburn. In fact, the first day of battle was June 23, 1314.[2])

John the Baptist plays a large part in the Holy Bloodline theory. Scholars generally believe Jesus was a follower or disciple of John, and several New Testament accounts report that some of Jesus's early followers had previously been followers of John. The Baptist is also mentioned by the Roman/Jewish historian Josephus, noting that he was considered a messianic figure himself and is referred to as the precursor or forerunner of Jesus.

In the Gospel of John, the fourth gospel, John the Baptist is described as "a man sent from God to bear witness to the light so that through him everyone might believe." In this light, John was seen to be Elijah, the prophet. However, John directly denies being the Christ or Elijah or "the prophet," instead describing himself as the "voice of one crying in the wilderness."

In any event, was there a clue in the date itself as to the secret that Brunet could only share with his superior in person? Brunet suggested

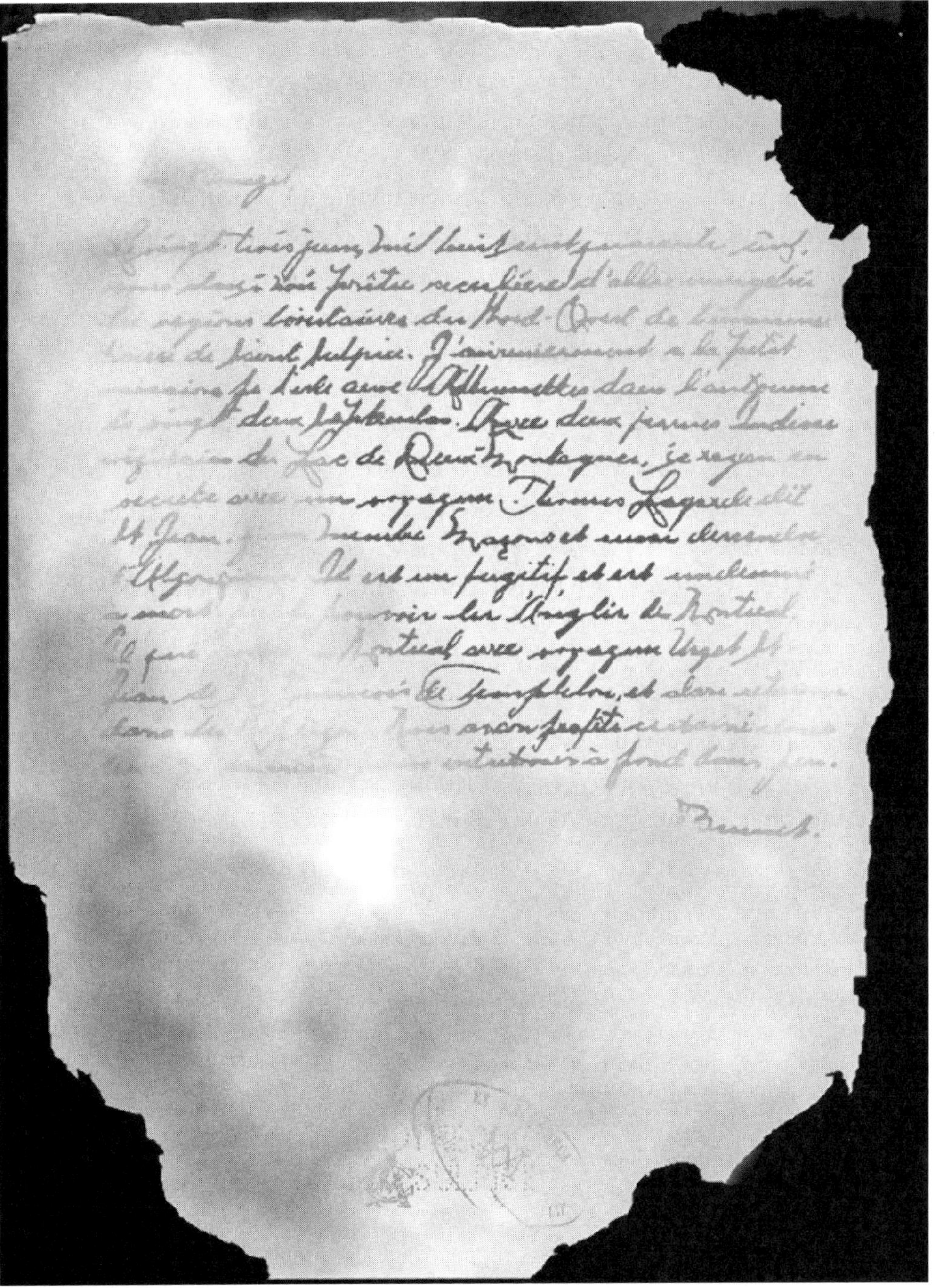

Fig. 1.3. Enhanced photograph of a copy of the original Brunet letter to Monsignor Bourget, Bishop of Montreal, dated June 23, 1845. Note the seal of the St. Sulpician Archives of Montreal at the bottom of the letter. Property of the author, William F. Mann.

even something more in his letter, identifying the voyageur as Thomas Lagarde dit St. Jean. Etymologically speaking, was Thomas seen as "the guard(ian) of Saint John (the Baptist)"? A "dit" name is a descriptive alias, or an a.k.a. of sorts, employed by early French Canadian families to distinguish one familial lineage from another. Compared to other aliases or nicknames that are given to one specific person, the dit names were adopted by families in relation to earlier occupations, the regions in France from whence they hailed, or some other distinctive aspect of the family's history.

In my previous two books I've shown that there are many facets to this entire story and that multiple levels of interpretation are required. If he had been schooled in the esoteric, Brunet could have buried multiple messages, codes, or clues within his letter, using the five elements, or keys of wisdom, that have been maintained in certain offshoots of Freemasonry. These Little Keys of Solomon, as they are known, allow the initiate to apply a variety of meanings on many different levels not only to increase the "secretiveness" of a ritual or message but also to trigger a higher level of understanding and knowledge.*[3]

Even to this day, every year in the early morning darkness of June 24, American and Canadian Masons climb Owl's Head Mountain, which is

---

*Kenneth MacKenzie, in his book *The Royal Masonic Cyclopedia,* goes to great lengths to explain that according to Canaan beliefs a pre-Flood patriarch called Lamech, who had three sons (the three apprentices), was the first to invent geometry. It is said that the first son taught geometry, another was supposedly the first mason, and the third was a blacksmith who was the first human to work with precious metals. Similar to the story of Noah, Canaan tradition maintained that Lamech was warned by Jehovah of the impending Flood caused by the wickedness of humanity. Consequently, Lamech and his sons decided to preserve their knowledge in two hollow stone pillars so that future generations would discover it.

One of these pillars was apparently discovered by Hermes Trismegistus, or Thrice-Great Hermes, who was known to the Greeks as the god Hermes and to the ancient Egyptians as Thoth. According to occult sources, the Emerald Tablet discovered by Hermes within the pillar, which in some stories is located in an underwater cave, is said to contain the essence of the lost wisdom from before the days of the biblical Flood. In other stories it is said that the mystic Apollonius of Tyana discovered this tablet in a cave. The first published version of the Emerald Tablet dates from an Arabic source of the eighth century CE, and it was not translated into Latin in Europe until the thirteenth century.

located south of Montreal along the Québec-Vermont border. It is here, in a natural rock bowl found on the mountaintop, that they perform the third degree ritual at sunrise. Surprisingly, what many of the modern-day Masons do not realize when they participate in the Owl's Head ritual on June 24 is that they are actually paying homage to an ancient pagan tradition.

The owl symbolism in fact can originally be traced back to the Hebrew/Akkadian goddess Lilith, a goddess of wisdom and magic who was depicted in many cases with owl's feet and wings and accompanied by two owls. Although it is said fraternally that the ceremony conforms to Antient, Free and Accepted Masonry and that "the old customs are carried out to the Masonic letter," the ceremony undeniably pays tribute to a far older, pagan Goddess ritual.

The key to the pagan origins of Freemasonry lies in the symbolic story of Hiram Abiff and the association or adoption of ancient initiation rites into the three basic degrees of Masonry. In Masonic lore the basis of the legend of Hiram Abiff is the semi-mythical story of the construction of King Solomon's Temple in Jerusalem. This building is regarded as the repository of ancient occult wisdom and symbolism by both the modern-day Freemasons and the Knights Templar. Kabbalistic traditions suggest that during the building of Solomon's Temple the craftsmen who came from Tyre with Hiram were paid in corn, wine, and oil. These specific sacrificial offerings were associated with the fertility cults of the dying gods such as Osiris and Adonis.

The same kabbalistic traditions tell of how Solomon supposedly carried King Hiram of Tyre off to hell by evoking a demon. However, this was not an act of vengeance. The story goes that when the king of Tyre returned from the depths, he told Solomon of all that he had seen and learned in the infernal kingdom. According to the Kabbalah, this was the true source of Solomon's wisdom. What this suggests is that Solomon was in actual fact a student of Hiram and was instructed by him in the pagan mysteries of the goddess Ishtar (also known as Astarte) and her story of the underworld.

Fig. 1.4. Historic picture depicting a Masonic gathering atop Owl's Head Mountain, Stanstead, Québec, following a sunrise ceremony commemorating Saint John the Baptist Day, June 24. Image provided courtesy of the Grand Lodge of Quebec.

Not to be mistaken with Arcadia, the Akkadian Empire from which the owl symbolism derives refers to the Semitic-speaking state that grew up around the city of Akkad, north of Sumer. The empire reached its greatest extent under Sargon of Akkad between 2296 and 2240 BCE. It was the first true empire in world history, and it flourished in one of the most fertile areas of the globe: the alluvial plain of southern Mesopotamia, which fed into the later Babylonian civilization.

ANTIENT, FREE AND ACCEPTED

Perhaps Brunet's letter speaks, in some oddly synchronistic way, to what I had written about in my previous two books. As I have noted, it was in *The Knights Templar in the New World* that I first explored the voyage of Prince Henry Sinclair, hereditary grand master of the Scottish Knights Templar, and his fellow knights. As established, this was the group who crossed the North Atlantic in 1398 CE in several ships to establish in Nova Scotia the first of many Rose Line settlements that ultimately stretched across North America.

I speculated in my earlier books that the hidden and underlying purpose behind Prince Henry Sinclair's daring and dramatic adventure was the need to establish a series of New World sanctuaries for the true Holy Bloodline—true living descendants of the union of Jesus and Mary Magdalene. And the individual sanctuaries that housed the direct descendants of the bloodline at one time or another are referred to as "Rose Lines." The derivation of the phrase Rose Line (conceived "under the rose") is as follows: In Greek mythology Aphrodite, the goddess of love, is said to have created the rose. The Romans turned Aphrodite into their goddess Venus. Rome was where Venus became the symbol of love and beauty. Cupid made the flower into a symbol of secrecy when he offered a rose to Harpocrates, the god of silence, in order to hush Venus's amorous escapades. As such, Roman dining room ceilings were decorated with roses, reminding guests to keep secret what had been said during dinner. Hence, *sub rosa,* "under the rose," became the term for discretion and confidentiality.[4]

In my second book, *The Templar Meridians: The Secret Mapping of the New World,* I delved more into how Prince Henry Sinclair came to possess D'Artt of the Antients, which was required to be able to reactivate a series of longitudinal meridians/rose lines across the New World. This enabled Prince Henry and those generations that followed him to locate and record the exact positions of a far-reaching network of Templar sanctuaries and focal points.

D'Artt of the Antients relates to those geometric axioms and mathematical proofs that were first developed and considered sacred in pre-Christian times by Greek philosophers and mathematicians such as Plato, Aristotle, Pythagoras, and Euclid. Indeed, it is simple Euclidean geometry upon which the geometric lessons of Freemasonry are based.

It is to Euclid that the proverb "there is no royal road to knowledge" is attributed. However, little is known of Euclid's life beyond the fact that he was born about 325 BCE and died about 265 BCE. It *is* known that he spent most of his life in Alexandria and that he taught mathematics at the university there and to private students for many years. His work fills a large part of the history of mathematics, with his greatest work being the *Elements of Mathematics,* which covered parts of arithmetic, a theory of numbers, algebra, and proportion, and all that was then known of geometry. The complete works consisted of thirteen books, and of these, seven were devoted to geometry. The books on geometry are usually separated from the others and together are known as Euclid's *Elements of Geometry* and more often simply referred to as *The Elements.* The reader will realize later on the real significance of the simple fact that *seven* of Euclid's works were devoted to geometry.

In *The Elements,* Euclid supposed that its reader could only use the ruler and compass and no other instrument. All of his drawings, proofs, and solutions are therefore based on and carried out by means of the straight line and circle. During and since Euclid's time other methods have been developed, but these belong to what is called higher geometry. It is Euclid's *elementary* geometry, the simpler form, that interests us here, in part given that this is the form that the Freemasons adopted for their use.

Now returning to the alternative name of this text of axioms and geometric proofs, D'Artt of the Antients, the next puzzle has to do with its label. Why is the word *Ancients* spelled A-n-t-i-e-n-t-s in this case? The "t" in antients actually suggests that God was responsible for the conveyance of the elementary laws of geometry directly to man. As will be demonstrated, the symbol T has played an intimate part in the conveyance of this knowledge throughout the ages. Not surprisingly, therefore, it continues to be promoted by certain Masonic bodies that the two main principles of Freemasonry (moral allegory and sacred geometry) have been passed down from a time before the Great Deluge, directly from God. Thus, the use of the phrasing "Antient, Free and Accepted Masons, or

A.F. & A. M.,"*[5] the key word here being *free,* implies that the principles and traditions are unencumbered by third party intermediaries such as priests or other mediums.

And why, in this situation, are two "t's" contained in the Old French word for D'Artt? As we have learned, the second "t" is representative of God or, on the same level, the earlier pagan Goddess. Thus, there is the suggestion of "God's Art" or the "Art of the Goddess." In this light this symbolism of the "t" was adopted by one of the first true monastic mystics, Saint Anthony.[6] Saint Anthony was also known as the patron saint of skin diseases, in particular ergotism, or Saint Anthony's Fire. He had a reputation as a healer in general and for this reason was the object of much devotion in the Middle Ages and during the Crusades.

THE HIDDEN SIGNIFICANCE OF SAINT ANTHONY

About the year 285 CE, at the age of thirty-five, it is said that Anthony crossed the eastern branch of the Nile and took up residence in some ruins on the top of a mountain. Here he lived almost twenty years in solitude. To satisfy his ever-growing group of followers he eventually came down from the mountain and founded his first monastery. But he chose for the most part to shut himself up in his cell upon the mountain until his death.

In Sassetta's famous painting *The Meeting of St. Anthony and St. Paul* (ca. 1440 CE) three scenes in one are presented. Anthony, in

---

*In many ways the description of the Eleusian ceremonies or rituals that Kenneth MacKenzie provided in *The Royal Masonic Cyclopaedia* resembles on a much grander scale the rites of the basic three degrees of Masonry.

In 1866 the English Societas Rosicruciana in Anglia was founded by Robert Wentworth Little on the basis of antient rituals that he purportedly discovered. Of particular interest is the fact that this body counted among its members Kenneth MacKenzie, who, at that time, was considered the utmost authority on Masonic symbolism and relationship. Had previous ancient societies possessed an understanding of the natural world in some manner beyond today's comprehension? Men such as MacKenzie, who spent all of their lives trying to decipher the countless rituals and symbolism, certainly believed this to be so.

the first scene, is shown setting out across the desert to find his companion, Saint Paul. In the second scene he blesses the centaur, a symbol of the pagan world, in a manner suggesting that the Christian Church adopted many symbols from its pagan roots. The third scene is where Saint Anthony finally meets with Saint Paul (bringing together the two rings of light that surround them in a symbolism reminiscent of the vesica piscis!). All of this takes place in a landscape dense with woods under a horizon high above the airy hills. In scene three, though, instead of sky there is an abstract gold ground that seems to emphasize a gold-rich land where there is a preciousness with which simple objects and events are treated. Could this be another sly reference to the blessed land of Arcadia?

What is missing in these enchanting scenes from the life of Saint Anthony is the completion of his ultimate task, the completion of the fourth scene: Saint Anthony burying Saint Paul in the cave with the help of the two lions. This omission provoked a flood of past literature and arguments with respect to the overall concept of the series of events. Is one to conclude that the Christian Church is not founded upon the rock of Saint Paul but the pagan symbolism that came before it and that the Church's sanctity is tainted by its demand for riches? In the eleventh to fifteenth centuries these were definitely part of the secret teachings of the Cathars and the Knights Templar.

Could Saint Anthony the Hermit's deeds be seen as the true path to Christendom? The Knights Templar certainly believed that to seek the light one had to retreat into the desert or the wilderness. It was the very first monks, Anthony and Paul, who in their independent withdrawal to the wilderness and shunning of all earthly possessions in the fourth century, and by using logic and reason, discovered a direct way to communicate with God.

Given as much, the generally held theory is that certain secret societies over the ages have either developed or come into the possession of a higher level of knowledge and skill, which directly relates to what are referred to in certain Masonic circles as the five mystery elements, or Little Keys of Solomon: astronomy, duality, numerology, androgyny, and (the hidden fifth element) etymology. It is also believed that through the proper application of these elements, or keys, in relation to ancient philosophy and Euclidian geometry, such as "squaring the circle," the initiate can achieve a higher level of wisdom. This allows the individual to not only understand the true meaning of God, the Creator, but also to be able to control the forces of nature and Earth. In doing so, when in perfect harmony and balance, the proper application allows the initiate to communicate directly with the Supreme Being.

SIGNS, SEALS, AND TOKENS

Coming full circle for the first time, could Thomas Lagarde dit St. Jean, deep in the Canadian wilderness in the mid-1800s, possess such powerful knowledge and wisdom? Even I am very skeptical as to the mystical abilities of one who appears to have spent most of his life in the bush trapping and trading. What is more likely is that the voyageur Lagarde, who had most certainly been initiated into Freemasonry, somehow during his travels into the interior had rediscovered or been shown by one of his fellow Algonquin the remains of another Rose Line settlement or a metal artifact relating to those Europeans who had come in pre-Columbian times.[7]

Mystery Hill, also known as America's Stonehenge, which is located just outside of Salem, New Hampshire, is one of the better-known sites of ancient travelers to America. But a lesser-known area, quite close to Nova Scotia, yielded some very interesting artifacts that link the Phoenicians to the New World. On Manana Island, which is located off the larger Monhegan Island of Maine, there are inscriptions identified by Barry Fell in his book *America B.C.*, as a Celtic script known as Hinge Ogam. The pointed runic characters differ from the seventy well-known varieties of Irish Ogam in that they lack symbols for vowels. Past epigraphers apparently have failed to understand these differences and therefore always considered the runes to be marks created by natural erosion. Barry Fell, in essence, cracked the code of a previously unknown writing system.

Certain evidence of an active sea trade between North America and the Mediterranean more than two thousand years ago was also found in the Bay of Castine, which is located about fifty miles northeast of Monhegan Island along the Maine coast. In 1921, at about forty feet below the water's surface and stuck in the mud, two ceramic amphorae dating back to the ancient Phoenicians were found. These led to the theory that thriving seaports grew in ancient times all along the eastern seaboard of the New World.

What Lagarde rediscovered would have been just as easily recognizable for two reasons. Native North Americans didn't work in metal until much later, and they never constructed their homes or fortifications using stone. Being a Freemason, Thomas would have surely recognized any signs, seals, and tokens possibly left behind by earlier Masonic travelers—or he could have recognized portions of Masonic ritual in native ceremonies. Or, maybe in his travels he was introduced to specific native tribes who displayed hidden European traits or physical characteristics that could only have been passed down from generation to generation.

Perhaps, on an even more intriguing level, Lagarde himself was a descendant of the Holy Bloodline and possessed oral traditions and artifacts that could prove his lineage. Native American lineage is matriarchal, meaning that descendancy is followed through the mother's ancestral line versus the more European patriarchal practice. Indigenous people also pass down their history through an oral tradition or by rote, relying on signs, seals, and tokens as a way of stirring a deeper memory, similar to that still practiced by Freemasons.

Information of this nature would have been of prime importance to the Order of St. Sulpice, for they were an offshoot of the Franciscans (the Brown Robes) and sworn enemies of the agents of the Roman Catholic Church, namely the Jesuits. It was not only the Jesuit Saint Dominic who, with the blessing of the church, became the instigator of the Spanish Inquisition, it was also the Jesuits, the Black Robes, who first moved inland from Montreal in 1639 and established the mission Sainte-Marie among the Huron.

The result of this folly was the obliteration of nearly all of those Huron/Wendat Indians who had heeded the call of the Jesuits to embrace God but only ended up with smallpox, which the first wave of Europeans had unwittingly brought with them. In retaliation the nonconverted, more warriorlike Iroquois burned the mission in 1649, killing the Jesuit missionaries Jean de Brebeuf and Gabriel Lalement and eating their hearts to ward off the evil spirits that had fallen upon their land.

THE REAL REASON FOR THE JESUITS IN CANADA

The underlying reason for the Jesuits' advancement into the Canadian wilderness was a more sinister one. I firmly believe that they had been entrusted by the inner circle of the Vatican to search out and destroy all remaining descendants of the Holy Bloodline along with any remaining guardians of it. Earlier reports by double agents such as Cartier and Champlain to the French monarchy had confirmed that there were at least native legends concerning white men who had gone westward before them. Also reported was that these great warriors wore "red, crossed sticks" on their chests and were shamans in their own right. Algonquin myth also spoke about fair-skinned, strangely dressed women accompanying the strange giants who wore metal on their heads and bodies.

Historically the Society of Jesus was founded as the Company of Jesus in 1540 by Ignatius Loyola. Saint Ignatius was originally a Spanish Basque soldier who, along with six other Spanish and French students from the University of Paris, started what has today become the largest religious order in the Roman Catholic Church. The term "Jesuit" was first applied to the society in 1544, but the order's name was eventually changed to the Society of Jesus by Pope Paul III. The stated objective of the society was to strengthen the Catholic faith in all lands while counteracting the spread of Protestantism. The Jesuits thus became the main instruments of the counter-reformation movement, and it is said that the preservation of the Catholic faith in France and other countries was largely due to their efforts.

One unconfirmed account places the Jesuits in Acadia as early as 1611. It is known for certain though that the Jesuits were on Isle Royale—Cape Breton—by 1629, where in August they established the first Jesuit mission and chapel at Sipo, a Mi'kmaq name meaning "gathering place," later renamed Fort Sainte Anne. Later that year a vessel left France carrying several more Jesuit missionaries. Unfortunately, it was shipwrecked somewhere in the vicinity of Canso, and fourteen priests lost their lives. Between the years 1630 and 1632, as the English were in possession of New France, the Jesuits were forced to abandon their work and retreat to France. When the French regained control of the area in July 1632, the Jesuits returned to Fort Sainte Anne, where they continued serving both the Mi'kmaqs and Acadians until 1641, when the mission at Saint Anne's was closed.

From 1632 to 1673 it appears that the Jesuits had gained control of all of New France, except for the colony at Montreal, through their relentless religious conversion of the Algonquin Nation. Thus for more than fifty years it was primarily the Jesuits who furthered any knowledge about the Canadian frontier. Most of what is known of their activities can be found in the many volumes of the published *Relations,* a massive work that brought together the reports of the missionaries' work in Canada.

The Jesuits meticulously kept their French administrators informed of events that occurred in the many regions of the New World, especially in the areas around the Great Lakes and between the St. Lawrence River and Hudson Bay. Here the English were making great attempts to penetrate the fur trade through the newly established Hudson's Bay Company. The Jesuits were also primarily responsible for the prevention of any real penetration from the south by the Dutch and their Iroquois allies until about 1648, again because of the spiritual guidance and self-imposed, authoritative direction provided to the Huron.

In 1657, Pope Alexander VII, who favored the Jesuits, placed all missionaries in New France under the jurisdiction of the archbishop of Rouen. The archbishop immediately appointed the superior of the Québec Jesuits as his vicar-general. This arrangement continued until June 1659, when the Jesuit bishop François de Laval came to Québec as the first vicar apostolic of New France, appointed by Pope

Alexander VII. Laval remained in Québec until 1662, when he returned to France, leaving the Indian missions in the care of the Jesuits.

A familiar side note to all of this is that Pope Francis, during a Mass held on the Canadian Thanksgiving, Sunday, October 11, 2014, canonized two seventeenth-century missionaries who spread Catholicism through what today is Canada. The Pope had done this alongside Québec cardinal Gerald Cyprien Lacroix and dozens of nuns and priests who made the pilgrimage to Rome. The first missionary canonized was none other than Saint François de Laval, and the second was the Ursuline nun Saint Marie de L'Incarnation, who, as the pope noted, had spread their faith "to the smallest and most remote parts of New France."

Back in 1663 the diocesan Seminary of Québec was founded under the title "Foreign Missions." The Jesuits also restored the Iroquois missions south of Lake Ontario. South of Montreal they founded the permanent mission of La Prairie de La Madeleine, which certainly suggests because of the veiled reference to the Magdalene that they had discovered something relating to an earlier Grail Refugees' colony located in the Lake Memphremagog/Owl's Head Mountain area south of Montreal.

It was in this area that René Goupil and the Jesuit father Issac Jogues were put to death by the Mohawks in 1642 and 1646, respectively. Furthermore, this was the home of Catherine/Kateri Tegakwitha, who was mysteriously labeled by Pope Leo XII in 1943 as the "Lily of Canada." She was also known as the "Genevieve of New France." On October 21, 2012, she was canonized by Pope Benedict XVI at Saint Peter's Basilica.

The story of the two martyrs and Catherine/Kateri Tegakwitha is again one of those odd little anecdotes, which is quite puzzling in that it's difficult to ascertain why this Iroquois/Algonquin maiden's name was added to those of the murdered René Goupil and Isaac Jogues for beatification and ultimately sainthood. Pope Leo XII had also declared that she had been born in the very same village where René Goupil and Father Jogues had shed their blood; otherwise there was no reason to even consider her for martyrdom.

The strangest thing arising out of this is that Catherine was born in 1656, some ten years after Father Jogues was murdered. Her father,

Fig. 1.5. Photo of stained-glass window found in Notre-Dame Basilica, which is located next to the Grand Seminarie du Saint Sulpice in Old Montreal. The left-hand window depicts one of the founders of La Congregation de Notre-Dame, Marguerite Bourgeoys; the right-hand window depicts Catherine/Kateri Tegakwitha. Marguerite is shown in her royal blue Franciscan robe; Catherine Tegakwitha is depicted in white with red stripes. Note the single stone tower that stands behind Marguerite Bourgeoys and the tepee that stands behind Catherine Tegakwitha. Photograph property of the author, William F. Mann.

it is said, was a chief of the Iroquois Turtle Clan, and her mother was Algonquin. Perhaps the real reason for her being recognized by the church was that Catherine was a descendant of the Holy Bloodline. She was the living proof sought by Goupil and Jogues during their earlier infiltration of the natives.

The origin of the name Iroquois is uncertain, although it seems to have involved a French adaptation of Indian words. Among the possibilities that have been suggested are a blending of *ierokwa* (meaning "they who smoke") and *iakwai* (meaning "bear"), or the Algonquin words *irin* (meaning "real") and *ako* (meaning "snake"), with the French *ois* (meaning "termination"). The French spelling roughly translates into "real snakes" or "rattlesnakes," which will take on a very significant meaning further along in the story.

In 1668 the French Jesuit father Marquette planted the cross at Sault Sainte Marie, and in the same year he set up a new mission at Chequamegon Bay near the western end of Lake Superior. When the Huron Indians that he worked among fled after several Sioux attacks, he followed them and moved the mission to the northern shore of the Straits of Mackinac, which are located between Lake Michigan and Lake Huron. It is here that a mission was established on a small island that is presently known as Beaver Island.

But it was up to a newcomer by the name of Louis Joliet and the indomitable Jesuit father Jacques Marquette to penetrate inland to the next Templar meridian, which was to be discovered at the 88 degree west longitudinal meridian mark—that is, 87 degrees 57 minutes west longitude to be exact. Located at the appropriately named present-day Oak Park, a neighborhood of Chicago fronting onto Lake Michigan, here was where Joliet would confirm the existence of an ancient Rose Line settlement/Templar nexus that signified the bridge between the Great Lakes and the Mississippi River basin. And like Champlain had done previously in Acadia at Green Oaks, they recognized that the meridians could be identified by the grove of oak trees that had been specifically planted as signposts directing them along the way!

With the death of Joliet in 1700 it appears as though the dominance of the French Jesuits across the new frontier died with him, given that the British had started to flex their collective muscles to the north and south of New France. The questions still remained, though, as to what had happened to the remnants of the Grail colonies, and where was the Templar treasure? The trail of Prince Henry Sinclair and his followers had definitely gone cold. It would be up to a number of British explorers to revive the quest in the early part of the eighteenth century.

Apparently, though, the English had a hand in the New World long before this. From his own records we know that in 1497, John Cabot (originally Giovanni Caboto from Genoa), on a mission on behalf the English sovereign Henry VII, was one of the first to report the sighting of a number of foreign fishing boats and temporary camps along the banks of Newfoundland. Following along the eastern seaboard using information gleaned from the fishermen of Bristol, Cabot was also one of the first to report on the whereabouts of the lost city of Norumbega.[8]

The Columbus Myth by Ian Wilson supports the claim that Bristol mariners, expelled from Iceland and searching for a new supply of cod, rediscovered Newfoundland some twelve years before Columbus. Wilson attempts to demonstrate that Bristol fishermen not only preceded Columbus but also his fellow countryman John Cabot to the shores of America by more than a decade. It seems beside the point to argue who rediscovered America around 1492, when all of the evidence points to pre-Christian exploration of North America. What is of importance in relation to Norumbega and the lost Seven Cities is the historical account presented by Wilson of Cabot's supposed voyage(s), which, like those of Columbus and Champlain, are full of suspicion and contradiction.

Of John Cabot's voyage (he reputedly sailed under the flag of England's King Henry VII from the west country port of Bristol to "discover" North America in 1497) there survives no journal, no biography, not a single document in his handwriting or even any remotely contemporary portrait. Yet he was hailed as a conquering explorer when, in 1756, the British required a claim to the New World.

Another belief—an earlier native belief attributed to the East Coast Mi'kmaq, a tribal nation that is part of the larger Algonquin Nation—tells of a man god, Kluscap, or Glooscap, who is said "to have arrived on their shores from the east" and then "went to the west." During his time with the Mi'kmaq, Kluscap/Glooscap came to know the ways of the Mi'kmaq, in turn sharing with them his knowledge and skills. Primary among those researchers who believe that Prince Henry Sinclair assumed the persona of Glooscap during his time with the Mi'kmaq was an American English teacher cum archaeologist of sorts by the name of Frederick J. Pohl.*[9]

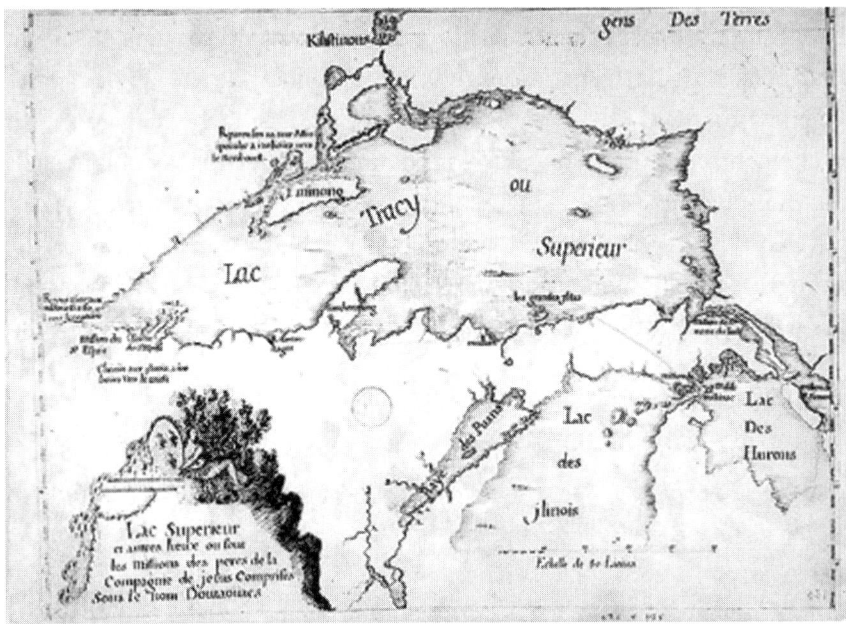

Fig. 1.6. Composite Jesuit map of 1675 illustrating the extent of inland exploration by various Jesuit explorers

*It should be noted that many people have accepted Pohl's premise that June 2, 1398, was the specific date of Sinclair's landing yet appear to have dismissed the notion that Sinclair and his men made more than one expedition to the New World. I think that several transatlantic journeys were made between the acceptable dates of 1395 and 1403 based upon the extensive recordings and evidence that indicate they brought with them the necessary provisions, tools, materials, livestock, and personnel to advance a large settlement of farmers and miners.

MORE EVIDENCE FOR PRE-COLUMBIAN CONTACT

As stated earlier, Frederick Pohl was one of the first to associate Prince Henry Sinclair with the oral legends of the Mi'kmaq by determining that there are seventeen striking similarities between Glooscap the man god and Prince Henry. This is not to say, however, that Sinclair should be assumed to be the ultimate Mi'kmaq entity, for Henry may have assumed the Glooscap persona for his own purposes. After all, Sinclair and his followers needed the help of the local natives on many different levels.

Ever since I can remember I have been totally enthralled by Pohl's books and the books of others relating to the transatlantic voyages of ancient mariners, ranging from Jason and the Argonauts to the Phoenicians, Carthaginians, the Irish monk Saint Brendan, and the Vikings. This excitement culminated in news of the discovery of the remains of the Viking settlement now known as L'Anse-aux-Meadows, which was discovered near St. Anthony, Newfoundland, in 1960. It was excavated in the 1970s by the Norwegian archaeological team of Helge Ingstad and his wife, Anne Stine Ingstad.

According to most books on the subject Brendan was born on the Dingle Peninsula in Kerry, southwest Ireland, in 484 CE. It is well known that Ireland was one of the few sanctuaries of learning in the Dark Ages, and Brendan was fortunate enough to attend school in Limerick, learning Latin, Hebrew, Greek, Gaelic, mathematics, and astronomy. It was in Ireland that any of the educated priests sought martyrdom by living as hermits in crude stone "beehive" huts on sea-swept islets in the Atlantic. Others cast themselves adrift in boats, putting their absolute faith in the hands of God. Brendan is said to have done this in 545 CE with fourteen other monks, safely reaching the Fortunate Isles, one of which later became known as Saint Brendan's Isle.

On Martin Behaim's globe, unveiled at Nuremberg in 1492, Saint Brendan's Isle was included among the lands west of the Canary Islands. Later on, expeditions were sent to look for it from both

Spain and Portugal, but it was never found. Several fifteenth-century maps show a vague but large island called Antilla across the western ocean. Brasil, yet another name for the Fortunate Isles, and Atlantis, the land of a forgotten civilization mentioned by Plato, were supposedly positioned somewhere in the same far seas to the west, but they too were never discovered.

L'Anse aux Meadows, carbon-dated to around the dated 1000, is the only site widely accepted as evidence of pre-Columbian transoceanic contact. Named a World Heritage Site by UNESCO in 1978, it is most notable for its possible connection with the attempted colony of Vinland established by Leif Ericson around the same period.

Interestingly, Pohl is still one of America's most widely prolific authors on the subject of pre-Columbian voyages, even though he died in 1991. Among his earlier works are *Lost America, Atlantic Voyages before Columbus,* and *The Viking Explorers,* which is a tale of the Norsemen's voyages to Greenland and North America in the eleventh

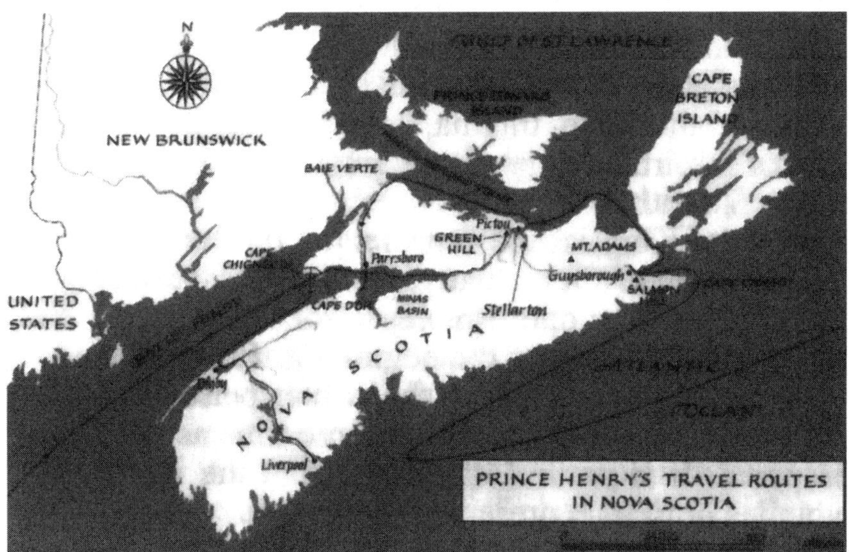

Fig. 1.7. Graphic depicting Prince Henry's travel route to Nova Scotia, according to Frederick J. Pohl. Taken from *Prince Henry Sinclair: His Expedition to the New World in 1398.*

century. Certainly Pohl's most infamous book is *Prince Henry Sinclair: His Expedition to the New World in 1398,* where through his interpretation of the Zeno Narrative he traces the route of Prince Henry's voyage to the New World.

Even though several Viking artifacts were discovered at L'Anse aux Meadows, many academics are still critical of the Ingstads and therefore dismiss the notion that the Vikings' Vinland is located somewhere along the northeastern shore of North America. But others such as author Barry Fell, in *America B.C.,* have also contended that not only did the Norse cross the North Atlantic but that diverse groups such as the Celts, Phoenicians, Egyptians, and Carthaginians did as well. Fell even goes so far as to speculate that King Solomon's mines were located in North America.[*10] Fell supported his theory of pre-Christian Celtic mariners by citing the hundreds of inscriptions found among stone ruins spread across Vermont, New Hampshire, and other eastern seaboard states of America, including the enigmatic Newport Tower, located in Newport, Rhode Island.

The Newport Tower appears on two maps that predate the colonial era by more than half a century. Giovanni de Verrazano mapped the area in approximately 1524 and listed the tower on his map and in his logs as a "Norman Villa." In his log notes he also described the native people who lived near the tower as "white European-Amer-Norse," because of their fair hair and skin and pleasant disposition.[11]

Michael Bradley in *Holy Grail Across the Atlantic* noted that the ruins at New Ross, Nova Scotia are generally similar in type of construction and style to the famous Newport Tower. However, in mentioning the Newport Tower, Bradley introduced a controversy that

---

*Author Robert Charroux, in addition to Pohl, has noted that before the discovery of the New World gold was extremely scarce in Europe, Asia, and Africa. Yet, according to biblical sources, in order to build his temple Solomon exchanged twenty-five cities for forty-four hundred pounds of gold from Hiram, King of Tyre. However, Hiram, who was Solomon's architect, was still forced to send several expeditions to the Ophir mines in order to meet a gold shortfall. Although these expeditions left from the Gulf of Aqaba in the Red Sea, their ultimate destination has never been determined; but it has been established that Hiram and Solomon's vessels were out at sea for forty-two days before reaching their destination.

crops up throughout his book and those of many other authors. The tower is a structure that apparently stood before Newport was founded in 1639. The problem is that conventional historians are unable to concede that it must have been built prior to any acceptable colonial periods. Again, however, evidence of pre-colonial European settlement was documented by Barry Fell in his *America B.C.,* as well as in Salvatore Michael Trento's *The Search for Lost America.*

Bradley also noted that the Flemish could also be considered to be of Norse descent. This is of particular importance to me personally, as I detail on pages 15–16 of the introduction. Interestingly, the twelfth century poet and troubadour Chretien de Troyes' story of the Grail was dedicated to Philippe d'Alsace, Count of Flanders. As such, the New Ross ruins and Newport Tower both have definite pre-fifteenth century Flemish/Norse characteristics, including their masonry technique of using uncut stones neatly fitted together. In Prince Henry Sinclair's time in the fourteenth century the Norse sagas were just being written down in Latin and formed the nucleus of Scandinavian lore. Earlier stories of the Celtic Avalon must have intertwined with

Fig. 1.8. Photo of the Newport Tower, Newport, Rhode Island, which is positioned in alignment with the four cardinal points and the winter solstice sunrise, among other archaeoastronomical alignments. Photograph property of the author, William F. Mann.

the Norse sagas to produce a blended version of the "Isle to the West."

Mercator's world map, published in 1569, also shows the exact location of the tower, which falls in an area labeled as Norumbega. The simple beauty of the location of the Newport Tower is that directly to the east and south of it lay nothing but the Atlantic Ocean. At night a small sliver of firelight coming from the interior of the tower must have been visible for upward of twenty nautical miles out to sea, but only to those who knew enough to approach the coastline on a true east to west or north to south bearing.

It was the earlier work of Pohl and the Ingstads that prompted contemporary author Michael Bradley to first speculate as to where Prince Henry Sinclair and his followers established their first Rose Line settlement in mainland Nova Scotia. Bradley's book *Holy Grail Across the Atlantic* positions a stone tower and walls at a small present-day community called New Ross, which overlooks Mahone Bay and the enigmatic Oak Island along the south shore of Nova Scotia. The author insofar goes to suggest that this is one of two castles depicted on the map that is associated with the Zeno Narrative, written, as noted earlier, by the great-nephew of the two Venetian Templar admirals who guided Prince Henry Sinclair and his followers on their voyage of 1398.

Curiously, in the lower left-hand corner of the Zeno map, in a country labeled Estotiland, are two illustrated stone towers, not one. Contrary to Bradley's summation, in the pages of *The Knights Templar of the New World,* I was able to demonstrate through the use of a geometric symbol shown to me by my late great-uncle, Frederic George Mann, a past supreme grand master of the Knights Templar of Canada, that at the small community of Green Oaks, Nova Scotia, deep in the woods, there remains the remnants of a stone tower. Close-up, enhanced aerial photographs have also revealed a number of concentric rings within the remnants of a Celtic earth fort, suggesting that astronomical alignments were recorded over time along a longitudinal meridian, making Green Oaks a true Rose Line settlement.

Through further research involving early sixteenth- and seventeenth-century maps, focusing on the map of 1566 attributed to Zaltieri, I was able to determine that indeed there were two stone towers

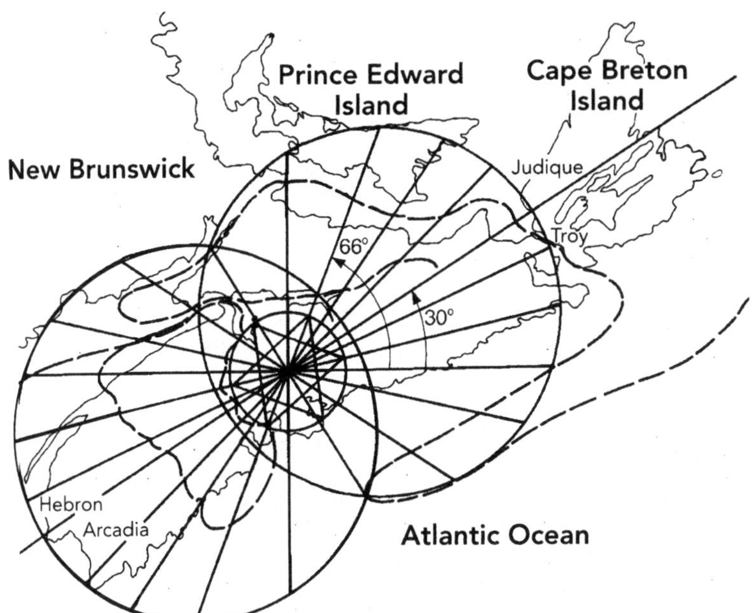

Fig. 1.9. Copy of an original drawing completed by the author demonstrating the application of the vesica piscis and Jewel of the Royal Arch to mainland Nova Scotia. Diagram copyright of the author, William F. Mann.

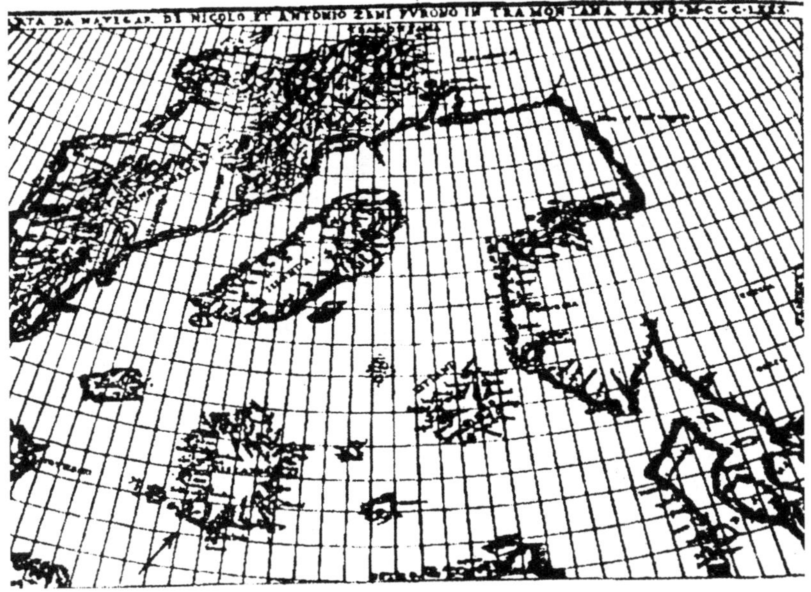

Fig. 1.10. Map contained in the Zeno Narrative, based on an equidistant azimuthal projection of the North Atlantic. Estotiland, with its two castles, is shown in the bottom left-hand corner.

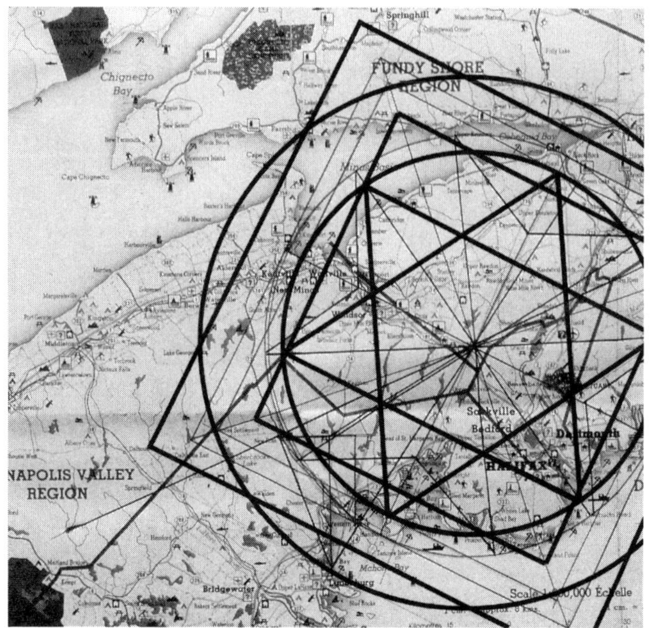

Fig. 1.11. Illustration depicting application of the Euclidian squaring of the circle and the resulting Jewel of the Royal Arch to mainland Nova Scotia, which led the author to the discovery of the remains of a Rose Line settlement at Green Oaks. Diagram copyright of the author, William F. Mann.

Fig. 1.12. Portion of the Zaltieri map of 1566 showing two medieval communities or castles labeled as Starnatana and Taina, located near the Bay of Fundy (Lago).

positioned on mainland Nova Scotia relative to the Bay of Fundy. The names given for these two medieval communities or castles, represented by the symbols of the stone castles, were, in Latin, *taina* (meaning "refuge") and *Starnatana* (meaning "Star of David"). Given what is suggested to date, the Star of David, or six-pointed star, definitely could be a sly reference to an early refuge or sanctuary of the descendants of Jesus and Mary Magdalene.

THE INITIATE

All in all, my journey so far over the past twenty years, over a lifetime actually, has been an interesting one to say the least. It stretches from the discovery of the remnants of a pre-Columbian stone tower in Nova Scotia, based on an application of sacred geometry and moral allegory embedded in my mind as a child, to the determination and discovery of a seemingly improbable longitudinal/latitudinal meridian grid pattern. This grid pattern, as stated earlier, when applied across North America, reveals a series of prominent strategic landmarks, stone circles, and medicine wheels, along with the remnants of earlier Indian villages or settlements.

What all of this has also led me to is an awakening of a previously unknown family heritage and my ensuing spiritual transformation, directly resulting in my current position as an executive grand council officer and grandhistorian/achivist of the Knights Templar of Canada, a Christian Masonic group of the highest order, as well as my becoming, just as importantly, an initiate of the Old Mide'win—the Grand Medicine Society of the Anishinabe/Algonquin Nation. In turn these associations have provided me access to the inner circles of two great "secret societies" and have given me the opportunity to meet some of what I consider to be the greatest people on Earth, unique individuals who have avoided the limelight that others seek so desperately.

These great and wise people, in turn, have encouraged me to finally reveal the full extent of what I have uncovered through logic and reason, including the final resting place of Prince Henry Sinclair and the last refuge of the Knights Templar in the New World. One of these people carries the native title of Keeper of the Prophecies.

Fig. 1.13. The author in front of the ceremonial tepee while attending an Algonquin spring fasting camp. Photograph property of the author, William F. Mann.

One such prophecy passed on to the native Algonquin shaman through a vision, just before the arrival of Champlain in 1604, was that the antient wisdom, including the knowledge and wisdom divined through the pre-Columbian strategic interaction between the Old World and the New World, had to go underground. The vision concluded that the antient wisdom had to be buried deep for at least four hundred years, until a time when mankind was willing and ready to accept an alternative history and all that it would reveal. The message spread throughout the Americas was that the native peoples were to abandon their ancient cities and take to the wilderness.

The time has now come to heed those visions and to return from the wilderness to reveal the lost "Art"!

Fig. 1.14. The author, Right Eminent Knight William F. Mann, shown following his initiation in 2007 as presiding preceptor of Godfrey de Bouillon Preceptory No. 3, Hamilton District No. 2, Sovereign Great Priory—Knights Templar of Canada. Photograph property of the author, William F. Mann.

2
A God for All Seasons

THE BEAR GODDESS

No one knows exactly what our earliest ancestors believed in from a spiritual perspective, but what *is* clear is that at some point humans started conceptualizing a Divine Being. Given the prevalence of the bear[1] throughout the Northern Hemisphere, for the peoples that resided there this was the logical choice of creature upon which to pin the notion of divinity.

I found it surprising that the British authors of *Holy Blood, Holy Grail* seemed to be more surprised by the fact that the Welsh word for bear is *arth* (as in "Arthur") than by the fact that Ursus, the Latin word for bear, is associated with the royal Merovingian line. Alternatively, Michael Bradley, in *Holy Grail Across the Atlantic,* provided sound reasoning associating the transfer of the Holy Grail from Arthur to the Merovingians circa 500 CE, when the Merovingian dynasty (the lineage that descended from the union of Jesus and Mary Magdalene) coalesced as such. Bradley noted that in the fifth century the invasion of the Huns, and more particularly the invasions of the Angles and Saxons and others into Britain, provoked massive migrations of all European tribes. This included the movement of the Sicambrian ancestors of the Merovingians into Gaul.[2]

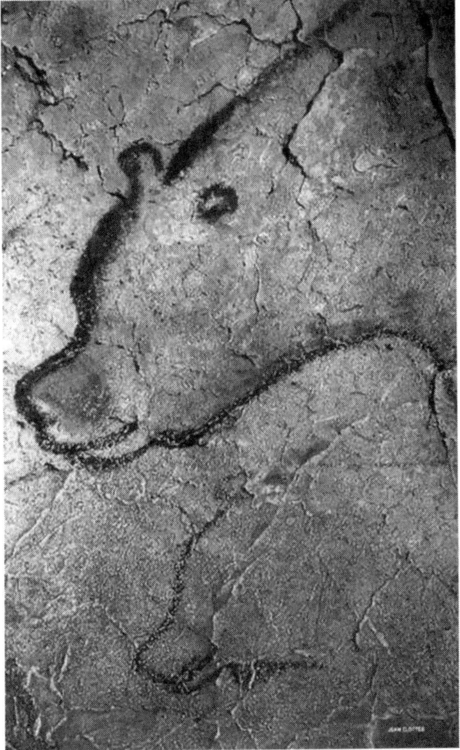

Fig. 2.1. One of the earliest images of a bear ever painted by man, appearing on a wall of the Lascaux caves, France

The two main legends attesting to Arthur's survival, the Avalon legend and the cave legend, both derive from the Celtic myth of the banished god Cronus, who sleeps in a cave on a western island until the dawning of a new golden age. A similar version of the cave legend is still part of the Arthurian lore of Glastonbury and Cadbury-Camelot. The legends tell of a king who sleeps in a cave, the doors or gates of which occasionally open so that the unsuspecting may catch a glimpse of him.

From all accounts it is because of Arthur's fall at the hands of his son Mordred that the golden age perished. However, because of the belief in Arthur's immortality, the ideal of the golden age is not lost. In many parts of rural Britain there remains a deep-rooted belief that

King Arthur still lies in his cave, awaiting discovery. Thus, the archetypal pattern reflected by the "lost king" has maintained a real influence on past and present religious and political movements, as well as on mythology and tourism.

We know for certain that the bear became one of the earliest observed symbols of life itself by our ancient ancestors and that the bear's various attributes metamorphosed over time into the earliest Goddess veneration. Starting some 20,000 years ago, during the Neolithic Period and the advent of stone tool construction, there is evidence of a bear cult in which the mother bear was seen as lord of the animals, a goddess as such, and was even considered to be the direct ancestor of humans.[3]

Mythologist Joseph Campbell and archaeologist Marija Gimbutas are well-known academics, particularly respected for their work on the goddess archetype and its origins. Indeed, Campbell claims that bear cults and clans are even older than the practice of shamanism, wherein the initiate dreams of contact with a higher spirit in his or her subconscious. Typically this is achieved by inducing an altered state of consciousness via the ingestion of mind-altering drugs, undergoing a fast, or experiencing sensory deprivation that may be brought on by long periods of time spent in a labyrinth or a cave.

Members of many ancient cultures, in an effort to try to *become* the bear itself, wore bearskins with the head still attached. The fierce attributes of the male bear as hunter and protector were admired by the human warrior-hunter as qualities to emulate and achieve. Fans of the movie *The 13th Warrior,* starring Antonio Banderas, will see this reflected in the depiction of the animalistic warriors of the Bear Clan, who were found in caves deep in the forest. Following the commands of the Mother Bear, these warriors emerged from the mountains to raid the more advanced agricultural communities springing up in the clearings of the Norse vales.

Younger fans of the animated Disney movie *Brave* will recognize Bear Goddess attributes assumed by the character of Queen Elinor and her spirited daughter Merida. The heroine, the wise queen, battles the ancient Bear Spirit found among the standing stones in order to protect her first-born daughter. The bloodline between mother and daughter and their matriarchal lineage is wonderfully yet subtly explored within the context of the earliest Scottish clan system.

The hibernation and birthing patterns of the bear correspond to the four seasons—spring, summer, fall, and winter—and thus connected the bear to Mother Earth and Nature herself. The female bear's fertility and motherly protectiveness were seen as special, mysterious gifts from nature, along with her lumbering sacrifice that allowed ancient man to kill her. This sacrifice provided both northern Europeans and Native Americans with food and with animal-skin clothing as protection against the cold.

Not surprisingly, this veneration of the bear in the form of the Goddess continued and strengthened throughout the Stone, Bronze, and Iron Ages, right up to the transition between pagan Roman and Roman-Christian beliefs, remaining thoroughly dominant as man shifted from a hunter-gatherer existence to one that was more agriculturally based. In the Lascaux caves in France, art featuring the bear and dating back to 17,000 BCE takes prominence among the art of other animals depicted. Many of these images of the bear reveal spears or darts penetrating the bear's body, with blood flowing from the mouth and nose. The hunter-gatherers who occupied these caves spiritually looked upon the animals as providers of both protection and sustenance, and, in drawing them on the cave walls before the hunt, they created a spiritual bond between themselves and the animals they hoped to kill—if the animal saw fit to offer itself up to them.

THE EVOLUTION OF THE BEAR GOD AND GODDESS IN VARIOUS CULTURES OVER TIME

One of Europe's most complete Neolithic agricultural villages is Skara Brae, a Neolithic settlement built of stone that is located on the west coast of Mainland, the largest island of the Orkneys. Skara Brae consists of eight clustered stone houses and was occupied from roughly 3180 to 2500 BCE. It is linked to other Neolithic structures also found on Orkney, such as the magnificent chambered tomb of Maeshowe, the Ring of Brodgar, and the Standing Stones of Stenness.

Maeshowe is a Neolithic chambered cairn and passage grave that replicates the female womb. It's been speculated that it not only venerated those earlier ancestors who were buried in its near vicinity but was also used in death/rebirth ceremonies replicating the four seasons in alignment with the bear's cycle. The entrance corridor of Maeshowe was designed intentionally to allow the direct light of the rising and setting sun to enter in to the chamber for a few days on each side of the winter solstice, illuminating the wall of the back cell with a lozenge-

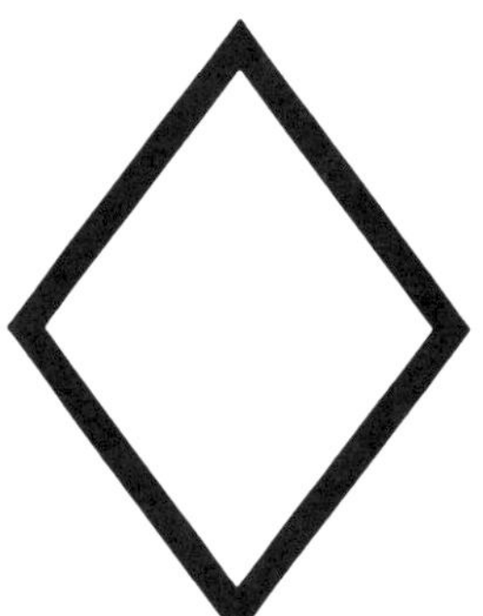

Fig. 2.2. Lozenge-shaped diamond of light exposed in the deepest recesses of the Maeshowe cairn during the rising and setting sun of the winter solstice. The Maeshowe cairn coordinates are approximately 59 degrees north latitude and 3 degrees 12 minutes west longitude. Symbol drawn by the author, William F. Mann.

Fig. 2.3. Sunlight penetrating the entrance shaft of Maeshowe at winter solstice. Photograph property of the author, William F. Mann.

shaped diamond. This is thought to signal the time when the mother bear retreats to the deepest part of her den during hibernation, during the gestation period, allowing her unborn to grow inside of her in a safe and warm environment.

The Grooved Ware people who built Skara Brae were primarily agriculturalists who raised cattle and sheep, harvested pastoral grains, and supplemented their diet with seafood. They are known as the Grooved Ware people because of their distinctive pottery, which incorporated the grooved lozenge as a central motif.

Fig. 2.4. Graphic comparison of the Neolithic Grooved Ware pottery and the later Egyptian and Greek pottery. Note the use of the diamond lozenge pattern on the Grooved Ware pottery.

One interpretation of the culture of the Skara Brae people suggests that Skara Brae was home to a variety of early sky-watchers engaged in astronomical and mystical ceremonies at nearby Neolithic sites. Similar ceremonies can be found in both Egyptian and Greek culture, marking the gradual transition between the Neolithic Age (dominated by stone construction), the Bronze Age, and the Iron Age. In many cases scenes of various religious ceremonies became the preferred motif found on the far more advanced and elaborate Egyptian and Greek pottery, whereas earlier Neolithic Grooved Ware pottery contained repeating geometric symbols and patterns (see figure 2.4 on p. 55).

The progressive development of ancient Egypt as a civilization is a fascinating study in itself, occurring in a series of distinct kingdoms: the Old Kingdom of the Early Bronze Age, the Middle Kingdom of the Middle Bronze Age, and the New Kingdom of the Late Bronze Age. The ancient Egypt of northeastern Africa was concentrated along the lower reaches of the Nile River in what is now the modern country of Egypt. Egyptian civilization came together in this region around 3150 BCE with the uniting of Upper and Lower Egypt under the first pharaoh.

Coming to rival the Hittite Empire, Assyrian Empire, and Mitanni Empire at the time, Egypt reached the pinnacle of its power during the New Kingdom in the Ramesside period. However, following the death of Ramesses II, Egypt entered a period of slow decline, being invaded or conquered by a succession of foreign powers (such as the Canaanites, Libyans, Nubians, Assyrians, Babylonians, Achaemenids, and Macedonians/Greeks), during which instability was brought on by political infighting among the various dynastic remnants.

It was during the many Egyptian kingdoms that the various bear attributes were distributed among individual gods, many of which related to the various planting and harvesting seasons that coincided with the rise and fall of the Nile. To the Egyptians, Ra was the ultimate sun god, the giver of life, and king of the gods until his son Osiris took over his throne. The son Osiris was the god of the underworld and the husband and brother of Isis, brother and mortal enemy to Seth, and father to Horus. Isis, the wife and sister of Osiris and the mother of Horus, was the goddess of magic, marriage, healing, and motherhood.

She was also shown to have a dual identity. On the one hand she was shown to be proud; yet on the other hand she deceived people, and she arranged for Ra to be killed so that her brother and husband could be king of the many gods who sat among them.

Significantly, belief in the divine and in the afterlife was ingrained in ancient Egyptian civilization from its inception, with pharaonic rule being based on the Divine Right of Kings. The ruling pharaoh was therefore seen as a divine manifestation above all else; whereas, the Egyptian pantheon was populated by gods who had supernatural powers and were called on for help or protection. However, the gods were not always viewed as benevolent, and Egyptians believed they had to be appeased with offerings and prayers. The structure of this pantheon changed continually as new deities were promoted in the hierarchy, but priests for the longest time made no effort to organize the diverse and sometimes conflicting myths and stories into a coherent system.

Eventually the Egyptian gods came to be worshipped in cult temples administered by priests acting on the pharaoh's behalf. At the center of the temple was typically the cult statue in a shrine. Generally temples were not places of public worship or congregation; however, on select feast days and celebrations a shrine showcasing the statue of the god was brought out for public worship by the priests—a practice that is continued to this day with statues such as the Madonna. Normally the Egyptian god's domain was sealed off from the outside world and was only accessible to temple officials. Common citizens were allowed to worship private statues in their homes, and amulets offered protection against the forces of chaos.

As the era known as the New Kingdom drew to a close in the eleventh century BCE, the pharaoh's role as a spiritual intermediary was de-emphasized when religious customs shifted to a direct worship of the gods. As a result, the Egyptian priests rather cleverly developed a system of oracles to communicate the will of the gods directly to the people. In this manner, the stature of the priests themselves became increasingly elevated.

In Greece similar transitions had taken place, with various gods assuming various attributes of the bear, although there was one significant difference between the Greeks and the Egyptians. In Greece the female priestess rose in stature over the male priest, assuming the oracle duties herself through her virgin state. In Greek myth a central theme surrounds the battle between the female and the male for supreme dominance, beginning with the supreme god, Zeus, falling in love with the huntress Callisto. It was Callisto and not his wife who bore Zeus a son named Arcas. As a result, in a fit of jealous rage, Zeus's wife, Juno, turned Callisto into a bear because of her affair with Zeus. Then one day Arcas was out hunting, stalking the bear who was his own mother. On seeing that Callisto's life was in danger, Zeus whisked her up into the night sky out of harm's way, where she lives on forever.

It is said that she can still be seen in the constellation Ursa Major, the Great Bear. In another version, Arcas is also sent skyward and becomes the adjacent Ursa Minor, the Little Bear. The Big Dipper, or Plough, is one of the more familiar groups of stars in this constellation, with the Mother Bear assuming the dominant position. Interestingly, the Druidic name for this group was Arthur's Plough, and the constellation was also seen as a bear in Native American and Hebrew traditions.

The Greek moon goddess of the hunt, Artemis, became a bear goddess who presided over all of nature.[4] She became the dual face of Callisto and was therefore seen as a protector of animals and had attendants called *arktoi,* or "bear girls." These maidens wore bearskins and masks and lived in the wild. Here, in the wilderness, the maidens would remain untamed, unwashed, and protected from men until they reached puberty and had developed the strength and maturity to choose whether to remain virgins in the temple of Artemis or to marry.

Similarly, in Roman mythology, Diana, the counterpart to the Greek Artemis, possessed the same general attributes yet forever remained a virgin. Artemis, on the other hand, was said to be desired and loved by many but ultimately possessed by none. Knowing this provides some insight into the thematic virgin/harlot overlay found in the Bible.

Like the Lovers tarot card, Artemis and Hekate are one, a lunar goddess of the life cycle with dual aspects. One stands at the beginning of the cycle; the other is at the end. One is young, pure, and beautiful, connected with young life, while the other is gruesome and connected with death. In Greek mythology, Hekate—whose temples and altars stood at gates, entrances, or in front of houses reminiscent of the gates of hell—is described as traveling above graveyards with her hounds, collecting poison, and then mixing potions of death. In another myth the hunter Aktaeon paid the penalty for spying upon the unclothed Diana as she bathed in the stream of a forest valley. So enraged was Diana at his arrogance that she turned him into a stag so that the very dogs with whom he hunted tore him limb from limb.

The early Greek goddesses were often given animal forms. Later, as civilization advanced, many of them took on human characteristics. Others were depicted as strange hybrids with human bodies and the heads of animals or birds. As previously indicated, the prevalent owl symbolism can be traced back to Athena. The one-eyed Greek goddess of wisdom has an owl as her companion sitting on her shoulder on her blind side, telling her all there is to see and know.

It is said through myth that only in cooperation with the owl can Athena see the whole truth. It was the Celts who believed that the owl carried the souls of the deceased into the Land of Youth, Tir nan Og or Avalon, the Isle of Apples. *The Four Branches of the Mabinogion,* a collection of Celtic myth and lore, tells a special story of the owl: Blodeuwedd is a woman made from nine flowers by a wise magician for the hero, Gwydion, who could not love a mortal woman. But in the end she betrays him, and as a punishment she is turned in to an owl.

As noted earlier, Marija Gimbutas was a Lithuanian American archaeologist known for her research into the Neolithic and Bronze Age cultures of Old Europe and for her widely accepted Kurgan hypothesis, which located the proto-Indo-European homeland in the Eurasian Steppe. Gimbutas's assertion that Neolithic sites in Lithuania and across Europe provided evidence for matriarchal pre-Indo-European societies

Fig. 2.5. A depiction of Athena and her owl on traditional pre-Christian Greek pottery. Note the two-dimensional quality and lack of perspective of the illustration at this time period.

was not well received in scholarly circles but became a keystone of the Goddess movement.*[5]

It was Gimbutas who first suggested that the Celts were the ones to

*In Greek religion, as described in the Orphic holy books from which Plato quoted verses, there are the accounts of the life, death, and miracles of Orpheus—the supreme singer and patron of poetry. What the Orphics did was to combine all of Apollo and Dionysus's "good" tendencies into the myth of Orpheus. Dionysus and Apollo themselves retained all of their darker secrets and habits. Once again we are struck with the notion of a fusion of ancient traditions, folktales, romances, and perhaps semi-historical memories into the dualistic concept of good and evil, young and old, virgin and harlot. Plato in turn saw the stories of Orpheus as one way for the common folk to be temporarily distracted from everyday tedium and the monotony of life.

merge the Bear Goddess and the Bird Goddess into a single deity.[6] As noted, this deity later became the Greek goddess Artemis and the Celtic goddess Artio—from which is derived the word *art.* Artio is considered to be the Bear Goddess herself. In addition, Celtic gods and goddesses had their counterparts in the Greek Eos, goddess of dawn; Aphrodite, goddess of love; Zeus; and Demeter, to name just a few.

In the early years of the third century BCE the Celts were masters of a vast area extending from Galatia in the East to all of southern Britain, including what is now Wales and Ireland in the West. The Celts reached the apex of their power later in the fourth century and thereafter entered a period of rapid decline. Most of what is known about the Celts has been passed down through the Welsh poets, who were primarily the earliest Christianized hermits to inhabit the land. During this time most Welsh poets/hermits did not solely portray the final resting place of the warrior as a Land of the Dead. One of the titles given this "otherworld" is Caer Feddwid—meaning "Court of Intoxication," or "Carousal"—and its staple drink was either a fermented honey or sparkling wine. Similar to the Irish monks, the Welsh poets at this time tended to inhabit small, cone-like shelters constructed of rough stone, which resembled bee-hives, believing that their closeness to nature provided them with the necessary inspiration.

The final resting place of the warrior was also named Caer Siddi, meaning "the Land of the Living." The significant point here is that any storyteller of this era, although obviously aware of the disparity, saw no inconsistency in conjoining the Land of the Dead and the Land of the Living as two aspects of the same otherworld. Here, possibly, is the earliest Christian attempt to reconcile the emerging concept of heaven versus hell with the earlier concept of the Land of the Dead versus the Land of the Living.

Around the same time, in 332 BCE, the Macedonian/Greek Alexander the Great conquered Egypt with little resistance from the Persians and was welcomed by the Egyptians as a supreme deliverer of the divine. In part this was because the administration established by Alexander's successors, the Macedonian Ptolemaic dynasty, was derived from an earlier Egyptian model. Alexander seized upon this orderly foundation and based his administration in the new capital city of Alexandria. This magnificent city showcased the power and prestige of Hellenistic rule and became a seat of learning and culture, the focal point of which centered on the famous Library of Alexandria.

Just as famous, the Lighthouse of Alexandria lit the way for the many ships that kept trade flowing through the city, given that the Ptolemies made commerce and revenue-generating enterprises, such as papyrus manufacturing, their top priority. It must be noted that Hellenistic culture did not supplant native Egyptian culture, however, as the Ptolemies supported time-honored traditions in an effort to secure the loyalty of the populace. The conquering Macedonians/Greeks built new temples in the Egyptian style, supported traditional cults, and portrayed themselves as pharaohs. Some new traditions did emerge though: Greek and Egyptian gods were condensed into composite deities such as Serapis, and classical Greek forms of sculpture influenced traditional Egyptian motifs.

Not surprisingly, an alternative to traditional religion was offered by Hellenistic philosophy. The most widespread of these systems was Stoicism, which taught that life should be lived according to the rational order that the Stoics believed governed the universe. Accordingly, human beings had to accept their fate, given that it was considered to be a mandate of divine will, and it was deemed that virtuous acts be performed for their own intrinsic value. But despite their efforts to appease the Egyptians, the Ptolemies were challenged by native rebellion, bitter family rivalries, and the general unrest of the inhabitants of Alexandria, which surfaced after the death of Ptolemy IV in 204 BCE.

In addition, as an ever-expanding Rome relied more heavily on imports of grain and other commodities from Egypt, the Romans took greater interest in the political situation of the country. Continued Egyptian revolts, ambitious Egyptian merchants, and powerful Syrian opponents from the Near East made this situation unstable, leading Rome to send forces to secure the country as a province of its empire, resulting in the ultimate disappearance of Egyptian culture. This signaled the end of an independent Egyptian dynasty.

The pagan Romans, after absorbing all that they considered

Fig. 2.6. A rare depiction of Hellenistic art through a sculptured figurine merging the best features of Egyptian and Greek culture. Compare her pose to that of the shepherdess in Poussin's *The Shepherds of Arcadia* (see figure 2.8 on p. 73).

worthwhile within Egyptian culture, in turn called the northern European Bear Goddess, Dea Artio. The goddess Artio was honored at Lughnasadh, a pagan festival celebrated when barley and corn were harvested. Following Constantine's conversion to Christianity after his successful battle at Milvern Bridge in 312 CE, Artio was integrated into early Christianity as Saint Ursula, a Latinized form of the Saxon *ursel,* meaning "she-bear." In the Gallo-Roman religion, Artio (as mentioned earlier) was the Bear Goddess and was worshipped at Berne, Switzerland (*berne* actually means "bear").

THE SYMBOLISM OF THE MERMAID

It was at Ephesus, at the famous temple of Artemis, that the last goddess—Diana of the Ephesians (the queen of Wisdom)—survived well into the fifth century CE. At this time the people were transferring their allegiance from the virgin huntress to the virgin mother, and it was in 471 at the Ecclesiastic Council of Ephesus that the seal of change was set. This final transfer of the goddesses' attributes is known as the Marian Devotion. Yet many people still consider the Marian Devotion to be the same devotion and sacrifices that had previously been given to mother goddesses such as Isis or Demeter.

Regardless of whether the Marian Devotion is purely Christian in origin, images such as that of the mermaid and mother bear have proved to be both endearing and popular throughout the ages. In the case of the mermaid, each age has provided this enchanting creature with new elements of her myth. Unfortunately, the mermaid has also become a victim of the repressive sexual attitudes of the church.

The mermaid as a siren figured prominently in medieval church decorations to symbolically serve as a vivid reminder of the fatal temptations of the flesh. As recently demonstrated through Disney's 2011 *Pirates of the Caribbean: On Stranger Tides,* mermaids were considered unable to possess souls of their own. Legend has it that one method for a mermaid to gain a soul was to marry a human being. Thus the legends of the all-seducing mermaids, anxious to acquire souls, arose—and became common among superstitious sailors.

The best-known form of this legend is Hans Christian Andersen's fairy tale *The Little Mermaid,* again popularized by Disney. But similar legends were to be found in the folklore of many countries. Celtic mythology included the sanctified Liban, a young woman who was drowned and transformed into a mermaid who, after five hundred years, enlisted the aid of an Irish saint, Saint Comgall, to save her soul. There was also the story of the mermaid of Iona who wept many bitter tears over her inability to leave her ocean home to gain her promised soul. According to legend, Saint Patrick allegedly had a custom of transforming pagan women into mermaids.

The animated Disney film *The Little Mermaid* is much more than just a fairy tale for girls. Rather, Ariel (the little mermaid) is a powerful metaphor for the plight of the divine feminine over the past several thousand years of Western civilization. Sadly, and true to form, Ariel's dream and desire is to gain a soul. In the Disney film, Ariel gains what she wishes for by saving the handsome prince, who is shipwrecked and dying, only to find that which she had found (her soul) to be lost again.

In her cave under the ocean, Ariel collects relics and artifacts from sunken Spanish galleons. Among her treasures is a painting by Georges de La Tour titled *Magdalene with the Smoking Flame.* In this painting the Magdalene is gazing at a candle burning on the table beside her, which is obviously meant to represent the lost Bride of the Church and the archetype of the Feminine Goddess. In this connection it is intriguing that the little mermaid is called Ariel, for Ariel is a symbol of the besieged holy city of Jerusalem.

Fig. 2.7. Sculpture of the little mermaid looking out to sea from the mouth of Copenhagen harbor. Photograph property of the author, William F. Mann.

In the animated Disney film, the little mermaid carries a book and a mirror, which are symbols commonly found in medieval art. The mirror is not just a symbol for feminine vanity but represents the role of Mother Earth—Nature—to manifest the divine in the flesh, just as the moon "mirrors" the sun. In ancient times the wisdom embodied by the goddess Sophia was called the "immaculate mirror" of divine energy.

The little mermaid's book supposedly represents all natural and spiritual law—science and revelation—and the quest in seeking to know God's precepts. Herein lays the proposed tenet that the Merovingians evolved from a union of Merovee's mother and a strange aquatic creature from beyond the sea. In other words, it is believed that the Merovingian dynasty resulted from a perfect balance of science and revelation—nature and spiritual essence.

There is very little evidence, though, as to the true origins of the Merovingians. They claimed descent from Noah, whom they regarded as the source of all biblical wisdom, for he was the master who survived the Great Flood. The Merovingians also claimed direct descent from ancient Troy. According to the research by the authors of *Holy Blood, Holy Grail,* the ancestors of the Merovingians were supposedly connected with Arcadia's royal house as well. It was this royalty who inhabited the actual Greek province of Arcadia, which dates back to antiquity.

Whether the Merovingians derived ultimately from Troy or from Arcadia or from Noah does not necessarily present a problem of origin. According to Homer and early Greek histories, a substantial number of Arcadians were present at the siege of Troy. (Troy was founded by settlers from Arcadia.) The very name Arcadia derives from Arkades, which means "people of the bear."

Not surprisingly, the bear was a sacred animal in both ancient Arcadia and Troy. And, like the many legends of the origins of various mystical warrior societies, the Merovingians assumed many of the larger-than-life attributes of the Akkadians, Trojans, and, for that matter, the Celts. In turn it was the Celts who would eventually play such a major influence on early Briton beliefs, including the aforementioned ever-growing legend of a local warlord named Arthur. Following the retreat of the Romans from Britain, it was Arthur who led those remaining Roman settlers against the marauding pagan hordes that swept down from the north. And it is said that Arthur wore a mantle displaying the bear's image.

THE BEAR IN CELTIC CULTURE

The Celts were a mysterious culture that emerged out of the Eurasian Steppe, taking advantage of Iron Age developments, including the refinement of the wagon wheel and a developed skill with the horse. To this day the living language of the Celts, Gaelic, still can be heard in places like Wales, the western shores of Ireland, the Scottish Highlands, western Cornwall, and Bretagne on the northwest coast of France. But the roots run far deeper. Six thousand years ago the forerunners of the Celts invented the Old European script, as it is now known, to become the world's earliest protolanguage.

What we do know of these ancient Celtic ancestors is derived from what remains of their Neolithic settlements in places like Heuneburg (in what today is Germany), Hallstatt in Austria, La Tene in Switzerland, and literally hundreds of archaeological sites across Europe and the British Isles.

Their lands stretched from Anatolia in Asia Minor (Celtic Galatia) north through the Macedonian Peninsula and the Balkans, Hungary, the Ukraine, and central Asia; from the Black Sea up the vast Danube River basin (from which the goddess Danu derives her name) to northern Italy; to eastern France, Spain, and Switzerland north of the Alps. Later they would migrate northwest to the British Isles in a constant search for iron and fertile lands.

In addition to what has been learned from their remaining artifacts, the Celts are known from the writings of the Mediterranean people, specifically from the Greek and Roman cultures. Unfortunately, these reports were written by men who feared the Celts and sought to destroy or enslave them and are therefore somewhat biased. The Romans certainly knew of the Celts and feared them for their sacking of Rome in the fourth century BCE. Julius Caesar wrote of firsthand encounters with them during the Gallic Wars in Gaul (France); Pliny the Elder specifically wrote of Druid and Celtic medicine.

Their religion, unfortunately, also largely remains a mystery. It is generally known that the Druids were the priests, judges, teachers, and magicians of their clans, though little that is known of their rites and ceremonies remain. This is because their knowledge was passed down orally, as was their sacred law. One thing that we do know is that theirs was a religion of unity with nature. The spirits of trees, rivers, rocks, and sky were ever-present, and the mighty oaks and the mistletoe that grew among them were seen to hold special meaning.

Sacred groves were common among the ancient Germans, Greeks, and Romans, as well as the Celts. The oak worship of the Druids is familiar to everyone in one form or another; indeed, there are still annual gatherings in sacred groves and woodland glades around the world. The majestic pillars of the early stone temples of the Egyptians and others obviously relate to the concept of entering the sacred grove of secret initiations. Famously, the main gate of the second Solomon's Temple was flanked by two giant stone pillars, which represented the pillars said to be used by Lamech and his sons to preserve the ancient knowledge that they discovered.

Within the circle of Freemasonry the twin pillars found at the main entrance of Solomon's Temple are known as Joachim and Boaz. Not only did Joachim symbolically represent the northern portion of Israel and Boaz the southern portion of the kingdom but the dual pillars also were meant to represent the balance between male and female. The pillars were also capped with bronze-cast flutes, respresentative of the traditional Canaanite fertility symbol, the lily. The lily is just one symbol of the ancient sacred feminine and is the origin of the fleur-de-lis symbol. The white lily depicted the faith and virginity of the priestess, while the blue lily respresented the fertility of the queen.

We know of the Celtic Morrigan, the great queen. We also have Morrigna, who is collectively deemed to be the goddess Trinity. She is always a personification of the ancient fertility goddess, descending in a direct matriarchal lineage from the dawn of time. Ironically, besides being seen as the bringer of life, she also is known as Panic, the raven of battle, bringer of fear and irrationality, who can undermine the courage of men in times of crisis and sometimes delights in doing so.

In terms of the bear, the Celts actually had two goddesses that took its form: Andarta (meaning "powerful bear") and Artio. Other cultures feature the Bear God Artaois, Ardeche, or Arthe, their names being taken from the root *art*. There are also many place-names—such as Artos or Arth—throughout northern Europe.

The Briton King Arthur (a form of Artios or Artiaus, a great god of antiquity) is, of course, associated with the bear. Midwinter is the time of Alban (Arthuran/the Light of Arthur) and the winter solstice. During this darkest period of the year people called upon the constellation of the Great Bear to light their way.

The bear is also thought to be ruled by the planet Mars. The legend of Arthur sleeping in an underground cave on the Isle of Avalon waiting for his day of awakening is reflective of the bear that hibernates in the winter in a sort of suspended animation. King Arthur, as Artios, was consort to Cerridwen, the Welsh triple goddess who possessed a magic cauldron. In the medieval Welsh romance of Culhwch and Olwen, Arthur was said to have gone to Ireland to recover this cauldron and in the process laid waste to one of the five provinces.

As noted, the Bear Goddess has been central to the notion of the earliest pre-Christian concept of the circle of life: birth, life, death, and rebirth. Also significant is that Greek warriors believed that it was the bear that, following death, acted as their guide to the subterranean underworld, or netherworld, where they would strive to be reborn to live a blissful life in Arcadia.

REFERENCING ARCADIA

The mythical Arcadia is associated with bountiful natural splendor, harmony, and was and is often seen to be inhabited by simple shepherds, in contrast to the heavenly mountaintop abode of the Greek gods. The concept of Arcadia differs from the traditional utopian vision in that Utopia is more often specifically regarded as unattainable, because civilized man is considered to be not of pure heart.

The simple inhabitants of Arcadia, conversely, were often regarded as having been granted the right to live in this land because they were without the pride and avarice that corrupted other regions. They were uncorrupted by civilization and the worship of false gods, and, above all, they had remained virtuous.

Probably the most famous reference to the mythical land of Arcadia is found in Nicolas Poussin's infamous painting *Et in Arcadia Ego . . .*, the title of which has been interpreted as "And in Arcadia I . . ."* This painting is otherwise referred to as *The Shepherds of Arcadia.* Poussin painted two versions of this work, the first in 1629 and the second version between 1640 and 1642, sometime just after being initiated as a Freemason in France. The reason for its infamy lies in the fact that from the day of its completion it was believed even by King Louis XIV that this painting (the second version) contained clues to the final resting place of the Templar treasure. This resting place was deemed not to be in the mythical Arcadia but in a real land that possessed all the qualities of the myth. Over the past four hundred years many have interpreted this area to be the south of France, in the Midi-Pyrénées region,†[7] yet to date no one has satisfactorily interpreted the painting's many layers of esoteric meaning.

That is, until now!

---

*The majority of references to the Poussin paintings and their relationship to the Rennes-le-Château mysteries found in this chapter are based on interpretations of the Rennes Parchments first presented by Henry Lincoln in *The Holy Place* and further decipherment that I developed. Although some of the original deciphers were presented in Gérard de Sède's *L'Or de Rennes,* I first learned of the decoding through *The Holy Place,* as well as Baigent, Leigh, and Lincoln's *Holy Blood, Holy Grail* (pp. 24–40). Therefore, most of the following notes and references identify these two sources as the origin of my investigation, although my own conclusions deviate from those of the British authors.

†The deciphered Rennes Parchments indicate that if one finds "the key," then one will find the treasure. To accomplish this is not as simple as it first appears. The original keys were supposedly given to Saint Peter, but, from the information presented, it is apparent that there are many keys intermixed throughout all ancient religions and myths. As we move forward through the *Templar Sanctuaries in North America* it will become clearer as to what the keys are, how they can be found, and how they can be applied.

UNLOCKING THE MYSTERY WITH ART

The next question appears to be: Who possesses the geometric and allegorical keys today? Does the Catholic Church, the Priory of Sion, or the Freemasons possess the keys that unlock the highest orders of the ancient mysteries? Or can the keys be discovered by any individual who has an inkling as to how the cord can be unraveled? In all secret mysteries, including those of the Catholic Church, lie the key elements of death, rebirth, and fertility. These elements are central to any understanding of the pagan origins of the myths of Osiris, Dionysus, Adonis/Tammuc, and even the brotherhood of Freemasonry.

In my two previous books I was able to demonstrate that this brilliant composition developed by Poussin was based on the two main principles of Freemasonry: sacred geometry and moral allegory. What many have failed to realize is that *The Shepherds of Arcadia* is not only a map of sorts but a clock. As such, it provides clues that the seeker of the truth must go back in time to the spiritual source, the origin of the Divine Being. Only then will the seeker of the truth understand the pre-Christian lineage from the Bear to the Goddess to Christianity. Only then will the seeker understand that they must look for clues pertaining to the Bear Goddess to "complete, or square, the circle."

In *The Templar Meridians* specifically, I demonstrated how a longitudinal/latitudinal meridian grid pattern could be applied to Poussin's painting, thus allowing the outline of the northeastern seaboard of North America to perfectly fit within the painting in relation to the four visible figures. To my own amazement I was able to determine that mainland Nova Scotia fit perfectly within the crook of the arms of the two figures that make up the inner circle. Not surprisingly, the diameter of the circle was determined by the length of their shepherds' crooks.

I was then able to apply the intertwining rings of the vesica piscis with the Jewel of the Royal Arch to mainland Nova Scotia and pinpoint exactly where the Rose Line settlement of the inner circle once lay. The young shepherd supporting the shepherdess actually is conveying the latitude where the center of the inner circle can be found. His left hand is displaying the index finger and the thumb. The castle tower at Green Oaks can be found just north of the 45th parallel.

We will enter into a more expanded discussion of what the gridlines reveal a little later in this chapter, but for now let's look at the painting's four figures a bit more closely.

In figure 2.9, hopefully the reader will now realize that the kneeling figure with the beard, which Poussin painted wearing an emerald green toga, is representative of Neolithic man and his desire to be the bear itself. He kneels before the goddess of Egyptian/Greek time in acknowledgment of her later transformation into the prime spiritual being. Poussin painted the goddess mainly in gold and blue to correspond with the Egyptian/Greek Hellenistic Bronze Age. The figure that she leans on, cloaked in red, represents on one level the pre-Christian Celtic people and their Druidic worship of gods of nature. It is the goddess and her guardian before whom the bear bows down.

Poussin has also hinted in the painting that the pre-Christian goddess figure, in her persona as the shepherdess of Arcadia, is definitely pregnant, in that she displays back pain with one hand while leaning on her shining knight for support. Here is the hidden fifth element that is exposed when the first four elements present a perfect square in harmony with nature. And, by connecting the four corners of the square, the hidden fifth element, the unborn child, is revealed. This is the shepherdess who presents "no temptation" because she is already bearing a child. By this, Poussin is referencing the Marian Devotion and the later evolving concept of the Madonna and Child.

The fourth figure might just be the most intriguing one. Dressed in a pure white toga, with his legs crossed and arm outstretched, this figure's relative positioning in relation to the underlying map appears to suggest that the spirit of Jesus himself, the man that the Romans crucified at one time, lay in a land once known as Arcadia. Accepting this scenario for the moment, could the other two figures nearest to him represent Mary Magdalene and Joseph of Arimathea? In turn, does this suggest that the guardians of an antient knowledge were instrumental in transferring the Holy Bloodline first to the Isle of Briton, the land of the bear, and then

Fig. 2.8. *The Shepherds of Arcadia,* Nicholas Poussin, 1640–1642. Reproduced courtesy of the Louvre Museum, Paris, France.

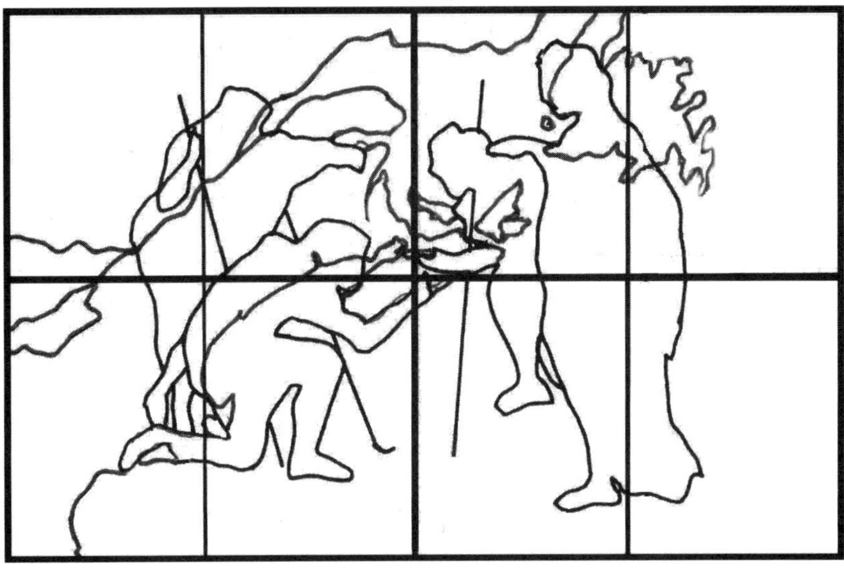

Fig. 2.9. Schematic of the four visible figures/elements contained in the painting *The Shepherds of Arcadia* depicting a hidden longitudinal/latitudinal grid (taken from *The Templar Meridians*) and the early lineage circle of the Goddess from the Stone Age through the Bronze and Iron Ages to Christianity. Diagram copyright of the author, William F. Mann.

to the Isle of Avalon—Arcadia? And could the manner by which the pattern of north–south rose lines/meridians splits the painting into four equal vertical parts denote a pattern of settlement that emanated westerly from the first Rose Line colony established in Arcadia?

Surely, on the same level, the kneeling figure in emerald green is meant to represent Saint John the Baptist, given that this figure is staring squarely at present-day Saint John, New Brunswick. Rather coincidentally, Saint John was established by Charles de La Tour prior to 1640, just prior to the date of Poussin painting *The Shepherds of Arcadia*. And notice how Prince Edward Island and Cape Breton, when combined, create an amazing set of wings for the shepherd who is physically supporting what evidently is a very pregnant shepherdess. Given that this supporting figure's colors are red and white in the painting,* it may be surmised that he is a symbolic representative of the Knights Templar, who may very well have recovered and then guarded the bones of the Holy Family, as well as guarding its bloodline. (This collection of bones may even have included those of Mary Magdalene, as Dan Brown has hinted.)

The manner in which Poussin chose to depict the knight is clearly his attempt at a rather cheeky depiction of an angel, or maybe more of a demon, who both supports yet hides behind the veneration of the female goddess. If this is the case, then Poussin was also conveying some hidden information he possessed concerning the descendants of the Merovingian bloodline, which supposedly descended from the union of Jesus and Mary Magdalene. Was it truly possible that the Holy Bloodline had made its way across the sea under the guardianship of the Knights Templar to find refuge in the New World?

Was Poussin relating his painting of Arcadia to a previously known location, or did he have an inkling that elementary geometry had to be applied to a specific location, one that he learned of during his two years in Paris through his relationships with Richelieu and Nicholas Fouquet, finance minister to Louis XIV? In retrospect, it makes sense that Poussin's first version of *The Shepherds of Arcadia,* painted in 1629, was nondescript in terms of geographic location. But its theme attracted

*The classic Templar robe features a red cross on a white background.

the interest of the French cardinal Richelieu, who could help Poussin pinpoint the allegory to a specific point on Earth.

CARDINAL RICHELIEU

In 1627, following his discovery of New France in 1604 and several subsequent transatlantic voyages, Samuel de Champlain sailed back to France again where he met with the powerful Cardinal Richelieu. It is during this meeting that Champlain convinced Cardinal Richelieu of the vast resources in Canada. More significantly, it is speculated that Champlain revealed what he had discovered about the inland movements of the Grail refugees. As a direct result, Cardinal Richelieu created the Company of One Hundred Associates and began recruiting investors. Champlain was also given the title lieutenant to the viceroy of Québec and became the governor of the colony, being provided with enough monetary support to establish a permanent settlement at Québec City.

When Samuel de Champlain died in 1635, Cardinal Richelieu replaced him with a provisional governor, Marc-Antoine Bras-de-Fer de Châteaufort, who was known to be a Knight of Malta. He would soon be named commander of Trois-Rivières ("Three Rivers") because in the following year King Louis XIII himself nominated the second official governor of New France—Charles Hualt, Sieur de Montmagny—also a high-ranking commander of the Order of Malta.

The French king's royal appointment of a Knight of Malta surely confirmed that the Order of Malta intended to make Québec City and all of New France their very own. Indeed, in 1624, before Champlain died, there seemed to have been a secret plan to turn over New France, including Acadia and Montreal, to the Knights of Malta. The curious thing here is that even though by all formal appearances Champlain supported the Knights of Malta, his actions appear to support the Knights Templar. To this end, apparently Champlain reluctantly agreed to Richelieu's direct orders that a church be established in Montreal through the Franciscan Recollets, who were later to be absorbed into the Children of St. Vincent—the Order of Saint Sulpice. It turns out that Richelieu was adamantly opposed to the Jesuits and was playing a dangerous game with King Louis XIII, a reported despot and bisexual who nonetheless relied heavily on Richelieu's advice.

From the very first day that Montreal was officially founded in 1642, the appointed governor, Paul Chomedey de Maisonneuve, who by all appearances was a Knight Templar, adamantly refused to take any orders from the sieur de Montmagny. Not surprisingly, the then established Jesuit clergy of Québec City repeatedly tried to force the first few devoted women in Montreal to join the nuns in what then was seen as the capital of New France. And every boat containing settlers bound for Montreal was pressed to stop in Québec City and not continue onward to Montreal. As such, it appears that there was an ongoing rivalry between the Knights of Malta, in partnership with the Jesuits who controlled Québec City, and the rather more nefarious group of Knights Templar, supported at this time by the Sulpicians who controlled Montreal.

It is said that Cardinal Richelieu's major goals were the establishment of royal absolutism in France and the end of Spanish Habsburg (Catholic) influence in Europe. Under Louis XIII's predecessor, Henry IV, the political threat posed by the religious dissent of the Huguenots, who had a considerable military force at their disposal, was initially tolerated. This all ended, however, when the Huguenot community was drawn into the larger political intrigues of the leading Protestant nobility and clergy, who mainly presided in England at the time. In direct response, Richelieu laid siege to the port of La Rochelle, which had once been controlled by the Templars but by then was a Huguenot center. The Huguenots were soundly defeated and the Peace of Ales was signed on June 28, 1629. Unfortunately, out of the more than 27,000 Huguenots who inhabited La Rochelle before the siege, fewer than 5,000 survived after declaring allegiance to the French crown and acceptance of the Catholic faith.

Somewhat orchestrated from behind the scenes, the later seizure by Spain in 1635 of the archbishop of Trier, who was under French protection, led to France's alignment with Protestant powers in the Thirty Years' War. Although contemporaries saw this alignment as a betrayal of the Catholic Church by one of its own princes, Richelieu remained orthodox in his views on the distinct relationship between church and state.

Through a stroke of genius, Richelieu succeeded in reducing the power of the Spanish and Austrian Habsburgs by manipulating the German princes to fight among each other. Then, through his usual guile and intrigue, Richelieu encouraged the French king to join the war against the Catholic Habsburgs, with the direct result that France gained rich territory along the Rhine, called the Alsace. As such, it was only through Richelieu's many intricate manipulations that King Louis XIII was able to centralize power in France and to quash the Holy Roman Empire controlled by the Habsburg dynasty.

A CLOSER LOOK AT *THE SHEPHERDS OF ARCADIA*

One of the biggest clues as to what lay in the New World, and along what Rose Lines, can be found in Poussin's *The Shepherds of Arcadia.* The second version of *The Shepherds of Arcadia,* painted by Poussin under the direct instructions of Cardinal Richelieu, would be obtained by Louis XIV in 1685 and hung in his private apartments at Versailles until his death. Knowing this, it is extremely odd that no one has ever considered it possible that Richelieu provided Poussin with specific geographical information; secret information that had been supplied to him (Richelieu) by one of the most intrepid and advanced explorers and cartographers of their time, namely Samuel de Champlain, who may himself have been playing both sides against the middle.

Amazingly, if one applies what is known about the discoveries of those secret agents such as Cartier and Champlain who explored the New World during the sixteenth and seventeenth centuries, a third underlying pattern to Poussin's painting *The Shepherds of Arcadia* is exposed. Minimizing the painting to simply illustrate the relationship between the four figures (actually, there are five figures if one includes the unborn child) as shown in figure 2.9 (p. 73) allows one to realize that Poussin positioned the shepherds and shepherdess over a very accurate map of the northeastern seaboard of North America and that the westerly border of the painting corresponds with the extent of Champlain's explorations into the heartland of the New World. Just as amazingly, if this is possible, the whole painting is aligned to a grid pattern that reflects a series of longitudinal meridians each separated by eight degrees!

Using these rose lines/meridians as a guide, the Christ-like figure's relative position definitely lies in Montreal. Was this possible? Could there possibly have been an earlier Rose Line settlement established in the early fifteenth or sixteenth century by the descendants of Prince Henry Sinclair and his followers? This settlement would have occurred after they had sailed west from Nova Scotia to Montreal and L'Ile Jesus (the Island of Jesus), where the Indian village called Hochelaga had once been visited by both Jacques Cartier and Samuel de Champlain. Could the Templars have been guided from Nova Scotia along the eastern seaboard and then along the inland waterways by the Mi'kmaq or their Algonquin brothers?

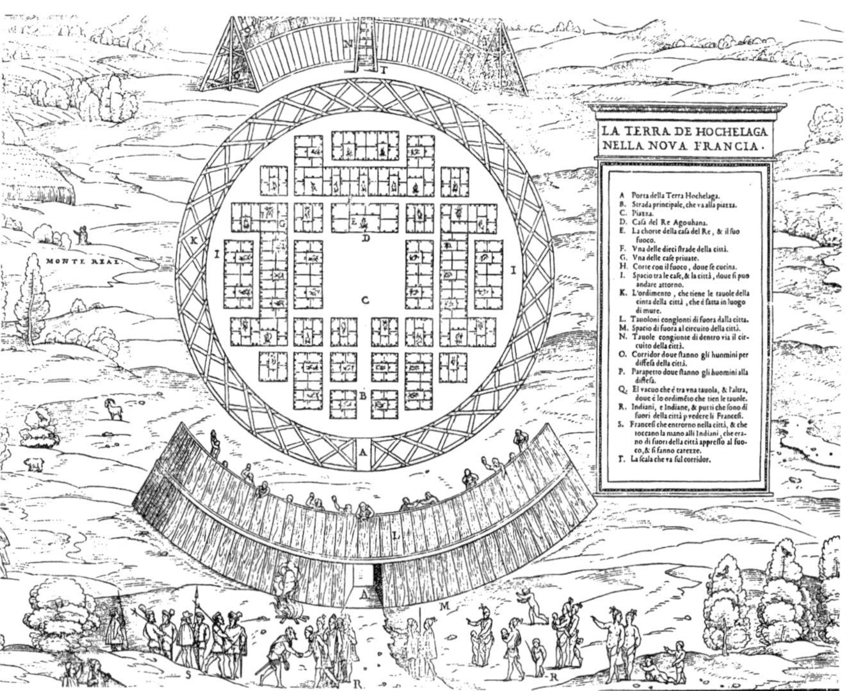

Fig. 2.10. Descriptive map of the village of Hochelaga as contained in Cartier's memoirs of his 1535 voyage. Note how the village is depicted as a perfect circle, replicating a Viking earth-ring fortress.

INSIGHTFUL NATIVE AMERICAN ORAL TRADITIONS

There exists to this day a local Mi'kmaq oral legend of the Mi'kmaq tribe who lived along the Shubenacadie River and one day just vanished. Could this tribe, specifically if it included the mixed blood of the Templars, have moved inland along with Prince Henry Sinclair, aiding him in his travels along the ancient native waterways and trails? It certainly now appears so. It appears even more reasonable when one considers that the Mi'kmaq was one of fifty-six nations making up the greater Algonquin Nation, which extended from the eastern seaboard inland to approximately where the 112 degree west longitudinal prime meridian falls along the foothills of the Rocky Mountains. The Algonquin or Wabanaki Confederation included the Malisett, Passamaquoddy, and Abenaki people as well as the then powerful Huron Nation, among others. It extended geographically as far south as Cape Hatteras on the coast of North Carolina and as far north as the southern tip of Hudson Bay.

Setting aside all conventional preconceived notions of early exploration in the New World for the moment, let's assume that the Grail refugees and their descendants probed inland among a number of major river routes between 1398 and approximately 1550 and that these routes converged on the Great Lakes. In support of this, rather convincing evidence of seemingly Grail-related activity has been found throughout Nova Scotia, New Brunswick, Québec, Ontario, Maine, New York, New Hampshire, Vermont, and Pennsylvania by interested scholars. And, as pointed out earlier, there are a number of plausible reasons as to why Prince Henry Sinclair, his inner circle, their descendants, and the natives who accompanied them moved inland toward the Great Lakes along the following rivers: the Saint John, the White, the Hudson, the Susquehanna, the Connecticut, the Allegheny, and the Genesee.

Let's also assume beyond speculation that these refugees possessed an infinite secret, which included the identity of the direct descendants of the Holy Bloodline. There is also now a strong belief that this group possessed a physical treasure of great wealth and significance. If true, this would eventually lead to (as the refugees surely would have considered each and every day) probes by agents of several European dynasties such as the Hapsburgs and the Catholic Church, who would have dearly loved to get their hands on the treasure and to obliterate all signs of earlier Grail occupation of the New World.[8]

To date there have been many possible explanations about what actually constitutes the Holy Grail. Some are as wildly far-fetched as two cruets containing the blood and sweat of Christ, or the bones and relics of Joseph of Arimathea, Saint Anthony the Hermit, or Saint Paul. The one sure fact is that whatever Saunière discovered (priest Bérenger Saunière, mentioned earlier, who had discovered the secret knowledge of the antient rose lines)—whether it was treasure or the keys to the treasure—it caused him to forego his religious beliefs for something far more valuable.

A strong contender for the source of Saunière's wealth may be found in the ancient and medieval history of Europe and, more particularly, the intertwining of the history of the Knights Templar and Rennes-le-Château. According to one popular explanation, the coded messages led Saunière to a cache of Visigoth gold, silver, and jewels hidden below the ancient church. An elaboration of this theory traced the treasure back to Solomon and the Treasure of Zion in the Holy Land. Other historians suggested that the Jewish treasure was taken to Rome by Titus and looted from the Roman treasury by Alaric the Visigoth in 410 CE. This is supported by the knowledge that what is now the tiny village of Rennes-le-Château was once a major Visigoth center and substantially fortified.

Another theory suggested that Saunière actually discovered several ancient tombs in which it was customary for the nobility to be buried in all their finery, complete with jewels and golden ornaments. Still another theory posits that Saunière found the sacred chalice Jesus once used at the Last Supper with his disciples or the lance once buried in the side of Christ at the moment of his death. Any such Christian relic would have accounted for Saunière's apparently unlimited supply of wealth.

Modern-day politico-religious societies such as the Priory of Sion and the Knights Templar continue to search for the holy "treasure" or links that confirm Jesus Christ as the rightful Messiah and provide direct proof of God's presence on Earth.

It would seem that the greatest treasure of symbolic and literary relevance to Western religious tradition and the Knights Templar included the legendary treasure of the temple of Jerusalem. And the contents of the Holy of Holies may have included the immense gold seven-branched candelabrum so sacred to Judaism, and possibly the Ark of the Covenant. This would warrant the references to Sion in the Rennes Parchments.

Speculations about the nature of the treasure aside, the intrigue and deflection that occurred during the early part of the fifteenth century along the eastern seaboard of the New World must itself have taken on a certain mystique among the existing aboriginal nations. It would also inevitably lead to the point where individual native tribes or whole nations would be forced to choose sides.

ANOTHER RATIONALE FOR INLAND MIGRATION

There is another strong rationale for the movement inland of the "lost" Templar/Grail refugees. These Europeans were in need of maintaining a certain level of Old World lifestyle because of the important persons in their midst. As well, they needed to be constantly prepared for a European attack from those parties of the Roman Catholic Church or others who might seek to do them ill. Because of this they would have needed to maintain a considerable standard of weaponry, and therefore they would have constantly probed inland for richer deposits of readily accessible metals and enough fertile land to be able to sustain ever-growing colonies.

It was the Canadian Shield, which extends as far south as New Hampshire and Vermont and encompasses the Great Lakes area, that offered what must have appeared to be a more than suitable area for agriculture. And, like Britain, this is also an area with a seemingly unlimited abundance of metals such as copper, nickel, tin, and iron ore, as well as the more mysterious rare earth metals titanium, manganese, and the extremely rare niobium. The significance of these deposits is that they were readily accessible by the practice of either crude open-pit mining or mining that took place just below the earth's surface, which was typical of the medieval technology practiced then. Beyond coincidence is the fact that many of these deposits are found along the many antient rose lines of the New World and that the natives themselves had a long and ancient practice of designating these areas as their spiritual centers.

Given that the Templars were engrained with a European military mentality, they would have approached every reconnaissance, excursion, settlement, and any other daily activity with strategic brilliance that could only have been gained through three centuries of constant battle. The Templars, along with their fellow initiates the Cistercians, also possessed probably the finest combination of skills of any culture anywhere in the world at that time. These skills spanned the disciplines of agriculture, mining and smelting, milling, forestry, navigation, astronomy, animal husbandry, and stonemasonry. This expertise would have allowed them to construct towers and fortified settlements related to archaeoastronomical alignments and to practice agriculture on a level that would have seemed absolutely foreign to the natives with whom they were interacting.

The idea of a series of holy refuges or secret Rose Line settlements in pre-Columbian North America centers on a plot that most historians would not even attempt to fathom, yet from a strategic point of view makes complete sense. The Templar refugees knew that they would forever be fighting a rearguard action. Therefore, their strategy must have been to have a settlement that was farther inland prepared and waiting for the necessary transfer of a Rose Line settlement whenever foreign ships were spied on the horizon. Then, like the knights on a chessboard, they could leapfrog their adversary to a sanctuary farther inland and to safety.

A FEW TRACKS LEFT BEHIND

Of course, even if the lines of communication with the Old World were intermittent at the best of times, rumors of New World colonies must have made their way back to the ports of Europe. Stories and myths would surely have passed among the Portuguese, English, and Basque fishermen who had been plying their trade just off the eastern seaboard along the Grand Banks during the fifteenth and sixteenth centuries. Yet as the veil of secrecy dipped once again over the New World activities of the Templars and the Grail refugees in the fifteenth and sixteenth centuries, it is suspicious that at least some additional rumors or clues cannot be found—either among the myths and legends of the Algonquin Nation or in the discovery of caches or ruins relating to these inland settlements. The simple truth is that the Templars were forever on the run, as they surely possessed something of infinite value. This meant that they would have constantly been on guard and have covered their tracks carefully and well.

Surely one of the best methods was to essentially blend into the native population in both manner and deed. But given their obvious skills in masonry, certain methods of stone construction would have been hard to disguise. Why then is it that a series of stone towers or at least their foundations, other than the Newport Tower, have not been found? The answer to this lies in the knowledge that those secret agents of the Holy Bloodline in later centuries deliberately assumed the very foundations of these settlements as their own and built upon them. This was done in much the same manner that churches and temples all over the world were typically built on earlier pagan sites.

A prime example of building upon earlier foundations is found in Old Montreal, where the Seminarie du Saint Sulpice and Notre-Dame Basilica are built upon the earlier foundations of a Templar settlement. This is supported by the very fact that the cornerstone of the original tower that stood on the site can still be found in the basement. The rectangular stone that the church proudly displays contains the signs and symbols of both the Templars and the Sulpicians.

This notion of building upon earlier goddess foundations is surely one of the underlying subliminal messages of Poussin's *The Shepherds of Arcadia.* The three dots that constitute the fifth word in the French title of the painting (*Et en Arcadia Ego . . .*) represent a time line of sorts, a sum total of the cycle of Goddess veneration, consolidating the

Fig. 2.11. Templar cornerstone found at the base of the Notre-Dame Basilica, on the site of the earlier Sulpician Church of Notre-Dame, Old Montreal. Note the Templar cross carved into the side of the stone. Photograph property of the author, William F. Mann.

earliest Divine Being beliefs through the period of Egyptian goddess and Hellenistic veneration to the Transformation of Jesus the man into the risen Christ—the Son of God. Here is the cycle of birth, life, death, resurrection, and ascension, reflective of the five main elements coyly positioned by Poussin within his painting, *The Shepherds of Arcadia.*

3
Out of the Wilderness

LIFE'S LITTLE TRICKS

Life has been playing little tricks on me ever since I can remember. Approximately thirty-six years ago I attended North London Polytechnic University in London, England, while completing my master's degree. Every so often I would take a short trip with some of my British classmates, and chance would have it that one such trip was to the south of France. After crossing the channel by car ferry, we drove south through the Midi-Pyrenees region, which includes the medieval communities of Carcassonne and Rennes-le-Château. We drove through this region for virtually no other reason than it was between us and the southern shoreline of France and its many trendy beaches, where we were aiming to go.

At the time I was totally unaware how this area of the world had played such an intimate part in the story of *Holy Blood, Holy Grail.*[1] Like any typical graduate student running on adrenaline and very little money, I was more interested in enjoying the amazing scenery and sampling what the region had to offer in terms of cheap drink and food and female companionship.

The authors of *Holy Blood, Holy Grail* and *Rennes-le-Château* have extensively detailed the background history of the Pyrenees and southern France and its spiritual connections to Catharism, which was based on earlier spiritual beliefs. In fact, they spend an inordinate amount of time explaining that the earlier Gnosticism and Hermeticism that emerged in southern France was in turn based in part on Manichaeanism, which is a branch of theology that is mainly concerned with the teachings of Mani, a mystic who lived in the third century CE. Perhaps the authors believed that it was critical to understand the fundamental tenets of Gnostic freethinking. Regardless of their intentions, according to the principles espoused by Mani, the human soul originated in the Kingdom of Light, to which it is continually trying to return. Hence, the human body was seen as the Kingdom of Darkness. This supports Gnostic Neo-Platonist and Hermetic thought, which posits that spirit is good and matter is evil. In a sense this principle may be interpreted as an attempt to weld the classical patterns of reincarnation onto the teachings of Christ whereby if a person can acquire the necessary inner spiritual knowledge they may escape from the prison of matter that is the body.

Part of our study routine was to draw, paint, and photograph as much as possible, filling a series of black sketchbooks with anything that inspired us. By chance, we happened upon some castle ruins, and, as it was a lovely sunny day, we decided to relax and picnic in the shadow of the stone walls. It turned out that the ruins were those of Château de Lagarde. As others relaxed and dozed in the grass after lunch I wandered among the ruins taking several pictures inside and out. The round stone tower was the most fascinating part of the fortress; the eleventh-century corbeled ceiling, which depicts a six-pointed star, had remained relatively intact.

The Château de Lagarde is located near the small medieval village of Lagarde, approximately five miles southeast of present-day Mirepoix in the French department of Ariège. The château was first constructed

Fig. 3.1. Castle ruins of Château de Lagarde, an eleventh-century stone fortress. The round tower is positioned in the foreground. Photograph property of the author, William F. Mann.

in the eleventh century by Garcia Ramirez, who held the many titles of Ramire de Navarre, King of Navarre, and Count of Barcelona. Château de Lagarde appears more as a fortress than even a castle, as the round tower dominates the structure. It was at this time that Ramirez was heading up a fight for independence of the kingdom of Navarre from the larger kingdom of Castile, and the Château de Lagarde was his defensive headquarters.

In the next century, following the loss of Jerusalem in July 1187 by Gerard de Ridefort, then grand master of the temple, it was the Templars who retreated to this same area of France. More specifically, the Templars retreated to Languedoc, the principality of the heretical Cathars. It is reasoned that they may have felt that the Languedoc area could become their New Jerusalem, because many wealthy landowners, who were Cathars themselves or sympathetic to Cathar beliefs, had donated vast tracts of land to the Order.

The Languedoc promoted religious tolerance, and, as a direct result, Greek, Arabic, and Hebrew, along with the Kabbalah—the ancient

Fig. 3.2. Ceiling of the round stone tower of Château de Lagarde, illustrating the six-pointed star. Photograph property of the author, William F. Mann.

esoteric tradition—was enthusiastically studied. However, not unlike the Roman Empire, complacency and decadence set in, and by 1208 the Roman Catholic Church had become increasingly threatened by the Cathar heresy.

Hence, under the direct orders of Pope Innocent III, a Holy Crusade was waged against the Cathars. In 1209 a northern army led by Simon de Montfort invaded the Languedoc, and during the next forty years approximately thirty thousand people were killed. This genocide, for it is the only truthful way to describe it, is now known as the Albigensian

Crusade. And although the pope initiated the crusade, it is best remembered for the fanaticism of a Spanish monk named Dominic Guzman, who created the tortures of the Holy Inquisition. Ironically, these same tortures would be perfected over the next century, just in time for their use on the Knights Templar, who refused to become engaged in the Albigensian Crusade.

Unlike the Roman Catholic Church, which remained fixated on the concept of the devil and hell as an all-encompassing, supreme form of evil, the Cathars thought that they knew the true nature of the devil. This statement may appear blasphemous from a Christian point of view, but it can be argued that the devil is only a symbol created by the church. On the other hand, the Cathars were eliminated as an outward force because of their inability to adapt to the orthodox teachings of their day.

The confusion may lie in the church's direct association of Satan to the devil and all that is evil. The Cathars considered all created matter the work of Rex Mundi/Satan, and, as flesh, Jesus could only be so related. What this implies is that we are all descendants of Satan and that the true House of God could be the House of Satan the Good, or Lucifer, and therefore Catholics should not be venerating Jesus Christ as the son of God.

In the Jewish Targum Samael, the birth of Cain is ascribed to a union of Satan and Eve. Masonic teachings indicate that Hiram Abiff descended from the line of Cain through Tubal-Cain, who, with his son, was said to be the only survivor of the superior race after the Great Flood. Masonic tradition also tells us that this race was created by the Elohim, "the serpent people," those of the fire snake.

By 1243 the Holy Crusade had leveled all major Cathar towns and forts except for a handful of isolated strongholds. Chief among the holdouts was the remote mountain citadel of Montsegur. Fighting against all odds, in March 1244 the fortress finally surrendered, and the Cathar heresy, at least officially, ceased to exist in the south of France. What is known is that the Cathars were wealthy, and rumors of a fantastic Cathar treasure spread. This treasure was supposedly kept at Montsegur, but when the fortress fell nothing of consequence was found.

During the crusades against the Cathars, Château de Lagarde came into the possession of Simon de Montfort, who in turn gave it to his lieutenant Guy de Levis, and this is the family to whom it has mainly belonged over the centuries. The Levis and Montfort families had intermarried for more than two centuries previously; Guy was married to Simon's sister, Guiburge de Montfort.

Again, as a post-graduate student exploring the area, I was totally unaware of any of the area's history. So as the sun began to set we made our way to the delightful medieval village of Lagarde itself, enjoyed a light supper, and then spent a peaceful evening sleeping under the stars alongside a small lane leading back into the countryside. But before we actually left the village in our beat-up rental van, I set off with my sketch pad to capture something of note that would be a reminder of such a perfect day. What I came upon was a plaque set into the plaster of a doorway of a small house. The plaque was labeled "Lagarde, France," and I thought it appropriate to record what I considered to be a very interesting family coat of arms. The funny thing was that I didn't realize how interesting the coat of arms would be to me personally until about five years ago when I earnestly studied the genealogy of my mother's side of the family.

The shield central on the coat of arms (see figure 3.3) is what I find most intriguing. The shield is divided into four quarters, or quadrants. The upper right-hand quadrant features two stone towers under a golden chevron on a black background, as does the lower left-hand quadrant. The lower right-hand quadrant features a semi-nude male figure reclining on a beach, and a blue background; the upper left-hand quadrant features a globe of the world, a notebook of sorts, and a navigator's compass on a green background.

Who were the original Lagardes who had named their little village after the family name? Or was it the other way around, with the local family taking the name of the village? The Château de Lagarde only has

Fig. 3.3. Lagarde coat of arms that was discovered on the wall of a home located in the small village of Lagarde, France. Drawing property of the author, William F. Mann.

one round stone tower, whereas the Lagarde coat of arms has two sets of two stone towers. Indeed, it appears that very little is known of the family's true origins other than the root of the name in Old French is *garde,* meaning "watch" or "protection." It appears probable then that the village was primarily formed around the garrison that first manned the nearby château, or fortress, in support of the kingdom known as Navarre.

What is known about the history of the area is probably more revealing at this time to the larger story being told here. Unfortunately, trying to follow the strategic intermarriages and prominent family lineages involved during the development and the ultimate absorption of the kingdom of Navarre into France is like trying to follow a single thread through a multilayered labyrinth. There are those, even to this day, who believe that the kingdom should be a separate state and as a result have recently committed horrible crimes against an innocent, non-suspecting population.

Given this context, as any present-day Basque will tell you, originally the kingdom of Navarre was a Basque kingdom, formalized in 778 CE when the Basques defeated a Frankish army at the Battle of Roncevaux Pass. Two generations later, in 824, the Basque chieftain Inigo Arista was elected king of Pamplona, in part due to support by the muwallad Banu Qasi of Tudela, thus establishing a Basque kingdom that developed and was later called Navarre. That kingdom reached its zenith during the reign of Sancho III of Navarre, comprising most of the Christian realms to the south of the Pyrenees, and even a short overlordship of Gascony during the early eleventh century.

When Sancho III died in 1035, the kingdom of Navarre was divided among his sons. Under the sons, it never fully recovered its political power, but its commercial importance increased as traders and pilgrims poured into the kingdom throughout the Way of St. James. This increase in pilgrims coincided with the widespread Christian pilgrimage associated with the First Crusade. Then, in 1200, Navarre lost the key western Basque districts to Alphonse VIII of Castile, leaving the kingdom landlocked.

The Navarre line of kings came to an end in 1234 when the remaining royal descendants strategically intermarried with the various French dynasties, consolidating northern Francia and southern Navarre to form the France that we know today. Generally speaking, the monarchs of the Franks ruled from the establishment of the more northern Francia from 486 to 870 CE.[2]

In the early fifth century, around the same time that the Celts were declining, the Sicambrians moved into Gaul, establishing themselves in what are now the Lowlands of Belgium and northern France. Prior to this the Sicambrians had maintained close contact with the Romans and had adopted their customs and administration. Following the collapse of the Roman Empire it was natural that the

Sicambrians would assume control of the already existing but vacant administrative structure in a region that came to be called the kingdom of Austrasie. The core of this kingdom is what is now known as Lorraine. Subsequently, the regime of the early Merovingians conformed to the customs and fashions of the old Roman Empire. And, as time went on, the Merovingian kingdom expanded to include the entire area of the earlier Frank dynasty.

During this time the Merovingian dynasty ruled until 751, followed by the Carolingian dynasty, which ruled until 987. The Capetian dynasty, the line of male descendants of Hugh Capet, then ruled all of France continuously from 987 to 1792 and again from 1814 to 1848. The branches of the dynasty that ruled after 1328, however, are generally given the specific branch names of Valois and Bourbon.

FOLLOWING THE BLOODLINE UNDERGROUND

The House of Valois was a cadet (the male-line descendants) branch of the Capetian dynasty, which succeeded the House of Capet and produced the kings of France from 1328 to 1589. A cadet branch of the family also reigned as dukes of Burgundy from 1363 to 1482. The Valois descended from Charles, Count of Valois, who lived between 1270 and 1325. Charles was the fourth son of King Philip III of France and reigned between 1270 and 1285. The Capetians based their claim on Salic law, which excluded females such as Joan II of Navarre as well as male descendants through the distaff line (such as Edward III of England) from succeeding to the French throne.

Charles's son Philip VI, who was called "the Fortunate," was therefore the first king of France from the House of Valois. He reigned from 1328 until his death in 1350 and was succeeded by his son John II the Good (Jean Le Bon), who ruled as king of France from 1350 until his death in 1364. At the age of thirteen John was married to

Bonne of Bohemia, daughter of John I of Bohemia. Their children were Charles V, who became king following the death of Jean II; Louis I, Duke of Anjou; John, Duke of Berry; Philip II, Duke of Burgundy; Joan, who married Charles II (the Bad) of Navarre; Marie, who married Robert I, Duke of Bar; Agnes and Margaret, who both died at the age of five; and Isabelle of Valois, who married Gian Galeazzo I, Duke of Milan. With so many children, Jean Le Bon ensured that the House of Valois would have plenty of heirs to continue the Valois hold over the French monarchy for centuries to come.

Charles VI, called "the Beloved" and "the Mad," succeeded to the throne and was king of France from 1380 to his death. Given that he was only eleven when he inherited the throne in the midst of the Hundred Years' War, the government was entrusted to his four uncles: Philip the Bold, Duke of Burgundy; John, Duke of Berry (Jean du Berry); Louis I, Duke of Anjou; and Louis II, Duke of Bourbon. Although the royal age of majority was fixed at fourteen, the dukes maintained their grip on Charles until he took power at the age of twenty-one. By this time, though, the financial resources of the kingdom had been severely diminished, and, upon his death in 1422, Henry VI of England, son-in-law of Charles VI, was proclaimed king of France, reigning from England through the War of the Roses, until 1471.

Meanwhile, one of the uncles, Jean du Berry, retreated to the southern Languedoc, where he immersed himself in the Kabbalah and Gnosticism and related art and religious symbolism. It was here that he became a notable art patron who commissioned, among other works, the most famous *Les Très Riches Heures,* the book of hours.*[3] The book of hours contains unlimited hidden references and symbolism to the

---

*The calendar illustrations in the the book of hours, painted by the Limbourg brothers under commission by Jean du Berry, are perhaps the most eloquent statements of painting during the Gothic period. Gothic art evolved from Romanesque art and lasted from the mid-twelfth century to as late as the end of the sixteenth century in some areas. The term *Gothic* was coined by classicizing Italian writers of the Renaissance, who attributed the invention—and what, to them at that time, was the nonclassical ugliness of medieval architecture—to the barbarian Visigoth tribes that had destroyed the Roman Empire and its classical culture in the fifth century.

Fig. 3.4. *Les Très Riches Heures* by John, Duke of Berry (Jean du Berry); a calendar panel of the month of November, the eleventh month, depicting the autumn harvest of acorns on which pigs are feeding. Note that the oak trees show trunks that are parallel to one another; the symbolism of the pig, which relates to Saint Anthony, is in the foreground. In the background stand two stone towers. Reproduced courtesy of the Cloisters Museum, New York.

Holy Family and Bloodline. Unfortunately, expenditures on Jean's art collection and sponsorship severely taxed his estates, and he was deeply in debt when he died in 1416 in Paris.

However, not all was lost with the death of Jean du Berry, for it was René d'Anjou, grandnephew to the duke of Berry (Jean du Berry), who in all probability provided the greatest wealth of material relating to the secret of the Holy Bloodline—the same bloodline that purportedly descended through the Frank and Merovingian kings and their familial lineage.[4] Born in 1408, René d'Anjou continued his great-uncle's work throughout his lifetime, not only as a major contributor to the formation of the Renaissance academies but also as one of the first proponents behind one of the Renaissance's favorite subjects—Arcadia. What is clearly evident is that René d'Anjou not only inherited his great-uncle's title and riches but also a great wealth of secret esoteric knowledge.

The Franks were a pagan Germanic (Visigoth) tribe that first came into contact with the Gallo-Roman provinces of Gaul in the first century. By the close of the fifth century they had become the most powerful of the Germanic tribes, and the Salian Franks had migrated to the Roman province of Belgica Secunda, which is now part of the Netherlands, Belgium, and northern France. In the days following the collapse of the western Roman Empire, the Franks created the most stable barbarian kingdom under the rule of Clovis, who became a Catholic and ordered his people to do the same.

The name Merovingian derives from Merovech or Meroveus in Latin; it was Merovech who was the next recorded king after Chlodio and it therefore is presumed that Merovech was Chlodio's son. After his father's death, it was recorded that Merovech went to Rome to gain support for succession against his brother, who solicited help from Attila the Hun for the same purpose. At the time, the historian Priscus wrote that he had seen Merovech and that "he was still very young and we all remarked the fair hair that fell upon his shoulders." According to Priscus, Merovech built a friendship with the Roman master of the soldiers, Aetius, and became Rome's ally in the Battle of the Catalaunian Plains (Catalaunum) where Rome and her allies fought Attila the Hun. Merovech the Frank is now labeled by historians as the root-historian of the entire Merovingian dynasty.

René's pedigree is as impressive as his inherited titles. His father was Louis II, Duke of Anjou and Provence, and his mother was Yolande of Aragon. His first wife was Isabelle, the ten-year-old heiress of Lorraine, daughter of Charles II of Lorraine and Marguerite of Bavaria. At the time of René's marriage, Charles, the dauphin of France, was married to René's sister Marie and had lived at the Angevin court for five years. By the time René was twenty, in 1429, he and Isabelle had four children: Louis, Yolande, Jean, and Marguerite. Marguerite became queen of England when she married Henry VI (of England) as part of the negotiations for a truce of the Hundred Years' War, otherwise known as the War of the Roses.

In 1419, René's great-uncle, Cardinal Louis, Duke of Bar, adopted René as inheritor of the duchy of Bar, and, with his great-uncle's death in 1430, René became the duke of Bar. Then, in November 1434, Duke Louis III of Anjou, René's elder brother, died while campaigning for Giovanna II of Naples. As a result, René inherited Anjou and Provence and, in addition, claims to the kingdoms of Naples, Sicily, and Jerusalem, which Giovanna confirmed on her death in 1435. Most interesting is that although René held the title of king of Jerusalem, he never exercised his right beyond accepting the title.

René was known as Good King René, and, in addition to being a royal duke and a titular king, he was an artist and a poet. It is said that he was intelligent, attractive, sensitive, tolerant, and fatalistic and saw himself as a chivalric knight in the tradition of Arthurian romances and the Grail. He also enjoyed jousting and planned many tournaments and even wrote a famous treatise on the form and creation of a tournament.

In René's own work, the Arcadian theme of an underground stream of knowledge, which is frequently symbolized by a fountain or a tombstone, appears to have been rich in symbolic and allegorical meaning. In addition, it appears to relate to the underground esoteric tradition of Pythagorean, Gnostic, Kabbalistic, and Hermetic thought. But it might also portray some very specific factual information—a secret of some sort—such as an unacknowledged and thus "subterranean" bloodline or, in reality, a labyrinth of settlements that existed in the New World/Arcadia during the fifteenth and sixteenth centuries.[5] Of course, this labyrinth of secret settlements that existed in the New World/Arcadia during the fifteenth and sixteenth centuries goes to the heart of this book, *Templar Sanctuaries in North America: Sacred Bloodlines and Secret Treasures.*

The concept of a subterranean bloodline promoted by René d'Anjou at this time is fascinating, to say the least. It almost appears as though certain of the French nobility were predestined to intermarry other similarly identified bloodlines, both for political purposes and to keep the stock strong and healthy. René's own bloodline, including the House of Lorraine, is a prime example of this type of controlled mixing of heraldic and genealogical purity. The same can be said for those Hebrew/Catholic northern branches such as the de Vere and de Mandeville families, who descended directly from the original nine knights of the Poor Fellow Soldiers of Christ and of the Temple of Solomon, which originated in Normandy and the north of France.

In 1449, René staged a series of plays known as pas d'armes. One of the most famous was called *The Pas d'Armes of the Shepherdess* wherein the Arcadian shepherdess presided over a tournament of knights whose identities represented conflicting values and ideas. Here is one of the first references to the shepherdess in terms of applying her thematic attributes in an art form. René then married his second wife, Jeanne de Laval, on September 10, 1454, shortly after the death of Isabelle in 1453. For Jeanne, René wrote *Regnault et Jeanneton,* a pastoral ode of ten thousand verses. The poem presented a debate on love between a shepherd and a shepherdess with a pilgrim wayfarer as arbiter.

Coming around again, Jeanne de Laval heralds from the same direct lineage as the later Jesuit bishop François de Laval, who came to Québec as the first vicar apostolic of New France, appointed by

Pope Alexander VII. Born in Siena, Pope Alexander VII's real name was Fabio Chigi; he was a member of the illustrious banking family of Chigi. Before being elected pontiff, Chigi served as inquisitor on the Island of Malta, where he resided mostly at the Inquisitor's Palace in Birga. At that time Malta was a fiefdom of the then combined Order of the Knights Hospitallers of the Sovereign Order of Saint John of Jerusalem and Knights of Malta—the same Knights of Malta to whom Samuel de Champlain would propose to deed all of New France!

Probably the most famous of all of René's literary works is the allegorical tale *Le Cuer d'amours espris,* "The Heart Smitten with Love." Finished in 1457, René not only wrote the story but also commissioned the illustrations, supervised their execution, and corrected the related text. Modeled on the previous *Roman de la rose,* this work is a return to the earlier knightly poetry, reflecting a quest for the Holy Grail in which a "green" knight and his attendant/apprentice try to free a damsel in distress through a number of gallant deeds.

One of the more famous illustrations contained in this work is *La Foutaine de fortune,* which illustrates the knight reflecting near a magical fountain while his attendant rests near the two horses. This painting has recently attracted the attention of many scholars, because it is said to illustrate the concept of the underground stream of esoteric thought, including the theme of Arcadia and its pastoral wilderness. It is also claimed that this work by René d'Anjou was one of the first, perhaps *the* first, to attempt to preserve the "most secret of secrets" by means of esoteric art. But even though several modern-day authors have realized the significance of this painting in terms of its underlying geometric composition, they have failed to grasp the rose line symbolism that pervades the painting. For example, if the reader refers to the copy of *La Fountaine de fortune* (see figure 3.5), it becomes obvious that the tree trunk, knight's lance, and right foreleg of the horse are positioned in such a manner as to represent a tripod.

The tripod is an ancient symbol representative of the Olympian god Apollo and secret societies in general. But it also suggests a surveying instrument that may have been used to determine a rose line or meridian, with the tree trunk of the oak itself representing the westerly

Fig. 3.5. René d'Anjou's *La Fountaine de fortune* is enriched with layer upon layer of "rose" symbolism relating to the underground stream of knowledge about the Holy Grail Bloodline. Reproduced courtesy of the National Gallery, London, England.

meridian. And although many authors claim that the painting shows the scene at sunrise, there is the faint hint that an eclipse is occurring. Then there is the clue that the fountain or source of the "underground stream" is located between the two oak trees that are parallel to one another, thus establishing three parallel longitudinal meridians. As such, it would come as no surprise to learn from my good friend Niven Sinclair that Prince Henry Sinclair's official seal* showed two oak trees, which acted in one way as flanking pillars of a sort.[6]

---

*The original seal of Prince Henry Sinclair is now held by Niven, who is also a direct descendant of Prince Henry. Although he is more than ninety years of age, Niven possesses a remarkable ability to comprehend very quickly the various relationships between the seemingly unconnected events and facts that I have presented to him over the past twenty years. For this reason and also because we are the closest of friends, I have chosen to acknowledge Niven first in the acknowledgments of this book.

In a simpler manner, in René's painting the tree trunk and lance combine to represent a splayed compass. Remember that the fourth quadrant of the Lagarde shield shows a globe, a navigator's compass, and a notebook on a green background. *La Fountaine de fortune* shows the attendant asleep on the green grass. But perhaps he is not really asleep. Perhaps he is contemplating how to apply the knowledge gained through the secret of being able to accurately predict the time and place of an eclipse.

The symbol that René adopted as his personal emblem is the Cross of Lorraine, the double-armed cross that became the emblem of the modern-day Knights Templar of Canada. It was also the emblem adopted by Charles de Gaulle and the Free French Forces during the Second World War. Some authors believe that the reason why the cross has two bars is that it is not the cross of the Crucifixion, but it is the cross-staff, an early surveying device for measuring angles to ascertain altitudes and bearings.

These same authors believe that the Cross of Lorraine is "symbolic of surveying, and thus of the concealment of the Secret and the preservation of the knowledge of its location by means of triangulation and the establishment of the meridian and parallel of the site."[7] Many treasure hunters have related this belief to a location in the south of France, but in *The Templar Meridians,* I demonstrated that a series of antient meridians also existed in the New World across the Atlantic Ocean.

It is easy to see symbolism in everything related to the search for the Holy Grail, even when none exists, but the significance of René's painting cannot be dismissed. René d'Anjou was a man of learning and influence in several courts and among the nobility of France and throughout all of Europe. In this position and through his marriages, he must have been privy to all kinds of court rumors relating to the secret activities of the Knights Templar in the New World.

As such, René's influence on the Renaissance and his role in establishing esoteric elite among certain ruling dynasties should not be underestimated. Sadly, on July 10, 1480, René died at Aix-en-Provence, and with him the notion of the sleeping white knight or

Fig. 3.6. A 1504 CE woodcut produced by one of northern Europe's most celebrated Renaissance printmakers, Albrecht Durer, depicting the explorer Amerigo Vespucci surveying the stars. Within the illustration there is also a great deal of hidden "rose" symbolism. Note the small, three-sided table with the tripod legs and the compass, square, and crossed sticks of Jesus's Crucifixion. The North Star is even shown as the eight-pointed, Templar cross.

king will lay silent until the dawning of a New Jerusalem. This is reflective of the theory of how an earlier age of symbolism, philosophy, and the application of sacred geometry came to relate to the quest for the Holy Grail.

LOGIC AND REASON

The literal translation of the word *renaissance* from French into English is "rebirth." The Renaissance as a historical period was part of a wider philosophical and symbolic trend toward realism in the arts based on a revival of the liberal philosophy or pre-Christian arts and sciences, including the use of geometry in the development of perspective.

In terms of my own perspective (no pun intended), geometry was always a strong suit of mine, both in high school and university, with mathematical equations and related geometric axioms and resulting solutions having the habit of jumping off the page at me. So to think that the "antient" initiates were unable to intuitively develop geometric progressions and mathematical equations to illustrate, test, and prove their theories is completely outside my way of thinking. The idea that ancient Greek philosophers played a pivotal role in the shaping of the Western philosophical tradition and provided the basis for the Renaissance is as natural and pure to me as the wilderness itself.

Greek philosophers always approached the big questions of life in a logical fashion, balancing science and allegory. The birthplace of Greek philosophy were the Greek cities of Ionia. Starting around 600 BCE these cities were at the intellectual and cultural vanguard of Greek culture, as Ionian people were the number one sea traders of the Mediterranean and their economy flourished. Miletus, the southernmost Ionian city, was the wealthiest of the Ionian Greek cities, thus becoming the main focus of the "Ionian awakening," a name for the initial phase of classical Greek civilization that coincides with the birth of Greek philosophy. It was here that the concept of observation followed by summation was considered to be of prime importance among the Milesian school. The Milesian mathematician and philosopher Thales even predicted an eclipse that took place in 585 BCE, and it seems he was also able to calculate the distance of a ship at sea from observations taken at two points.

The Ionian city of Miletus was ruled by a local aristocracy that consisted of powerful trading families who had the leisure to enjoy and patronize education and the arts. The Milesians were known as daring sailors and traders, and it is speculated that they had through some manner inherited the secret knowledge of the Phoenicians. They also had connections to the empires of Egypt and Persia but also had the independence to develop a new culture out of what was imported. Given that the first Greek philosophers came from Miletus suggests that Persia had a particularly powerful influence over the development of Greek philosophy. This could explain why Eastern Orthodox Christianity, which has clearly been influenced by Persian Zoroastrianism, spread through Syria and Ionia to the rest of Greece and Egypt centuries later.

On the other hand, Pythagoras is considered one of the finest Ionian thinkers outside the Milesian school. Although Greek, Pythagoras was originally from Samos, an offshore Ionian settlement, which allowed him freedom from the Milesian school beliefs. Influenced by the Greek Orphic traditions, his philosophical approach combined science with religious beliefs, and, as a result, his philosophy has a dose of mysticism. Mathematics, in the sense of demonstrative deductive arguments, certainly began with Pythagoras. Indeed, he is credited as the author of the first known mathematical formulation, the Pythagorean Theorem, which states that the square of the longest side of a right triangle equals the sum of the squares of the other two sides.

Then, around 500 BCE, the Sophist school began in Athens. In a way the Sophists represented a new political era in Athenian life, especially because they were linked with the new educational desires of the Greeks. It was about this time that Greek culture started to struggle with the idea of conserving past philosophical foundings or allowing Greek philosophy to logically evolve. It was at this same time that Socrates became the pivotal figure in Greek philosophy and was considered the wisest among all philosophers.

Socrates was unusual among his peers in that he combined a humble spirit and a strict agnosticism with a method that challenged conventional assumptions and intolerance for unclear thinking. Because of this, Socrates gradually earned enemies from the various sectors of Athenian society. He was, consequently, put on trial and condemned to death. However, as Athenians did not like to condemn a citizen to death, this was merely a formal sentence, and he was offered the possibility of escape. He refused to do so and obeyed the jury's decision by drinking a mixture containing poison hemlock, which ended his life.

Hence, Plato and Aristotle became and still are considered to be the two most important Greek philosophers because of Socrates' untimely death. As a result, it is their work and not the work of Socrates that has been the main focus of interest for students of philosophy. This is because, unlike most of their predecessors, what they wrote about survived in an accessible form and partly because Christian thought, which was the dominant thought in the Western world during the Middle Ages and early modern age, contained a high dose of Platonic and Aristotelian influence. Of course, many of the Christian faithful will argue otherwise, but the golden thread of thought is absolutely clear.

Among other topics, Aristotle's interests covered a wide scope, including ethics, metaphysics, physics, biology, mathematics, meteorology, astronomy, psychology, politics, and rhetoric. Interestingly, after himself being a student of Plato for almost twenty years, Aristotle was the tutor of Alexander the Great. Aristotle was also the first thinker who systematically developed the study of logic. Some of the components of Aristotelian logic existed long before Aristotle, such as Socrates' ideas on exact definition. Argumentative techniques found in Zeno of Elea, Parmenides, and Plato, and many other elements traceable to legal reasoning and mathematical proof, were also earlier concepts readily adopted by Aristotle.

As we have seen before, the building upon earlier foundations tends to erase those earlier references. For example, while Rome was expanding, Greece started to decline. Thankfully, though, the western Mediterranean was left relatively untouched by Alexander the Great. After the first and second Punic Wars, dating from 264 to 241 BCE and 218 to 201 BCE, Rome was more interested in neutralizing Carthage and controlled Syracuse, which were the two leading city-states of the western Mediterranean. After this Rome continued its expansion by conquering the Macedonian monarchies during the second century BCE, followed by Spain, France, and Britain.

As discussed previously, Rome's influence in the cultural life of Greece was not significant despite its expansion and military superiority. On the contrary, the influence of Greece on Roman culture was deep and long lasting. Roman gods became associated with the Olympian deities, Hellenic art, literature, architecture, philosophy—even the language captivated most educated Romans. Rome's bureaucracy was far superior to Greece's in building roads, implementing social cohesion, creating effective systematic legal codes, and military tactics, but for the rest Romans looked to Greece and adopted a wide range of beliefs for their own benefit. It can be said that Roman science, art, and philosophy were all just a mere plagiarism of the Greeks.

Like all good things, though, they always come to an end. In the case of the Roman world, debauchery and pestilence ultimately reduced its population. Adding to this, unsuccessful military campaigns increased expenditure and taxes while resources diminished and the entire Roman fiscal system crashed. One direct result is that early Christian religion developed during this time in Rome, thanks in part to the bureaucratic slaves who embraced Christianity from the start. Christianity was the one religion that provided the slaves with hope of everlasting freedom.

It was during this time of Plotinus that the world showed few signs of hope, which could explain why the ideal and eternal world of Neo-Platonic ideas was an appealing refuge. This shift of attention from the real world to the otherworld was adopted by pagans and Christians alike, whose philosophies revolved around the idea of an eternal and heavenly afterlife. The resemblances between Platonic and Christian thought are so strong it's evident that later Christian theologians used many of the ideas of Plotinus to cement their philosophy through the Council of Nicea. It was here that a number of telling gospels were rejected for inclusion in the Bible and the central tenet of Jesus as the Son of God was formally adopted, as told through the Nicene Creed, which is still used on a daily basis in the Roman Catholic Church.

Clearly, to anyone with the eyes to see, Platonism played a central role in shaping early Christian theology. This early Christianity combined Platonism, some philosophical beliefs from the Stoics and Orphism, esoteric aspects traceable to cults of the Near East, and morals and history acquired from Judaism. Even Saint Augustine refers to Plato's ideas as "the most pure and bright in all philosophy."[8] Knowing this and what we have learned about its pagan origins, it can be said that Christianity has undergone many changes during its long history, but it is important to note that during the Renaissance its philosophy revolved largely around ideas derived directly from the Greeks.

MORE CLUES IN RENAISSANCE ART

Most Renaissance artists indeed paid homage to the earlier Greek philosophic foundations, which had come together to form Christianity. Aside from Nicolas Poussin, one of the most famous Renaissance painters was Raphael, who received the prestigious commission to decorate with frescoes the rooms now known as the Stanze di Raffaello in the Apostolic Palace in the Vatican. One of the four resulting frescoes, known as *The School of Athens,* or *Scuola di Atene* in Italian, has long been deemed to be Raphael's masterpiece.

It was painted between 1509 and 1510. Plato and Aristotle appear to be the central figures in the rather ambitious portrayal of the Greek school. They are shown debating the merits of *Timaeas,* Plato's work that discussed the logic and deductive reasoning behind the physical versus the spiritual world. The building depicted in Raphael's painting (see figure 3.7) is in the shape of a Greek cross, which some have suggested was intended to show a harmony between pagan philosophy and Christian theology.

There are two sculptures in the background. The one on the left

Fig. 3.7. Raphael's painting of *The School of Athens* (1509–1510), depicting Plato and Aristotle as the central two figures discussing Plato's dialogue *Timeaus*.

is the god Apollo, god of light, archery, and music. He is shown holding a lyre. The sculpture on the right is Athena, goddess of wisdom in her Roman guise as Minerva. The main arch above the two central characters shows a design called the meander, an "infinite" design using continuous lines that repeat in a series of rectangular bends, which originated on pottery of the Greek Geometric Period and then became widely used in ancient Greek architectural friezes.

What's interesting about how the arch is depicted is that by following Plato's upward-pointing hand the central keystone is hinted at but barely seen, which is suggestive of the need to find the secret key (stone) to unlock the hidden meaning in the painting. This could be said to be a symbol of Plato's claim that ultimate reality (the forms) lies beyond what we experience. Plato holds a copy of his work *Timaeus,* and Aristotle holds a copy of his *Ethics* while describing the Earth and the wide realm of moral teaching with his extended hand in a parallel horizontal gesture.

Aristotle thought that the ordinary empirical world is more real than Plato's world of forms. Could it be that Raphael is suggesting that the key leading to that point where heaven and earth meet can be determined by the intersection of specific longitudinal and latitudinal lines, reflective of the hand gestures of the two Greek philosophers? The figure depicted in the forefront of the painting, positioned "on the square," is said to be Euclid. It's therefore most interesting that Raphael shows Euclid in the painting falling on the side of Plato, essentially aligning logic and reason with geometry.

Of course, one of the best known of the Greek mathematician philosophers to prove his theories through geometry is Euclid, who we mentioned briefly earlier. As noted, he is often referred to as the father of geometry. He is also referred to as Euclid of Alexandria as he lived in Alexandria, Hellenistic Egypt, between 323 and 283 BCE. And, as previously noted, his most popular work, *The Elements,* is thought to be one of the most successful textbooks pertaining to the history of mathematics.

In the treatise, the properties of geometrical objects are deduced from a small set of self-evident transformations, or axioms, thereby establishing the *axiomatic* method of mathematics. Euclid thus imposed a logical organization on known mathematical truths by the disciplined use of logic. It was through logic that Euclid actually concluded that a square could be constructed with the same area as a given circle using the axiomatic method of mathematics.

Thus, "squaring the circle" became the challenge of constructing a square with the same area as a given circle by using only a finite number of steps with a compass and straightedge. But the solution to the problem of squaring the circle by compass and straightedge has been proved to be impossible using the infinite, or *transcendent,* value of pi.

Conversely, it is possible to construct a square with an area arbitrarily close to that of a given circle if a rational numerical value such as 3.14 is used as an approximation of the number for pi. However, this is only an approximation and does not meet the constraints of the ancient rules for solving the problem.

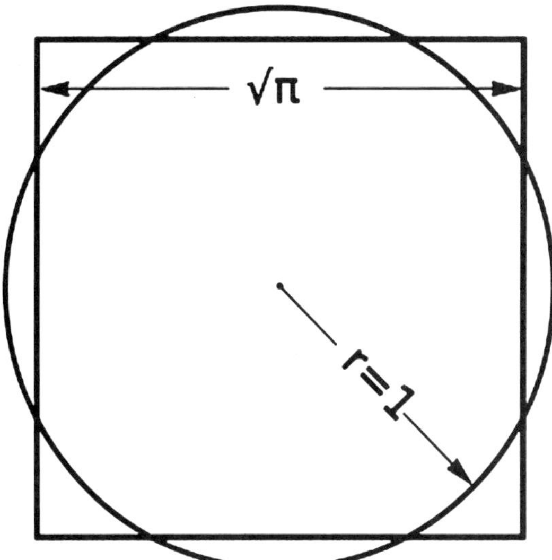

Fig. 3.8. Diagram illustrating Euclid's "squaring the circle," wherein theoretically the square has the same area as the circle. Illustration developed by the author, William F. Mann.

THE GENIUS OF POUSSIN

It is said that after reading *The Elements* even the Renaissance painter Poussin tried his hand at "squaring the circle." But being a man of extraordinary learning and intellectual sophistication, Poussin realized very quickly the transcendence of the number for pi, quickly relating it to the need for a transformation to the concept of metamorphosis. Thus, Poussin was able to apply logic and reason to the philosophical transformation of the Divine Being, following the golden thread from the Bear to the Feminine Goddess, to the Olympian Gods, to the basic Christian tenets, and, ultimately, to the absolute faith required to accept the conversion of Jesus to the Son of God.

Even so, in his painting *The Shepherds of Arcadia* (figure 2.8 on p. 73), Poussin secretly acknowledges the inevitable discovery of the truth concerning the union of Jesus and Mary Magdalene. The thread here suggests that the shepherdess is indeed a representation of Mary Magdelene, the wife of Jesus, and the unborn child that she carried even as Jesus was crucified. Given this reasoning I find it truly amazing that Poussin was able to take geographic information provided to him by Cardinal Richelieu and others, rationalize it through logic, and transform it through deductive reasoning. Thus Poussin was able to create a painting that transcends its two-dimensional surface, through a third- and fourth-dimensional transformation, ultimately achieving a hidden fifth dimension.

In much simpler terms, Poussin applied the esoteric understanding

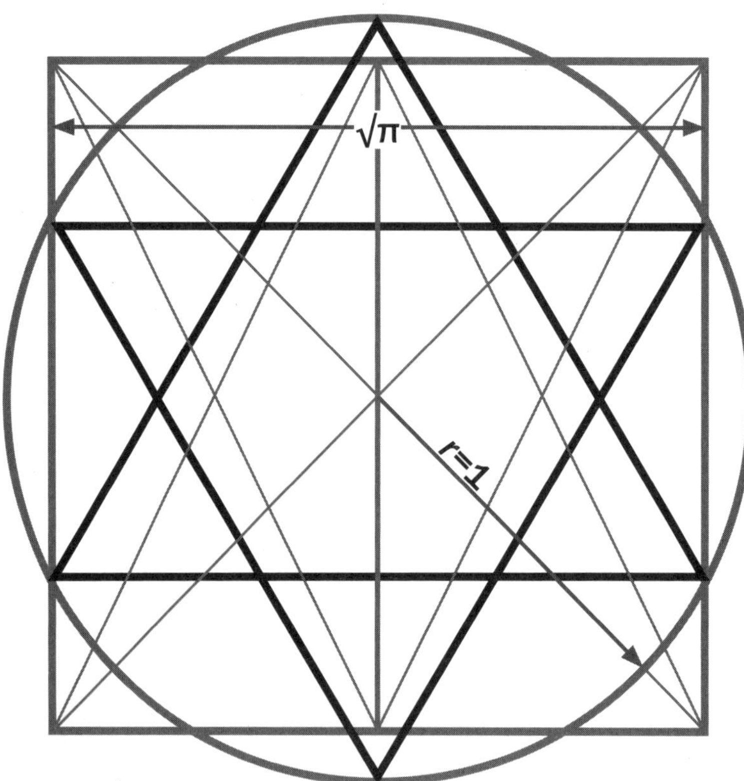

Fig. 3.9. A geometric demonstration of the concept that through "squaring the circle," using only a compass and square, the initiate is able to construct the inner six-pointed star and, in so doing, achieves a higher level of understanding and knowledge. Diagram property of the author, William F. Mann.

and knowledge that he had gained by embracing several systems of belief or elements—Pagan, Jewish, Christian, Stoic, Pantheistic—along with the principles that he had gained through initiation into Freemasonry to create a multilayered canvas of signs, seals, and tokens. This layering of moral allegory and sacred geometry was playfully based on a philosophy of balanced harmony between heaven and earth, between the real world and the spirit world, and the concept of squaring the circle. In Poussin's case, his transformation to a level of pure genius could be represented by the Jewel of the Royal Arch—the Seal of Solomon—which represents, in Freemasonry, a movement to a higher level of degree or order. Clearly, in Masonic circles, it is the royal arch that the intiate

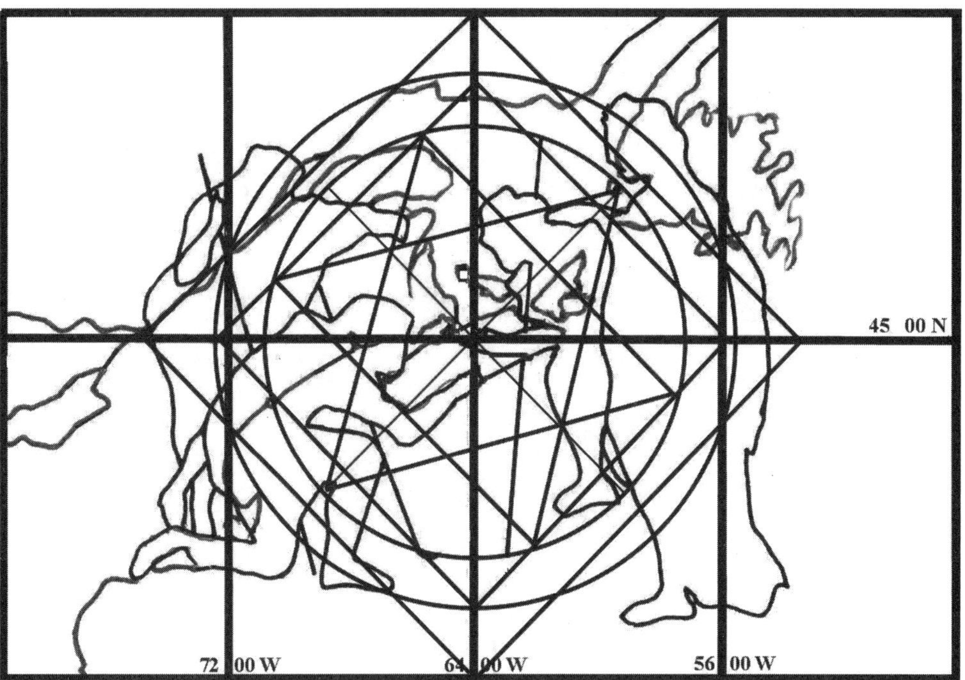

Fig. 3.10. A dual application of the geometric squaring of the circle positioned on the exact center of mainland Nova Scotia, revealing the Jewel of the Royal Arch. Note how the two shepherds define the perimeter of the inner circle with their staffs and how the square is positioned to align with the 45th-degree parallel. Also note the perfect square diamond lozenge falling on the 45th parallel. Diagram copyright of the author, William F. Mann.

must pass through if he wants to achieve any one of a number of higher levels or degrees.

Within *The Shepherds of Arcadia* the two shepherds depicted by Poussin as members of the inner circle are meant to be the antient initiates who have the knowledge and understanding to apply sacred geometry across both land and sea, thus allowing them to define the location of their refuges—their two stone towers—by longitudinal and latitudinal coordinates. The placement of the two rings, one on top of the other, also suggests that eclipses were used to establish relative longitudinal/latitudinal positioning of various Rose Line sanctuaries across North America.

During total lunar eclipses, the moon passes into Earth's shadow, causing the planet to darken the face of the moon. However, instead of making the moon go completely dark, it shines with a rosy copper hue because it reflects light from the sun coming through Earth's atmosphere. For example, on Wednesday, October 8, 2014, in the early morning hours, a stunning total lunar eclipse was visible over parts of North and South America. At its fullness, the moon took

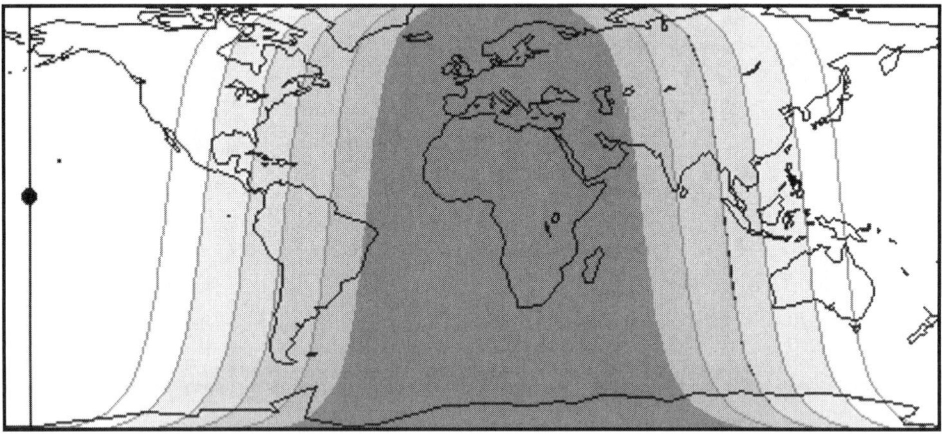

Fig. 3.11. A diagram calculated by NASA illustrating the visibility of a total lunar eclipse across Earth's surface from the east to the west on the evening of October 8, 2014. The gradient illustrates the degree of visibility of the event, with the darkest area representing the greatest eclipse. The gradient pattern represents intervals of the moon's transit. Taken from NASA website eclipse.gsfc.nasa.gov/LEsaros/LEsaros127.html.

on a glowing coppery red hue, which makes it appear mysteriously translucent. Hence, the name given to this phenomenon is the blood-red moon, which eerily relates on another level to the bloodline of the moon goddess.

Nicolas Poussin was certainly familiar with solar and lunar eclipses. His 1635 painting of *Helios and Phaeton with Saturn and the Four Seasons* appears to be a prelude in many ways to the many layers of symbolism found in *The Shepherds of Arcadia.* The painting depicts the sun god Helios with his son Phaeton. Surrounding Helios is his entourage—the Four Seasons. Phaeton is depicted on one knee, begging his father to let him drive his chariot across the sky for one day. Helios allows it, but his son lacks the skill to control the chariot and horses, dropping the sun. But before the sun can immolate Earth, Zeus destroys the chariot with a thunderbolt and sends Phaeton into the river Eridanus.

ESTABLISHING AN ACCURATE LONGITUDE

This notion of a series of antient longitudinal/latitudinal meridians spanning the globe—established through continual observations and timing of eclipses—is not a new concept, but to associate it with the Goddess suggests both a pre-Christian and secret society connection. It not only suggests that through the union of Jesus and Mary the bloodline of ancient kings, including the House of David and Tribe of Benjamin, continues to this day but also that an antient knowledge has been perpetuated as well—a secret knowledge that among other things allowed the highest of initiates to establish over the centuries their relative position on Earth's surface. During a time when the church was promoting the concept that the Earth was flat, this secret information represented pure power in terms of trade and natural resources. Needless to say, the holders of such knowledge would very quickly realize the necessity to veil it in layers of esoteric and religious symbolism that outwardly fell under the sanction of the church.

As first demonstrated in *The Knights Templar in the New World,* a method did exist that allowed for the establishment of an accurate longitude long before the development of the chronometer in 1773 by John Harrison.[9] The only known method of establishing longitude prior to this had been by timing an eclipse, either of the sun or the moon. However, there are two problems that had to be overcome when determining an accurate longitude. The first was that someone had to be able to accurately predict when the eclipse was going to occur. The second was that two parties, one west of the other, had to simultaneously record the time of the eclipse in local time. This way if the parties involved compared the relative observed hour of eclipse wherever they were and multiplied it by 15 to convert time into arc (1 hour of time = 15 degrees of longitude) between the base station and another station, then the result was the longitude west of the base station.

Returning to *The Shepherds of Arcadia* for a moment, remember that the figure hiding behind the goddess, yet supporting her, was painted by Poussin in a manner and style that suggests he was not only a shepherd but also a Knight Templar acting as a guardian. The supposition that the Templar figure is indeed a Masonic initiate is confirmed by the placement of his foot resting on a squared stone. (I've often wondered if the Templar figure is a sly depiction of the artist himself.)

In *The Knights Templar in the New World* it was also demonstrated how the proper application of geometry, including the Pythagorean Theorem, could be applied across mainland Nova Scotia. As well, with a balancing of moral allegory, it was demonstrated how the mirror image of Oak Island, with its planted grove of red oaks, could be determined to be Green Oaks, Nova Scotia—with its planted grove of swamp white oaks, which are otherwise known as green oaks.

All of this leads to the reasonable deduction that there definitely were antient ways of determining specific longitudinal and latitudinal positions on Earth. It could also be speculated that the original Templars rediscovered this knowledge during their excavations beneath the ruins of the Temple of Solomon, along with the knowledge that pre-Christian settlements had been established in the New World by certain inner circles of Celts, Phoenicians, Carthaginians, Egyptians, Hebrews, and even the Greeks and the Romans.[10]

My second book in this trilogy, *The Templar Meridians,* is certainly based on conclusions that were not derived from a glorious flash of revelation but on extensive and well-documented research by several authors, all the while mingled with some intuitive and determined insight of my own relating to the pre-Columbian exploration and settlement of North and South America. Included in this ever-expanding circle of authors is the most interesting couple, Lionel and Patricia Fanthorpe. Located in Cardiff, Wales, Lionel Fanthorpe is quite unique in that he is a priest, a journalist, an author, and an entertainer who, along with his wife, Patricia, has co-authored at least ten books pertaining to the mysteries of Rennes-le-Chateau, Oak Island, and the Knights Templar. One may think that being a British priest and investigator into ancient mysteries and hidden knowledge is inherently conflicting, but the logic and reason portrayed by the Fanthorpes is truly remarkable. In a similar vein, hopefully, the fact that I am currently a high-ranking officer of the Knights Templar of Canada, as well as an inititiate of the Grand Medicine Society of North America, does not in any way impede my ability to be objective in what is about to be revealed for the first time.

4
Old Habits Never Die

IN PERFECT HARMONY

By now, hopefully, the reader will have realized that the missing two elements in the puzzle are *logic* and *reason,* embodied in the *form* and *spirit* of Saint Paul and Saint Anthony. These two elements complete the sum of 7, numerologically speaking 1 + 2 + 3 + 4 + 5 + 6 + 7 = 28, or 4 x 7. (The number 7 represents the perfect number.) We find the first four elements contained in Poussin's painting *The Shepherds of Arcadia* in perfect harmonic concordance, thus allegorically completing the square and revealing the hidden fifth element. Add to this the sixth and seventh elements, Saint Paul and Saint Anthony, and we arrive at a prime number that can be divided only by the number 1 or the number itself. Anyone who frequents any of the seemingly infinite number of gaming casinos across North America will quickly realize the iconography of having four 7s lined up in a row: *Jackpot!*

In the iconic Greek panel depicting Saint Anthony and Saint Paul (see figure 4.1), note the placement of the hands: Saint Anthony's are arranged to form a right-angle triangle and Saint Paul's are positioned to indicate that a specific line measurement (the traditional Celtic measurement of ell?) is also necessary to determine how the antient meridians can be determined. Perhaps the two saintly halos denote a

Fig. 4.1. Iconic Greek panel depicting Saint Anthony (on the right) and Saint Paul (on the left) in the desert. The line and equilateral triangle have been inserted by the author to demonstrate the hidden message behind the positioning of the hands.

potential measurement between two eclipses. Also note the two lions flanking Saint Paul. This is significant in that it is said that Saint Paul was buried in the desert by Saint Anthony with the assistance of two lions.

The resulting deductive reasoning derived from all of this symbolism suggests that one of the major messages to be found in Poussin's most enigmatic painting lies in the phrase "And in Arcadia I (am) the sum total," of the seven elements taken from the earliest pagan worship, Pantheistic/Hellenistic, Pythagoreum, Judaic, Marian Devotion, Platonic, and Stoic philosophies.

In support of this deductive reasoning, in Poussin's painting the kneeling Green Man can be seen on the basic of levels to represent the earliest pagan element divined by Neolithic man. The goddess, cloaked in gold and blue, can be seen to represent the dualistic Pantheistic/Hellenistic era of Egypt and Greece. The third figure, the knightly initiate dressed in red and white is a disciple of Pythagoras, who in turn was a disciple of Euclid. He is the (Masonic) initiate who understands the power behind the application of sacred geometry. The fourth figure, representative of Jesus the man, represents Old Testament Judaism.

The fifth element, the unborn child, represents the previously described concept of the Marian Devotion wherein devotion to Mary predestines the observer to heaven. Many devout Catholics believe that Mary, the Virgin, is the only female who warrants devotion of this nature, but it will be seen that there are several Marys involved at this level. It is said in some circles that the devotion of the Virgin Mary was actually developed by Saint Dominic as a way of countering the role accorded to women by the troubadours and, perhaps to a lesser extent, by the Cathars. But it is here that we move to the acceptance of the Madonna and Child as a religious icon or holy concept.

In this light Poussin is seen to be rejecting the concept of the virgin birth and the unborn child being considered the Son of God, as the alpha and the omega . . . the beginning and the end. Through Poussin's analogous completion of the square, the first four elements combine in perfect harmony to produce the hidden fifth element, namely the offspring of the holy union between Jesus and Mary Magdalene. In other words, the only way for there to be a Holy Bloodline child was to accept that Jesus was only a man and that he was married to a woman, Mary Magdalene.

All of this suggests that Saint Anthony and Saint Paul are representatives of the earliest Christian philosophy and theology, the foundations of which most Renaissance painters believed were taken from pre-Christian Greek freethinking. Even the Catholic Church officially recognizes Saint Anthony and Saint Paul as the cofounders of Monastic Christianity and thus conduits between pre-Christianity and Christianity. If Poussin's painting indeed holds a number of clues regarding the location of the physical remains of the Holy Family, then David Teniers's enigmatic painting *St. Antony and St. Paul Fed by Ravens,* which builds upon Poussin's earlier foundations within *The Shepherds of Arcadia,* should be examined in the same light.

This suggests that Saint Paul, as painted by Teniers, represents the Greek philosophy of logic, which is associated with the Greek philosopher Plato and his theory of Forms. In the simplest of terms, the theory of Forms or theory of ideas argues that "Form" can only be recognized intuitively. In a way, Saint Paul was one of the first to understand that the early Christian concept of a "one and only god" was formed by many of the concepts that came before, and, as such, one could apply logic and reason to the existence of God.

All of which brings us to Saint Anthony, the seventh element when the two paintings are combined. It should come as no surprise, but it is said that Poussin was a fervent believer in Stoicism, to the point that he earned the nickname "the philosopher painter." Even he himself admitted as such through a series of letters to one of his best patrons and good friend, Paul Fréart de Chantelou. Poussin's following of Stoicism suggests that he approached each of his subject paintings in the "spirit" that the subject matter dictated and that he painted the underlying truth, no matter what it suggested. If he had been provided with secret information concerning the Holy Bloodline he surely would have worked this underlying concept into his painting.

David Teniers the Younger would have known of Poussin's beliefs, in that he painted *St. Anthony and St. Paul Fed by Ravens* some ten years after Poussin completed *The Shepherds of Arcadia.* In painting *St. Anthony and St. Paul Fed by Ravens* in the manner that he did, Teniers was paying tribute to a fellow genius in the only way that he saw fit. As a fervent student of alchemy, Teniers realized the transformation that had not only taken place in Poussin physically but in his philosophical reasoning as well. Teniers must have realized and deeply admired the fact that Poussin had achieved a higher level of spiritual understanding and consciousness that very few painters in the world ever achieve. The beauty of this is that in doing so Teniers also achieved the same level of spiritual understanding and comsciousness that transcends time and space. To be able to incorporate within hidden layers the elements of someone else's masterpiece in one's own painting is again true genius in itself.

Fig. 4.2. *St. Anthony and St. Paul Fed by Ravens by* David Teniers the Younger, 1652–1654. Reproduced courtesy of the Ashmolean Museum, Oxford, England.

MORE CLUES TO TENIERS'S UNDERSTANDING

It comes as no surprise that the painter David Teniers the Younger is viewed by modern-day art critics on the same elevated plane as Poussin and Raphael. He was born in Antwerp in 1610 and became an apprentice under his painter-father, David Teniers the Elder, and soon surpassed his father in talent and reputation. In 1632, Teniers* was admitted to the prestigious Saint Lucas Painter's Guild located in Antwerp and would ultimately be initiated into the Foundation of the Antwerp Academy of Fine Art in 1664.[1]

Teniers the Younger became famous for his depictions of rural and pastoral landscapes, incorporating a range of everyday, mythological,

*Like Nicolas Poussin, Teniers was a painter who liked to paint subjects that had been illustrated centuries before by earlier masters such as Titian. Teniers's works have a technical freshness, though, when compared to that of other Renaissance painters, through straightforwardness in means and intent. This makes them worthy of the closest scrutiny in our search for esoteric symbolism and hidden meanings.

and classical scenes and figures in much the same way that Poussin had done. During his lifetime Teniers moved in the highest circles of society and had an extremely rewarding career, both from a professional and social perspective. In 1637 he married the daughter of Jan van Brueghel the Elder, Anna, and as a result gained full access to the painting elite of Flanders. Anna's guardian was another great of the time, namely Peter Paul Rubens.

In part because of these connections, Teniers moved to Brussels in 1651 to become court painter in the service of the Spanish governor of the southern Netherlands, Archduke Leopold Wilhelm I von Habsburg. It was here that Teniers took on the influential position of administrator of the archduke's extensive collection, thus ensuring him access not only to a wide range of great masters but also to royal gossip and secrets of every nature. One of his pioneering achievements was the production of the first-ever illustrated catalog of a collection of paintings, namely the archduke's collection, titled *Theatrum pictorium.*[*2]

Teniers's patron, Archduke Leopold Wilhelm I, was the youngest son of Holy Roman Emperor Ferdinand II and Maria Anna of Bavaria, daughter of William V, Duke of Bavaria. As his elder brother became Emperor Ferdinand III, Leopold was instead invested with a number of prince-bishoprics when he came of age. A prince-bishop is a bishop who at the same time is the civil governor of some secular principality, thus combining the roles of church and state. In Leopold's case, his official titles included the prince-bishoprics of Halberstadt (1628–1648), Passau (1625–1662), Breslau (1656–1662), Olmütz (1637–1662), and Strasbourg (1626–1662). In a way this presented Leopold with almost the same extraordinary power and influence over state matters

*Leopold Wilhelm's collection came to number more than thirteen hundred works, including paintings by Holbein, Pieter Bruegel the Elder, Van Eyck, Raphael, Giorgione, Veronese, and more than fifteen works by Titian. This exceptional accumulation of masterpieces now forms the heart of the Kunsthistorisches Museum in Vienna. Most of these paintings had only recently been acquired by the archduke from the collection of the Duke of Hamilton (who was executed in 1649 following the Royalist defeat in the English Civil War). The Hamilton paintings, which included numerous prized works by Titian, became the jewels of Leopold Wilhelm's collection of Italian art.

as possessed by his older brother, the Holy Roman Emperor.

It comes as no surprise to learn that Archduke Leopold Wilhelm I was educated by the Jesuits. This wasn't because he was personally suited to the priesthood but because this was common practice for later-born sons of important Catholic dynasties in order to guarantee them an income that befitted their rank and status. In the case of Leopold Wilhelm I, in 1626, when he was only twelve, he became the official successor to his uncle Archduke Leopold V, as bishop of Strasbourg and Passau.* His installation as bishop of Halberstadt in 1627 and archbishop of Magdeburg in 1629 was more problematic, though, because these territories lay in the predominantly Protestant region north of the Holy Roman Empire, and the Catholic bureaucracy was effectively no longer in place.[3]

Leopold Wilhelm I's appointments must be seen in the context of the interests of his father, Emperor Ferdinand II, who in 1629 demanded the restitution, to the Catholic Church, of all ecclesiastical territories that had fallen into Protestant hands after 1522 during the course of the Reformation. These demands would lead to the Thirty Years' War.

In the two bishoprics of Brandenburg and Magdeburg, Leopold Wilhelm was the last Catholic prince-archbishop, given that the territories were subsequently allocated to adjacent secular Protestant states. Halberstadt was given to Brandenburg in 1648; in Magdeburg in 1635 the archbishopric was officially secularized and given to Duke August of Saxony.†[4]

---

*One very interesting fact about Leopold Wilhelm's lineage is that his parents were double first cousins as they shared all four grandparents. Therefore Leopold only had four great-grandparents, being descended from each of them twice. Further back in his ancestry there is more pedigree collapse due to the close intermarriage between the Houses of Austria and Spain and other Catholic monarchies.

†Emperor Otto I, the first Holy Roman Emperor, was the founder of the archbishopric of Magdeburg and is still buried in the town's cathedral. Prior to the Thirty Years' War, Magdeburg was one of the largest German cities and a notable member of the Hanseatic League, which earlier became the greatest archrival for trade against Norway and its Scandinavian allies. The city is best known for the 1631 sacking of Magdeburg in that the bitterness that it caused hardened Protestant resistance during the prolonged thirty-year conflict.

In 1637, Leopold Wilhelm I was also appointed bishop of Olmutz. No sovereign rights were attached to this office because the diocese was located in the Margraviate of Moravia, which belonged to the Habsburg monarchy. The bishopric was, however, endowed with ample funds for Leopold to support his many patronages of the arts. Similar motives also played a role in the case of the bishopric of Breslau in Silesia, where Leopold Wilhelm I was appointed bishop in 1655. The hand of the Jesuits is evident in these appointments in that no singular person should have received the staggering number of rich appointments that Leopold received. In a way it appears that Leopold was being seen to in the same manner that René d'Anjou was accommodated from both a secular and financial perspective. This is not to suggest that either were unwilling pawns in a larger game of chess but, again, that the invisible hand of fate appears to have an immense influence on affairs across Europe over many generations.

In Leopold's lifetime he not only became the predominant patron of David Teniers the Younger but was also an extremely influential benefactor to a number of artists, writers, and scientists, including many who were involved in alchemy. When the tomb of Childeric I,* an early Merovingian king of the Salian Franks and father of Clovis I, was discovered in 1653 by a mason doing repairs in the church of Saint-Brice in Tournai, it was Leopold Wilhelm I who funded the full excavation and had the find published in Latin.[5]

In addition, Leopold Wilhelm I was grand master of the Teutonic Knights from 1641 until his death in 1662. The position as head of this chivalric Catholic order came with religious and military duties. These included serving as a general in the Thirty Years' War and the

---

*Childeric's tomb was discovered not far from the twelfth-century church of Saint-Brice in Tournai, Belgium. Numerous precious objects were found, including jewels and gold, gold coins, a gold bull's head, and a ring with the king's name inscribed on it. Some three hundred golden bees were also found, which had been placed on the king's cloak. The treasure went first to the Habsburgs in Vienna, then was a gift to Louis XIV. During the French Revolution, Napoleon insisted during his coronation that Childeric's bees be attached to his royal cloak as symbols of the earlier French Empire. Napolean also insisted that he, instead of the church, crown himself as Holy Roman Emperor.

Franco-Spanish War, which occurred between 1635 and 1659, and also serving as governor of the Spanish Netherlands from 1647 to 1656. Clearly Archduke Leopold Wilhelm I von Habsburg came into the possession of significant information concerning the secret activities of the Knights Templar in the New World and conveyed those secrets to Teniers when Teniers was in his employ until 1662 when Leopold passed away.

When Teniers himself died in 1690 he was venerated as one of the most important Flemish masters of the seventeenth century, alongside Peter Paul Rubens, Anthony van Dyck, and Jacob Jordaens. Similar to Poussin's methods, a habit of his was to paint many variations of the same subject on different occasions. His version of *St. Anthony and St. Paul Fed by Ravens,* executed between 1952 to 1954 (often referred to as *St. Anthony and St. Paul in the Desert*), has become his most famous and enduring painting. In many ways the painting of *St. Anthony and St. Paul Fed by Ravens* has taken on the same level of mythical proportions as has Poussin's *The Shepherds of Arcadia.*

SAINT ANTHONY'S ROLE IN THE MYSTERY

It's important to understand that Anthony and Paul were, in reality, mere hermit monks who sought to understand the concept of God and how one could connect with him directly. As such, that is how Teniers depicted them in this painting. Obviously, the veneration afforded them by their followers, during and after their lifetime, caused the church to canonize them and to mold their story to meet acceptable church dogma and tenet.

It's said that Anthony the Hermit was sustained for the last forty years of his life in the wilderness on only bread and water, for he apparently lived well beyond the age of one hundred years. The painting by Teniers of Saint Anthony and Saint Paul suggests that this bread was really manna from heaven that was delivered by ravens. Because of this early belief, the Christianized Saint Anthony is seen as the patron of the faith of the Blessed Sacrament. Saint Anthony is also seen as the patron of sailors and mariners, shipwrecks and starvation, Portugal and Brazil, oppressed and poor people, elderly people and travelers, and, rather surprisingly, expectant mothers and Native Americans. Above all else, why expectant mothers?

The official story goes that, before his death, Saint Anthony visited his monks, for he was then the head of a desert monastery, and told them that he would not die among them. His orders were that he should be buried in the earth beside his mountain cell by two of his disciples, Macarius and Amathas. The story goes that after hastening back to his solitary existence on Mount Kolzin near the Red Sea, he soon died, whereupon his disciples followed his orders and buried his body secretly in that place.[6]

The life of Saint Anthony could easily have inspired the Knights Templar and even the Knights Teutonic in their allegorical quest for the Grail. Any noble knight would surely have related to Anthony's discarding of all earthly treasures and comfort in his quest for wisdom and his desire to be close to God. Other stories tell of Saint Anthony's ongoing struggle with the many temptations of the flesh, to which the Templars must have also related, although the notion that all Templars were celebate appears almost too much to fathom.

The logic therefore follows that Prince Henry Sinclair and those Templars who accompanied him across the wilderness of the New World starting in 1398 would have also taken solace in the knowledge that the prior spiritual actions of Saint Anthony were reflected in their own actions. Rather coincidently, Saint Anthony is the patron saint to whom one prays to recover a lost or stolen article. Perhaps "that-which-was-lost" is nothing more than the wisdom of the antients, which, among other things, allowed them to feel closer to God.[7]

Luke 19:10 states, "For the Son of Man came to seek and to save the lost." Many biblical scholars believe this to be an allegorical reference to the restoration of the word of God, of the good in man or the restoration of the Holy Kingdom (Jerusalem). In the widest of Freemasonry circles, that-which-was-lost refers to the "lost word"—the *TETRAGRAMMATON*. In Greek it signifies a word of four letters. It is the title given by the Talmudists to the name of God, Jehovah,

Fig. 4.3. Teniers's painting of *St. Anthony and St. Paul Fed by Ravens,* overlaid by a longitudinal/latitudinal rose line/meridian pattern. Note how the horizontal and vertical lines coincide with the pattern of the frame and how the vertical center of the painting is defined by the Crucifixion cross. Also note that the central horizontal meridian aligns with the eyes of Saint Anthony. Overlying grid copyright of the author, William F. Mann.

which in the original Hebrew consists of four letters (JHVH).

Setting aside this philosophical pretext for the moment, Teniers's painting without a doubt reveals an underlying series of antient meridians established across the landscape. The central meridian is established by the crucifix, or cross, which splits the painting into two equal parts. In the "east" half of the painting there is light, representative of urban civilization. In the "west" half of the painting we find Saint Anthony in the dark wilderness, or desert, debating with Paul whether to follow the hidden reasoning that lies in his small library of books or the entirely spiritual logic represented by Saint Paul. It's no coincidence that Teniers painted the two saints sitting in the dark. Here they are waiting for the one adept who can solve the mystery of the puzzle.

It is known through historical records that Anthony the Hermit was born in a village south of Memphis in Upper Egypt in 271 CE. Following the death of his parents, as tradition has it, he heard those now famous words of Christ to the rich young man: "Go, sell what thou hast, and give it to the poor, and thou shalt have treasure in Heaven."[8] Soon thereafter Anthony became a model of humility and charity, virtue and redemption, selling his estate and giving the profits to the poor. It is told that his only food was bread, with a little salt, and he drank nothing but water. It is further told that he never ate before sunset and often ate only once in three or four days. When he rested it is said that his only bed was a rush mat or the bare ground.

The official story is that at the age of thirty-five Anthony was determined to withdraw from civilization and thus retired in absolute solitude. He crossed the Nile, and on a mountain near the east bank, then called Pispir, now Der el Memum, he found an old fort into which he shut himself and lived there for twenty years without direct human contact. Apparently food was thrown to him over the wall. It is said that he was at times visited by pilgrims whom he refused to see; however, gradually a number of would-be disciples established themselves as a colony of ascetics in caves and huts around the mountain. The disciples constantly begged Anthony to come forth and be their guide in the spiritual life. Finally, in approximately the year 305 CE, he yielded to their requests and emerged from his retreat, and it is said, to the surprise of all, that he appeared to be as when he had gone in—not emaciated, but vigorous in body and mind.

For five or six years he devoted himself to the instruction and organization of the great body of monks that had grown up around him. But then he once again withdrew into the inner desert that lay between the Nile and the Red Sea, near the shore of which he fixed his humble abode on a mountain where the monastery that bears his name, Der Mar Antonios, still stands. It was here that he spent the last forty-five years of his life in seclusion. However, he did not live as strictly as he had at Pispir, for he freely saw those who came to visit him, and he crossed the desert to Pispir with considerable frequency.

It was on only two occasions that he went to Alexandria: once after he came forth from the fort at Pispir to strengthen the Christian martyrs in the persecution of 311, and once at the close of his life, to preach against the Arians. Apparently he died at the ripe old age of 105, with Saint Jerome, in his writings, placing Anthony's death in 356 or 357 CE. As previously noted, at Anthony's own request his grave was kept secret by the two disciples who buried him to prevent his body from becoming an object of reverence.

SAINT PAUL'S ROLE IN THE MYSTERY

Paul the Hermit, also known as Paul the First Hermit and Paul of Thebes, was an Egyptian hermit and close friend to Saint Jerome, who also became his biographer. Born in Lower Thebaid, Egypt, the official story says that Paul was left an orphan at the approximate age of fifteen and hid during the persecution of the church under Emperor Trajanus Decius. The story continues with Paul going into the desert at the age of twenty-two to avoid a planned effort by his brother-in-law to report him to authorities as a Christian and thereby gain control of his property.[9]

It is said that Paul soon thereafter found that the life of a hermit was much to his personal taste, and so he remained in a desert cave for the rest of his reportedly very long life. His contemplative existence was only disturbed by Anthony (the Hermit), who visited the aged Paul. In this story Anthony also buried Paul, supposedly wrapping him in a cloak that had been given to Anthony by Saint Athanasius. According to the most accepted version of the legend, and as mentioned earlier, two lions assisted Anthony in burying Paul.

Other church writings have it that it was God himself who revealed Paul's existence to Anthony. Yet Anthony still took three days before discovering his cave. It is said that after seeing a thirsty she-wolf run through an opening in the rocks Anthony followed her to look for water and found Paul. Apparently the two religious adepts knew each other at once and praised God together, passing the night in prayer. At dawn Paul told Anthony that he was about to die and asked to be buried in the cloak that had been given to Anthony by Saint Athanasius.

The official church story goes on to say that Paul asked this of Anthony in order to be in communion with Saint Athanasius, who was seen as the invincible defender of the faith against the Arian heresy.

Fig. 4.4. Detail taken from the painting *Mary Magdalene at the Foot of the Cross,* as found in the Monastery of Sainte Marie de Oia along the Way of St. James. Note the placement of the skull and crossbones, along with the capital letter "G," which signifies a Masonic Templar connection. Also note the very apparent depiction of a pregnant Mary Magdalene.

Here we find, once again, official church doctrine being applied to what at first appears, by all simple logic and reason, to be a story of two ordinary men who longed to understand the true story of Jesus and Mary Magdalene and their relationship to God.

TOO MANY MARYS

It is officially acknowledged by the church that among the first followers of Jesus were three women: Mary Jacob and Mary Salome (the mothers of the apostles John and James, respectively) and Mary Magdalene. It is also said that after the Crucifixion the Romans exiled the three Marys from the Holy Land along with their black Egyptian servant, Sarah. The story goes that the four females were put on a ship with neither sail nor oar and set adrift in the Mediterranean Sea, where after many storms they miraculously found their way safely to the southern French shores of Camargue, to the town that would become known as Les Saintes-Maries-de-la-Mer. And it was from here that the three Marys spread Christianity throughout the European continent until they died.

According to another story, Mary Magdalene and Lazarus left the Holy Land around 53 CE and arrived in Massilia (Marseilles). There, each year on February 2, the local people celebrate the arrival of Mary Magdalene and Lazarus. It is said that upon their arrival they installed themselves in a necropolis on the south side of the Lacydon River, taking care of the ill and preaching the Christian faith. After about a decade, apparently Mary Magdalene headed to nearby Sainte Baume, where she prayed to Saint Michael to chase out a sea monster, the Tarasco, from the cave where she allegedly spent the remaining days of her life.*

Less known is the legend that her sister Martha also went to Avignon. This legend imparts that Saint Martha went to Avignon, but then she was asked by the people of Tarascon, just south of the city, to appease the Tarasco—the same sea monster that had fled to Tarascon upon her arrival in Avignon. The official story goes that by showing the sign of the cross and using holy water, she appeased the monster that had been rising from the waters of the Rhone to devour children and livestock. In short, there are several legends that tell of how France was

*There is another lingering episode to this legend and it relates to the supposition that Lazarus was in fact Mary Magdalene's brother. In the church at Rennes-le-Château, above the altar, is a picture of Mary Magdalene washing Jesus's feet. This took place when Jesus was dining at the house of Simon the Pharisee who was of the House of Bethany. It is recorded that none of the disciples were present, so the question remains: Who is the person in the background? It is most likely Lazarus, because, if he was Mary's brother and also of the House of Bethany, he surely would have been living there at this time. If the legend of Mary Magdalene and Lazarus's flight to Marseilles is in any way true, it makes sense that the widow of Jesus would have been accompanied by her closest blood relative—her brother.

Christianized by those who had witnessed the miracles of Jesus and the Passion themselves, namely the Marys.

In 950 CE, Rabanus Maurus, the bishop of Mayence, wrote that Martha had converted the people of Tarascon and that she lived, until her death, in a prayer house constructed on the site where she tamed the sea monster. A church now stands on the site, having assumed the original foundations for its own purpose. According to church records, excavations were carried out in Tarascon in 1187, and bones—believed to have been Martha's*—were found.[10] The discovery of Martha's bones rather conveniently followed in the wake of the discovery of the supposed relics of Lazarus that had been unearthed in Tarascon in 1146. These combined relics are currently housed in the crypt of Saint Victor, in Marseilles. Inside the crypt is also a Black Madonna, the Notre-Dame de Confession said to have been sculpted by Saint Luke himself.

This belief or knowledge that some members of the early Holy Family of Christianity had escaped to France remains part of the local lore in that part of the world. It also hasn't hurt the local pilgrimage trade that continues to this day.

Pilgrimages to Tarascon began as early as the thirteenth century, and when Good King René inherited the Provence in 1435 he initiated local feasts in Martha's name; they are held on or around June 24 (Saint John the Baptist day) every year, and continue to this day.

However, it is the nearby communities of Sainte Baume and Saint Maximin that really became the very cradle of Magdalene veneration in France, with the Catholic Church definitely capitalizing on earlier legends and the almost too convenient discoveries of relics and such in the area. Saint Maximin is referred to as the "third tomb of Christianity," because a skull identified as being that of Mary Magdalene was found there. For centuries the cave at Sainte Baume has been a site of pilgrimage for those wanting to see the cave where she allegedly spent the last years of her life.

---

*In 1974, carbon dating showed that the skull currently on display as that of Mary Magdalene in Saint Maximin was that of a woman who had died in the first century CE, that she was between fifty-five and sixty years old, and, according to anthropomorphic studies from 1978, four feet eight inches tall and of Mediterranean origin.

As early as the fifth century monks tried to enhance access to the cave, and later, even kings on pilgrimage stopped here for prayer. For their convenience the company of Chemin des Roys was installed to take them up to the cave on horseback. Every year even now local boys on horseback celebrate the event through a reenactment of the journey from the sea. After anointing their spears in the surf, they ride up into the mountains to the hillside cave, where they ceremoniously bury their spears.

The big breakthrough, though, came in 1279, when the bones of Mary Magdalene were said to have been found at nearby Saint Maximin. Charles II, Count of Provence and nephew of King Phillip III, supposedly had a dream on December 9, 1279, about a tomb at the foot of the oratory of Saint Maximin. Pursuing his dream, he rather conveniently found a document from 710, which supposedly said, "Here rests the body of Mary Magdalene." Again, rather conveniently, the document itself has since disappeared. A year later, in 1280, King Phillip III officially recognized the finding as genuine, and from 1295 onward, Charles II, Count of Provence, gave his entire fortune to building a basilica to hold the bones. Ironically, in 1300, Saint Maximin became a required stop for all converted Cathars—the very heretics who, in the south of France, were convinced that Mary Magdalene had been married to Jesus!

Obviously, in southern France there is a consistent legend of the movements of the Holy Family and how they left their legacy—and bones—behind. Though most academics and the church itself pass all of this off as mere legend, it has worked to the church's advantage, given that the various locations fall on the Way of St. James, the main pilgrimage route to Santiago de Compostela in Spain.

TOO MANY SARAHS

There is yet still another version of the legend of the Marys arriving in Provence. The gypsies of France, or Romas, as they prefer to be called, tell this version around their caravan campfires. The gypsies describe Sarah as a "Provençal gypsy" who had arrived in France prior to the

Marys having done so. After having had a vision of the coming of the ship that contained the three Marys, it is said that Sarah waded out into the tumultuous sea and saved them when their boat capsized in a violent storm off the Camargue coast. She later converted to Christianity and spread the word of Christ among members of her own gypsy band.

To the Catholic Church, Sarah remains officially unrecognized. To the gypsies, however, the true story is quite clear. Sarah is their patron saint, so annually on May 24, for as long as anyone can remember, gypsies from throughout Europe descend upon Les Saintes-Maries-de-la-Mer to venerate Saint Sarah in prayer and music. Thousands of gypsy caravans now fill this small town in France that has become a crossroads of gypsy prayer and dance every year around May 24th, much to the chagrin or delight of the local residents.

It is not known when and why this Sarah became so sacred to the gypsies, but it was some time after the Romas arrived in Europe in the early 1400s. The devotion may have started after René d'Anjou gave the order to excavate an oratory—where the two Marys were allegedly buried—in December of 1448. It is said that the excavations revealed several human heads arranged in the form of a cross and the bodies of two women, which were assumed to be the two Marys. Apparently an altar of compacted earth was also found, as well as a smooth marble stone that was later to be called "the Saints' pillow." This pillow is currently visible inside the small church that was built on the same spot that the saints' heads were said to have been found.

At a ceremony in the presence of Good King René and his first queen, Isabelle, it is recorded that the relics of the two Marys were piously placed in two reliquaries and stored in the upper chapel of the church. Though the reliquaries themselves were destroyed at the time of the French Revolution, the local priests apparently had the foresight to hide the relics separately; so after the revolution two new reliquaries were made and the bones reinserted in them. Maybe the priests had a second set of relics available in anticipation of just such a calamity? Rather curiously, Sarah's bones have never been found; thus it is a statue of her that is displayed in the annual gypsy procession that honors her every year.

Why is a gypsy servant girl like Sarah venerated in this way? For some it is because she is depicted as a Black Madonna. The reason for this is the side story that Sarah was an Egyptian servant—an unnamed black woman—who was pregnant with Jesus's first child, and that child, a girl, was called Sarah. Still another line of reasoning posits that Sarah was Jesus's daughter and that she was already twelve years of age when she and the Marys arrived in southern France.

Alternatively, Eastern Orthodox tradition says that Mary Magdalene died and was buried in Ephesus, where her original home supposedly still stands, and that Pope Leo VI took her relics to Constantinople.[11] There is therefore within the Eastern Orthodox church officially no rationale for her voyage to France, even though the French landscape is dotted with relics and legends of her presence there. Could it be that the church has perpetuated the legend of Sarah, the Egyptian servant, because it neatly deflects the question of the other Sarah, who may have been Jesus's consort or in fact his firstborn?

There certainly appears to be a great deal of confusion over which Mary went where after the Crucifixion. Another legend has it that the Virgin Mary lived her last days on Earth in a small stone cottage on Mount Koressos to the south of Ephesus in Turkey. The foundations of the house were supposedly rediscovered through the miraculous visions of a German nun named Anne Catherine Emmerich, who apparently remembered detailed directions and descriptions of the house after emerging from the visions. It is said that her directions were intimately followed by Father Julien Gouyet of Paris in 1881 and by two Lazarist missionaries from Izmir in 1891. The small stone house that now stands on the very site is said to have been built on the discovered foundation of an earlier structure. Today the Virgin Mary's House is a must visit for pilgrims and cruise ship tourists alike who come from far away to visit the house rebuilt as a chapel, to sip the waters of an adjoining spring said to have curative powers, and to enjoy the pine-shaded mountaintop location.

If any of these legends of the Holy Bloodline are true, then it must be asked if there is any definitive evidence of a child. What child of the union of Mary Magdalene and Jesus might have survived in western Europe to be the eventual ancestress of the Francia/Navarre dynasty? And, where is there a child mentioned in the legends of Mary Magdalene? This question always appears to come around to Sarah, the adolescent refugee girl on the boat, whose name means "princess" in Hebrew. Is it really possible that she is the forgotten child of the *sang real* of *The Da Vinci Code*—the "blood royal" of Israel's kings?

The child called Sarah might very well have been the origin for the "little lost princess" of Western fairy tales who is eventually found and united with the handsome prince. There is an interesting passage in the Book of Lamentations (4:8) that describes the plight of the royal princes of the House of Judah, the lineage of the Davidic kings: "Their faces, once white as milk, are now black as soot. They are not recognized in the streets." Might this passage be reflected in the dark skin of the saint called Sarah the Egyptian? Or is her darkness a symbolic reference to her combined royal bloodlines, including the line of

Fig. 4.5. *The Mystic Marriage between Christ and the Church, Psalm 44,* in *Les Tres Belles Heures,* commissioned by John, Duke of Berry, and painted by the Limbourg brothers. Note how the bride, Mary Magdalene, is portrayed as being pregnant. Reproduced courtesy of the Musée Conde, France.

the Davidic kings of Judah and the Tribe of Benjamin, through Mary Magdalene, which originally came out of Egypt? Don't forget that the infant Jesus fled to Egypt with his parents, Joseph and Mary, when they feared that King Herod was searching to kill the child. There are also lingering questions relating to the untold gaps in Jesus's early adult life. Many fringe authors claim that a good part of Jesus's early adult life was spent in Egypt, where he became a master of the Egyptian mysteries, otherwise known as a mystic. So there is definitely an Egyptian connection to the story.

The notion of a Holy Grail family is a powerful symbol on many levels. The chalice is intimately connected with the sacred cauldron of creativity so explicitly illustrated by the vesica piscis, which is representative of Jesus Christ. But the symbol of the two adjoining circles is also irrevocably associated with Mary Magdalene. Pre-Christian beliefs dictated that when the Bride is restored, the wasteland is healed and the crops and herds thrive—the desert blooms. This is the age-old promise inherent in the mystery surrounding the sacred union—the partnership of the archetypal Bride and Bridegroom.

A CONSOLIDATION OF PHILOSOPHY

As Poussin has demonstrated, the reconciling in one's mind of the probability of Jesus being married to Mary Magdalene requires a consolidation of philosophy, once one's mind is free of religious predetermination. In the same light, one of the greatest freethinking philosophers to reconcile in his mind the right of man to transcend to a "god king" status was the Roman Boethius.

Anicius Manlius Severinus Boethius, commonly called Boethius, was a Roman philosopher of the early sixth century. He was born in Rome in 489 CE to the ancient and prominent Anicia family, which included emperors Petronius Maximus and Olybrius and many consuls. His father, Flavius Manlius Boethius, was consul in 487 after Flavius Odoacer (an Italian soldier) deposed the last Roman emperor during the fall of Rome.[12]

Boethius's best known work is the *Consolations of Philosophy,* written during his imprisonment for conspiring with the enemy, which deals with many problems of metaphysics as well as of ethics. It is a far-reaching treatise on the being and nature of God, of providence and fate, of the origin of the universe, and of the freedom of the will. In medieval times it became one of the most popular and influential books pertaining to philosophy and a favorite study of statesmen, poets, and historians as well as of philosophers and theologians.

Within his *Consolations of Philosophy,* Boethius engages in a conversation between himself and Lady Philosophy (with himself really) regarding topics such as the nature of predestination and free will. He speaks about the nature of free will versus predestination when he asks if God knows and sees all, or does man have free will in all of his actions? In the *Consolations,* Boethius answers religious questions without reference to Christianity, relying solely on natural philosophy and the classical Greek tradition. Thus he truly believed what he discussed with himself through the correspondence between faith and reason. Boethius, writing as a Platonist who is also a Christian, came to the now accepted conclusion that the truths found in Christianity would be no different from the truths found in philosophy.

Boethius himself entered public life at a young age and was already a senator by the age of twenty-five. His negotiation and persuasion skills would serve him well as he was consul in 510 in the kingdom of the Ostrogoths, and in 522 his two sons also became consuls to the conquerors of Rome. Sadly, Boethius was imprisoned and eventually executed in 525 by King Theodoric the Great, who suspected him of conspiring with the Eastern Byzantine Empire, although it was never proved. King Theodoric the Great was king of the Ostrogoths, ruler of Italy, regent of the Visigoths, and a patricius of the Roman Empire who reigned following the fall of Rome.

Coming around again, in a similar light to both Boethius and Nicolas Poussin, David Teniers the Younger was able to consolidate natural philosophy and pre-Christian philosophy in the Greek tradition. This in turn allowed him to build upon the very foundations that Poussin had hidden in plain sight in his painting of the Arcadian shepherds pointing at the tomb, along with the message *Et in Arcadia Ego*. . . . For certain, Teniers is the initiate that Poussin knew in his heart would eventually come along—the initiate who would be able to transform the antient signs, seals, and tokens through another allegorical story.

As noted earlier, Teniers was also a lifelong student of alchemy and alchemy's own transformation from the spiritual plane to more of a science. As an antient initiate who understood the hidden art, it certainly comes as no surprise that David Teniers the Younger was fascinated by

Fig. 4.6. *The Alchemist* by David Teniers the Younger, 1680. This painting is a self-portrait, made when David Teniers was seventy years old. However, note the similarity in character between the alchemist and the portrayal of Saint Anthony in Teniers's *St. Anthony and St. Paul Fed by Ravens.* Reproduced courtesy of Palazzo Pitti, Galleria Palatina, Florence, Italy.

alchemy and that he created a number of paintings based on the subject. One of his more famous paintings, appropriately named *The Alchemist,* is a graphic and honest portrayal of himself as an aging alchemist practicing his art. But it was also during the seventeenth century that the art of alchemy started to disappear, being absorbed into the new discipline known as chemistry, which had been named such by Robert Boyle, the "father of modern chemistry."

THE INFLUENCE OF ALCHEMY

The start of Western alchemy generally can be traced back to Hellenistic Egypt, where the city of Alexandria was a center of alchemical knowledge. Alchemy retained its prominence through most of the Greek and Roman periods. Here, elements of technology, religion, mythology, and Hellenistic philosophy, each with their own much longer histories, combined to form the earliest known records of alchemy in the western portion of Eurasia. Although it was Zosimos of Panopolis who wrote what are today considered to be the oldest books on alchemy, the strange figure Mary the Jewess is credited as being the first nonfictitious Western alchemist.[13] Rather surprisingly, even though both Zosimos and Mary lived in Egypt under Roman rule, they were free to practice the art of alchemy.

Mary the Jewess is said to be the inventor of the tribikos—the very first distilling equipment. The tribikos was a kind of alembic glass jar with three varied arms that was used to obtain substances purified by distillation. No one knows for sure whether Mary the Jewess was its inventor, but Zosimos credits the first description of this instrument to her. Through her writings, as quoted by Zosimos, first appears the notion of the old withered widow who possesses witchlike powers and is taken to the cave or forest. In this manner it is no coincidence that Mary the Jewess and Mary Magdalene became synonymous with witchcraft during the Dark Ages.

As noted previously, it was the same Zosimos of Panopolis who maintained that alchemy dated back to pharaonic Egypt, where it was the domain of the priestly class, though there is little to no evidence for his assertion. To suggest a continuous thread to the earlier mystical periods, chemical writers used classical figures from Greek, Roman, and Egyptian mythology to illuminate their works and allegorize alchemical transmutation, even if there was no direct correlation between symbol and process. The earliest alchemists even went to the extent to include the pantheon of gods related to Isis and Osiris and many others in hopes of securing their favor and supposed powers during their alchemical processes.

Not surprisingly, the central figure in the mythology of alchemy is Hermes Trismegistus (or Thrice-Great Hermes), in part because of his supposed possession of the Emerald Tablet of antient wisdom. Hermes and his caduceus, or serpent-staff, were among alchemy's principal symbols. According to Clement of Alexandria, it was Hermes Trismegistus who wrote what were called the *Hermetica,* the forty-two books of Hermes, covering all fields of antient and esoteric knowledge. It is generally understood that the *Hermetica* forms the basis for Western alchemical philosophy and practice, called the hermetic philosophy by its early practitioners.

Some early alchemists, including the aforementioned Zosimos of Panopolis, indeed highlighted the spiritual nature of the alchemical quest, which is symbolic of a religious transformation and regeneration of the human soul. This approach continued in the Middle Ages, as metaphysical aspects, substances, physical states, and material processes were used as metaphors for spiritual entities, spiritual states, and, ultimately, transformation.

Rather surprisingly, practitioners and patrons such as Melchior Cibinensis and even Pope Innocent VIII existed at one time or another within the ranks of the church. It's said that Martin Luther even applauded alchemy for its consistency with Christian teachings. During this period both the transmutation of common metals into gold and the universal panacea symbolized evolution from an imperfect, diseased, corruptible, and ephemeral state toward a perfect, healthy, incorruptible, and everlasting state. Hence, the philosopher's stone represented a mystical and spiritual key that would make this evolution possible. But many individual lives were wasted over the centuries in pursuit of that fleeting state of perfection.

It was through the eyes of a variety of esoteric and Hermetic practitioners in the seventeenth century that the heart of alchemy became even more spiritual than physical. During this period the transmutation of lead into gold was presented as an analogy for personal transmutation, purification, and perfection. This approach is often termed "spiritual," "esoteric," or "internal" alchemy versus the more practical sciences that evolved out of alchemical practices by men such as Robert Boyle and those of the early Royal Society.

As noted, it was during the height of the Renaissance in the seventeenth century that alchemy broke into more distinct schools, placing spiritual alchemists in high contrast with those working with literal metals and chemicals. Most spiritual alchemists during this period also incorporated some physical elements. Examples of a purely spiritual alchemy can be traced back as far as the sixteenth century, when Jacob Boehme used alchemical terminology in strictly mystical writings. Another example can be found in the work of Heinrich Khunrath, who lived between 1560 and 1605. He viewed the process of transmutation as occurring within the alchemist's soul.

Another prominent alchemist of the seventeenth century was Johann Joachim Becher, who was born in 1635. Becher was a German physician, alchemist, precursor of chemistry, scholar, and adventurer best known for his development of the phlogiston theory of combustion and his advancement of Austrian cameralism. Coincidentally, like Teniers, Becher also gained the archduke Leopold Wilhelm I as a benevolent patron for most of his life.

In 1666, Becher was made a councilor of commerce at Vienna, where he had also gained the powerful support of Leopold's brother, Ferdinand II, the Holy Roman Emperor of the Spanish Netherlands. It is said that several times over the next few years he was sent by the emperor on a secret mission of some sort to the Netherlands. Remember that this was approximately another ten years after Teniers completed his painting of Saint Anthony and Saint Paul. Could there be a hidden connection between Teniers, Becher, Leopold, and his brother the emperor? Regardless, in 1669, Becher published his classic treatise on alchemy, *Physica subterranean.**

Even Sir Isaac Newton, the famous seventeenth-century British mathematician and scientist, was an alchemist who practiced the art with a passion. Over time, he wrote more than a million words on the subject, but none of them were printed until his papers were rediscovered in the middle of the twentieth century. Most scholars now concede that Newton was first and foremost an alchemist, as it has become obvious from his writings that the inspiration for his laws of light and theory of gravity came from his alchemical work.

It is written that as a practicing alchemist Newton spent days locked in his laboratory; some have even suggested that he succeeded in transmuting lead into gold. Perhaps that explains one of the oddest things about his life: at the height of his career, instead of accepting a professorship at Cambridge, he was appointed director of the Royal Mint with the responsibility of securing and accounting for England's repository of gold.

Surely during his lifetime David Teniers the Younger was familiar with and exposed to the spiritual and physical alchemical writings and treatises of both Becher and Newton. This would have occurred through his many travels on behalf of the archduke Leopold Wilhelm I, ostensibly seeking out the many works of art that would ultimately make up the archduke's collection. And, most certainly, as an initiate in D'Artt of the Antients, Teniers would have consolidated the philosophies of those around him, specifically Poussin's, to transform his own canvas into a larger treasure map—a map that spanned the breadth of North America in order to unveil the last refuge of the Knights Templar in the New World.

---

*Becher's last book was a chemistry text published in 1682. Unfortunately this was the same year that he died. The book contains fifteen hundred chemical processes (remarkable for its time), including one for making a philosopher's stone to turn lead into gold, which unfortunately turned out to be like many of his earlier theories: unsuccessful. His many other contributions to modern science, however, can never be challenged.

BALANCE, HARMONY, AND UNITY: AN ERA OF SPIRITUAL ILLUMINATION

What information did the archduke provide to Teniers in 1652 that allowed the painter to build upon the underlying philosophical foundations and geometrics that Poussin hid in his painting *The Shepherds of Arcadia*? Given the archduke's prince-bishopric stature across the Spanish Netherlands, which encompassed most of Europe at the time, along with his position as grand master of the Teutonic Knights as well as his lifelong connection to the Jesuits, it comes as no surprise that Leopold was in possession of every bit of information that both the Spanish and French Jesuits had wrung out of their two-pronged exploration of the New World.

Beginning in the sixteenth century, following the explorations of Coronado, Spain established Jesuit missions throughout New Spain, which consisted of Mexico and portions of what is today the southwestern United States. And as previously noted, by the middle of the seventeenth century French Jesuits had penetrated beyond New France into unknown territories at the headwaters of Lake Superior and the Mississippi.

Consolidating all of this information, David Teniers the Younger placed not only Saint Anthony and Saint Paul into a remarkably accurate map of most of North America (see figure 4.7 on p. 146) but also aligned, in perfect harmony, Poussin's previous five elements, or figures, with the two figures of Saint Anthony and Saint Paul. Here again are the seven major elements that support the question behind Jesus's transformation from a man to the Son of God. As an alchemist himself, Teniers would have recognized the significance of the harmonic concordance between these seven elements. Spiritually speaking, he had achieved the creation of the philosopher's stone, turned lead into pure gold, embraced body and soul, and transcended time and space.

In 2003, on the evening of November 8 and into the early morning of the next day, a total lunar eclipse was the distinguishing feature in an exceedingly rare astrological chart that was highlighted by a six-planet (Sun, Moon, Jupiter, Mars, Saturn, and Chiron) alignment known astrologically as a Grand Sextile.

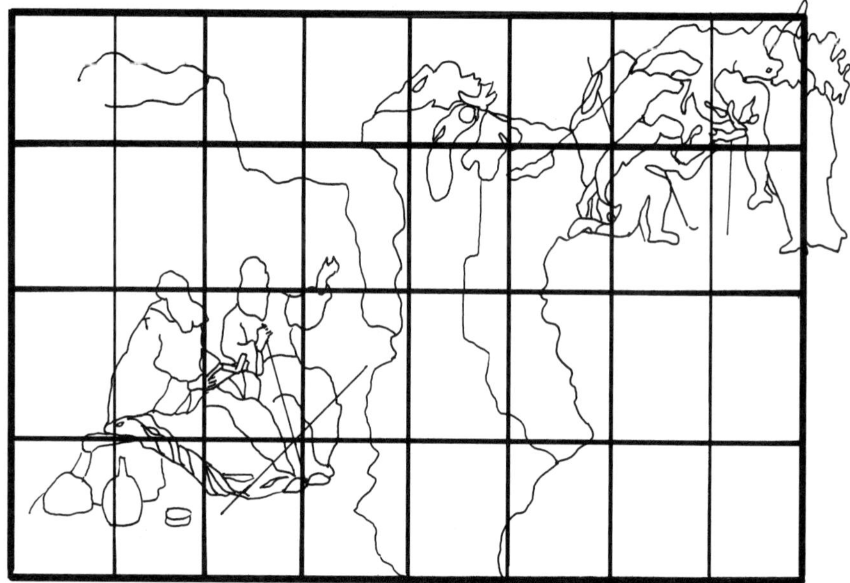

Fig. 4.7. Illustration combining the seven elements, or figures, of both Nicolas Poussin's *The Shepherds of Arcadia* and David Teniers the Younger's *St. Anthony and St. Paul Fed by Ravens,* revealing the underlying longitudinal/latitudinal grid pattern and corresponding mapping of what would have been known of North America by the mid-seventeenth century. Diagram copyright of the author, William F. Mann.

Actually, in astronomy Chiron is an asteroid. But in astrology it is considered a planet because of its strong influence on human life. Chiron is the only planet of the third level that cannot be seen with the naked eye. It is a medium, connecting planet, which is reflected in its position in the solar system. Situated between Uranus and Saturn, just on the border between the lower and the higher planets, it is named after the centaur Chiron of Greek mythology.

Esoterically known for millennia as the Seal of Solomon or Star of David, the symbolism embodied in the Grand Sextile alignment speaks of ultimate Balance, Harmony, and Unity. The spiritual/metaphysical importance of this most unique arrangement of planets became the focal point of a worldwide new age celebration known as the Harmonic Concordance in 2003.

Thus it can be said that the perfect alignment of the seven elements, or figures, in Teniers's painting embody a pattern that speaks to an ultimate combination of Balance, Harmony, and Unity. This perfect alignment allowed Teniers to achieve the ultimate spiritual/metaphysical transformation from revered painter to that of true genius, transcending to the highest level of understanding, knowledge, and wisdom.

Among the Algonquin people, the Seven Fires prophecy is an Anishinabe prophecy that marks phases, or epochs, in the life of the people on Turtle Island, which is the Native American name for the North American continent. The seven fires of the prophecy represent key spiritual teachings for North America (Turtle Island) and suggest that the different colors and traditions of all human beings can come together on a basis of trust and respect.

The prophecy predates the arrival of the Europeans and was originally taught among the practitioners of the Old Mide'win. It is said to contain information for the future lives of the Anishinabe, which are currently in the process of being fulfilled. Unfortunately, there is still a time line controversy among the many Anishinabe elders as to what period we are in presently, but most agree that we are moving from the seventh to the eighth and final fire.

The Eighth Fire is to be seen rising like a phoenix from the teachings of the Seven Fires prophecy. The teaching suggests that if enough people—of all colors and faiths—turn from materialism and instead choose a path of respect, wisdom, and spirituality then environmental and social catastrophe will be avoided, and an era of spiritual illumination will unfold.

5
Castles in the Sky

THE ROLE OF SAUNIÈRE IN THE ONGOING MYSTERY

There is another one of those odd little stories, again coming out of southern France, that plays into the whole concept of initiates building upon earlier foundations for their own purposes, all the while masking prior secrets or activities. This time, though, instead of disguising the clues the new constructions and artworks have provided a different set of keys to unlock the mystery of the whereabouts of the Templar sanctuaries in the New World.

Not surprisingly, the story of the small village of Rennes-le-Château, which is located in southern France, was initiated at the end of the nineteenth century when the veil of darkness and an esoteric subculture in Europe had clouded everything that seemed to relate to the real question of the antient rose lines. And the little village of Rennes-le-Château did not receive any great interest until three British authors first pieced together a number of varying factors in the 1970s and related them to the present-day activities of a rather mysterious European fraternity known as the Priory of Sion.[1] After conducting extensive research, Michael Baigent, Richard Leigh, and

Henry Lincoln wrote *Holy Blood, Holy Grail,** which reads like a murder mystery of sorts, centering as it does on a "treasure story" that is linked to Rennes-le-Château and the Holy Bloodline.

Part of the story began on June 1, 1885, when the village received a new parish priest, Abbé Bérenger Saunière. In 1891, Saunière started a modest restoration of the village church that in 1059 had been consecrated to Mary Magdalene. With the advent of this restoration, the first of many strange events occurred. During the renovations Saunière apparently discovered that one of the two archaic Visigoth columns that supported the altar stone was hollow, and inside were four parchments preserved in sealed wooden tubes.[†2]

Two of the parchments were comprised of genealogies, the first dating from 1244—the year that Montsegur, the last heretical fortress of the Cathars, surrendered to northern French forces led by Simon de Montfort—and the other was from 1644. In the 1780s an earlier priest of Rennes-le-Château, Abbé Antoine Bigou, had evidently composed the additional two, which appear to be encoded Latin texts. Both of the latter two parchments have subsequently been deciphered, and the following interpretation of them has appeared in many books devoted to Rennes-le-Château.

> BERGERE PAS DE TENTATION QUE POUSSIN TENIERS GARDENT LA CLEF PAX DCLXXI PAR LA CROIX ET CE CHEVAL DE DIEU J'ACHEVE CE DAEMON DE GARDIEN A MIDI POMMES BLUES
>
> (SHEPHERDESS, NO TEMPTATION, THAT POUSSIN, TENIERS, HOLD THE KEY; PEACE 681, BY THE CROSS AND

---

*As stated earlier, but bears repeating, a great deal of the material used in this book that you now hold in your hands, concerning the life and death of Bérenger Saunière and the mystery of Rennes-le-Château, originally derived from Gérard de Sède's *L'Or de Rennes*. However, the bulk of the background material is taken from *Holy Blood, Holy Grail*.

†It also has been suggested that the legendary Emerald Tablet eventually found its way to Rennes-le-Château and was ultimately discovered by Bérenger Saunière, but this has never been confirmed.

THIS HORSE OF GOD, I COMPLETE—OR DESTROY—THIS DAEMON OF THE GUARDIAN AT NOON. BLUE APPLES.)[3]

Additional interpretation from the second parchment includes the following:

> A DAGOBERT II ROI ET A SION EST CE TRESOR ET IL EST LA MORT.
>
> (TO DAGOBERT II, KING, AND TO SION BELONGS THIS TREASURE AND HE IS THERE DEAD.)[4]

The story goes that following his discovery, Saunière was sent to Paris by his superior, the bishop of Carcassone, with instructions to seek out the Abbé Bieil, director general of the Seminary of Saint Sulpice, which falls on the ancient prime meridian that passes through France. Having duly presented himself to Bieil, Saunière then spent three weeks in Paris in the company of Bieil's nephew Émile Hoffet, who was a known occultist.

It was during this time that Saunière was also introduced to Emma Calve, who would purportedly become his longtime lover. Calve was also known to be a high priestess of the Parisian esoteric subculture.

During his stay in Paris, Saunière spent time in the Louvre where it is recorded that he purchased reproductions of three paintings. One was a portrait of Pope Celestine V by an unidentified artist. The second painting was *St. Anthony and St. Paul Fed by Ravens* by David Teniers the Younger, and the third was Nicolas Poussin's second edition of *The Shepherds of Arcadia.*

Upon his return to Rennes-le-Château, Saunière had become a different man and undertook a series of rather mysterious projects; apparently he had acquired a great deal of money and a newly defiant attitude toward the church. In the churchyard, for example, Saunière erased the headstone inscription found on the sepulchre of Marie de Blanchefort, the Marquise d'Hautpoul, not knowing that the inscriptions on the tomb had already been copied by a local historian. The reasoning behind this rather oddly violent gesture for a Catholic priest to be involved in cannot be fully explained.

Fig. 5.1. La Tour Magdala, Rennes-le-Château, France. Photograph property of the author, William F. Mann.

A replica of a medieval tower—La Tour Magdala—which was designed to house Saunière's ever-growing library, was built across another ancient meridian. As well, a rather grand country house called the Villa Bethania (presumably in honor of the House of Bethany) was constructed; Saunière himself never occupied it. Finally, the village church was restored in a most unusual fashion througout, including this Latin inscription that was carved in the arch above the entrance:

TERRIBILIS EST LOCUS ISTE
(THIS PLACE IS TERRIBLE)

Inside the church, reliefs were installed depicting the fourteen stations of the cross; however, they each deviated from accepted scriptural accounts in some manner. For example, Station VIII depicts a small child and her mother kneeling before Jesus, with the child wearing a plaid Scottish tartan. Just as oddly, on January 22, 1917, Saunière died after having inexplicably fallen ill on January 17, which is the day attributed to Saint Anthony's birthday. Somewhat more mysteriously, the morning following his death Saunière's body, clad in an ornate robe adorned with scarlet tassels, was placed upright in an armchair on the terrace of La Tour Magdala, and, one by one, as mourners from the village filed past, many of them plucked a tassel from the garment.[5] This action symbolized an acknowledgment of the earlier Merovingian kings, given that Merovingian royalty, including the last king, Dagobert, had worn tasseled mantles adorned with bees.

ENTER THE PAPACY

The conclusion put forward in the book *Holy Blood, Holy Grail* is as unorthodox but as fascinating as the Rennes-le-Château mystery itself; but let us not forget that the conclusion is the same one that's been promoted since medieval times. Baigent, Leigh, and Lincoln's theory supports the old Cathar belief that Mary Magdalene was the wife of Jesus and that offspring were produced. These authors even hypothesized (again, not the first time that the theory was put forward) that after the Crucifixion, Mary Magdalene, either pregnant or with at least one child, was smuggled to an overseas refuge by her uncle, Joseph of Arimathea.

As previously noted, this was the first modern-day suggestion that there is indeed a hereditary bloodline descended directly from Jesus and that this Holy Bloodline has perpetuated itself to this day. One direct result of this theory is the recent rash of books on this very subject, including Laurence Gardner's *Bloodline of the Holy Grail,* Keith Laidler's *The Head of God,* and many, many more, including the most famous of them all—the novel by Dan Brown—*The Da Vinci Code.*

Given the recent popularity of this topic, however, I'm always surprised that it has never dawned on the millions of followers of this story that the mystery behind the village of Rennes-le-Château could represent nothing more than a giant ruse—an extremely effective ruse to prevent those misguided Grail treasure seekers from looking beyond

Europe to the western horizon and the New World. In much the same way, if the Grail treasure hunter does make the leap across the Atlantic Ocean, Oak Island becomes the next effective ruse.

The geometric axioms found in the paintings by Teniers and Poussin have already been exposed in earlier chapters; so what role does Pope Celestine V (1215–1296) play in all of this, in that his coronation was the subject of one of the two paintings that Saunière bought while in Paris? Interestingly enough, the ascetic life of Pope Celestine V appears in many ways to emulate the earlier lives of Saint Anthony and Saint Paul and even Saint Francis, except for one minor detail: Pietro di Murrone (Pope Celestine V) ultimately assumed the mantle of the papacy, even though that was a post he held for only five months.[6] And in assuming the papacy, according to the painting *Allegory of the Coronation of Celestine V* (see figure 5.2 on p. 154), he also appears to have intentionally assumed only one, not two, keys to it. Indeed, this is corroborated in Dante's *Inferno* when the Prince of the Pharisees says, "I can open and close Heaven as you know, with the two Keys, that my predecessor, Celestine, did not prize."

But what are these mysterious keys of the papacy that the prince refers to, and how do they possibly figure into our story?

Officially, the crossed keys in the coat of arms of the Holy See symbolize the keys of heaven that were entrusted to Simon Peter by Jesus. The gold and silver keys are said to represent the power of loosening and binding. The triple crown represents the pope's three functions as "supreme pastor," "supreme teacher," and "supreme priest"; and the gold cross on a monde (globe) surmounting the tiara symbolizes the sovereignty of Jesus (see figure 5.3 on p. 154).

Unofficially, and alchemically, the color gold is representative of the male sun and light. The color silver is representative of the female moon and its shadowy darkness. When bound together, is the hidden message meant to convey that only through a perfect combination of the sun and the moon (an eclipse?) or a male and female (Jesus and Mary Magdalene?) will heaven's doors be open? Remember that half of Teniers's painting of Saint Anthony and Saint Paul is bathed in light and the other half is bathed in darkness. Will this same concept, when

Fig. 5.2. *Allegory of the Coronation of Celestine V.* The painter is unknown, but the date on the painting indicates that it was done in the sixteenth century. Note that in it, Pope Celestine V only possesses one of the keys to the papacy. Reproduced courtesy of the Louvre Museum, Paris, France.

Fig. 5.3. The papal keys of heaven, one gold and one silver, bound together to form the symbol X, a Hooked X in fact. Note the right angle, or 90-degree angle, formed at the nexus (the point where the keys cross one another).

applied through the proper keys, lead to the purest silver and gold that is said to make up at least part of the missing Templar treasure?

Perhaps the keys to the message lie in the simple notion of light being balanced by darkness, of black being balanced by white. If this concept is applied to the simple analogy of a checkered black-and-white chessboard, then we find four castle towers, one in each corner of the board, or two sets of each, one white and one black. Saunière was definitely providing a series of clues when he built La Tour Magdala, with its round stone watchtower attached to the square library of knowledge. These two elements, the circle and the square, are required to square the circle. In chess there is a classic movement known as the knight's tour, which is a sequence of moves of a knight on a chessboard such that the knight visits every square only once. If this notion is combined with the underlying geometric solutions found in a combination of the paintings by Poussin and Teniers, then, similarly to the hermit saints, the key is to take to the mountaintop wilderness, moving from castle to castle, always three steps ahead of your opponent.

A PAPAL TIME LINE

Pietro di Murrone (Pope Celestine V) was born around 1215 CE and became a Benedictine monk at the young age of seventeen, eventually becoming a hermit in the wilderness of Monte Murrone and later Monte Majella in Italy.[7] It is said that he strove to emulate the simple spiritual life of John the Baptist, seeking solitude and discomfort, believing that suffering brings one closer to God. Similar to Anthony, as news of Pietro's simple life spread, other monks who desired to be closer to God were drawn to his humble mountaintop cell.

As a result a religious community formed around him at Monte Majella, and in 1264 the Order of the Celestine Monks was officially recognized by Pope Urban IV, who had been the Latin patriarch of Jerusalem between 1255 and 1261. This was during the time when Acre was the headquarters of the Knights Hospitaller following the success of the Third Crusade. However, it wasn't until 1261 that Jacques Pantaleon, who originated from Troyes, Champagne, France, was anointed Pope Urban IV. The Order of Celestine Monks was one of Pope Urban IV's last acts before he died in 1264. His successor would be Honorius IV, who ruled until 1288, and then Pope Nicholas IV, the first Franciscan to become pope and who ruled between 1288 and 1292.[8]

In 1292, after the death of Pope Nicholas IV, the cardinals met to elect a new pope but reached a stalemate. At that time the officers of the church were as political as they were spiritual, and the cardinals were split into two polarized factions, each one aligned with a powerful (Italian) dynasty. As a result the church was without a pope for more than two years while each faction blocked the nominees of the other. Then, perhaps in absolute desperation, one of the cardinals nominated Pietro as the next pope, and the rest of the conclave quickly approved of this.

At first Pietro adamantly refused the papacy, but after the cardinals pressed him to accept, and several very important people including King Charles II of Naples came to his mountain cell to convince him, Pietro relented. The king subsequently urged him to come to the city of Aquila, in the kingdom of Naples, to be crowned. Pietro thus traveled from his mountain hermitage to Aquila with an entourage of kings and princes, cardinals and bishops. The story goes that he rode on the back of a donkey amid royal carriages, knights, and chargers. Finally he was consecrated and crowned Pope Celestine V in the cathedral at Aquila on July 5, 1294.[9]

Within weeks of assuming the office of pope, Celestine V wanted to abdicate, given that most of the cardinals in Rome had quickly turned against him because he appeared to favor the kingdom of Naples over the church. At this point the southern state of Italy was much more aligned with the Angevin Empire (House of Anjou) than it was to Rome and the Vatican. However, such an act was unprecedented, and some cardinals implored him to stay while others tried hard to convince him to leave.

At last Celestine V realized that as pope he could influence changes in church law. He put forward a rule that would allow popes to abdicate, and, after harsh debate among the cardinals, it was accepted as papal law. Celestine V then quickly abdicated, returning to his mountaintop cell, where he died in 1296. It may interest some that this papal law was never used again until Pope Benedict resigned on February 28, 2013.

Coming around again, the story picks up with Pope Celestine V being very quickly sainted in 1313 by none other than Pope Clement V, who was the pope who cooperated with the king of France at the time, Philippe IV, to orchestrate the downfall of the Knights Templar in 1307. Recently, though, it was determined that Pope Clement V was pressured by the king to denounce the Templars and that, in fact, Clement issued the Chinon Parchment on July 2, 1308, which declared that the Templars were not guilty of heresy but were guilty on other counts, and he ordered them to disband. Regardless, a massive raid had been previously orchestrated against the Knights Templar on Friday, October 13, 1307, wherein many of their numbers throughout France, including Grand Master Jacques de Molay, were captured and imprisoned. De Molay would be burned at the stake, but it is said that with his last breath, in spite of the seven years of captivity and torture he had endured since his arrest, he recanted the confession that he had previously made under duress. He also called upon his persecutors—Pope Clement and King Philippe—to join him within the year before the court of God and to account for their own sins.

As noted, by the end of the year both Philippe and Clement were dead, and the mystique and arcane knowledge surrounding the Templars had consequently grown to epic proportions, as had the legend of their secret treasure, which vanished under the cloak of darkness along with eighteen galleys of knights from the port of La Rochelle on that infamous Friday the 13th.

FROM FRANCISCAN TO RECOLLET

Francis of Assisi, from whom the current Pope Francis has taken his name, was born Giovanni di Pietro di Bernardone in 1181 CE. He was an Italian Catholic friar and preacher but was never ordained to the Catholic priesthood. Regardless, he founded the men's Order of Friars Minor, the women's Order of St. Clare, and the Third Order of St. Francis, which allowed both men and women.[10]

Saint Clare of Assisi was one of the first followers of Saint Francis of Assisi. Through the encouragement of Francis of Assisi, she established the Order of Poor Ladies, a monastic religious order for women in the Franciscan tradition, and wrote their Rule of Life, which is the first monastic rule known to have been written by a woman. Following her death the order was renamed in her honor as the Order of St. Clare, commonly referred to today as the Poor Clares. It is said that Lake Saint Clair and the Saint Clair River in the Great Lakes region of North America were named in her honor by the Recollets in 1679 on her feast day, August 11. Interestingly, Mission Santa Clara, founded by Spanish Franciscan missionaries in northern California in 1777, has also given its name to the university, city, county, and valley where it sits.

Francis came from a very wealthy Catholic Italian family, even fighting as a soldier for Assisi. Apparently, while going off to war in 1204, he had a vision that directed him back to Assisi, where he set off on a pilgrimage to Rome after shunning all of his possessions. The experience in Rome moved him so much that he vowed to live in poverty for the rest of his life. From then on, soon after Francis returned home to Assisi and began preaching on the streets, he attracted many followers. His order, by then known as the Franciscans, was authorized by Pope Innocent III in 1210.

In 1219, Francis went to Egypt in an attempt to persuade the sultan to put an end to the conflict of the Second Crusade. Following his failure to do that, he returned to Assisi, where he withdrew increasingly from the affairs of men. According to official records of the the church, it is said that it was in 1223 that Francis arranged for the first Christmas nativity scene to be displayed to the public, because by this time his only companions were the animals who flocked to him. And, in 1224, he received the stigmata, making him the first recorded person to bear the wounds of Christ's passion. He died on October 3, 1226, leaving behind a legacy that included a thriving monastic community, which still exists around the world to this day.

Fig. 5.4. The Franciscan monastery, Il Sacro Convento, and the lower and upper Church of St. Francis of Assisi: were begun immediately after his canonization in 1228 and completed in 1253. Compare the outline and features of the monastery with the mountaintop castle depicted in the far background of Teniers's painting of *St. Anthony and St. Paul Fed by Ravens* (figure 4.2, p. 122). They are far too identical to not be the same. Photograph property of the author, William F. Mann.

What is relatively unknown is that the Recollets, the monastic order that came to New France at the start of the seventeenth century with Samuel de Champlain, were a reformed branch of the Franciscan family. The stated main objective of the Recollets was to observe more strictly the Rule of Saint Francis, and, like other semi-autonomous branches, their governance came under the aegis of the French minister general of the Franciscans at the time. Recall that the Recollets were replaced by the Jesuits after 1626 and left New France but returned in 1670 at the express wishes of the French king at the time, Louis XIV, the Sun King, in consultation with his closest advisor, the minister of finance, Jean-Baptiste Colbert.

The early missionary goal of the Recollets in New France was to undertake simple work among the indigenous people who lived there. They planned to do this by initially gaining their confidence. This work was not without its challenges, though, as language proved a difficult barrier to overcome. However, the Recollets persevered and eventually developed extremely close connections with the natives, especially with the Hurons and the Algonquins. In many cases the Recollects would ensure that their convents were constructed in indigenous settlements, unlike the Jesuits, who distanced themselves from the native encampments. This way the Recollects quickly learned about the natives' beliefs and customs. The natives would readily teach them their language and welcome them into their lodges.

As missionaries and explorers, the Recollets were known for their simple and austere life. Curiously, in 1763, British authorities forbade them to receive novices, and thus the order disappeared in 1849 when the last Canadian Recollet, Father Louis Demers, died in Montreal. Did the attempts of the British authorities to have the Recollects die out have something to do with the Recollets' extensive exploration into the North American wilderness in the seventeenth century? Were the British somehow threatened by the reach that the Recollects enjoyed in North America?

One well-known Recollet was Father Louis Hennepin. Born in 1626 in the Spanish Netherlands (Belgium), he was one of the greatest explorers of the interior of North America during the seventeenth century. At the direct request of Louis XIV, who had finally been able to acquire Poussin's *The Shepherds of Arcadia* in 1685 as his own, Hennepin accompanied René Robert Cavalier, Sieur de la Salle, on his 1675 exploration of the North American interior through Québec and the Great Lakes. Hennepin was present at the construction of Fort Crevecoeur (near present-day Peoria, Illinois) in January 1680, and in February of the same year La Salle sent Hennepin and two others as an advance party to search for the Mississippi River.

Throughout several midwestern states, such as Michigan, Illinois, and Minnesota, the name Hennepin has been memorialized through its attachment to a variety of natural landmarks and modern-day constructions and place-names. For example, Hennepin Island is in the Mississippi River at Saint Anthony Falls, Minnesota, which lies just outside of Minneapolis/Saint Paul. Although it is no longer an island, it extends into the river, and houses the Saint Anthony Falls Laboratory at the University of Minnesota, a five-unit hydroelectric plant owned by Xcel Energy, and the Main Street substation that serves downtown Minneapolis. There is also Father Hennepin Bluffs Park, which lies on the east bank of the Mississippi River adjacent to Hennepin Island.

The party followed the Illinois River to its junction with the Mississippi and then the Missouri. Shortly thereafter, Hennepin was captured by a Sioux war party and carried off for a time into what is now the state of Minnesota. In September, Hennepin and the others were surprisingly given canoes and allowed to leave, eventually returning to Québec. Hennepin returned to France, and his order mandated that he must never return to North America.

Two great waterfalls were brought to the Old World's attention by Louis Hennepin. The first was Niagara Falls, with the most dramatic flow of any waterway in North America. The second was Saint Anthony Falls in what is now Minneapolis/Saint Paul, the only waterfall on the Mississippi River. Not surprisingly, it was Hennepin who curiously named these falls after the father of Monastic Christianity, for Hennepin would clearly have recognized that the Recollets' way of life was based on the beliefs and foundational lifestyles of earlier Franciscans, Cistercians, and the original hermit saints.

What is just as curious is the fact that David Teniers the Younger, in his painting *St. Anthony and St. Paul Fed by Ravens,* had not only depicted the Franciscan monastery found in Assisi but also depicted the figure of Saint Paul wearing the brown robe of a Recollet. In the same painting, the brown robe of Saint Anthony is partially concealed by a Jesuit's black robe. Could this be another key relating to the secret geographic information already known of the New World by 1652? The answer to why Saint Anthony is wearing the outer black robe over a brown robe will be answered later in this story. The question to be answered at this point is: Was Hennepin, a white man, exploring the native environment for the first time, or was he following earlier mapping and information provided by those Jesuit priests and Franciscan friars and earlier secret Templar explorers who had preceded him?

Who really were the competing chess masters of the late seventeenth century who were racing their chess pieces across North America in order to be the first to recover the Templar treasure? Was Cardinal Richelieu, who now appears to be a Knight Templar/Mason in disguise, working secretly with the Recollets and St. Sulpicians, directly competing with the Habsburg archduke Leopold Wilhelm I, who represented the Knights Teutonic and the Jesuits?

THE KNIGHT'S TOUR

No matter how one tries to reason where every individual initiate or every fraternal group falls in the overall mystery, the question always comes around as to what exact antient knowledge did Prince Henry Sinclair and his followers possess that allowed them over several centuries to always be out in front of their enemies? It certainly makes total sense that those of the inner circle of Knights Templar who intermarried with North America's indigenous people would be exposed to information and secret knowledge that the various nations possessed with respect to the relative geography of North America; but there most certainly appears to be something more "magical" to the knights' knowledge of the North American continent.

In both *The Knights Templar of the New World: How Henry Sinclair Brought the Grail to Acadia* and *The Templar Meridians: The Secret Mapping of the New World* it is clearly demonstrated that the Knights Templar possessed a collection of antient writings and maps that originated from pre-Christian times, even perhaps from a time before the

Great Flood. For close to two centuries the Templars certainly enjoyed a rather unique position between the established church and state. And this exalted position most certainly related in some way to what the original nine knights had discovered during their excavations under the ruins of the temple in Jerusalem.

According to most books on the subject, the Order of the Poor Fellow Soldiers of Christ and of the Temple of Solomon was founded in 1118 CE, nineteen years after the capture of Jerusalem during the First Crusade. The declared objective of the original nine knights was to keep the roads and highways safe for pilgrims. However, there is very little evidence of their having done so, and the true objective of the first Knights Templar may never be known. Many historians agree, though, that these knights discovered something hidden beneath the Temple of Solomon that confirmed, among other things, the very existence of Jesus.[11]

In 1127, after nine years in the Holy Land, most of the nine knights returned to their ancestral homes in France, and, in January 1128, at a church council in Troyes, the Templars were officially recognized as a religious-military order. This was mainly due to their patron, Bernard of Clairvaux, who was originally a follower of the Roman Catholic Carthusian order and was later instrumental in establishing the Cistercian order. The recognition awarded the Knights Templar at this juncture does indeed suggest that the knights discovered something of tremendous religious and historical value in Jerusalem, given the rapidity of their rise in stature.

The Templars, at least outwardly, were sworn to poverty, chastity, and obedience, and they enjoyed virtual anonymity due to a papal bull that had been issued by Pope Innocent II in 1139. It stated that the Templars would owe allegiance only to the pope and to no one else. One result was that over the next two decades throughout Europe, younger sons of noble families flocked to join the Order's ranks. And, because on admission to the Order a man forfeited all his possessions, including his land, Templar holdings quickly proliferated.

As a result, in a mere twenty-four years after the Council of Troyes, the Order held substantial estates throughout most of Europe, the

Holy Land, and points east. Hence, by the mid-thirteenth century, the Templars had become powerful enough to be involved in high-level diplomacy between nobles and monarchs throughout the Western world and the Holy Land. The Order's political activities were not confined to the Christian world, though, as ties were forged with the Muslims also. As well, the Templars commanded respect from Saracen leaders far exceeding that accorded any other Europeans. There are even unsubstantiated stories that the Templars developed a loose alliance with the religious sect known as the Nizari Assassins. (This may come as a surprise to the modern-day gamers who spend their days pitting the Assassins against the Templars while playing *Assassin's Creed.*)

At the same time, the Templars created and established the institution of modern banking and, in effect, became the bankers for every throne in Europe and for various Muslim potentates. But the Templars did not only trade in money. Through their ongoing relations with people of the Islamic and Judaic cultures they came to learn and to accept new areas of knowledge and new sciences.

Throughout this period the Templars essentially controlled a veritable monopoly on the best and most advanced technology of their age and contributed to the development of surveying, mapmaking, road building, and navigation. They possessed their own seaports, shipyards, and fleets, both commercial and military; their major fleet was based in La Rochelle, France. It is said that one of the main reasons for the Order's mercurial rise in stature was that they also possessed the finest map library of its time, including a number of rare portolan maps of unknown origin.

AN ANTIENT KNOWLEDGE RELATING TO ASTRONOMY, NAVIGATION, AND MAPMAKING

Harvard professor and author Charles Hapgood, in his *Maps of the Ancient Sea Kings,* spent many years examining the earliest "port-(t)o-lan(d)" maps in the light of their information about Earth that was presumably unknown at the time the maps were made.[12] Hapgood has certainly demonstrated that some of these maps were copied and recopied through the centuries from vanished originals formerly kept in the great library of ancient Alexandria. He also demonstrated that these maps possess startlingly accurate knowledge of lands as yet undiscovered (according to history as we have learned it) when the original and even the copies were made, including the existence of North and South America and Antarctica.

For example, the 1519 Piri Reis map, accidentally discovered in the old Imperial Palace in Constantinople in 1929, is one such portolan map, which has amazing, inexplicable accuracy. Based on a larger equidistant azimuthal projection, it shows the American continents more accurately than any map drawn two hundred years later.

As was first demonstrated in *The Knights Templar in the New World,* a geometric application of the Seal of Solomon, the inner jewel, can be applied to an equidistant azimuthal projection of the world (see figure 5.5 on p. 166). In this manner distances between two points on Earth could be accurately calculated using simple geometry if the latitudinal and longitudinal position of both points were known. This is the exact basis upon which the concept of the Templar meridans was developed. The meridans are, in essence, a series of previously undiscovered longitudinal rose lines, or secret meridians, in a geometric pattern that encompasses the whole world.

Ley lines, also known as dragon lines, are straight lines or trackways passing over and through the landscape. They were first brought to light by the amateur archaeologist Englishman Alfred Watkins in 1921. Throughout Europe these trackways, or ley lines, are marked by standing stones, megaliths, earthworks such as barrows and mounds, holy wells, and other assorted, prominent, natural or man-made landmarks. Surely, given that these ley lines exist across Europe, it definitely appears reasonable that antient rose lines/meridians of the same nature were established around the world and that there is the potential of connecting the thousands of megalithic sites that exist all over the globe.

This very simple explanation concerning the thousands of megalithic sites positioned throughout the world certainly raises a fascinating concept: if a specific society or societies were able to establish their relative positions around the globe by both latitude and longitude through the simplest geometry, then these same societies would be able to map their

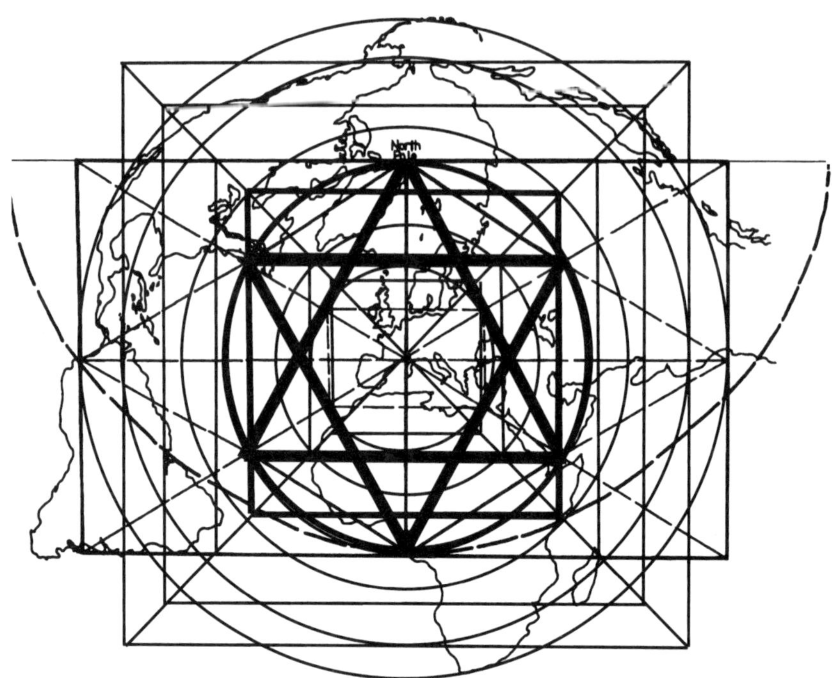

Fig. 5.5. Application of the squaring of the circle to an equidistant azimuthal projection of the world, centered on the port of Marseille, the ancient Roman port of Marsilia. Note how the various tangents extending outward in accordance with the concentric circles provide for the relative calculation of bearing and distance between various ports. For example, there is a direct correlation between the Templar port of La Rochelle, France, and mainland Nova Scotia. Diagram copyright of the author, William F. Mann.

relative positions in relation to one another. One direct result would be the development of incredibly accurate maps. From the perspective of a trade monopoly, this knowledge would have represented pure power.

In *The Golden Thread of Time* author, inventor, and master navigator Crichton E. M. Miller has demonstrated quite effectively how a simple construction that resembles an ancient Celtic cross can be used to measure the angle of the sun. Through simple mathematics Creighton demonstrated that he was able to determine one's latitudinal or longitudinal position anywhere on Earth's surface. In fact, the instrument was so successful in determining latitude and longitude that Miller was granted a patent for his surveying, navigation, and astronomy instrument.[13] With the simplest of materials Miller was able to determine his relative position on Earth to within 30 nautical miles, or ½ of 1 degree. What may initially appear an unacceptable inaccuracy is explained by the tilt of Earth's angle against the ecliptic, as caused by precession. (In simpler terms, Earth wobbles a little!)

This instrument allowed the ancient mariner to fix longitudinal and latitudinal positions at sea and on land, as established above, to an accuracy of half a degree. To put this into perspective, with Earth's surface measuring 360 degrees, or 21,600 nautical miles, the measure of inaccuracy is less than one-quarter of 1 percent.

Miller believes that the cross, and the methods of its use, was one of the greatest treasures to be found by the Knights Templar in their excavation of Solomon's Temple. He further believes that this discovery led to the immense power and wealth of the Templars. It was this material wealth that would finance a new style of architecture, namely the building of the great Gothic cathedrals in Europe, beginning with Chartres in France.

At this juncture it's extremely rewarding to realize that like-minded experts in various scientific disciplines, such as Charles Hapgood and Crichton E. M. Miller, have come to the same conclusion: an antient knowledge relating to astronomy, navigation, and mapmaking did exist and has survived to this day.

ETYMOLOGICALLY SPEAKING . . .

Remember the five elements contained in the Little Keys of Solomon: astronomy, dualism, numerology, androgyny, and etymology. Even though some academics consider them to be nothing more than a medieval grimoire, or book of magic, developed during the fourteenth or fifteenth century, according to the mythology included in the document, King Solomon originally wrote the book for his son Rehoboam and commanded him to hide it in the king's tomb upon his death. Allegedly, the book was later discovered by a group of Babylonian philosophers while repairing Solomon's tomb.

It's evident that both Poussin and Teniers believed that the Little Keys of Solomon was the basis of Solomon's wisdom, in that their compositions adhere to the elements contained in Solomon's treatise.[14] In the composite of the paintings *The Shepherds of Arcadia* and *St. Anthony and St. Paul Fed by Ravens* it's been demonstrated how all seven elements, or figures, can adhere to the first four little keys. There are certainly various elements of astronomy, dualism, numerology, and androgyny in how Poussin and Teniers relate the seven figures to one another.

From an astronomical perspective, the ancient Greeks and Romans knew there to be only seven original planets; each presumed to be circling Earth according to the complex laws laid out by Ptolemy. They were, in increasing order from Earth (in Ptolemy's order): the moon, Mercury, Venus, the sun, Mars, Jupiter, and Saturn.

By the first century BCE, during the Hellenistic period, the Greeks had begun to develop their own mathematical schemes for predicting the positions of the planets. Based on geometry rather than the arithmetic of the Babylonians, these schemes would eventually eclipse the Babylonians' theories in complexity and comprehensiveness. In this manner they accounted for most of the astronomical movements observed from Earth with the naked eye. These theories would reach their fullest expression in the *Almagest* written by Ptolemy in the second century CE and superseded all previous works on astronomy to the point that it remained the definitive astronomical text in the Western world. Ptolemy's theories were even supported by early church doctrine for thirteen centuries until the advent of the early telescope.

Conversely, the Pythagoreans (followers of Pythagoras) in the sixth and fifth centuries BCE developed their own independent planetary theory. This suggested that the center of the universe was a "Central Fire" and that around this central element revolved the sun, the moon, Earth, and other planets. Then, in the third century BCE, Aristarchus of Samos proposed that the Earth and the planets revolved around the sun. This was generally known as a heliocentric system. Unfortunately, to many early Renaissance astrologers, including Galileo, who paid for his beliefs with his life, the church continued to be unaccepting of any theory other than the Earth being the center of the universe. This was commonly known as the geocentric system, and church doctrine would not officially change until the early nineteenth century.

With this in mind, what if we were to reexamine in greater detail the seven elements identified within the composite of *The Shepherds of Arcadia* and *St. Anthony and St. Paul Fed by Ravens* to the prior idea that they represented on one level a planetary alignment of harmonic concordance? First of all, the kneeling figure in Poussin's painting *The Shepherds of Arcadia* has been earlier identified on a variety of levels as Neolithic man, the Green Man, the god Zeus, but he could also represent the sun. See how his is the only figure to cast a shadow on the tomb? The female figure, with her blue and gold clothing, obviously represents Mother Earth and the moon, which has such an effect on Earth, specifically during an eclipse. From a dualistic perspective she is both mother and wife in this situation, given that she is already pregnant. Logically she presents no further temptation to the other figures, in accordance with the Rennes Parchment. Above all else she is seen as a goddess of love and beauty, who possesses the greatest gift of all—the gift of life.

The figure in red hiding behind the goddess, the Celt, the antient initiate, the Templar, is most definitely representative of Mars, the warrior/guardian. The ephemeral, androgynous Jesus-like figure dressed all in white is Mercury, being the closest of the planets to the sun. Jesus, in the form of the Roman god Mercury, was the messenger to the people. But Mercury is the smallest and potentially the most insignificant planet, always in the sun's shadow. Poussin was definitely providing a hidden comment here: Even though the Templars purportedly acted as guardians to the Holy Bloodline, they also used it to deflect their own true purposes. As to what the true purpose, raison d'être, of the Templar Order was and possibly still is will have to wait to be revealed.

Then there is the unborn child, whose existence is tantamount to the whole notion of a Holy Bloodline continuing to this day. In the harmonic concordance that was identified earlier in chapter 4, this unborn child obviously represents the planet Chiron. It's interesting that this planet, being a minor planet in the outer solar system, is invisible to the naked eye and was only officially discovered on October 18, 1977, by Charles Kowal from images taken two weeks earlier at the Palomar Observatory in San Diego, California.

So in the scheme of things, where does this leave Saint Anthony and Saint Paul within this harmonic concordance? Saint Paul can be viewed as Jupiter and Saint Anthony as Saturn, given that these two planets were once considered to be the farthest planets from Earth. At one time Saturn was considered to be a planet older than the sun. Saint Anthony is definitely considered to be the oldest ascetic monk. Notice how the two figures are placed in the foreground and away from the other elements in the composite of Poussin and Teniers's paintings (figure 5.6 on p. 172). Ancient mythology also originally presented Saturn and Jupiter in vigorous interactions, much like the stories of Anthony and Paul's ultimate encounter in the desert.

Etymology is the hidden fifth element and is defined as the history of words, their origins, and how their form and meaning have changed over time. By extension, the phrase "the etymology of a word" means the origin of the particular word. As we have seen through both Teniers's and Poussin's rather dry sense of humor, it can also mean "a play on words." A prime example is the reference to the planet Chiron. The word can be pronounced as "Sharon," a derivation of Sarah.

But the origin of a particular word also can be applied to the notion that modern-day place-names have been derived from either original native words or in terms of what originally occupied that place. In this manner there are modern-day place-names across North America that can provide not only a hint as to the location of pre-Columbian Templar sanctuaries but also relate in some manner to the Templar meridians. One just has to realize what the key words are and how they relate to the larger story of the unveiling of the last refuge of the Knights Templar in the New World.

Figure 5.6 (p. 172) demonstrates in a fascinating way what happens when some of the key place-names have direct references to, or derivations from, specific words, figures, and colors—such as bears, crows, snakes, leys, meridians, oaks, castles, Saint Anthony, Saint Paul, Saint Clair, black, white, red, and green. To enable the reader to better associate the relative places and their geographic locations in relation to the established rose line/meridian grid, the table below highlights the longitudinal and latitudinal positions of some of the key locations (compare with figure 5.6 on p. 172). A tolerable error in accuracy of half a degree surrounding the longitudinal/latitudinal grid coordinates has been determined in relation to that identified by Crichton E. M. Miller through his work with his navigational instrument known as the Celtic cross.

Position	Place-Name	Latitude	Longitude
A1	Debert, Nova Scotia	N 45°26'12"	W 64°07'23"
A2	Castle Hill Lighthouse, RI	N 41°27'43"	W 71°21'43"
A3	St. Clair, Pennsylvania	N 40°43'04"	W 76°11'23"
A4	Indian Mound, Tennessee	N 36°30'03"	W 87°41'37"
A5	IXL, Oklahoma	N 35°31'21"	W 96°23'18"
A6	Oakwood, Ohio	N 40°06'55"	W 87°46'44"
B1	Castle, Oklahoma	N 35°27'53"	W 96°22'12"
B2	Santa Clara, Colorado	N 37°36'00"	W 104°48'00"
B3	Mount Ogden, Utah	N 41°12'97"	W 111°52'39"
B4	Castle, Oregon	N 45°49'04"	W 119°49'52"
B5	Shiprock, New Mexico	N 36°41'15"	W 108°50'11"
B6	Castle Fin, Illinois	N 39°28'12"	W 87°44'00"
B7	Oak Park, Wisconsin	N 41°52'55"	W 87°48'05"
C1	Green Oaks, Nova Scotia	N 45°14'56"	W 63°26'07"
C2	Owl's Head Mountain, Québec	N 45°01'44"	W 72°17'34"
C3	Midland, Ontario	N 45°00'23"	W 79°58'19"
C4	St. Paul Road, Middle Inlet, Wisconsin	N 45°15'30"	W 87°58'57"
C5	Crow Wing, Minnesota	N 45°36'49"	W 96°05'52"
C6	Camp Crook, South Dakota	N 45°32'54"	W 103°58'29"
C7	Crow Peak, Montana	N 45°47'06"	W 111°53'54"
C8	Crowbutte, Washington	N 45°50'49"	W 119°50'0"

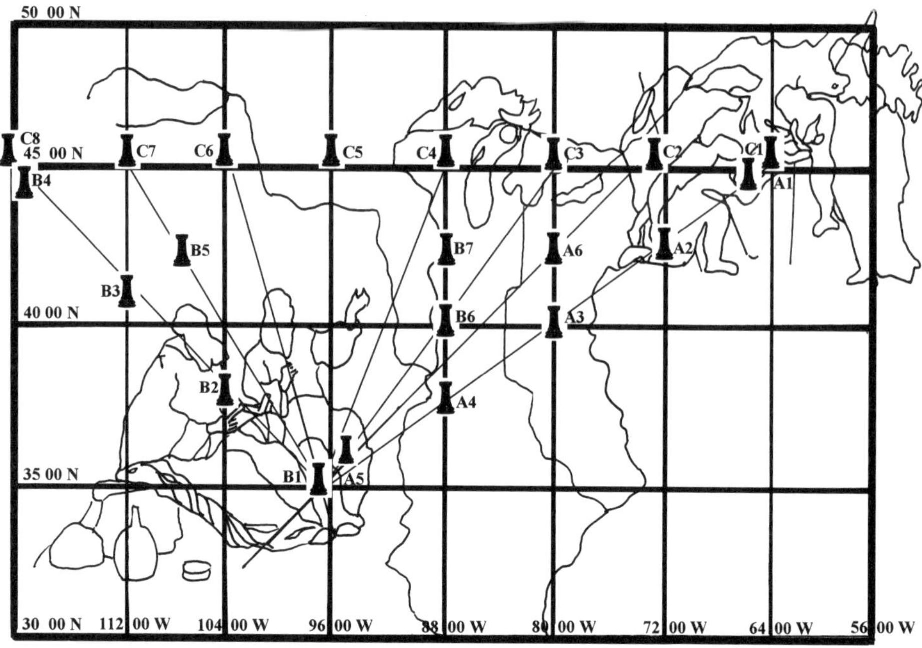

Fig. 5.6. Composite diagram of the seven elements of Poussin's and Teniers's most famous paintings, which illustrates the hidden relationship between key modern-day place-names across North America and the underlying longitudinal/latitudinal grid pattern. Note that at the outer points of the largest triangle two castles are depicted. Diagram copyright of the author, William F. Mann.

Note in figure 5.6 how the 40-degree north parallel transverses across Saint Anthony's ears and eyes, and the same latitudinal grid line travels across the mouth of Saint Paul. Teniers appears to be suggesting that between these two men they should "speak no evil, hear no evil, see no evil" of those gods that came before Christianity.

If one refers back to figure 4.2 (see p. 122), Teniers's painting of *St. Anthony and St. Paul Fed by Ravens,* the raven delivering manna to the two saints is geographically located at Sault Sainte Marie, where Lake Superior joins Lake Michigan and Lake Huron.

Sault Sainte Marie is one of the oldest French settlements in North America. It was at the crossroads of the fur-trade route, which stretched some three thousand miles from Montreal to Sault Sainte Marie and to the country north of Lake Superior. After the visit of the French explorer/voyageur Étienne Brûlé in 1623, the French called this location Sault de Gaston, in honor of Gaston, Duke of Orleans. The duke of Gaston was the favored brother of King Louis XIII of France. In 1668, though, French Jesuit missionaries renamed it Sault Sainte Marie and established a mission on the river's south bank. Later a fur-trading post was established by the French, and the settlement expanded to include both sides of the river. Could the Jesuits renaming the settlement in honor of Sainte Marie be another coy acknowledgment that direct descendants of Jesus and Mary Magdalene spent some time at this strategic location before once again moving westward?

Officially it is said that the present-day city's name originates from Saults de Sainte-Marie, archaic French for Saint Mary's Falls, a reference to the rapids of Saint Mary's River. Etymologically the word *sault* comes from an archaic spelling of *saut* (from *sauter*), which translates most accurately in this usage to the English word "cataract." This in turn derives from the French word for "leap" or "jump." Citations dating back to 1600 use the "sault" spelling to mean a "cataract," "a waterfall," or "rapids." Again, there appears to be an emphasis of the early explorers on areas where significant waterfalls are located. Practically speaking, the locations and distances between major rapids or waterfalls would have been mapped by the early explorers as accurately as possible to indicate where portages would be required and how far a paddle it was between them. They also would have been seasonal gathering places where the natives would congregate to fish during the spawning runs, which provided ample opportunity for trade and other interaction.

Also note the geometric relationships of the various place-names in the table on page 171 in relation to points A5 and B1 in that they form a number of right-angle triangles from which accurate distances and bearings can be determined using the Pythagorean Theorem. Points A5 and B1, rather coyly located on the right kneecap (a lookout?) of Saint Paul, were obviously used as a major transit station during the ancient surveying of North America. In Teniers's painting the walking stick held by Saint Paul along with Saint Anthony's broken stick forms an X of sorts. What place-name happens to lie at this cross-point of the triangle and what is its significance?

Located at the nexus of the crossed sticks held by Saint Paul is a very small town that is located just between Oklahoma City and Tulsa, Oklahoma: the town of IXL. The town's population in 2010 was approximately fifty. The funny thing is that the origin of the rather mysterious word has never been determined. Some have speculated that the place-name IXL is one of those onomatopoeic words that phonetically imitates, resembles, or suggests the source of the sound it describes. (A very simple example would be a cat's "meow.") In this case, though, the hidden suggestion is that the place-name translates into "I excel; thus, I transcend." Teniers certainly exceeded every expectation in developing the many hidden layers of his painting *St. Anthony and St. Paul Fed by Ravens.*

But this isn't even the start of Teniers's genius. Three miles directly south of the town of IXL (35°31'21"N, 96°23'18"W) is Castle, Oklahoma (35°28'31"N, 96°23'3"W). Nine miles south is the small town of Bearden (35°21'29"N, 96°23'18"W). And slightly northwest of IXL is Keystone Lake (36°23'06"N, 96°30'50"W). Hence the suggestion that, as Saint Paul appears to be explaining to Saint Anthony, logically the "key (to finding the) stone (is to determine geometrically the north–south rose line) I (and then to find the ape-)X (and apply it to a right-angle) L (triangle.)" In reverse, the message can read: "Find the bear's den and castle at the point of the keystone."

Not surprisingly, I've found that there's always some sort of quirky coincidence that pops up once in a while when I put pen to paper. While I wrote about the place-name of IXL and Keystone Lake, Oklahoma, there continued a raging debate between environmentalists and industrialists over what is labeled the Keystone XL Pipeline. The Keystone XL Pipeline is an intended oil pipeline system in Canada and the United States, which has been commissioned since 2010. It is proposed to run in its entirety from the Western Canadian Sedimentary Basin in Alberta to refineries in Illinois and Texas and also to, of all places, oil tank farms and an oil pipeline distribution center in Cushing, Oklahoma. The first three phases of construction have already been completed, and a bill approving the construction of the Keystone XL Pipeline extension was passed by the Senate on January 29, 2015, and by the House on February 11, 2015. But President Obama vetoed the bill on February 24, 2015, arguing at that time that the decision of approval should rest with the executive branch; and then, in November 2015, the president ultimately rejected the bill outright.

All of what's been discussed in this chapter raises so many questions. Sometimes people read into things in order to see what they want to see when nothing's really there. Why was a point in Oklahoma used as the major intersection or one of the major transit stations for mapping North America in pre-Columbian times? What if a more logical and reasonable way of thinking had been applied to this question? Maybe the spiritual layering of moral allegory and sacred geometry should be set aside for the moment, and the critical point to the composite drawn should be analyzed in terms of the historical and geographical information that is known in relation to Oklahoma.

6
Happy Trails to You!

ALL THAT GLITTERS . . .

Approximately fifty years after Columbus first sailed to the New World in 1492, Spaniards came northward out of Mexico across the Sonora Desert to investigate what is now present-day Arizona, New Mexico, Texas, Oklahoma, and Kansas. Always accompanying the Spanish explorers were Catholic priests or friars, given that the Catholic Church had declared that all of the New World was to be rid of pagan demons and converted to Christianity. The priests and friars were well educated; thus notes were made and reports were submitted to the proper authorities both in Mexico and in Europe.[1] In this way a considerable store of knowledge was accumulated about the land and people of the Great Plains and Rocky Mountain foothills.*

Just as importantly, extensive maps with fairly remarkable accuracy were created; many of the clergy had also been trained in the fields of astronomy, basic triangulation, and distance calculation. Given that Mexico and Sonora were essentially dry with few rivers, the Spanish explorers traveled with trains of horses and pack mules following ancient

*It must be remembered that the Spanish expeditions of de Soto and Coronado, along with the Franciscans who accompanied them, were undertaken a century and a half before the French explorer La Salle and more than two and a half centuries before Lewis and Clark. The expeditions were the natural outflow of the experiences of Cortés, and of Pizarro in Mexico and Peru, as well as the voyages of Christopher Columbus.

Indian trails. This provided the mapmaker with the best opportunities to survey the countryside.

The various explorers' efforts were prompted by rumors of seven golden cities, known collectively as Cibola. It was the Spanish friar Marcos de Niza who said that he had once discovered it in 1539 CE. These towns, with buildings said to be made of gold, quickly assumed an important status in the Spanish ethos. The vast wealth discovered among the Inca and Aztec Empires had stimulated the Spanish appetite for more gold and silver and enticed them to further explorations in "New Spain."[2]

Friar Marcos de Niza* was a Franciscan friar who was born in Nice, France, which was at that time under the control of the Italian House of Savoy. He went to South America in 1531, and after serving the Franciscan order zealously in Peru and Guatemala, he was rather mysteriously chosen to explore the country north of Sonora, the wealth of which had been depicted in earlier accounts of the wanderings of Alvar Nunez Cabeza de Vaca and Estevanico, his Moorish companion.

Friar Marcos thus left Culiacan, Mexico, in March 1539, crossed southeastern Arizona and penetrated to the Zuni Pueblo, which lies in present-day New Mexico, before returning in September to Culiacan. He apparently saw Cibola only from a distance, yet nonetheless embellished his report, *Descubrimiento de las siete ciudades,* to make it appear that he had visited the Seven Cities. This led Francisco Vazquez de Coronado, with Friar Marcos di Niza as his guide, to take his expedition party in 1540 back to the Zuni Pueblo where they spent the winter months.

From New Mexico in April 1541, Coronado's expedition continued eastward, looking for another supposedly wealthy place at that time called Gran Quivira,† and they crossed through the Texas and Oklahoma

---

*Many academics have claimed that Friar Marcos was a complete fraud, having turned back near the present-day Mexican-American border without ever reaching Cibola and that he was part of a secret conspiracy with Mexican viceroy Mendoza to promote exploration of the north.

†Recent archaeological evidence suggests that Quivira was actually located near the great bend of the Arkansas River in central Kansas. The remains of several Indian settlements have been found near Lyons along Cow Creek and the Little Arkansas River, along with articles of Spanish origin dating from Coronado's time.

Panhandles before arriving in late July in Kansas at a Wichita Indian village that was presumed to be their destination, Quivira.[3] They found no gold or silver there, though. Ending his trip in utter disappointment, Coronado returned to New Mexico and then traveled back to Mexico in 1542.

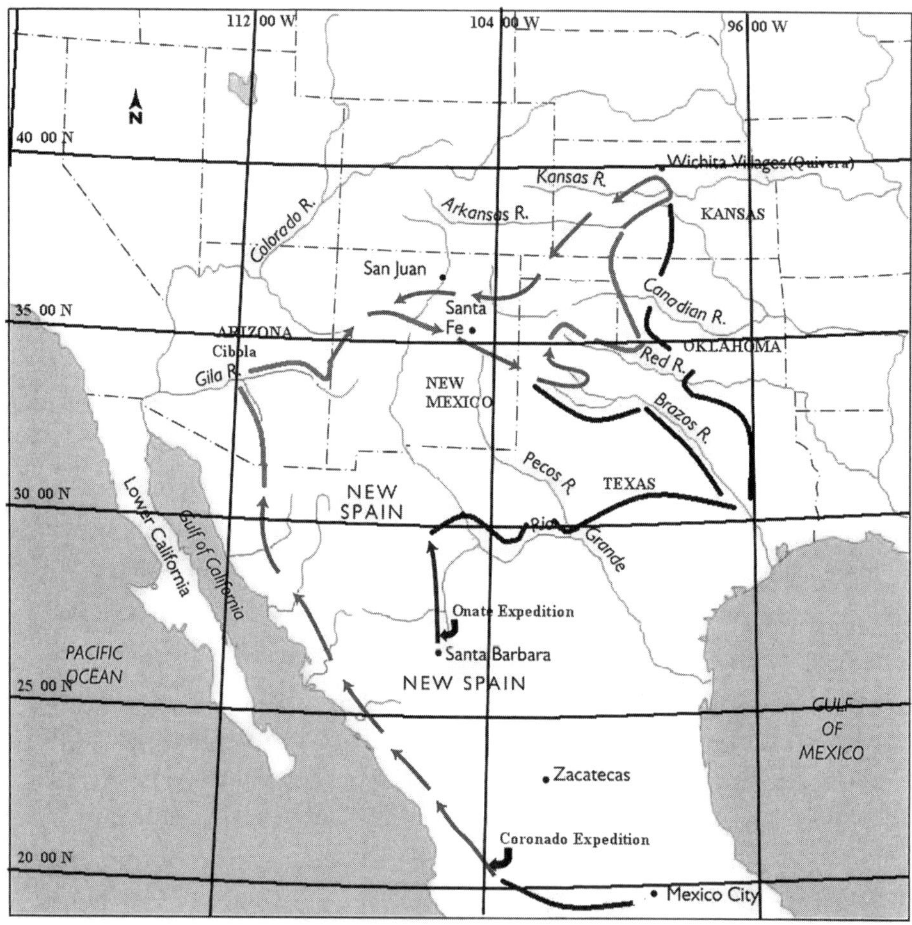

Fig. 6.1. Diagram illustrating the determined routes of the early Spanish explorers, Coronado and Onate, who ventured north from Mexico between approximately 1540 and 1600 into the present-day states of Arizona, New Mexico, Texas, Oklahoma, and Kansas searching for Quivira. *The Templar Meridians* latitudinal/longitudinal grid has been superimposed on top of the routes to demonstrate how they correspond to the rose lines. Note how the two routes are mostly defined by the four-grid quadrants. Diagram developed by the author, William F. Mann.

Meanwhile another Spanish expedition had penetrated the interior from the east. In 1539, Hernando de Soto began an exploration designed to find gold and converts in "La Florida." The men traveled farther and farther westward and reached west-central Arkansas before Soto died of a fever in May 1542.

Most historians now credit Soto's men with crossing into and exploring eastern Oklahoma. The best evidence, based on geographical description, indicates that scouting parties from the Soto expedition traveled into eastern Oklahoma via the Arkansas River. It was left to Luis de Moscoso Alvarado, who succeeded Soto in command, to lead the party out of Arkansas across the southeastern corner of Oklahoma along a well-known Indian trail that crossed the Red River into Texas.

Next came Andres do Campo, a Portuguese soldier, and several other Franciscans, including Friar Juan de Padilla, who had been with the Coronado expedition on its journey from present-day New Mexico to Kansas and back. Interested in establishing a mission to convert the Wichita people, they returned to Quivira in the spring of 1542. The Wichita people were targeted because their rivals, the Spanish, believed that they possessed specific knowledge concerning the lost seven cities. But in 1544 they were attacked by a party of Kaw (Kansas) Indians, who killed Padilla and held Campo and two others captive for a year.

After escaping, the prisoners fled due south across the center of Oklahoma and crossed Texas into Mexico. Legend says that the men commemorated Padilla's death by taking turns dragging an enormous wooden cross the entire length of their journey. Campo's description of the more direct route from Mexico to Quivira commanded some notice among Spanish officials, who later considered but decided against undertaking another expedition along the more direct route to search for the golden cities.

A generation later others became interested in the Quivira story. A small party led by Francisco Leyva de Bonilla and his lieutenant Antonio Gutierrez de Humana left Mexico for the north, wintered among the pueblos (native villages) in 1591, and without permission from the Spanish government headed east in search of Quivira. It is said that they traveled across what is today the Oklahoma Panhandle on their way north to Wichita settlements in Kansas in 1592–1593, where they both died.

Then finally, in 1598, the Mexican governor Juan de Onate established a colony in north-central New Mexico, the first "official" European colony west of the Mississippi River. One purpose of settling so far north of Mexico was to provide a base of operations from which to seek the fabled wealth that had eluded Coronado. Based on knowledge gleaned from previous expeditions, Governor Onate decided to seek Quivira in 1601. He led his expedition eastward, following the main Canadian River across the Texas Panhandle, and then turned north at the Antelope Hills and traveled across most of Oklahoma.

But as Coronado had done before him, Onate found nothing remarkable at the large Wichita village in Kansas, causing him to return to his new colony soon after arrival. This quietly ended a sixty-year period of Spanish exploration into a small portion of a region that would eventually make up part of the Louisiana Purchase. The vast area that contained present-day Oklahoma technically remained French Louisiana from 1682 to 1763 and then was returned to the Spanish before the French once again obtained it, finally selling the vast wilderness to the United States in 1803.

It would therefore be left to the French/Métis explorers and voyageurs of the early 1700s traveling west from St. Louis to penetrate into the deep West to establish the fur trade among the Plains Indians, including the Mandan. Then they engaged the indigenous tribes of the foothills of the Rockies, all the while setting the stage for Napoleon to consent to the Louisiana Purchase.

WHAT JEFFERSON KNEW

In anticipation of the completion of the Louisiana Purchase, in October 1803, President Thomas Jefferson was successful in having Congress pass a bill to sponsor an upcoming expedition called the Corps of

Discovery. Congress thus approved both the bill and the president's choice to lead the corps, Meriwether Lewis, an army captain and distinguished brother of the Antient, Free and Accepted Masons. In turn Lewis chose William Clark, who was also an army captain but not a Mason at the time, as his second in command.

It now appears that Jefferson knew exactly what he wanted to achieve in promoting Lewis to lead the expedition. On the surface of things Jefferson wanted to find a continental route to the Pacific, but internally he fully expected Lewis to rediscover the antient rose lines and even perhaps the descendants of earlier Knights Templar and the Holy Bloodline.

Thomas Jefferson was particularly insistent that all observations were to be taken with extreme accuracy and that they were to be recorded in such a manner that they could be read and replicated by others. It was Jefferson's intent that all records were to be submitted to the war office so that final calculations could be made later by several qualified individuals working at the same time. To ensure against a possible loss of records, Jefferson directed the explorers to make several copies of their notes and to give them to their most trustworthy companions for safekeeping.

In a letter dated June 20, 1803, Jefferson tells Lewis:

> *Beginning at the mouth of the Missouri, you will take observations of latitude and longitude, at all remarkable points on the river, and especially at the mouths of rivers, at rapids, at islands, and other places and objects distinguished by such natural marks and characters, of a durable kind, as that they may with certainty be recognized hereafter. The courses of the river between these points of observation may be supplied by the compass, the log-line, and by time, corrected by the observations themselves. The variations of the needle, too, in different places, should be noticed.*

> *The interesting points of the portage between the heads of the Missouri, and of the water offering the best communication with the Pacific Ocean, should also be fixed by observation; and the course of that water to the ocean, in the same manner as that of the Missouri.*
>
> *Your observations are to be taken with great pains and accuracy; to be entered distinctly and intelligibly for others as well as yourself; to comprehend all the elements necessary, with the aid of the usual tales, to fix the latitude and longitude of the places at which they were taken; and are to be rendered to the war-office, for the purpose of having the calculations made concurrently by proper persons in the United States.*[4]

Rather more mysteriously (if that's possible at this point), Thomas Jefferson had earlier advised Lewis to urge any whites he met west of the Mississippi to head back east and also ordered Lewis to be on the lookout for Welsh-speaking Indians! Sadly, after successfully reaching the Pacific and then returning via the Columbia and Missouri Rivers to much fanfare and jubilation in 1806, over the following years Lewis became despondent and suicidal until he met his death at an inn just south of Nashville, Tennessee, called Grinder's Stand, on October 11, 1809.

All of this makes for fascinating speculation into the early formation of the United States and the question of what the early founding fathers, including Thomas Jefferson, knew about the lost Templar sanctuaries. With this in mind, remember that Teniers completed his painting in 1654. For the moment, though, it's the secret information that was gleaned before then by the Spanish Franciscans who stayed behind after the so-called conquerors—conquistadors—had left, which is the most compelling facet of this overall mystery!

THE FRANCISCANS AND ENIGMATIC INDIANS

One of the very first missions in the new territory, then known as Pimeria Alta, was established by the Franciscan friars accompanying Onate's expedition of 1598. However, like many of the more than forty missions that were to be established over the next hundred years, this mission was burned to the ground by the local natives. To their credit, though, this didn't stop the Franciscans, who appeared compelled by some unknown hand to penetrate ever farther into the new territory. Especially influential was the Franciscan father Alonso de Benavides, who directed the founding of ten temporary missions between 1625 and 1629 and thereafter continuously promoted the Franciscan effort, even after returning to Spain.[5]

One of the few who enjoyed some earlier success among the indigenous people was Franciscan friar Juan de Salas, who came to New Mexico in 1613 or 1622 and founded the original San Antonio Isleta Mission, which was dedicated to Saint Anthony, of course. In his later writings after he returned to Spain, Father Benavides says that the Pueblo Indians had a special fondness for Salas.

Legend has it that, in 1629, Jumano Indians went to the original mission, now known as the Old Isleta Mission, and asked for religious guidance, stating that they had come at the request of the mysterious "woman in blue," Maria de Agreda. It is said that while they were living alongside a stream some three hundred miles east-southeast of Old Isleta they were visited by what appeared to be a vision of a nun.

The real woman in blue was the early Spanish nun Sister Maria de Jesus de Agreda, who lived between 1602 and 1665. She is also known as Mary of Agreda and Maria of Agreda. Surprisingly, it is said that during her life she not only survived the Spanish Inquisition but advised the king of Spain and preached Christianity in the American Southwest, most notably in Texas, New Mexico, and Arizona.

There she is revered as the legendary woman in blue because of the miraculous nature of her preaching. The widespread effect of her missionary work in America, for which she is revered to this day, is cited in numerous historical texts of the time.

This stream was erroneously thought to be the Arkansas River but has now been identified as the present-day Concho River in Texas. Apparently Salas and fellow friar Diego Lopez followed the natives, but they found nothing when they arrived at the native village, or pueblo, Isleta Pueblo. This pueblo is again the subject of another one of those strange discrepancies, because it is actually the name of two pueblos of the ancient Tiwa tribe of remote Shoshoncan Indians. The original Old Isleta (meaning "islet") Pueblo was so named by the Spaniards because of its position on a tongue of land projecting into a stream somewhere close to today's Albuquerque, but its actual location has been the subject of considerable debate.

In 1680, Spanish settlers and Tiwa (Tigua in Spanish) Indians were driven from the Old Isleta Pueblo by the Pueblo Revolt, during which the native population rose up against the steady influx of Spanish settlers. They traveled southward to El Paso del Norte, where El Paso, Texas, exists today. Mexico Governor Antonio de Otermin, at this time representing the crown of Spain, established the Ysleta Mission (Ysleta del Sur Mission) here for the refugees. The current San Augustin de la Isleta Mission was founded on the site of the Ysleta del Sur Mission that was burned during another native uprising in 1682.[6]

The real question arising out of all of this is who were the Shoshoncan Indians referenced above? It has been noted that the Shoshoncan traditionally spoke the Shoshoni language, which is part of the Numic languages branch of the larger Uto-Aztecan language family. Assuming that the Shoshoncan were of the Southern Shoshone, they were sometimes called the Snake Indians by neighboring tribes. But the Shoshone were known to have three large divisions, not four: the Eastern Shoshone, who occupied Wyoming, northern Colorado, and Montana; the Northern Shoshone, who occupied eastern Idaho, western Wyoming, and northeastern Utah; and the Western Shoshone, who occupied Oregon, Idaho, and Utah.

So where did the Southern Shoshone come from? It is said that these Southern Shoshone were of the Tiwa people. But nothing is known about the Tiwa, or Tigua, people before their encounter with the Coronado expedition other than they occupied a series of pueblos, or concentrated habitations, all along the Rio Grande.

WHERE THE RIVERS GLISTEN

The Rio Grande is listed as the fourth or fifth longest river system in North America, depending on how you measure it. It is a natural highway of sorts in that it meanders close to two thousand miles, flowing from south-central Colorado all the way to the Gulf of Mexico. The river is formed by the joining of several streams at the base of Canby Mountain in the San Juan Mountains, just east of the Continental Divide. Perhaps the ancient Shoshoncan came down from the mountains along the glistening rivers when the prophecies or visions instructed the people, through their shaman, to scatter from their cities. Perhaps they foretold of the strangers who would come seeking others who had come before them.

Importantly for Spain, the prior activities of the somewhat misguided Spanish explorers over a sixty-year period made it possible for that nation to lay tentative claim to the region, despite the fact that ownership seemed to offer little in the way of economic compensation. The Spanish held very little understanding of the power that the many rivers flowing both westward to the Gulf of California and eastward into the Mississippi and the Gulf of Mexico held in terms of commercial travel potential, even though they had mapped most of the major rivers and their tributaries.

Aside from the Rio Grande, one of the very first rivers to be mapped by the Spanish was the Gila River, which has its source in western New Mexico. It flows southwest from the Black Range Mountains, then westward into Arizona, and then along the southern slope of the Gila Mountains through a series of canyons. Emerging from the mountains into the valley southeast of modern-day Phoenix, the river bends sharply southward along the Gila Bend Mountains, then it swings westward again near the town of Gila Bend. It flows southwestward through the Gila Mountains in Yuma County, and finally it empties into the Colorado at Yuma, Arizona.

Like its namesake, the Gila monster with its webbed feet and meandering body and long tail, the Gila River is joined by many tributaries, including the San Francisco and San Simon Rivers. Farther downstream at San Carlos Lake it is joined by the San Carlos River. It also picks up the San Pedro River and then is joined by the Santa Cruz River south of Casa Grande before receiving its last two major tributaries, the Agua Fria and Hassayampa Rivers, from the north.

Although the Gila River flows entirely within the United States, the headwaters of two tributaries—the San Pedro River and the Santa Cruz River—extend into Mexico. Spanish explorer and missionary Juan de La Asuncion was most probably the first Spaniard to see the Gila River in 1538, after following one of the two rivers that extend into Mexico. Then, in 1540, Hernando de Alarcon became one of the few early Spaniards who was actually known to have used a boat to explore north of Mexico. He sailed up the Colorado River and the Gila River; maps drawn by his expedition show the Colorado River as the Miraflores or Brazos de la Miraflores.

It was the Hohokam people (also called the Gila River people) who lived on the banks of the Gila River for at least a thousand years before the arrival of Spanish explorers. The Hohokam created large, complex civilizations along the Middle Gila River between 600 and 1450 CE. Quite ingeniously, these agriculturally based civilizations depended largely on irrigation, and it's been determined that over time more than two hundred miles of complex irrigation channels were built. The upper Gila was inhabited by the Mogollon culture over most of the same time period, in settlements like those at the Gila Cliff Dwellings National Monument, which the good friar, Marcos di Niza, most likely mistook for Cibola.

Other cliff dwellings found close to the present-day town of Campe Verde, Arizona, were built and used by the Sinagua people—

a pre-Columbian culture closely related to the Hohokam—sometime between approximately 1100 and 1425 CE. The main structure is comprised of five stories and twenty rooms and was built over the course of three centuries. It is known as Montezuma Castle and is situated about ninety feet up a sheer limestone cliff, facing the adjacent Beaver Creek that drains into the perennial Verde River, a tributary of the Salt River—the largest tributary of the Gila River.

Montezuma Castle National Monument is located at the coordinates of 34°36'40"N, 111°50'02"W, which is relatively close to the Prime Templar Meridian of 111°57'W. In this instance the name Montezuma does not relate to the Aztec emperor but is a mythological god who figures prominently in the religion of the Pueblo Indians. It was the Pueblo Indians who held that their god-king Montezuma was conceived in an ancient pueblo during the union of a beautiful virgin and a pinyon pine nut. The legend says that, although weak as a youth, Montezuma was chosen to be their unlikely leader and surprised everyone with his miracles, including the ability to produce rain.

Fig. 6.2. Montezuma Castle, Arizona, located at 34°36'40"N, 111°50'02"W. Photograph property of the author, William F. Mann.

Other legends among present-day Arizona and New Mexico tribes relay that Montezuma was the name of a great king and lawgiver of the remote past who ruled over a vast empire, including Mexico. It is said that he is buried inside a particular mountain in Arizona that allegedly bears his image. It is also said that, above all else, Montezuma taught the people how to follow the sun and the stars and the moon across the sky and how to build adobe pueblos.

Setting aside these legends for the moment, if Coronado had indeed followed the Gila River to the east he would have encountered six major rivers roughly parallel to one another and running from the northwest to the southeast. From west to east, these rivers are the Rio Grande, Pecos, Brazos, Red, Canadian, and Arkansas. The Red, Canadian, and Arkansas all drain into the mighty Mississippi; the Brazos, Red, and Rio Grande drain into the Gulf of Mexico.

The source of the six rivers has been the subject of considerable speculation and legend over the years. Putting aside the notion of the fountain of youth or manna from heaven for the moment, the source of the Red River is a particularly interesting geographic phenomenon. The Red River rises near the edge of the northwestern slope of the Llano Estacado Mesa in two forks in northern Texas and southwestern Oklahoma. The southern and largest fork, which is about 120 miles long, is generally called the Prairie Dog Town Fork. It is by the confluence of the intermittent Palo Duro Creek (*palo duro* meaning "hard wood" in Spanish) and Tierra Blanca Creek (*tierra blanca* meaning "white land").

The Llano Estacado lies at the southern end of the western high plains eco-region of the Great Plains of North America. It is part of what was once called the Great American Desert. The term Great American Desert was used up until the start of the twentieth century to describe the western part of the Great Plains east of the Rocky Mountains, from the 112th degree longitudinal meridian to about the 104th meridian. The area is now usually referred to as the High Plains, and the original term is now sometimes used to describe the arid region of North America that includes parts of northern Mexico and the American Southwest. Again, for avid movie buffs, this is the area that's been featured in a number of Clint Eastwood movies, including *High Plains Drifter.*

Why is all of this geographic information of southwestern North America another important element to this story? Interestingly, as noted previously, Teniers's painting is sometimes misnamed *St. Anthony and St. Paul in the Desert.* Could the Great American Desert be the sly reference to where the two saints can be found, lifting back the many veils of hidden symbolism and sacred geometry applied by Teniers during the initial composition of his masterpiece?

In Teniers's painting, there is definitely the hint that the two saints, in their hidden persona as an early Spanish Jesuit priest and a Franciscan friar, are consulting their notebooks, logs, and maps with respect to their archaeoastronomical positions. Could the crossed sticks be a subtle reference to the secret knowledge relating to the use of the Celtic cross in determining latitudinal and longitudinal positions?

ANCIENT ARCHAEOASTRONOMERS

Archaeoastronomy has widely been defined as the study of how people in the past understood the elements and the movements of the night sky and how they used these endless cycles in their cultures. All over the world ancient peoples have studied the position of the stars and planets in the night sky and the movement of the sun across the horizon throughout the year. Also of prime importance is the movement of the moon and its many phases across the horizon on its eighteen-to-nineteen-year cycle.

As noted previously, knowledge of these cycles helped ancient people to know when to plant their crops, migrate, celebrate religious holidays, and to otherwise advise them about other important events of the year. To ensure the correct dates for rituals and monitoring the return of the growing season a calendar with some degree of accuracy would have been necessary to their very existence.

The Hohokam were one of these ancient peoples. It was the Hohokam who built the famous ancient pueblo Casa Grande in what is now Arizona. When compared to traditional pueblo construction, it uncharacteristically consisted of multiple structures surrounded by a compound wall (see figure 6.3 on p. 190). Indeed, the Hohokam were a very

Fig. 6.3. The ruins of Casa Grande, Arizona; an early photo taken around 1900. The Casa Grande Ruins National Monument is located at 32°59'49"N, 111°31'55"W.

mysteriously advanced people. Similar to the Acadians and their construction of a series of dikes in the salt marshes of Nova Scotia for agricultural purposes, the Hohokam constructed an array of simple canals combined with weirs, using the waters of the Salt River and the Gila River.

It was between the ninth and the fifteenth centuries that the Hohokam built and maintained an extensive irrigation system that allowed them to cultivate several varieties of cotton, tobacco, maize, beans, and squash. As well, they harvested a vast assortment of wild plants, which were used for traditional medicine purposes. Later on they also used extensive dry-farming systems, primarily to grow agave for food and fiber. Their reliance on canal systems of irrigation, vital in their less than hospitable desert environment and arid climate, provided the basis for the aggregation of rural populations into stable cities. Yet, like most of the American indigenous people, they readily abandoned their urban centers and took to the wilderness mid-fifteenth century.

The largest structure on the Casa Grande site is what remains of a four-story structure that was abandoned by 1450 CE. The structure is made of caliche using the traditional adobe processes and has managed to survive the extreme weather conditions of the Sonora Desert for about seven centuries. The large house consists of outer rooms surrounding an inner structure. The outer rooms are three stories high; the inner structure is four stories high.

Casa Grande, similarly to Montezuma Castle, lies very close to the Prime 111°57' W Templar north–south longitudinal Meridian at exactly 111°31'00" W. The manner in which the four walls of the larger inner tower line up with the cardinal points of the compass—north, south, east, and west—suggests that Casa Grande was at one time used as an astronomical tower in much the same manner as the Newport Tower.

Evidence certainly suggests that the Hohokam people incorporated their knowledge of astronomy into Casa Grande's architecture. It appears that they used a window in the west wall to record the setting sun on the summer solstice (June 21). Other windows and doors at Casa Grande align with the sun or moon at significant times of the year. (The vernal equinox—March 21—also appears to be an important point in time in determining when to plant crops.)

Just to the northwest of Casa Grande lies the enigmatic Chaco Canyon, located at 36°03'37"N, 107°58'01"W. Chaco Canyon was initially inhabited by the ancient Pueblo people beginning around 2900 BCE. During the period of 850 through 1150 CE these indigenous people constructed large structures called kivas. Strangely, archaeologists have determined that around 1150 CE the settlements were abandoned, possibly because of prolonged drought but also possibly because of an infusion of strange-looking white men and women.

It is not entirely clear why the Pueblo people abandoned their extensive settlements in the mid-twelfth century. Factors examined and discussed by present-day archaeologists include global or regional climate change, prolonged periods of drought, cyclical periods of topsoil erosion, environmental degradation, deforestation, religious or cultural change, and even influence from Mesoamerican cultures. There is one enduring theme that has been dismissed by the same academics, though: that being the arrival of mysterious white men and women from the east. Enduring Pueblo legends and prophecies tell of this event and the coming of additional whites, although these would be hostile to the natives. In as much, this appears to be a similar theme across the ancient Native American population.

From an archaeoastronomical perspective, one of the more prominent structures from the Chaco culture includes Casa Rinconada, which was built between 1070 and 1110 CE. The symmetry axis defined by the two T-shaped doors is aligned with the north–south longitudinal line. Shortly after sunrise on the summer solstice, as the sun rises, a beam of light shines through a lone window on the north-northeast side of the kiva and moves downward and northward until it illuminates, on the interior west wall, one of the five larger, irregularly spaced niches in the kiva.

Nearby, at the top of Fajada Butte along a narrow ledge, is a sacred Native American site that was constructed by the ancient Anasazi around 1000 BCE. It has been given the modern-day moniker of Sun Dagger, and on the day of the summer solstice a slender beam of sunlight passes between two rock monoliths and bisects the center of a spiral-shaped petroglyph. Two parallel daggers bracket the larger spiral at the spring and fall equinoxes.

Coming back to the notion that David Teniers the Younger used the notebooks and maps of the early Spanish Jesuit and Franciscan priests and friars that were conveniently provided by Archduke Leopold Wilhelm I, it's certainly possible to accurately place the figures of Saint Anthony and Saint Paul into the Great American Desert.

Judging by the simplified drawing of the main elements found in the foreground of Teniers's painting (see figure 6.4), what is immediately recognizable is that Saint Anthony is sitting on top of a Gila monster, which easily relates to the latitudinal/longitudinal positioning of the Gila River. Here again is an example of the Renaissance painter's rather dry sense of humor. It is said that Saint Anthony was forever tempted by demons and visions and, as such, could only find relief in the wilderness. In this case Saint Anthony, in the Great American Desert, has certainly managed to control his very own personal demon by sitting on him!

Notice how Saint Anthony is also sitting atop a rough flat-topped stone known as a mesa. Again, in relative terms, the Gila River skirts

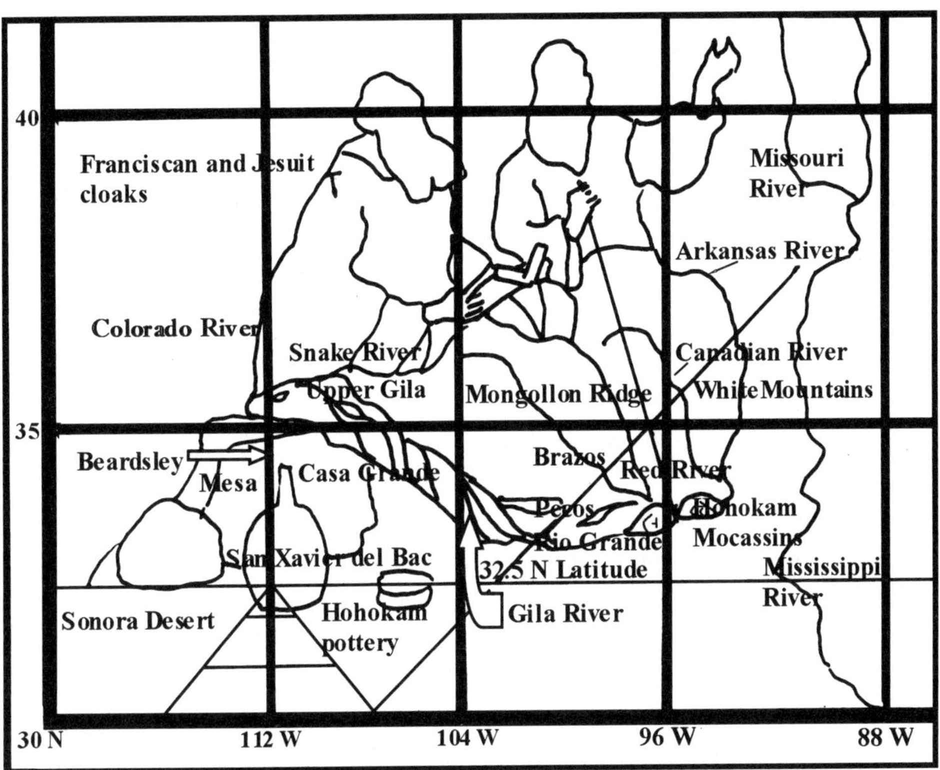

Fig. 6.4. Schematic diagram of the bottom left-hand corner of Teniers's painting *St. Anthony and St. Paul Fed by Ravens,* which demonstrates the relationship between the main elements of the painting and their relative geographical place-names in the American Southwest, based on *The Templar Meridians.* Diagram copyright of the author, William F. Mann.

the Gila Mountains near present-day Mesa, Arizona (33°24'54"N, 111°49'53"W), which rather conveniently falls within the 112-degree west longitudinal meridian's tolerance. And, again, the history of Mesa dates back at least two thousand years to the arrival of the Hohokam people, who used the small tributaries of the Gila River to feed their extensive irrigation system.

The funny thing is that Teniers has chosen to hide the stone that Saint Paul is sitting on. Nevertheless, I would wager that the stone is intended to be the perfect ashlar (the keystone) of the Masonic lodge. In this way, using the analogy of shaping the rough stone into the perfect cube, Teniers was conveying that as the initiate progresses through the degrees of the lodge he becomes shaped and perfect.

Not surprisingly then, there is a black mesa located in Oklahoma's Panhandle along the tri-state border with Colorado and New Mexico. Black mesa takes its name from the layer of black lava rock that coated the mesa about 30 million years ago. The top of the plateau is Oklahoma's highest point, at 4,973 feet above sea level, which allows for a perfect 360-degree sighting of the surrounding landscape and the daytime and nighttime sky. Black Mesa corresponds nicely to figure 6.4 in that its summit coordinates are 36°55'55"N, 102°59'51"W.

I could go on and on calling out these individual relationships, but it is now surely beyond doubt that Teniers's genius transcended time and space. Other examples can demonstrate how the flowing robes of the two saints relate to the relative positioning of the six main southwestern rivers, as well as the two main mountain ranges: the Mogollon Ridge and the White Mountains. The ancient clay pottery shown in Teniers's painting just below Saint Anthony and easily relates to the geographical area known as the Sonoran Desert surely denotes the Shoshoncan, Anasazi, and Hohokam people.

Again, the analogies are almost endless! The key to the overall mystery, though, is not to get hung up on any one relationship but instead to constantly look beyond it. Remember the message: "And in Arcadia I (am) the sum total." The key is to be able to take whatever geographical information and moral interpretation can be gleaned from the two paintings and to consolidate the total of that into an overall summation. It's "Elementary, my dear Watson, elementary!" as Arthur Conan Doyle's most famous fictional character was wont to exclaim.

"YES, BUT WHAT DOES IT ALL REALLY . . . *MEAN?*"

So, where do all of these elements lead? The summation is that Prince Henry Sinclair had thousands of years of accumulated antient knowledge at his disposal. As the hereditary grand master of the Knights Templar of Scotland and guardian of the Grail, he had been raised and initiated for the singular purpose of ensuring that the final resting place of the Templar treasure and the Grail refugees—the Holy Bloodline—would never be discovered by the noninitiated.

Over the centuries, though, there have been men who have gained an inkling as to where the Prime Templar Meridian lies and where lies the last refuge of the Knights Templar in the New World. The French explorer Pierre de La Vérendrye is one such man, as was the British explorer David Thompson and President Thomas Jefferson. Another one of those unique individuals with insights as to what lay in the West was Brigham Young, who was the driving force behind the movement of the Latter-Day Saints and their settlement of the western United States.

INTO THE DESERT

Brigham Young was the second president of the Church of Jesus Christ of Latter-Day Saints (the Mormon Church) from 1847 until his death in 1877. He followed in the footsteps of the church's spiritual founder, Joseph Smith.

Young, being a man of immense spiritual faith and energy, founded Salt Lake City and served as the first governor of the Utah Territory. Young was also controversial in that he had a total of fifty-five wives, producing fifty-six children by sixteen of those wives.[7] After his predecessor, Smith, had been killed by an armed mob in Nauvoo, Illinois, Brigham Young led his followers, the Mormon pioneers, in an exodus through the midwestern desert. Whether this trek was a result of divine intervention, secrets conveyed to him by his predecessor, or just sheer ambition, we do not know. What we *do* know is that he was a daunting force throughout his entire life and singularly guided the Mormon Church through its darkest period. He led its congregation to what they saw as a promised land, the New Jerusalem, eventually settling at the Great Salt Lake valley in present-day Utah.*

---

*One little-known fact about Brigham Young is that the great English writer Arthur Conan Doyle based his first Sherlock Holmes novel, *A Study in Scarlet,* on Mormon history—even mentioning Brigham Young by name.

Joseph Smith had earlier based the establishment of the church on teachings that he said were delivered to him by the angel Moroni, who directed him to a buried book of golden plates inscribed with a Judeo-Christian history of an ancient American civilization. But some modern-day authors have actually presented a very interesting alternative theory to Smith's official version of the story as to how the golden tablets were delivered to him. They speculate that, given that Smith was a known treasure hunter and engager of religious folk magic in his earlier years, in the wilderness surrounding where he grew up—Palmyra, New York—he had actually discovered bound copper tablets that recorded the travels of the much earlier Knights Templar and the Holy Bloodline during the earliest generations of their movement in the New World.*[8]

Henceforth the story goes that, following the often difficult reading and interpretation of the tablets, Joseph Smith wrote the Book of Mormon, which was published in Palmyra on March 26, 1830. Afterward the ever-expanding Mormon congregations received threats of mob violence. These threats were such that the congregations, over several years, moved their growing settlements initially to Kirtland, Ohio, and then to Jackson County, Missouri, and then finally to Nauvoo, Illinois, where Smith was initiated into the Nauvoo Masonic Lodge before his untimely demise.† Following Smith's death several claimants to the role of church president emerged during the succession crisis that ensued, before Brigham Young claimed the leadership

*I first heard this alternative hypothesis from the author Michael Bradley prior to his writing *Swords at Sunset.* At the time I was quite tentative about the hypothesis, given that Smith was such a spiritual and revered historical figure. However, as my own research developed I found it quite plausible that Smith discovered in upper New York state a cache that had belonged to the Grail refugees as they moved westward so many hundreds of years ago. In his early life, prior to his marriage to Emma Smith, Joseph Smith's stated occupation was that of treasure hunter.

†New York Grand Lodge records show that Joseph Smith was initiated into Freemasonry and raised to the degree of Master Mason on May 7, 1818, in Ontario Lodge No. 23 of Canandaigua, New York. Smith and several prominent Mormons, including Brigham Young, after becoming Freemasons founded a lodge in Nauvoo, Illinois, in March 1842. Those records show that Smith remained a Freemason until his death. Presently the Church of Jesus Christ of Latter-Day Saints (LDS) takes no position supporting or opposing Freemasonry.

through sheer willpower and the support of the Quorum of the Twelve Apostles.

Young was considered by both his followers and enemies alike to be the "American Moses" for helping to settle much of the American West. During the thirty years between the Mormons' arrival in Utah in 1847 and Young's death in 1877, Young directed the founding of 350 towns in the Southwest.[9] Thereby the Mormons became the most important single entity in colonizing the vastness between the Rockies and the Sierra Nevadas, and today it is said that the Mormons control the vast majority of the economy of Utah. This state was originally known as the State of Deseret.

But Brigham Young is also known for being the instigator of the Mormon Rebellion, which was a prolonged armed confrontation between Mormon settlers in the Utah Territory and the armed forces of the United States government. The confrontation lasted from May 1857 until July 1858, and unfortunately it was not bloodless. At the height of the tensions, on September 11, 1857, more than 120 California-bound settlers from Arkansas, Missouri, and other states, including unarmed men, women, and children, were killed in remote southwestern Utah by a group of local Mormon militiamen.[*10]

It was first claimed that the migrants had been killed by Native Americans. The motives behind the incident, later called the Mountain Meadows Massacre, remain a mystery. The rebellion itself had a few notable skirmishes but was generally resolved through negotiations between Mormon representatives and those of the United States.

In the aftermath of the Mormon Rebellion the federal government became stagnant because of a congressional stalemate between the Republicans and the Democrats. As a result, very little was done with respect to the Mormon issue, and in 1860 sectional strife had split the Democratic Party into northern and southern wings, indirectly leading to the election of Abraham Lincoln, a Republican, in 1860, with the American Civil war following soon after.

---

*For those who love a well-written novel, modern-day author Steve Berry used this episode in Mormon history as the central focus of his recent bestseller, *The Lincoln Myth*.

Along with the Republican majority came legislation meant to curb the Mormon practice of polygamy. Probably the best known piece of legislation is known as the Morrill Anti-Bigamy Act of 1862; however, President Abraham Lincoln did not enforce any of the laws meant to curb the Mormon practice. Instead, Lincoln gave Brigham Young tacit approval for the Mormons, in essence, to remain autonomous. In exchange, the Latter-Day Saints agreed not to become involved in the American Civil War.[11]

There is a popular concept in Mormon folklore that supports the practice of polygamy. As far back as 1853 a prominent Mormon writer and philosopher by the name of Orson Pratt had written that Jesus was married—possibly to Mary Magdalene; Mary, sister of Lazarus; and/or Martha—and that Jesus may have been a polygamist and had children. Pratt was a leader in the LDS movement and an original member of the Quorum of the Twelve Apostles under Joseph Smith and himself had seven wives and forty-five children. Pratt was also a supporter of Brigham Young from the start, and later, in Utah, Pratt's strong analytical and writing skills led Brigham Young to assign him to produce sermons and pamphlets for the Church of Jesus Christ of Latter-Day Saints.[12]

Not to be condescending in any way toward the Mormons, but could there be an underlying reason as to why the church is known as the Latter-Day Saints? The phrase "latter-day saints" implies the existence of earlier saints. Could these earlier saints have been Saint Anthony and Saint Paul? And is it possible the golden (or copper) tablets that Smith found contained hints of the prime rose line/meridian that the Mormons should ultimately seek?

The Great Salt Lake City meridian and base marker, with the coordinates of 40°46'04"N, 111°54'00"W, is located at the intersection of South Temple Street and Main Street. This marker defines the southeast boundary of Temple Square and serves as the originating point of the city's street-numbering system. In honor of the momentous feat that the marker represents, the Mutual Improvement Associations of the LDS Church and Utah Pioneer Trails and Landmarks Association erected a plaque in 1932.

The plaque, Marker Number 12, reads:

> **LATITUDE 40°46'04"—LONGITUDE 111°54'00"**
> **ALTITUDE (SIDEWALK) 4327.27 FT.**
>
> FIXED BY ORSON PRATT, ASSISTED BY HENRY G. SHERWOOD, AUGUST 3, 1847, WHEN BEGINNING THE ORIGINAL SURVEY OF "GREAT SALT LAKE CITY," AROUND THE "MORMON" TEMPLE SITE DESIGNATED BY BRIGHAM YOUNG JULY 23, 1847. THE CITY STREETS WERE NAMED AND NUMBERED FROM THIS POINT.
>
> DAVID H. BURR, FIRST U.S. SURVEYOR-GENERAL OF UTAH, LOCATED HERE IN AUGUST 1855, THE INITIAL POINT OF PUBLIC LAND SURVEYS IN UTAH, AND SET THE STONE MONUMENT, STILL PRESERVED IN POSITION.
>
> AN ASTRONOMICAL STATION, ITS STONE BASE STILL STANDING 100 FT. N. AND 50 FT. W. OF THIS CORNER WAS ESTABLISHED BY GEORGE W. DEAN, U.S.C.&G. SURVEY, SEPTEMBER 30, 1869, TO DETERMINE THE TRUE LATITUDE AND LONGITUDE; IT WAS USED TO OBTAIN CORRECT TIME AT THIS POINT UNTIL DECEMBER 30, 1897.[13]

Most amazingly, the Great Salt Lake City meridian and base marker is only four arc-minutes off the exact longitude of the Prime Templar Meridian that I identified in my previous book, *The Templar Meridians: The Secret Mapping of the New World.* Rather prophetically, if one follows W. North Temple Street westerly from Temple Square to reach the Prime Templar Meridian, one must physically cross the Jordan River to reach the Prime Templar Meridians' coordinates! And notice that the plaque acknowledges that Orson Pratt was the one to receive the honor of fixing the exact spot of the meridian and base marker.

The city plan of wide streets and consistently numbered, uniform blocks proposed by Brigham Young was certainly visionary in itself. Contained within Temple Square proper are the Salt Lake Temple, Salt Lake Tabernacle, Salt Lake Assembly Hall, the Seagull Monument, and two visitor centers. Located on the block west of Temple Square, the

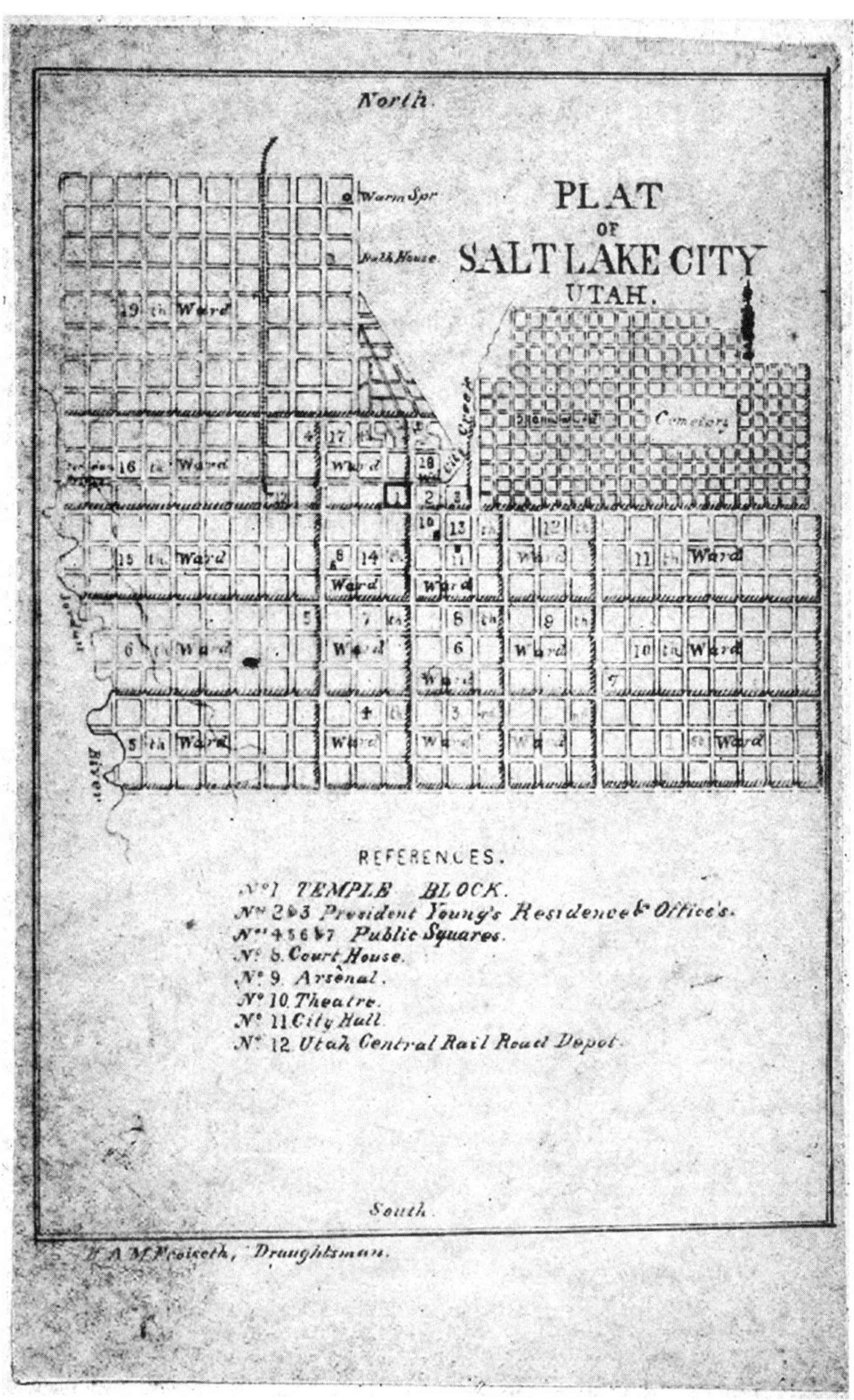

Fig. 6.5. Plat of Salt Lake City

Family History Library is the largest genealogical library in the world. It's said that the library holds a vast array of genealogical records for more than 110 countries, territories, and possessions. It is open to the general public at no charge, and the staff members are extremely professional and courteous.

Why are the genealogical records of so many people around the world so important to the Mormons? The official response is that Mormons believe that the family unit can remain intact in heaven. Their central theme is that all mankind will have the opportunity to hear and accept or reject the gospel of Jesus Christ, whether in this life or the next.[14] Of course, if someone has passed on to the next life without the opportunity, how can they be baptized and have the other necessary rites performed? Mormons believe this can be done by proxy, meaning a living family member can stand in place of one who is dead. As such, the rites of baptism, endowment, and sealing of families together for those who have died are done in LDS temples throughout the world.

The Mormon Church also believes that its members are part of the original ten lost tribes of ancient Israel that were said to have been deported from the kingdom of Israel after it was conquered by the Neo-Assyrian Empire in about 722 BCE. However, the Mormon Church claims through inspired patriarchal blessings to its members throughout the world that most members are descendants of the Tribe of Joseph through Joseph's sons Ephraim and Manasseh, making the total number of tribes twelve. The LDS Church believes that scattered descendants of Ephraim from Europe, Scandinavia, and other parts of the world have been led by the guiding hand of God to settle in the Americas along with the descendants of the Lamanites and others—and that the Americas are a promised land of liberty for those who have been led there.

The Bible records that the first three kings of Israel (Saul, David, and Solomon) reigned over all the tribes, but after the deportation, ten of the tribes went north as the kingdom of Israel and two of the tribes, Judah and Benjamin, went south as the kingdom of Judah. It is said that Jesus belonged to the House of David, which descended from the Tribe of Judah; Mary Magdalene was of the House of Bethany, which belonged to the Tribe of Benjamin. Perhaps this is taking certain latitudes at this time, but even though the Mormon Church officially no longer believes in the union of Jesus and Mary, their extensive DNA/genealogical records would surely register a unique "hit" through the many DNA testing sites that have recently proliferated via the Internet, including those directly controlled by the LDS Church. This definitely suggests that the Mormons assume descendants of the Holy Bloodline have survived to this day and that even some members of the Church of LDS are derived from the bloodline and that the LDS Church will be very interested when a specific DNA and associated markers register on the charts.

7
North by Northwest

THE NORSE

So many individual questions remain, but hopefully the answer to the larger question as to where the final New World sanctuary of the Knights Templar and the Holy Bloodline can be found is coming into focus. Assuming that the reader has been able to follow the knights' tour across North America to this point, their pattern of settlement from east to west should also be increasingly evident. And hopefully with the historical background that has been presented in relation to the establishment of New France and New Spain, it's become more than plausible that the painters and esoteric initiates Nicolas Poussin and David Teniers the Younger were privy to the secret information and mapping of New France and New Spain that was provided by their respective benefactors.

Yet there is still something missing from the larger puzzle: There's the outstanding question as to what *was* the exact secret knowledge known by Prince Henry Sinclair and those who accompanied him on his journey across the wilderness? What we do know is that the Templars' native North American allies and blood brothers facilitated the multi-generational movement of the Grail refugees from one Rose Line sanctuary to another between 1400 and 1600 CE. And logic therefore dictates that as the refugees moved west they would have naturally cohabitated with their native relations at long-established Indian encampments.

Fig. 7.1. The Gokstad Viking ship, late ninth century, Viking Ship Museum, Oslo, Norway. Photograph property of the author, William F. Mann.

Why, then, do mysterious stone ruins and rune stones scattered across North America suggest that separate Rose Line settlements with stone fortifications were established along the antient Templar meridians? Perhaps the answer lies in these structures' archaeoastronomical alignments. Or perhaps it was because the indigenous people were primarily nomadic and therefore didn't maintain permanent structures that could be shared. Or just perhaps Sinclair and his entourage didn't entirely trust their native allies enough to live with them (and vice versa) due to lasting memories of the rather tenuous relationship that had existed between the natives and their antecedents in the New World: the Vikings!

Remember that most of the inner circles of Templars, including Prince Henry Sinclair himself, were direct descendants of those original knights who had come from Normandy. Those ancestors had fought alongside William "the Bastard," who ceremoniously became William the Conqueror after defeating and killing his rival Harold Godwinson at the Battle of Hastings on October 14, 1066. William himself was a descendant of Rollo, who was probably the greatest of the Viking raiders. Rollo first began raiding in the late ninth century in the area of northern France that would become known as Normandy.

Sometime before 911, Rollo and King Charles the Simple of France reached an agreement whereby the northwestern county of Rouen, which later became the regional district of Normandy, was granted to Rollo from the king. Normandy was then used as a base when Danish/Norse attacks on England were renewed at the end of the tenth century, culminating in William's defeat of Harold about six miles from William's castle at Hastings in East Anglia (present-day East Sussex, England).[1] Consequently, after the consolidation of his power in England and a confirmation of his Christianity, William, by then the duke of Normandy, became the first Norman king of England, reigning from 1066 until his death in 1087.

It is recorded that after pledging their undying blood allegiance to William, upward of twelve Saint Clair knights supported him at the Battle of Hastings. It's not surprising then that these Saint Clair knights were also descendants of Rollo. In part, Rollo's claim to the crown traces back to the Norse sagas *Orkneyinga* and *Heimskringla,* which together present a direct lineage of Rollo going back to Fornjot, the very first king to emerge and reign over Finland and Kvenland. The claimed line leading to Rollo also includes Rognvald Eysteinsson, an impressive individual in his own right who was the founder of the earldom of Orkney.

The *Orkneyinga* saga relays that Rognvald was made the earl of More by the Norwegian king Harald Fairhair. Rognvald had accompanied the king on a great military expedition wherein the islands of Shetland and Orkney were cleared of Vikings. Remember that at this time the islands of Shetland and Orkney belonged to Norway. The Vikings had first raided Norway before continuing on to Scotland, Ireland, and the Isle of Man. The *Orkneyinga* narrative tells us that during this campaign Rognvald's son Ivarr was killed, and Harald granted Rognvald the islands of Orkney and Shetland to compensate for his personal loss. Quite surprisingly, Rognvald himself then decided to return to Norway, giving the northern isles to his brother Sigurd Eysteinsson. Sigurd had been the front man (first to attack) on King Harald's ship, and after sailing back east the king gave Sigurd the title of earl. Picking up on the story, the *Heimskringla* states specifically that Sigurd was the first earl of Orkney, which is the position that Prince Henry Sinclair would eventually assume through Queen Margaret of Norway, the widow of King Haakon VI of Norway.

Coming full circle again, Prince Henry Sinclair would also eventually hold the title of earl of Orkney under the banner of King Haakon of Norway. Prior to this he succeeded his father, William Sinclair, as baron of Roslin, Pentland, and Cousland, a group of strategic properties in Lothian, Scotland, which by the time that Henry was born in 1345 was the seat of the Scottish St. Clairs, or Sinclairs. Roslin, or Rosslyn, Castle thus became the central stronghold of the French/Scottish Knights Templar following their escape in 1307 from France, ultimately becoming a hotbed for French/Scottish Rite Freemasonry and its associated Templarism.

At this point it is important to reemphasize that Norway controlled the Orkney Islands during the fourteenth century and was in fierce competition with the Hanseatic League, which controlled most of the Baltic trade. As emphasized previously, the Hanseatic League, which was also known as the Hansa Teutonica, was a confederation of commercial merchant guilds and their market towns, which dominated trade along the coast of northern Europe.* From the thirteenth to seventeenth centuries, the confederation stretched from the Baltic to the North Sea and inland.[2]

Obviously the fierce battle was not only over supremacy of Scandinavian and Baltic sea trade but was also the continuation of a battle between the Teutonic Knights and Knights Templar for the ultimate treasure that had disappeared from Jerusalem following the First Crusade. Less than obvious was what appears to have been a secret agreement between Queen Margaret, who was by then the widow of King Haakon VI, and Prince Henry Sinclair. In exchange for Sinclair's seagoing services in protecting the Orkneys against the Hanseatic League, Margaret, as queen regent of Norway, provided invaluable information to Prince Henry confirming the extent of Norse exploration in the New World.

Modern-day historians certainly now acknowledge that Viking seafarers set sail for the New World around 1000 CE. A popular Icelandic saga tells of the exploits of Leif Eriksson, a Viking chieftain from Greenland who sailed westward to what was then termed an unknown land. According to the saga, Eriksson stopped for a bit on what is now presumed to be Baffin Island (in Canada) before heading south to a place he called Vinland. The saga goes on to say that it was on Baffin Island that he walked the coast—named Helluland, which is an Old Norse word meaning "stone-slab land."

---

*Members of the Hanseatic League were both individual Low German merchants and towns where these merchants held citizenship. However, not all of the towns with Low German merchant communities were members of the league. Hanseatic merchants could also come from settlements not ruled by German town law.

Fig. 7.2. A bust of Anne Stine Ingstad and Helge Ingstad that stands outside of the Viking Ship Museum in Oslo, Norway, with an archway that is indicative of the joining of the Old and New Worlds. Photograph property of the author, William F. Mann.

It is now also widely accepted that Bjarni Herjolfsson, in 986 CE, was purportedly blown off course by a severe storm on his way from Iceland to Greenland and that he most likely ended up in Newfoundland. There are many, however, who believe that he sailed all the way down the eastern seaboard, even entering the Gulf of Mexico. Learning of Bjarni's earlier journey, Leif Eriksson is said to have established a colony in this New World. This colony has been presumed to be the L'Anse aux Meadows site uncovered by Anne Stine Ingstad and her husband, Helge Ingstad. However, it is thought to have been very short-lived due to its remoteness and the attacks on it by Native Americans indigenous to the area.

Anne Stine Ingstad and her husband, Helge Ingstad, discovered the remains of the Viking settlement at L'Anse aux Meadows in 1960. Before then the couple had only theorized that the Avalon Peninsula in Newfoundland would have been the most logical place for a Viking landing in the New World. The story is that the couple asked various fishermen along the peninsula whether they were aware of any physical anomalies in the landscape. One such local eventually took them to the exact spot where the remains of a Viking settlement lay under a foot of silt and grass. Upon recognizing the mounds for what they really were, the Norwegian couple set about to excavate them, uncovering a variety of Viking relics that confirmed their conjectures, thereby becoming heroes in their native Norway.

The small settlement discovered at L'Anse aux Meadows is today thought to have been a strategically positioned base camp for exploration down both the St. Lawrence River and southerly along the eastern seaboard, possibly as far as Norumbega. Many early maps show Norumbega extending as far south as North Carolina, including the Newport Tower, in Newport, Rhode Island. More recently, though, archaeologist Patricia Sutherland, an adjunct professor of archaeology at Memorial University in Newfoundland and a research fellow at the

University of Aberdeen in Scotland, discovered a second Viking camp in the Tanfield Valley, on the southeast coast of Baffin Island.

Sutherland's team discovered more than twenty whetstones that bear grooves containing traces of copper alloys such as bronze—materials known to have been made by Viking metalsmiths—which was unknown among the Arctic's native inhabitants. Sutherland states that the site shows evidence of several occupations and several radiocarbon dates indicating that the valley was indeed occupied in both the tenth and fourteenth centuries. The microscopic streaks of bronze, brass, and smelted iron that Sutherland and her colleagues detected—clear evidence of European metallurgy—give way to the notion that this was another strategically positioned Viking base camp, leading to the copper deposits of Isle Royale via Hudson Bay.

Published in October 2012, a *National Geographic* article written by Heather Pringle and Patricia Sutherland speculated that parties of Viking seafarers traveled across the North Atlantic sea to the Canadian Arctic to trade and barter with the indigenous Dorset/Inuit people. Sutherland believes that Viking traders likely offered bits of iron and pieces of wood that could be carved into figurines and other goods in exchange for valuable walrus ivory, Arctic furs, and other indiginous materials. What's most amazing about this whole premise is that it has always been thought that the Vikings and North American indigenous people had no friendly contact whatsoever.

The Canadian Museum of History, located in Gatineau, Québec, across the river from Ottawa, has just put on display a small, wooden carving found on Baffin Island, attributable to the Dorset/Inuit people, which has been carbon-dated to the fourteenth century. What's even more amazing is that the figurine displays a monklike figure in a European habit, providing irrefutable proof that the Dorset people came into contact with Europeans prior to generally acknowledged seventeenth-century contact. The museum's director of research and content, David Morrison, Ph.D., has even gone so far as to state that out of the thousands of artifacts and relics currently in the museum's possession this tiny figurine is by far the museum's most valuable piece.

Further evidence discovered by Patricia Sutherland suggests that the indigenous Arctic hunters known as the Dorset people had also camped at the site over a series of generations. This certainly raises the distinct possibility that they had made friendly contact with the Vikings, in that the indigineous people would not have repeatedly returned to the site if the Vikings on any occasion had been violent toward these trading partners. Indeed, a Native American woman may even have voyaged to northern Europe with the Vikings, according to a provocative new DNA study that was recently published online in the *American Journal of Physical Anthropology.*

Then there is the intriguing speculation presented online by Donald Wiedman of Toronto, who was born and raised in St. François, Laval, Québec. Although he has no academic credentials as an archaeologist or historian, he nonetheless has uncovered what definitely appears to be a Viking earth ring—the base of a wooden palisade—that looks incredibly similar to the Fyrkat Viking earth ring in Denmark that is located at 56°37'24"N, 9°46'14"E.[3]

Wiedman speculates that the St. François, Laval, location is the settlement site of the Thorfinn Karlsefni 1009 CE expedition. In part this speculation depends on the notation in the sagas that the Karlsefni settlement was known for its peaceful relations between the indigenous people and the Norsemen. The sagas say that the two sides bartered furs and gray-squirrel skins for milk and red cloth over several seasons. Gray squirrels are common to this area and not found farther north, toward the Arctic Circle, so the logical conclusion is that the Baffin Island camp could not have been the Karlsefni settlement.

Fyrkat is a former Viking ring fortress in Denmark, dating from 980 CE. It is located near the town of Hobro, some distance from the end of the Mariager Fjord in northern Jutland (mainland Denmark). The fortress is strategically positioned on a narrow piece of land, a promontory of sorts, with a large stream on one side and swampy areas on the other sides. It would have enabled control of the traffic on the mainland route between Aalborg and Aarhus, Denmark.

What I find most fascinating about Donald Wiedman's discovery is the relative location and place-name—St. François, Laval—of the earth fortress. Located at the extreme east of Île Jésus, its exact location is again a promontory of sorts, bound on the north by the Rivière des Mille Îles and to the south by the Rivière des Prairies. Lying on the coordinates of 45°36'N and 70°49'W, the fortress was strategically located in a manner that allowed for the control of the native trade between the Algonquin and Iroquois Nations that are known to have inhabited the area. (Recall that this area was also the home of Catherine "Kateri" Tegakwitha.)

Strategically, Rivière des Mille Îles rises at the narrowing of the Lac des Deux-Montagnes (Lake of Two Mountains), the area where the Ottawa River widens as it feeds into the St. Lawrence at Montreal, and flows west to east. It joins the Rivière des Prairies at the eastern tip of Île Jésus, which shortly thereafter joins the St. Lawrence at the eastern tip of the Island of Montreal. As its name suggests, the river contains many small islands that are part of the Hochelaga Archipelago. From a relative positioning, the ring fortress at St. François, Laval, is approximately 80 degrees west and 11 degrees south of the Frykat ring fortress,

Fig. 7.3. A 1955 air photo of Frykat ring fortress, which is located at Hobro, on the mainland promontory of Denmark just outside the present-day city and port of Aarhus. The entrances to the fortress are aligned to the four cardinal points.

which strongly suggests an archaeoastronomical relationship between the two Viking sites.

Could the place-name of the settlement site be a subtle clue, relating in some way to the previously noted Jesuit bishop, Saint François de Laval? As mentioned, it was in 1674, fifteen years after his arrival in New France, that Laval was appointed the first bishop of Québec by Pope Alexander VII. Remember that this date closely follows the date that *St. Anthony and St. Paul Fed by Ravens* was painted by David Teniers the Younger. As discussed, Laval's diocesan territory originally included the territory contained in Teniers's painting, extending even to the foothills of the Rocky Mountains, which corresponds to the land of the entire, larger Algonquin Nation. And, again, Laval was canonized for his stated pastoral work among the aboriginal people of New France and for trying to defend the natives from being exploited by European merchants, who attempted at that time to control the inland fur trade.

François de Laval was a member of one of the most powerful generational families of Norman origin in France—the Montmorencys—a family that over the years provided numerous grand masters to the French crown and to various knightly orders. This family line included Henry de Montmorency, who was grand master of the Knights Templar in 1574.* Knowing this, perhaps there is more to François de Laval than first meets the eye. It certainly appears that the bishop knew a great deal more about the rose line positioning of inland earth forts, castle ruins, and other stone evidence of Norse exploration and settlement in New France than has just recently come to light.

The bishop certainly would have been privy to one very important fact that surrounds the Vikings. The earliest marauders coming south from the larger Denmark Nation starting in the eighth century may have been pagans, but those who sailed west in the tenth and eleventh centuries were definitely early Norse Christian. In many cases monks

---

*Relatively close to St. François, Laval, Québec, is the aptly named Montmorency Falls on the Montmorency River. Some ninety-eight feet higher than Niagara Falls, it is the highest waterfall in the province of Québec. It was given its name in 1613 by Samuel de Champlain, in honor of Henri II, Duke de Montmorency, who served as viceroy of New France from 1620 until 1625.

were even purported to be among the early seafaring Norse Christians. These men were by no means unsophisticated and were guided by information provided to them by the various head monks who had been secretly sanctioned by the Cistercians and, more often than not, were also descendants of the St. Clairs.

In fact, a surprising number of the earliest northern European abbeys are directly connected to the Sinclair family. This includes Eynhallow, built under the direction of a Sinclair who came from Melrose in 1117 CE, and Tintern Abbey, built by the son-in-law of Robert Sinclair.[4] The son-in-law's name was Fitz-Hamo (the son of Hamo), suggesting another strategic maritial alliance between the Sinclairs and a different branch of the early Norse settlers. Many other Cistercian abbeys were founded in the twelfth century throughout the Orkney Islands, in Scotland, in Surrey and Essex in England, around Hereford (what was once part of Wales), and in Wales itself.

Eynhallow is known as the Holy Island of the Orkneys. Local Orkney fairy tales across the island that speak of the Finfolk (little people) suggest that the Hildaland spoken of in the Norse sagas and Eynhallow were one and the same. In the summertime it is said that the Finfolk were believed to dwell on the magical, invisible island of Hildaland, returning to their beloved undersea kingdom of Finfolkaheem in the winter. Although it may be that their summer residence, Hildaland (meaning "hidden land"), was made up of a number of distinct islands, in time it came to be regarded as one. Of course, Orkney is also made up of a series of islands.

RELIGIOUS MANEUVERS

Much can be said about the Cistercians who accompanied not only Prince Henry Sinclair on his journey but whose spiritual leader—the highly influential Saint Bernard of Clairvaux—was the figurehead and promoter of the Second Crusade. The Cistercian order was also often called the Bernardines, after their founder. As previously mentioned, they were also known as the White Monks in reference to the color of the *cuccula,* or white choir robe, worn over their habits. Remember that the medieval Knights Templar also wore a white mantle. In contrast, the Benedictine monks wore black cucculas.

But one really needs to go back some hundred years, before the Cistercians' true success, to understand the underlying foundations of their order. In 1098 CE, after recovering from the initial onslaught of the original Viking raiders, a Benedictine abbot by the name of Robert of Molesme left his monastery church of Cluny Abbey in Burgundy with a small group of followers under the blessing of Pope Urban II. It bears repeating that it was Pope Urban II, along with Peter the Hermit, who had instigated the First Crusade. Robert's small group acquired a plot of marshland just south of Dijon called Cîteaux (the Latin is "Cistercium"). Cisteaux means "reeds" in Old French, and it was under a new abbot—Alberic—that the group flourished. It was at this time that they switched to the white habit. The belief was that they had found the true white light and purity of God.

From a strategic perspective, Alberic turned out to be more of a diplomat than an abbot, forging a mysterious alliance with the dukes of Burgundy. In 1108, Alberic died and was soon succeeded by Stephen Harding, and by 1111, under Stephen, the ranks had grown exponentially at Cîteaux, along with the monastery's coffers. That same year a supremely eloquent, strong-willed mystic named Bernard arrived at Cîteaux to join the order. He had come from Cluny Abbey with thirty-five of his relatives and friends.

As they say, the rest is history.

In 1115, Count Hughes de Payens of Champagne deeded a large tract of land some forty miles east of Troyes to the order. Subsequently Bernard led twelve monks there to found the Abbey of Clairvaux, again within the duchy of Burgandy. Rather amazingly, this single abbey led to the establishment of thriving abbeys across all of Europe, including parts of Scandinavia. This explosive expansion may have been due in part to the fact that, by 1129, Clairvaux Abbey may have become the temporary repository of some or all of the original Templar treasure that

Fig.7.4. Early thirteenth-century woodcut that depicts Bernard of Clairvaux giving his blessing to a Poor Knight of the Temple before going off to the Second Crusade

had been brought back from Jerusalem by the original nine knights, led by the aforementioned Champagne nobleman Hughes de Payens.

Rather coincidently, it was in 1129 that the Order of the Knights Templar was officially sanctioned by the church at the Council of Troyes, which was led by Pope Honorius II, who had been made a cardinal by none other than Pope Urban II. One could definitely say that the "fix was in" around the start of the twelfth century in the heart of Burgandy.

Pope Paschal II was pope from August 1099 until his death in 1118, being consecrated as pope in succession to Pope Urban II. Not surprisingly, Father Pascalis and Bernard of Clairvaux were both monks at Cluny. It therefore again comes as no surprise that the first bishop of America was appointed during Paschal II's reign, nearly four centuries before Columbus's first voyage across the Atlantic. It is recorded that Bishop Erik, or Henricus, Gnupsson was born in Iceland and was specifically given domain over the the provinces of Iceland, Greenland, and Vinland, quietly including Norumbega and the Newport Tower.

It was also Pope Paschal II who issued the papal bull *Pie postulatio voluntatis,* which in February of 1113 confirmed as a religious order the Hospital of St. John of Jerusalem, later known as the Knights Hospitaller. Currently in Canada this order has combined with the Masonic Knights Templar order and is known as the Sovereign Great Priory of the United Religious and Military Orders of St. John of Jerusalem, Palestine, Rhodes, and Malta, and of the Temple. (I am presently a grand council officer of the combined Order and, as such, can also be considered to be a Knight of St. John and a Knight of Malta.) The 1113 CE papal bull also confirmed the Hospitaller order's acquisitions and donations in Europe and Asia and exempted it from all authority save that of the pope, similar to what was granted to the Knights Templar in 1129 through the Council of Troyes.[5]

The Council of Troyes was a pivotal moment in the early history of the Order of the Temple, otherwise known as the Poor Fellow Soldiers of Christ and the Temple of Solomon. The assembly marked the church's formal approval of a formal rule (regulations for the observance of a religious life) for this group of knights as set out by Bernard of Clairvaux. It was in 1127 that their leader, the Champagne knight Hughes de Payens, first toured the West to seek backing for the Templar order and also to recruit men for a planned crusade against Damascus. It appears that he was more than successful, soliciting large grants of land and money in Champagne, Flanders, and Anjou. It was the lesser-known papal legate, Matthew of Albano, who presided over the Council of Troyes where Hughes, supported by Bernard, set out the basic precepts for his knights. The Order was to be governed by a grand master, who would fall under the jurisdiction of the patriarch of Jerusalem. The churchmen present dissected Hughes' proposals and with the guiding hand of Bernard of Clairvaux a rule of seventy-two clauses was drafted. This approval for the new Order by the pope thus enabled it to attract substantial support over the next few years and laid the foundations for its long-term existence.

Coming full circle again, during the fourteenth century Prince Henry Sinclair's position as hereditary grand master of the Knights Templar of Scotland was still recognized by the Kalmar Union (although the original Order of the Knights Templar had been officially disbanded in 1308 by Pope Clement V). The Kalmar Union, or Union of Calmar, was formed to counter the Hanseatic League. It brought together Danish, Norwegian, and Swedish interests, along with Venetian interests, from 1397 to 1523. It was orchestrated by none other than the magnificent Queen Margaret—the daughter of King Valdemar IV of Denmark—who herself had been strategically married to King Haakon VI of Norway and Sweden to counter the Hanseatic League. As we know, this relationship with Queen Margaret provided Sinclair with the seafaring knowledge, as well as with direct assistance from the Venetian Zeno family. Entrusted as Sinclair no doubt was with both the Templar treasure and relics and living members of the Holy Bloodline, nothing was left to chance. Prince Henry Sinclair's absolute authority over the secret voyage was thus secured.

Logic and reason definitely lead to the conclusion that Prince Henry and his trusted followers knew without a doubt where they were going in the New World by following the antient rose lines/meridians. And, without a doubt, Prince Henry and his trusted followers absolutely knew what they would find when they got there. Just to make sure, earlier generations had left hidden signs, seals, and tokens carved in stone and planted in oak groves across North America for the initiated to recognize.

CARVED IN STONE

The coastal and inland waterways of both North and South America certainly lent themselves to extensive exploration and settlement not only by the Norse but also by those who came before them; so there should be no suggestion that the Vikings were the first New World explorers. Of course, waves of ancient mariners, beginning with the most ancient of mariners, Neolithic man, and continuing on to include the Phoenicians, Carthaginians, Egyptians, Celts, Greeks, Roman, Chinese, Libyans, Hebrew, and Irish, all took their turn in what now appears to be the longest and most highly secretive and lucrative trade monopoly in history. Each wave built upon information passed down or gleaned from prior transatlantic journeys. Their explorations focused not only on exploiting natural resources such as animal furs, antlers and tusks, and the immense deposits of copper found at Isle Royale in Lake Superior but also extended, as previously mentioned, to other base metals, including gold and silver, and scarce earth minerals such as titanium and manganese.

It is thought that each of the major rivers of North America—including the St. Lawrence, Mississippi, Ohio, St. Croix, Missouri, Yellowstone, Arkansas, Canadian, Red, and Rio Grande—as well as the Gulf of Mexico and Hudson Bay, played a major role in the inland exploration of North America by making up a collective highway system upon which the explorers could travel. But what shouldn't be forgotten in all of this is the one common denominator, namely the indigenous people of the Americas. From all of the evidence presented so far, one

Fig. 7.5. Schematic diagram illustrating the major rivers of the United States

can only surmise that the native peoples recognized the true benefit of receiving these foreigners with grace and diplomacy, for the Indians had peace and prosperity in mind. Also true was the fact that the foreigners had items that the Indians coveted in trade, including metal goods and fish hooks—both of which would have been prized by the natives. Some native legends even tell of how Glooscap taught the Mi'kmaq to fish with nets weighted down by lead beads.

With this in mind there's surely a great deal of evidence to suggest that the early Norse Christians, among others, traveled extensively within the New World to reopen various trade centers and to confirm the archeaoastronomical information already in their possession. This suggestion probably comes as no surprise to many. Given that there is a substantial amount of archaeological evidence suggesting that the Nordic presence in America actually dates back well over eight hundred years, it's logical to assume that the Norse followed a well-established trade route that incorporated several base camps that ancient explorers and traders had used for centuries.

As discussed earlier, Swedish farmer Olof Ohman unearthed a Viking relic in Minnesota in 1898, which is popularly known as the Kensington Runestone. Unfortunately, this discovery ignited a heated debate about the stone's authenticity that continues to this day. That said, I believe that the authenticity of this ancient marker has now been proved beyond a doubt by Scott Wolter. It demonstrates, with irrefutable proof, that medieval explorers from northern Europe reached the center of North America at least 130 years before Christopher Columbus.[6]

Scott, who is my good friend and colleague, is a certified forensic geologist and, as we have established, the host of the TV show *America Unearthed.* He admirably took up the case of the Kensington Runestone more than a decade ago. His microscopic analysis of the ruts that formed the glyphs revealed that oxidation residue surrounded each of the characters, demonstrating that the modern overscoring had been done on top of the ruts. Significantly, Scott's ongoing work and constant findings relating to the mysterious Hooked X found in the carved message support the first geological analysis of the rune stone, which when conducted in 1910 also found the stone to be genuine.

The Kensington Runestone is not an isolated Viking artifact. On the contrary, it's one of several Norse marker stones discovered in North America, many of which have been found in the very heart of North America, namely Oklahoma. The three Heavener Runestones, as they are now known, found in Heavener, Oklahoma, seem to offer further evidence of a Viking/Norse presence in North America. The Heavener Runestones have all been dated to the early eleventh century, which would make them several centuries older than the Kensington Runestone, predating it by some three hundred years.

Another runestone—the Vérendrye Runestone—so named for its discovery by the sieur de la Vérendrye, was discovered in 1783, near Minot, North Dakota, more than a century before the discovery of the Kensington Runestone. Mysteriously, the rune stone discovered by Pierre Gaultier de Varennes, Sieur de la Vérendrye, was shipped back to France, by the Jesuits no less, where it disappeared, never to be seen again.

Pierre Gaultier was born at the St. Sulpician Mission in Trois-Rivières, Québec, which at the time was a major Algonquin settlement and trading area. Pierre was the youngest son of René Gaultier de Varennes, who came to Canada as a soldier in 1665, and Marie, who was the daughter of Pierre Boucher (the appointed governor of Trois-Rivières) and a mother who was of Algonquin descent. Here again is a prime example of the strategic intermarriage between a French family of lesser nobility (Gaultier) and the native Algonquin. Interestingly, the Gaultiers came from the Anjou area of France; Varennes and La Vérendrye were two of their ancient estates.

Another stone, the Poteau Runestone, was discovered in 1967. This stone is a bit more controversial (if that's possible), given that most of its characters are said to belong to the Elder Futhark language, which was in use in the second to eighth centuries. Then there is the Shawnee Runestone, which was found in August of 1969 in Shawnee, central Oklahoma, approximately one mile from the North Canadian River. The North Canadian River, a tributary of the larger Canadian River, together with the Arkansas River, again figures very prominently in the early Spanish and Jesuit explorations.

A MESSAGE TO THE WISE

An interesting theory put forward by Scott Wolter is that the inscription on the Kensington Runestone contains a secret, multilayered code relating to the Holy Grail/Holy Bloodline, similar to the code that researchers discovered at Rennes-le-Château in France. Even Scott was pleasantly surprised to discover Templar crosses alongside some of the runic inscriptions, much like the crosses found on the cornerstone of the Church of Notre-Dame in Old Montreal.

Scott Wolter believes that the runestone was intended to act as a boundary deed and surveying marker along the Continental Divide in much the same way that the Salt Lake City meridian and base marker established the Mormons' prime meridian. This is something I also firmly believe, in that it was a common practice among the Europeans but is foreign to the indigenous people of North America. Native North Americans see themselves as stewards of the land and not in any way as an owner of the land. Therefore, land claims are foreign to them.

The funny thing is that if the Holy Bloodline is ultimately proved beyond a doubt, the Kensington Runestone and other runestone markers may one day end up in the International Court of Justice, which is located in The Hague. One day these stone markers may provide the necessary evidence that North America can be rightfully claimed by a partnership consisting of the Holy Bloodline, the Knights Templar, the Cistercians, and their blood brothers, the Native Americans.

Even in 1566, when the Venetian mapmaker Bolognino Zaltieri drew up his famous map, the area west of the Mississippi and north of New Spain was shown as Avacal and Terra in Cognita, meaning "unrecognized land." He showed Larcadia, La Nova Franza, Quivira Pro, and even Terra de Norumbega, but nothing beyond this. Or did he? The translation of the Old Venetian word *avancal* means "to advance, to bring forward, to raise to a higher degree."

Here once again is a hidden clue that this was the land of the antient initiate who had attained a higher understanding and thus was responsible for the advancement of the Holy Bloodline to the west.

Fig. 7.6. Zaltieri's map of 1566, which incorporates most of the geographical information available at the time. Courtesy of the British Library, London, England.

Remember that the Zeno map, which accompanied the Zeno Narrative, was produced in Venice around the same time: 1555.

It would have been extremely important to the Venetians, in their own battle of shipping supremacy with the Genoans during the twelfth to seventeenth centuries, to conceal any knowledge of a far-off land that offered so many trade prospects. Remember that the Zeno family had offered their services to Prince Henry Sinclair in ensuring that the Templar New World expedition would arrive at Arcadia safely. Not to lessen their involvement in any manner, it now appears as though their participation in Prince Henry's expedition was also in part self-serving, which of course would have been readily accepted by the other involved parties.

What this also suggests is that even in the sixteenth and seventeenth centuries there appeared to be a concerted effort, although rather covert, by a secret society or rival secret societies to establish a future claim to North America. As noted in the introduction to this book, even to this day it appears as though the battle is still raging in some royal circles in anticipation of what may yet be discovered.

With this in mind, the Canadian government has recently made a particular spectacle of the discovery of one of the sunken ships from the British Franklin expedition, which in 1845 set out in two ships, the HMS *Terror* and HMS *Erebus,* to find the Northwest Passage via Hudson Bay. The expedition, led by Sir John Franklin, set sail from Greenhithe, England, on the morning of May 19, 1845, with a crew of 24 officers and 110 men. The ships stopped briefly in Stromness Harbour in the Orkney Islands in northern Scotland (the islands were formally transferred into Scotland's ownership in 1468). From there they sailed to Greenland with HMS *Rattler* and the transport ship *Barretto Junior.*

Further investigation determined that the discovered ship was the HMS *Erebus,* which then prime minister Stephen Harper personally confirmed on Wednesday, October 1, 2014, in the Canadian House of Commons. In response, Queen Elizabeth II personally congratulated Prime Minister Harper and the Canadian government on behalf of all the British people in what she claimed was a most tremendous discovery.

The Franklin expedition was doomed right from the start, because its leader, Sir John Franklin, obviously was not privy to the earlier secret information and knowledge relating to the New World. In addition, when the two ships got stuck in the ice just off King William Island in James Bay, the expedition appeared not to take advantage of the local knowledge and offer of assistance from the local Dorset people. As a result, the entire expedition perished over the next few seasons but not before some crew members had resorted to cannibalism. Ultimately the shifting ice broke up the two abandoned ships, and they sank to the bottom of James Bay.

Sadly, in 1854, John Rae of the Rae-Anderson Arctic expedition, while surveying the nearby Boothia Peninsula for the Hudson's Bay Company, discovered further evidence of the lost men's fate and reported back to the British admiralty on his findings, which included the rather grim evidence of cannibalism among the crew. This led to Rae being ostracized and having his rather distinguished career shattered. He died a broken man, and it would not be until 2014 that his reputation would be posthumously restored.

During the Rae-Anderson expedition, John Rae made it all the way northward on snowshoes beyond Hudson Bay to Repulse Bay with two other men. At Repulse Bay, which is directly atop the Arctic Circle, he found several Inuit families who had come to trade relics. The Inuit told Rae that four winters previously some other Inuit had met at least forty white men who were dragging a boat south. They described their leader as a tall, stout man with a telescope, obviously referring to John Franklin. The men had communicated with gestures that their ships had been crushed by ice, and they were going south to hunt deer, declining the Inuit's help. When the Inuit returned the following spring they found about thirty corpses and signs of cannibalism. One of the artifacts Rae bought from the Inuit was a small silver plate that was engraved on the back with the name Sir John Franklin, K.C.H. With this important information Rae chose not to continue exploring. Instead, he left Repulse Bay on August 4, 1854, as soon as the ice had cleared, only to be received back in London with ridicule over his concluding remarks about the cannibalism that had occurred among the starving crew. The ridicule was relentless and led by none other than Franklin's widow, Lady Jane (Griffin) Franklin, who would come to be known as "the heroic widow who refused to believe in her own widowhood."

The rather Monty Pythonish irony to the whole situation is that millions of dollars have been spent over the past 150 years by several expeditions, both British and Canadian, seeking the remains of the two ships. The ultimate location of HMS *Erebus* was determined when someone finally listened to the oral stories of the native people in the area, who pinpointed exactly where the ship lay from stories that had been passed down from one generation to another. If the Canadian and British governments are looking for a solid claim to the Canadian Arctic, and maybe more, then they should look to those who are still considered to be the "adopted children" of Queen Victoria—the First Nations people.

Perhaps a page should be taken out of Lewis and Clark's playbook. In 1804, after pushing up the Missouri River from their base camp in St. Louis, the expedition wintered in Fort Mandan, North Dakota, surviving only through the kindness of the native Indians. But the expedition would next be entering the territories of the Shoshone and Blackfoot, two First Nations that were still proud warriors and fiercely protective of their role as guardians of the western plains, including the foothills of the Rockies.

Rather coincidently, the native wife of a French trapper hired at Fort Mandan to act as an additional interpreter turned out to be the long-lost sister of the Shoshone Indian's leader, Chief Cameahwait. The trapper's name was Toussaint Charbonneau, and his wife's name was Sacagawea. Due to the later writings of historian Grace Raymond Hebard and novelist Emery Dye, Sacagawea was to be become a legendary figure. There were also whispers that Sacagawea was herself a member of the Holy Bloodline.

The presence of Charbonneau's Indian bride would no doubt facilitate negotiations in that she had an amazing capacity for various languages, along with the fact that her original tribal nation—the Shoshone—were horse traders who lived near the source of the Missouri, which lay at the foot of the Rocky Mountains and the nearby Columbia River. Of course, horses would be particularly useful, if not essential, for the success of the expedition if it was to cross the Great Divide.

ALL SORTS OF INDIANS

Remember the telling remarks made by Jefferson advising Lewis to be on the lookout for Welsh-speaking Indians? In 1832, George Catlin, who was a lawyer, frontiersman, and pictorial historian, lived for several months among the Mandan Indians near the site of present-day Bismarck, North Dakota. Catlin noted in his own journals that the Mandan were distinctly different from all other Native American tribes that he'd encountered, not least because most of them were "nearly white," with light-blue eyes.[7]

Catlin also deemed the Mandan to be "advanced farther in the arts of manufacture" than any other Indian nation. Their lodges were equipped with "more comforts and luxuries of life." To add to the mystery, William Clark, who by this time was both a Mason and governor of Missouri, personally told Catlin before he started up the Missouri that he would find the Mandan a strange, half-white people. Obviously the genetic strain that produced the Mandan with blond hair "fine and soft as silk," blue eyes, and fair skin was certainly well entrenched and originated well before 1832.[8]

Catlin's affirmation in his own journals that he knew of no contact between the Mandan and Europeans prior to their encounter with Lewis and Clark in 1804 means that he was probably unaware of the earlier English and French expeditions along the Missouri. Aside from David Thompson—a British Canadian fur trader, surveyor, and mapmaker acting on behalf of the North West Company (a fur-trading business)—it is recorded that the sieur de la Vérendrye had visited the Mandan in 1795, guided by a Metis trapper and voyageur by the name of Jean-Baptiste Trudeau. News of this encounter even reached Thomas Jefferson, with the president securing Trudeau's journals in 1803. Rather coincidently, roughly two hundred years later, on October 19, 2015, Canadians elected as their 23rd prime minister Justin Pierre James Trudeau, whose mother just happens to be a Sinclair.

As highlighted earlier, it was the Algonquin—Pierre Gaultier de Varennes, Sieur de la Vérendrye, who took an expedition from his forts in present-day Manitoba to what is now North Dakota in search of a rumored tribe of "white, blue-eyed Indians." Along the banks of the Missouri River, Varennes apparently found a stone pillar with a small stone tablet inscribed on both sides with unfamiliar characters that the Blackfoot called hoodoos. Jesuit scholars in Québec would later describe the writing on the stone as Tartarian—a runic script similar to

Norse runes. This is the same stone tablet that was rather mysteriously shipped to France and from there disappeared into the Jesuit archives.

Varennes's own notes and drawings show that he located the Mandan village in what is now MacLean County, North Dakota, between Minot and Bismarck, on December 3, 1738. He described the village as a large and well-fortified town with 130 "round" houses laid out in streets. What is of interest here is that the fort's palisades and ramparts were not unlike Viking earth ring fortresses, with a dry moat around the perimeter. Many of the Mandan were described as having light skin, fair hair, and "European features."[9]

Once again we are struck by the fact that there existed a group of "white Indians" who displayed European characteristics both in appearance and military technique. And isn't it rather coincidental that the French nobility and Jesuits would be the ones to first discover a stone cairn with Norse runic script carved into one of the stones? Remember that the Norse earl Prince Henry Sinclair and his Templars would have been well aware of the significance of carved symbols and would have spoken a form of Gaelic that, in later years, could be mistaken for Welsh.

So were the descendants of Sinclair and his party perhaps "the Welsh-speaking Indians" that Jefferson referred to? Or was Jefferson referring to some other party? (You will have to continue reading to the end of the book to find out!)

Earlier initiates would surely have established stone cairns as surveying markers of sorts—cairns that could have acted as beacons across the Great Plains if fueled with coal or some other suitable material. Amazingly, the description of these cairns is very similar to those that were previously identified in great numbers along the antient meridian identified at Owl's Head Mountain, Québec. They are also very similar to the stone "beehive" cairns illustrated on Desceliers's map of 1550 (see figure 7.7).

Desceliers was one of the leading figures of the Dieppe school of cartographers. Between 1530 and 1560 he produced several world maps, now very rare, that reflected the geography of the St. Lawrence River and New France, as had been determined by Jacques Cartier's exploration of

Fig. 7.7. A portion of the 1550 version of Desceliers's world map, which shows the known lands of the New World as explored by Jacques Cartier. The Desceliers map is unusual in that the landmass is drawn with north pointing upward but all other illustration and labeling in the Northern Hemisphere is inverted. Reproduced courtesy of the British Library, London, England.

those areas. His crowning glory was the world map, or planisphere, that he produced in 1550. The original parchment map appears in a mid-sixteenth-century atlas manuscript compiled by an unknown person from the French Dieppe group of portolan mapmakers.

Desceliers's 1550 map is another anamoly containing layers and layers of hidden symbolism and geometric axioms. It is obvious that Desceliers based his most famous maps on firsthand accounts of the three earlier expeditions (1534, 1535, and 1541) of Jacques Cartier to the New World. During Cartier's first expedition in 1534, it was at Hochelaga (located on an island in the St. Lawrence River) that the native inhabitants told Cartier many tales of wealthy kingdoms such as Seguna and the Saguenay, which lay up the great Hochelaga River (the St. Lawrence).

The people of these mysterious kingdoms, Cartier was to learn, dressed themselves in cloth like that of white men and wore ropes of gold around their necks that contained plenty of precious stones. It was also learned that the country of "Canada" extended much farther to the west and that it was enclosed by immense lakes and guarded by waterfalls of great height. Most of all, the natives made it clear that the land to the west contained copper, gold, and silver, the same metals that had been used to make the weapons carried by Cartier and his men.

Desceliers's first version of a map recording Cartier's direct description of European-looking Indians was created in 1544 and was more illustrative than geometric in nature. This version illustrates a group of four women in European dress, along with a group of bearded natives. Cartier is shown introducing himself to the inhabitants, while the natives stand nearby, next to the clergy who accompanied Cartier on his journeys.

What is fascinating about this illustration is that the four women it depicts appear to be of rather unique or noble stature. In fact, the central female figure is dressed all in red with a gold cord about her waist and a gold necklace around her neck. The women also appear to be guarded by natives who possessed metal weapons and had beards. Is this just Desceliers's fanciful imaginative rendering of Cartier's exploits, or is there some truth to what the natives had relayed to Cartier? Could the prominent "European" woman be a member of the surviving Holy Grail Bloodline, and could the three women attending to her represent the three daughters of Prince Henry Sinclair?

MORE SYMBOLISM IN THE EARLY MAPS

Both of Desceliers's world maps of 1544 and 1550 were drawn with north pointing upward but with any illustration or labeling found within the Northern Hemisphere inverted. Desceliers's second version of the same map, created in 1550, is in reality a rather sophisticated application of the esoteric "completion of the square." Of course the one symbol that stands out above all the rest on the 1550 version is the unicorn, which in medieval times represented Jesus. The funny thing is that on Desceliers's map of 1550 there are two inverted unicorns. The first striking feature of the two unicorns to be highlighted is that their eyes are pierced by the relative latitudinal and longitudinal meridians, which complete the square.

It could be surmised that the unicorns were another symbol denoting the positions of two significant Rose Line settlements that lie along the longitudes denoted by the ancient 80°00'00"W meridian, more accurately located at 79°57'00"W. It would be remiss of me at this point not

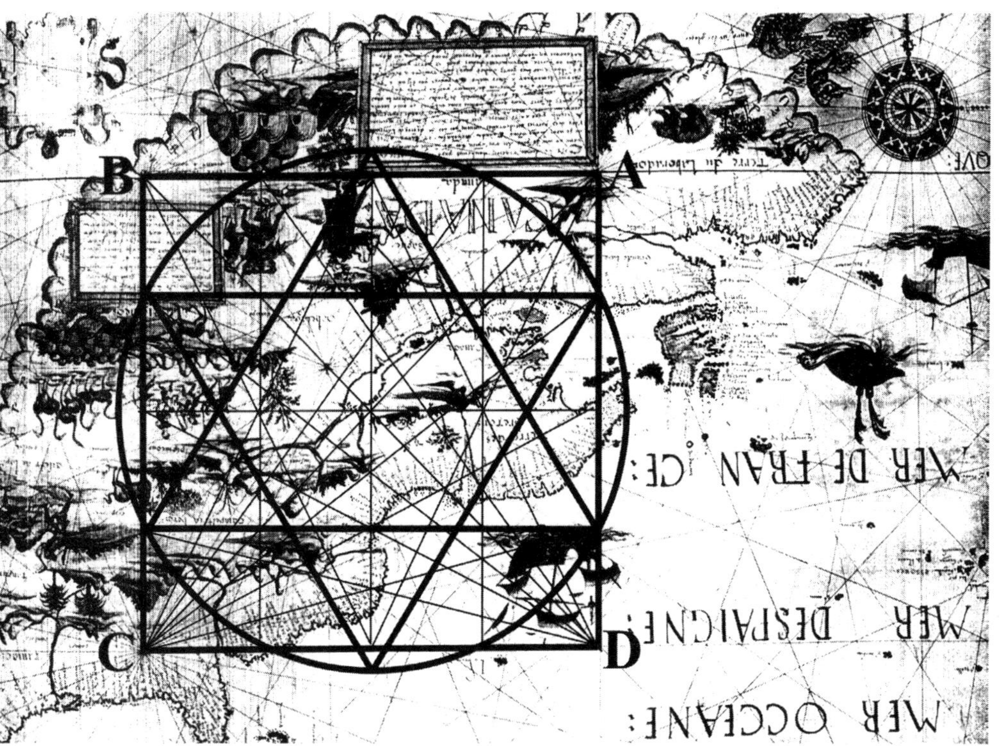

Fig. 7.8. An overlay of the geometric "squaring of the circle" on a portion of Desceliers's 1550 map showing the eastern seaboard of North America. Note how the construction of the square relates to the axiom points shown on the map and also note the stone beehive found outside the square, suggesting that various stone cairns can be found in the Terra in Cognita that lay outside of the known territory. Diagram copyright of the author, William F. Mann.

to mention to the reader that the modern-day community of Meridian, Pennsylvania, is located at 41°00'00"N, 79°57'00"W, exactly where one of the unicorns stands. The other unicorn stands at the modern-day community of Meriden, New Hampshire, which is located along the 71°57'00"W rose line meridian at 43°00'00"N latitude. Readers may find it interesting that the rather famous painter Maxfield Parrish (1870–1956) lived in Meriden, New Hampshire, at an estate called "The Oaks." Logic suggests that the painter named his estate as he did because of the rather mysterious grove of majestic oaks that was most likely present on the site prior to the construction of the house.

Following the geometric completion of the square (see figure 7.8 on p. 231), the coordinates and corresponding modern-day place-names of the four corners of the square are as follows: a) Port Burwell, Labrador—60°00'00"N, 63°57'00"W; b) Ottawa Island, Hudson Bay—60°00'00"N, 79°57'00"W; c) Charleston, South Carolina (more specifically the Morris Island lighthouse)—32°30'00"N, 79°57'00"W; and, d) Bermuda (more specifically the St. David's Island lighthouse)—32°30'00"N, 63°57'00"W.

MORE MOVES ON THE CHESSBOARD

Cartier's last voyage to Canada was delayed until 1541 due to what has been attributed to a rather curious mixture of court intrigue and conflicting ego. Just prior to the expedition's departure on October 17, 1540, the French king François I ordered the Breton navigator to return to Canada to lend weight to a colonization project at the mouth of the Saguenay River, where he would be the "captain general."

However, on January 15, 1541, Captain Jean François de La Rocque, lord of Roberval and a Huguenot courtier, rather abruptly supplanted Cartier as captain general by a new order of the French king. Authorized to leave by Roberval, who was awaiting the delivery of artillery and merchandise, Jacques Cartier departed from St. Malo on May 23, 1541, with seven ships and created a new base near Cap Rouge, roughly located at the mouth of the St. Lawrence River.

From there Cartier went forward to explore the Saguenay River to its source, only to find out that this river was a dead end. Cartier and his men then returned to Cap Rouge. However, contrary to his first two encounters with natives of the region, this time the natives harassed Cartier so much that he left Cap Rouge after one winter because of dwindling supplies. By then most of his men were sick with scurvy, and, rather mysteriously, Roberval had not arrived with supplies by the spring of 1542 as was planned. At this time, instead, Roberval was leading five vessels containing fifteen hundred people across the Atlantic to settle Acadia (Nova Scotia) at a new settlement named Charlesborg-Royal, which also failed in its attempt to be a permanent colony.

The crossing of Roberval's fleet would take more than three months, leading one to question Roberval's navigational abilities or his motives for delaying his arrival. Leaving the St. Lawrence, Cartier finally found Roberval in the harbor of St. John's, Newfoundland. Roberval then ordered Cartier to return to Cap Rouge, but Cartier refused and left with his ships that night, landing in St. Malo, France, in September. Bitter and broken, Jacques Cartier would never return to the New World.

It is here that a critical juncture in our story has been reached. In all probability, the Huguenot—Roberval—appears to have delayed his arrival to the New World approximately two years to give the Grail refugees of both Acadia and New France ample warning to move their Rose Line settlements to the west, as it would be another sixty-four years before the arrival of Samuel de Champlain. Just as certain, the secret initiates knew that the stone cairns that Desceliers depicted on his maps as beehives would lead all those with the eyes to see across North America to the gravesite of some extremely important personages, including that of Prince Henry Sinclair himself!

With this in mind, it bears repeating that a major portion of the Templar treasure would have been buried with this esteemed guardian of the Grail—Prince Henry Sinclair—in order to consecrate the ground around him and to honor his past achievements. If at all true, then does this notion relate in some manner to the real reason why Lewis and Clark moved so quickly westward from the settlement of Mandan?

The race was definitely on, but Lewis and Clark's journals record that it inexplicably took fifty-three days to go around the great falls of the Missouri and that the expedition split at this point to separately explore the surrounding countryside. With the specter of late fall and winter quickly settling into the Rocky Mountains, what was so important for the expedition to stop at this point for fifty-three days? Did Captain Meriwether Lewis, an esteemed Mason and confidant of Thomas Jefferson, have the inside track as to where he might find the last refuge of the Knights Templar in the New World?

A CLOSER REVIEW OF THOMAS JEFFERSON

Of all the revolutionary visionaries in America none is more enigmatic than the third president of the United States—Thomas Jefferson. We touched on him earlier, but it's worth taking a closer look at him now.

Although Jefferson's membership in Freemasonry has never been proved, his understanding of the most important tenets of Freemasonry and Rosicrucianism is evident in all of his major endeavors. Jefferson succeeded Benjamin Franklin as minister to France in 1785, and it is speculated that during this period he was introduced to the teachings of the Jesuit-trained illuminist Adam Weishaupt.

It is also suspected that during Jefferson's time in France he became privy to the secret knowledge of the Holy Bloodline, the Templar meridians, and the earlier explorations of Prince Henry Sinclair in the New World. What is known for certain is that he utilized the harmonic architecture of Freemasonry in all of his designs. One of Jefferson's most cherished architectural precepts was the "circle within the square." Both the combination of a dome or rotunda set within a square, as is found in his famous home, Monticello; or a dome set within a rectangle, as is incorporated in our nation's capitol building, are perfect examples of Jefferson's understanding of and appreciation for this motif.

During his lifetime Jefferson developed an extraordinarily balanced set of interests as well. In addition to being a naturist and musician, he could converse expertly on art, science, religion, physics, astronomy, law, and literature. He also spoke several languages and could read the classics in the original Greek and Latin. Rather intriguingly, it is said that

Jefferson disliked priests because of what he felt were their dogmatic distortions of Christ's teachings. He was branded an atheist as a result. More modern analyses label him as a dualist.

Regardless of his religious beliefs, he was also a man of great foresight. During and after his extended stay in France, Jefferson collected maps and books about North American geography. He also read and reread the accounts of the explorations of La Salle, Hennepin, Charlevoix, LaHontan, and Jean Bossu and delved into the *Histoire de la Louisiane,* which was written by Le Page du Pratz. Always on the lookout for new information, he even laid his hands on a copy of the journal of Jean-Baptiste Trudeau. As noted previously, Trudeau was the former Montrealer who eventually settled in St. Louis and who had earlier guided the Vérendrye expedition all the way to the rather enigmatic Mandan Indian lodge.

8
The Entrance to the Lodge

Fig. 8.1. *Self-Portrait,* 1650, by Nicolas Poussin. Note the stark clarity found in the artist's facial features, with the right side of his face bathed in light and the left side in the shadows. Note also that the second framed painting, which represents the second degree, displays the visage of a goddess. Reproduced courtesy of the Staatliches Museum, Berlin, Germany.

ON THE SQUARE

Nicolas Poussin was born in the small town of les Andelys, France, in 1594. As outlined previously, he moved early in his career to Rome and only returned to France once in 1640 for a period of two years, under direct orders from Cardinal Richelieu. And, although somewhat unusual, this episode is not the most mysterious incident in his lifetime of secrets. What has to be the most intriguing aspect of Poussin's life is that by 1650 he definitely was a Master Mason!

In a self-portrait that is clearly dated 1650 (see figure 8.1 opposite), the painter is proudly signaling to the world that he is a Master Mason by showing off his Masonic ring. In a similar self-portrait painted in 1649 (see figure 8.2 below), he centered his head in the middle of a background square, slyly hinting that he was "on the square," but at that time wasn't so bold to, or didn't choose to, show off his ring. His 1649 self-portrait does not portray the clarity that his 1650 self-portrait possesses. In this light, what could have compelled Poussin to outwardly declare in 1650 what he had only hinted at a year before?

Fig. 8.2. *Self-Portrait,* 1649, by Nicolas Poussin. Note the square embedded in the wall behind Poussin's head and the faint outline of a circle, which again is suggestive of Euclid's theoretical "squaring of the circle." Reproduced courtesy of the Staatliches Museum, Berlin, Germany.

Many of the other paintings that Poussin completed following his return to France in 1640 are known to contain hidden Masonic symbolism that would only be recognizable to an initiate of the Craft. The funny thing is that the question as to where and when Poussin was initiated has never been properly answered, although all of the evidence suggests that his initiation was conducted by a number of prominent Scots who fought for France during the Thirty Years' War. These included a lord, a general, and a spy, among others! This aspect will be examined in more detail further into the story.

The 1650 version of Nicolas Poussin's self-portrait is to a fellow initiate definitely revealing in many ways, allowing the informed viewer to understand that by this time Poussin was privy to the secrets of the lodge. First and foremost, proudly displayed on the pinky finger of Poussin's right hand for all to see is the Masonic ring of the Blue Lodge, containing the compass and square. Next, the three framed paintings in the background are indicative of the first three degrees of Masonry. Poussin's 1650 self-portrait is primarily painted with varying degrees of blue paints. These hues definitely suggest the three basic degrees of the Blue Lodge. Notice how the corners of the three paintings are arranged in a manner suggesting that Poussin was indeed "on the square."

But one of the most telling clues of all can be found in what lies behind the three paintings. Here is the inner door of the Masonic lodge, the archway. It is through this door that the candidate is first challenged by the Inner Guard, who asks the candidate at the point of a sword what it is that he seeks. If the proper password is given by the companion Master Mason (the conductor) who accompanies the candidate, the candidate is allowed access into the inner sanctuary whereby his life is changed forever. It is said that Masonry takes good men and makes them better. In Poussin's case, what he learned through his initiation allowed his subconscious to evolve to the highest point possible.

Freemasonry is often described as a fraternal organization that is based on a ritualistic system of elevating degrees. The three basic degrees of traditional Blue Lodge or Craft Masonry that are common to both York Rite (English) and Scottish Rite Masonry are those of the Apprentice, Fellowcraft, and Master Mason. There are several additional degrees that vary with country and jurisdiction and are administered by various bodies, but it has always been said that the first three degrees are all that a Mason is required to achieve in his lifetime.

THE ROYAL ARCH

According to Antient, Free and Accepted Masonry, though, it was believed that there was a fourth basic degree, which was encompassed in what is now known as the Royal Arch. In fact, the United Grand Lodge of England still recognizes that pure Antient Masonry consists of three degrees and no more: those of the Entered Apprentice, the Fellowcraft, and the Master Mason, the latter of which in this case includes the Supreme Order of the Holy Royal Arch. This inclusion has been subsequently interpreted to suggest that the Holy Royal Arch was not an additional degree but merely the completion of the Master Mason degree.[1]

The legend behind the fourth degree, or Mark Master Mason's degree, is an interesting one and very significant to the story contained in this book. It is said that in ancient days a young craftsman found in the quarries of Tyre a stone of peculiar form and beauty that was marked with a double circle containing certain mysterious characters that greatly excited his curiosity. Having his curiosity thus piqued, he presented the stone to the Mark Master Mason as a work of his own. But because the stone was neither a single nor a double cube but oddly shaped, it was rejected and cast forth among the rubbish. Some time afterward, when one of the arches in the foundation of the temple was nearly completed, the keystone was missing. Sadly, it had been carved in the quarries by Hiram Abiff himself and was marked with his mark. A search was made for it in vain, but then the prior discovery of the young Fellow Craft was recollected, and, among the rubbish, the identical stone was found, which was used to complete the work.

The Royal Arch is today contained within different Masonic bodies around the world as either a separate entity (Supreme Grand Royal Arch Chapter of Scotland) or part of a larger order. In York Rite Masonry, for example, the Holy Royal Arch Chapter is a separate order from Craft Freemasonry, although sponsorship is required by a Craft Lodge.

Similar to Craft Freemasonry, the Royal Arch conveys moral allegorical and ethical lessons. In the three degrees of the Craft the candidate is presented with a series of degrees, which in many ways speak to the practical aspects of becoming a better person. But it is said as man also has an essential spiritual aspect to his nature, the Royal Arch is said to further develop this latter aspect by a contemplation of man's inner nature.

In Royal Arch Chapter the teachings of the Royal Arch are conveyed using a ritualized moral allegory based on the Old Testament, which tells the story of the return of the Hebrews to Jerusalem from Babylonian captivity to rebuild the city and the temple. In clearing the ground where Solomon's Temple once stood in preparation for the foundation of a new temple to be laid, the candidate makes a number of important discoveries that require an interesting and illuminating explanation of the nature of God.

By adding a transcendental dimension to the practical lessons of Craft Freemasonry, the Royal Arch is seen as an extension of the preceding degrees. The philosophical lessons conveyed are considered to be appropriate to that stage in a candidate's Masonic development. The Royal Arch Mason degree is said by many to be the most beautiful degree in all of Freemasonry in that it bridges Craft Freemasonry to a series of higher degrees. York Rite Freemasons who reach this degree may continue to Cryptic Masonry or go straight to the Order of the Knights Templar.

Cryptic Masonry takes its name from the word *crypt,* which has its origins in the Greek language, meaning "a concealed place or subterranean vault." Indeed, the degrees of Royal Master and Select Master in Cryptic Masonry deal with the concealed vault, which is known to be under the ruins of the Temple of Solomon. Similar to the common elements found in all Royal Arch bodies, the Cryptic story tells of how the secrets of the very nature of God came to be placed in the secret vault below the Temple of Solomon, where they are later discovered by three masons, or sojourners. (Does the story of the three local youths who discovered the vault on Oak Island sound familiar?)

Once the vault is discovered and penetrated, the three masons come upon nine arches where various secrets were deposited. (On Oak Island the three youths dug down and discovered nine oak platforms. On the ninth platform it is said that they discovered a smooth stone that contained a secret coded message.) In a slight variation in the degree, the candidate represents a well-known mason in the employ of King Solomon, who stumbles by accident into the secret vault where three grand masters are in conference. Through interpretation of antient writings on the vault's arches, the candidate attains a higher level of understanding and knowledge.

Fig. 8.3. An early graphic depiction of the lowering of one of the workmen who discovered the secret vault below the Temple of Solomon. As reenacted during the thirteenth degree of the Scottish Rite, it is known as the Royal Arch of Solomon or the Knight of the Ninth Arch. The ritual has a strong association to the story of the original Knights Templar who discovered a great treasure below the Temple of Solomon following the First Crusade.

The Royal Arch is also the subject of the thirteenth degree of the Scottish Rite of Freemasonry, with basically the same allegorical story being played out except in a more theatrical manner. As noted, it is known as the Royal Arch of Solomon (Knight of the Ninth Arch). Like other degrees encountered in Scottish Rite Masonry, this degree is also known by other names: the Royal Arch of Enoch, the Royal Arch, and the Royal Arch Ecossais (Scottish Royal Arch). In Hebrew the name Enoch is Henoch, which means "to initiate, instruct, teach, and dedicate."[2] In Freemasonry, Enoch has naturally become a symbol of initiation and of the acquisition of knowledge and understanding.*

THE INVOLVEMENT OF CARDINAL RICHELIEU

In this light this knowledge and understanding surely suggests that Richelieu must have dangled something of immense esoteric value in front of Poussin to have coerced him back to France in 1640, for it is obvious that the painter was neither a French royalist nor a patriot. Nor was Poussin desirable of any monies. Accordingly, it now appears that Richelieu must have arranged for Poussin to be initiated into the most exclusive secret fraternity at the time, namely the Freemasons. It also suggests that Richelieu himself was a high-ranking member of this very exclusive lodge.

Curiously, French Freemasonry is traditionally said to have originated in 1688 with the Royal Irish Regiment. The royalist regiment followed the Catholic James II of England into exile in France after he was deposed in 1688 in what has come to be known as the Glorious Rebellion. The first French Masonic Lodge is said to be constituted under the name La Parfaite Egalite of Saint-Germain-en-Laye.[3] To the contrary, it's now apparent that a form of Freemasonry existed in France

*There are many scholars who believe that the Book of Enoch was published before the Christian era by some unknown Semitic race. It is also believed that the actual author of the book believed himself to be inspired in a post-prophetic age and borrowed the name of an antediluvian patriarch (Enoch/Henoch) to authenticate his own enthusiastic foretelling of the coming Messiah.

prior to its official beginning, as evidenced by the ring on Poussin's hand.

Cardinal Richelieu has never been associated officially with Freemasonry or for that matter with any other esoteric secret society. His lasting influence over the French monarchy, however, was no doubt due in part to the extensive spy network that he had developed across France and abroad. Voltaire argued that Richelieu started wars for no other reason than to enhance his own power, and the famous French novelist Alexandre Dumas even created a literary character based on Cardinal Richelieu. One of the main villains in his classic work *The Three Musketeers* is Richelieu.[4]

Of course Richelieu was also famous for his patronage of the arts. Most notably he founded the Académie Française, the learned society responsible for matters pertaining to the French language. In 1622, Richelieu was elected *proviseur,* or principal, of the Sorbonne, where he presided over the renovation of the college's buildings and over the construction of its famous chapel, where he is now entombed.

Richelieu was also known by the moniker l'Eminence rouge (meaning "the red Eminence"), from the red shade of a cardinal's clerical dress and the "eminence" style that he adopted as cardinal.[5]

The most famous painting of Richelieu was completed by Philippe de Champaigne, who was the only artist allowed to paint him enrobed as a cardinal. Champaigne was known to have painted the cardinal *eleven* times in his telltale robe, with his 1637 portrayal being the most famous of the eleven (see figure 8.4 on p. 244). On an esoteric level, the number 11 assumes prime significance in that it represents, numerically, transcendence to a higher level. In this specific painting perhaps it is not what lies in the foreground that is the clue to Richelieu's association with the Holy Royal Arch. The cardinal himself, in assuming the rightful pose, appears to be suggesting that hiding behind his cardinal's biretta, the three-peaked hat, are not only the secrets of the Holy Royal Arch but also the secrets of the two oak trees, the two pillars, that lie beyond.

What is known for certain about Philippe de Champaigne is that he was born into a poor family in Brussels during the reign of the Habsburg

Fig. 8.4. *Cardinal Richelieu,* 1637, by Philippe de Champaigne. Note how the artist cleverly arranged the painting's composition from foreground to background, leading the initiated viewer's eye through a progression of Masonic levels. The cardinal is shown solidly on the square. By following his right hand, one is led through the royal arch to a courtyard, an inner square of sorts, where the cardinal must forego his status within the church garment. The cardinal is shown wearing the eight-pointed star of the Knights Templar. Reproduced courtesy of the National Gallery, London, England.

Netherlands by the archduke of Austria Albert VII von Habsburg and Isabella Clara Eugenia of Spain. At a young age Champaigne became a pupil of the landscape painter Jacques Fouquieres after coming to his attention. Then in 1621 he moved to Paris, where through a series of fortunate events he worked with Nicolas Poussin on the decoration of the Palais du Luxembourg under the direction of Nicolas Duchesne. It was Duchesne's daughter whom Champaigne married. Afterward he returned with his wife to Brussels to live with his brother, and from there he developed a reputation for portrait painting. On many occasions he was summoned to Paris by Cardinal Richelieu, where it is said he became reacquainted with Poussin in 1640. Perhaps, under Richelieu's guiding hand, Philippe de Champaigne was initiated alongside Nicolas Poussin.

THE SPREAD OF FREEMASONRY IN EUROPE

What is known about the spread of Freemasonry in Europe outside of France is that the first Italian lodge was said to have been set up in Florence in 1731. Seven years later the Catholic Church published *In Eminenti,* the first papal bull against Freemasonry. The various Italian states refused to register the papal bull, however, as the situation was delicate throughout all of Italy at the time. The Medici dynasty was waning and the real political power had just passed to Francis III Stephen, Duke of Lorraine, brother-in-law of the Holy Roman Emperor Charles VI of the House of Habsburg, and husband of Maria Theresa. In 1739, Cardinal Corsini, the nephew of Pope Clement XII, personally asked the duke of Lorraine to arrest the Freemasons and to hand them over to the Inquisition's tribunal, but the request was never fulfilled. Francis III Stephen would instead go on to become Francis I, Holy Roman Emperor.*[6]

The United Grand Lodge of England was formed in 1813 and remains to this day as the governing body for the majority of Freemasons

*It is said that Francis took a great interest in the natural sciences and was also a member of the Freemasons.

in England and Wales. It also oversees lodges in other predominant Commonwealth countries outside of the United Kingdom. The United Grand Lodge claims to be the oldest Grand Lodge in the world, by descent, from the first Grand Lodge of England formed in London in 1717. Not surprisingly, June 24, Saint John the Baptist Day, is often cited as the founding day of Grand Lodge Freemasonry.

On the other hand, the Grand Lodge of Antient, Free and Accepted Masons of Scotland, although officially founded in 1736, holds records of the Lodge of Edinburgh (Mary's Chapel), which date from 1599.[7] Furthermore, Mother Kilwinning Lodge, a Masonic lodge in Kilwinning, Scotland, is reputed to be the oldest lodge not only in Scotland but also the world. It attributes its origins to the twelfth century and is often called Mother Kilwinning Lodge No. 0.

The Kilwinning Masonic Lodge No. 38 (3 + 8 = 11) is in Orkney itself; this is the home of the famous Kirkwall Scroll. The scroll is made of strong linen cloth; painted on it in blue oil are scenes from the history of the children of Israel. This scroll is certainly a unique piece of craftsmanship and is regarded as the Masonic lodge's first treasure of antiquity.

The origins of the Kirkwall Scroll, its age, who made it, and what was its intended use are still questions whose answers are shrouded in mystery; but there is some evidence in the records of this lodge to indicate that the scroll was used in Masonic rituals in Kirkwall as early as 1786. Several symbols on the scroll are known to relate to the Knights Templar, and other symbols display a remarkable similarity with symbols found in the Mi'kmaq native culture.

Significantly, before the transfer of Orkney to Scotland in 1468, William St. Clair, Earl of Orkney, is recorded in Kilwinning Lodge as holding the appointment of patron of the Masons of Scotland. This position was hereditary and was held by the descendants of the earl until 1736, when the last William St. Clair, Earl of Rosslyn (Roslin and Rosslyn are interchangeable in this instance), resigned his appointment before the Grand Lodge of Scotland only to become its first elected grand master.

It was the last William St. Clair who also signed the charter that authorized the formation of the Kilwinning Lodge No. 38. Not surprisingly, the Masonic buildings of Kilwinning Lodge are built on the very ground where Kirkwall Castle once stood. This is the castle that was originally the stronghold of Prince Henry, from whence his Templar fleet set out for the New World in 1398 CE.

Conversely, it was the earlier William St. Clair, third Earl of Orkney, Baron of Roslin, and first Earl of Caithness, who between 1446 and 1456 was responsible for the construction of Rosslyn Chapel, which is located at the village of Roslin, Midlothian, Scotland. The chapel, built some 150 years after the dissolution of the original Knights Templar, contains many Templar symbols, such as the two riders on a single horse that appears on the medieval seal of the Knights Templar.

It is said that William wanted in some way to permanently commemorate in stone the sailing of his grandfather—Prince Henry Sinclair—to the New World some fifty years before. Several arches in Rosslyn Chapel display plants such as maize (corn) and aloe (cactus), which were at that time only native to the Americas. And to this day, Rosslyn Chapel clearly displays a series of carved stones directly related to Masonic initiation, which includes carvings demonstrating the three basic degrees, including the Royal Arch.

One of the prime stories behind the Roslin Sinclairs is certainly interwoven with the Douglases, Freemasonry, and the medieval Knights Templar. It was in 1329 that the Knight Templar Robert the Bruce died. But before his death he had expressed the wish that his heart be removed and taken to Jerusalem and buried in the Knights Templar Church of the Holy Sepulchre. Thus, Bruce's heart was transported to the Holy Land by none other than the hereditary grand master of the Scottish Templars, Sir William Sinclair, along with Sir James Douglas, Sir William Keith, and at least two other knights. It was Douglas who had been given the task of carrying Bruce's heart in a silver casket hung around his neck.

Their journey took them through France and Spain, where they met up with King Alfonso XI of Castile and León, who encouraged them to accompany him on his campaign against the Moors of Granada. On March 30, 1330, at the Battle of Tebas de Ardales, the Scots, riding in the vanguard, were surrounded. According to a fourteenth-century chronicle, Douglas removed the silver casket containing Bruce's heart from his neck and hurled it into the attacking Moors.

To be honest, although the Moors were ultimately defeated, the battle was ill planned from the very start and ended up more as a fiasco, with Douglas and his contingent foolishly pursuing the fleeing enemy. The story goes that, unfortunately, Sir James outran the rest of his men and found himself far out in front with only ten or so followers. Too late, he tried to turn back to rejoin the main body. Unfortunately for Douglas, the more agile Moorish cavalry saw their opportunity, rallied, and counterattacked. In the running fight that followed Douglas saw Sir William St. Clair surrounded by a body of Moors, trying to fight his way free. With the few knights still with him, Douglas rode to the rescue, but all were killed, including Sir William St. Clair and the brothers Sir Robert and Sir Walter Logan.

Most historians say that this bold action rallied the king's own knights, who won the day, but not before most of the Scottish knights perished. Only Sir William Keith survived, because he had broken his arm earlier and therefore did not participate in the battle. The story goes that Sir William Keith valiantly retrieved the silver casket from the battlefield and completed the task, ensuring that Bruce's heart was buried as he had wished.

COURT INTRIGUE AND POSSIBLE COMPLICITY IN THE MYSTERY OF THE TEMPLAR TREASURE

Some scholars maintain that it was King Louis XIII who personally commissioned Poussin in 1640 to paint his most famous painting, *The Shepherds of Arcadia,* and not Cardinal Richelieu as most scholars assert. Louis XIII was a monarch of the House of Bourbon who ruled as king of France between 1610 and 1643 and king of Navarre (as Louis II) from 1610 to 1620, following the merging of the crown of Navarre with the French crown. In 1610, Louis XIII had succeeded his father, Henry IV, as king of France and Navarre a few months before his ninth birthday. His mother, Marie de' Medici, acted as queen regent during Louis's early years. However, abuse of her powers and ceaseless political intrigues by Marie and her Italian favorites led the young king to take power in 1617. He accomplished this by exiling his mother and executing her followers, including Concino Concini, who was the most influential Italian attending the French court at the time. Concini was reputed to have been Marie's lover.[8]

Subsequently, the reign of Louis XIII "the Just" was primarily marked by struggles against Habsburg Spain through the Thirty Years' War. France's greatest victory in the conflicts against the Habsburg Empire during this period came at the Battle of Rocroi in 1643, just five days after Louis's death.[9] This victory, which was largely attributed to the courage and veracity of Scottish mercenaries—the Scots Guard—marked the end of Spain's military ascendancy in Europe and foreshadowed French dominance in Europe under Louis XIII's son, King Louis XIV.

The Royal Scots or Scots Guard was first raised in 1633 as the Royal Regiment of Foot by Sir John Hepburn under a royal warrant from King Charles I, specifically for service in France to the French king. It was formed from a nucleus of Hepburn's previous regiment, which had been in existence since 1625, originally in the service of the Swedish crown—King Gustavus Adolphus.* When Hepburn arrived in France the Scots Guard absorbed the remnants of a number of other Scottish mercenary units that had fought for Sweden. By 1635 the regiment had swelled to some eight thousand men.

Unfortunately, Sir John Hepburn was killed at the siege of Saverne, France, in 1636. The regiment was then taken over by his nephew Sir John Hepburn, who was also killed in action the following year. Lord

*King Gustavus Adolphus is still known as the greatest king in Swedish history, and it is said that he commanded the greatest army to have fought in the Thirty Years' War. Unfortunately, his death in 1632 was considered a tragedy and helped ensure that the Thirty Years' War would end in a stalemate rather than outright victory for one side or the other. Regardless of the outcome, he laid the foundation for the Swedish Empire and made Sweden the dominant power of northern Europe throughout the seventeenth century.

James Douglas was then appointed the new colonel, and the name of the corps was altered to the Regiment de Douglas, in recognition of the French/Scottish ties. Lord James Douglas was a direct descendant of Sir James Douglas, who had earlier died at the Battle of Tebas de Ardales in 1330. By 1640 the regiment numbered some twelve hundred fierce and loyal Scotsmen. The regiment fought with distinction under this same name even beyond when Lord "Jamie" Douglas was killed in a skirmish between Arras and Douai on October 21, 1645, in an attempt to take back the city from the Habsburgs.

Prior to the lord's death, though, it has been speculated that he, along with several other prominent Scots involved in the Thirty Years' War, such as general Sir James Hamilton, the first Duke of Hamilton, who was Charles I's chief adviser in Scottish affairs, and the enigmatic Sir Robert Moray, had established a "field lodge" in France sometime between 1640 and the end of the war in 1648. The existence of this field lodge also explains how Poussin could have been initiated as a Freemason prior to 1650. Cardinal Richelieu would surely have been associated with these prominent Scots. This makes a great deal of sense, given that the House of Hamilton and House of Douglas are interwoven throughout the history of both Scotland and France by marriage, by deeds, and through the fraternal bond of Freemasonry.[10]

Interestingly, Sir George Hamilton of the Royal Scots became the first earl of Orkney on January 3, 1696. He was the fifth son of the duke of Hamilton and had been a company officer in the regiment in 1684, when his uncle the earl of Dumbarton was colonel. In January 1692 he had been made colonel of the Fusiliers, but after distinguishing himself at the Battle of Steenkerque during the Nine Years' War he was appointed colonel of the Douglas regiment that same month. The battle was won by the French under Marshal François-Henri de Montmorency (again, here is a significant intertwining of family names) against a joint English-Scottish-Dutch-German army under Prince William of Orange. By this time the Royal Scots had stopped being mercenaries on behalf of the French and were fighting on the English-Scottish-German-Dutch side.

A book could be written about the life and times of Sir Robert

Moray. Born in 1609, Sir Robert Moray was, at various times, a Scottish soldier, statesman, diplomat, judge, spy, freemason, and natural philosopher. He was considered to be a favorite of Cardinal Richelieu and was a prominent member of the group of twelve who led the formation of the Royal Society. Experienced in military engineering, he was appointed quartermaster general of the Scottish Army, which invaded England in 1640 in the Second Bishops' War and took Newcastle upon Tyne. Above all else, he was a political survivor.*[11]

Lodge records show that several prominent Freemasons who were already members of the Lodge of Edinburgh, including James Hamilton, initiated Moray into Freemasonry on May 20, 1641.[12] What is rather interesting about this is that although Moray was initiated into a Scottish lodge, the event is known to have taken place south of the border on English soil at a field lodge. Thereafter, he regularly used the five-pointed star, his Master Mason's mark, on his correspondence, proudly displaying his affiliation for all of those "with the eyes to see" (see figure 8.5 on p. 252).

Meanwhile, an important act in the Thirty Years' War was played out by the Swedes, who were being led throughout the war by their dynamic king Gustavus Adolphus. A turning point in the long and arduous war came in the Second Battle of Breitenfeld in 1642, which occurred just outside of Leipzig, Germany. It was here that the Swedish field marshal Lennart Torstenson defeated an army of the Holy Roman Empire led by Archduke Leopold Wilhelm I of Austria. He was the same Archduke Leopold who would later become patron to David Teniers the Younger.

During the last few years of the Thirty Years' War, between 1643 and 1645, Sweden and Denmark also fought each other in what is known as the Torstenson War. The result of that conflict and the conclusion of the Thirty Years' War at the Peace of Westphalia in 1648, which is

*The list of Robert Moray's accomplishments goes on and on. He was a confidant to Charles I and Charles II and the French cardinals Richelieu and Mazarin (Richelieu's successor). He is best known, however, for being one of twelve individuals who in 1660 laid the groundwork for the formation of the Royal Society and was influential in gaining its royal charter and formulating its statutes and regulations.

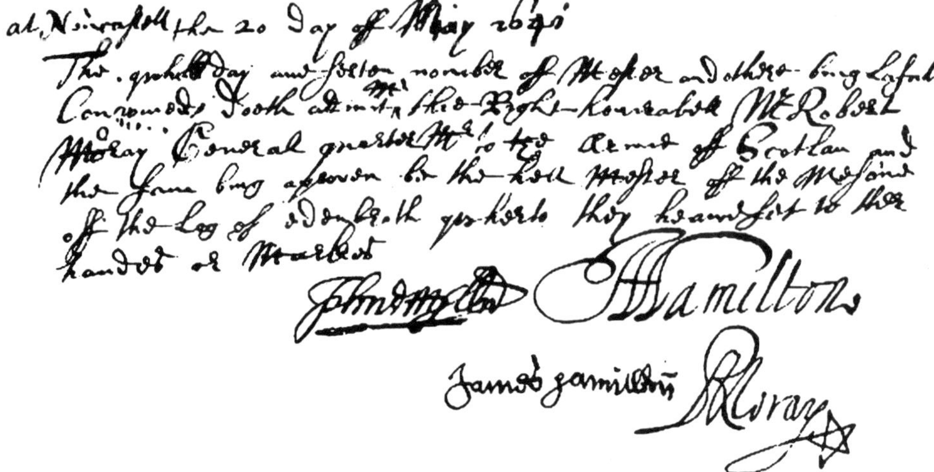

Fig. 8.5. Facsimile of initiation record of Sir Robert Moray into the Lodge of Edinburgh, dated May 20, 1641, which displays Moray's distinctive Master Mason's mark—the pentagram—or is it representative of Venus? Note the signature of General Sir James Hamilton and the elaborate scroll intertwining his first and last initials. Courtesy of the Masonic Lodge of Edinburgh.

quietly said to have been orchestrated by Masonic forces on both sides, helped establish postwar Sweden, France, and the Netherlands as predominant forces in Europe.[13]

THE CHESS GAME RESUMES

Regardless of the question as to what came first—Scottish Freemasonry or French Freemasonry—and whether either contained the Holy Royal Arch, it is quite evident that from the fourteenth to seventeenth centuries there was a free mixing of ideals between Scotland and France due to the alliances formed between the reigning monarchs and their top advisers. In many ways it can be said that the various kings were nothing more than figureheads on a chessboard and that the game was played by the hidden chess masters who made their moves and countermoves from the shadows.

Remember that the most powerful piece on the board is the queen. During this period, potential queens were certainly used to trap future kings, in more ways than one. The key is also to remember that multiple chessboards were being played—all at the same time—spanning the Old World and the New World, and a move on one board could prompt another move some two hundred years later on another board.

One such all-encompassing move was played when the notion that the Merovingian dynasty was a direct descendancy of the fruit of the union of Jesus and Mary Magdalene was first introduced.* As early as the thirteenth century the Cistercian monk and chronicler Peter of Vaux de Cernay claimed it was part of Cathar belief that the earthly Jesus had a relationship with Mary Magdalene and that their descendants had survived as part of Merovingian royalty.† As a result, various royal dynasties across Europe used this purported Holy Bloodline descendancy to restore themselves to a god-king status.

Another rather intriguing move followed the death of Lord James Douglas in 1645. With great pomp and circumstance that was ensured by Richelieu, Douglas's body was returned to Paris and buried at the Abbey of Saint-Germain-des-Prés beside other members of his family, which included William Douglas, tenth Earl of Angus, who was his grandfather. The Benedictine Abbey of Saint-Germain-des-Prés is located just beyond the outskirts of early medieval Paris and was the burial place of the Merovingian kings of Neustria.‡ Access to the Left

*The point to remember here is that from the first time the notion of a Jesus/Magdalene union was introduced there never has been an offering of definitive proof, thus enabling the Roman Catholic Church to readily dismiss any such claims as soon as they were introduced.

†Peter de Vaux de Cernay was a Cistercian monk and chronicler of the Albigensian Crusade. His *Historia Albigensis* is one of the primary sources for the events of that crusade against the Cathars. The chronicle is believed to have been written from 1212 to 1218. His uncle was bishop of Carcassonne for some years after 1212; he had been specifically appointed by Simon IV de Montfort to preach against Catharism. The oddity is that Peter went out of his way to make sure that the Jesus/Magdalene claim was stated by and associated with the Cathars, even though his uncle's objective was to dismiss the Cathars' claims.

‡One little-known fact about the abbey itself is that from 1275 to 1636, its pillory (whipping post) was located in the current Place d'Acadie, perhaps as a silent tribute to those persecuted knights who had made their way across the Atlantic Ocean to a place that was secretly known as Arcadia or Acadia/Acadie.

Bank of the Seine, where the abbey is located, was originally across the Pont de l'Alma (bridge), which is located near the modern-day Pont de l'Alma tunnel where Princess Diana was killed.

In pre-Christian times the Pont de l'Alma (meaning "bridge of the souls") was a pagan sacrificial site where human sacrifices were regularly made. By the time of the Merovingian kings, the Pont de l'Alma was an underground chamber or vault where the kings were buried. It is also said that the site was where the Merovingian kings of Europe came to fight to the death to settle disputes. They came to Pont de l'Alma because it was believed that whoever was killed there would go directly to heaven. The earthly practice was to divert the river, entomb the king in the chamber, and then re-divert the river along its original course. In other places Merovingian kings would be entombed in a hollowed out oak tree trunk that would be placed beneath a diverted stream or river. The abbey itself was founded in the sixth century by Childebert I, who was the son of the Merovingian king Clovis I. Here again is a prime example of the early Christian faith building upon earlier pagan foundations.

Another intriguing chess move occurred in 542 CE. While fighting in Spain, Childebert aborted his siege of Zaragoza when he heard that the inhabitants had placed themselves under the protection of the martyr Saint Vincent. It is said that in gratitude the bishop of Zaragoza presented Childebert with the stole of Saint Vincent. The story goes that when Childebert returned to Paris he erected a church to house the relic and dedicated it to the Holy Cross and Saint Vincent.*

This Saint Vincent should not be confused with Saint Vincent de Paul. The earlier Saint Vincent of Saragossa, who concerns us here and who was also known as Vincent Martyr, Vincent of Huesca, or Vincent the Deacon, was born in the third century and is the patron saint of Lisbon, Portugal, and Valencia, Spain. He was born at Huesca, then in the principality of Aragon, and martyred under the pagan Roman emperor Diocletian around the year 304 CE.[14] According to legend,

*There could be a double entendre here. Throughout history there has been a reference to the Children of St. Vincent, which many believe to be an inference to the Order of St. Sulpice. Perhaps in a different light the Merovingians could be considered to be the children of an earlier Saint Vincent.

after being martyred and thrown to the scavengers by the Romans, ravens protected Saint Vincent's body from being devoured by the larger vultures until his followers could recover the body. The legend continues that his body was taken to what is now known as Cape St. Vincent, where a shrine was erected over his grave and to this day is apparently guarded by flocks of ravens.

THE MEROVINGIAN LINE OF KINGS

By 558 the Catholic faith had swept through Roman Gaul, but there were still many who practiced the pagan ways. In spite of sporadic opposition, St. Vincent's Church in Paris was completed by Childebert, the Frankish king, and dedicated by Germain—then bishop of Paris and Childebert's chief counselor—on December 23, which was apparently the very same day that Childebert died. The bishop would later, in 754, be canonized as Saint Germain in recognition of his relentless attempts to stamp out the last vestiges of paganism throughout Gaul.[15] The church, seen as a dominating Christian presence over pagan Paris, was frequently plundered and set on fire by the marauding pagan Normans in the ninth century but was rebuilt in 1014 and rededicated—in 1163 by (none other than) Pope Alexander III—to Saint Germain of Paris. The abbey continues to this day as the Abbey of Saint-Germain-des-Prés, having first been reconsecrated as such in 754 in the prescence of Pepin III (the "Short") and his son, Charlemagne, who by this time was King of the Franks and Holy Roman Emperor.

The Merovingian king was briefly succeeded by Chlothar, who divided the combined kingdoms of Neustria and Austrasia among his four sons, which led to a great deal of infighting over the following years. Eventually the area of Paris fell into the hands of Chlothar's son Sigebert, a despot of unlimited cruelty, who died without producing a male heir. Chlothar had reigned alone over all the Franks since 613, but in 623 he was forced to make Dagobert I the king of Austrasia by the Merovingian nobility of that region, who wanted a king of their own. When Chlothar reluctantly granted Austrasia to Dagobert, he initially excluded the Alemannic regions—Alsace, the Vosges, and the

Ardennes—but shortly thereafter the Austrasian nobility forced him to also concede these regions to Dagobert I.

The rule of a Frank from the Austrasia heartland actually tied Alsace more closely to the Austrasian court. King Dagobert I thus created a new duchy (the duchy of Alsace) in southwest Austrasia to guard the region from Burgundian and Alemannic aggressions. Recognizing the strategic advantages of strengthening ties with Alsace, Dagobert then made his courtier Gundoin, who hailed from Alsace, the first duke of this new area. Hence, Alsace lasted as its own duchy until the end of the Merovingian dynasty. As king, Dagobert I also made Paris his capital, where he would be responsible for the construction of the Saint Denis Basilica. Dagobert I was the first Frankish king to be buried in the Saint Denis Basilica, and legend says that he actually died in the abbey while praying.[16] Remember that the Rennes Parchments claim that the treasure lies with Dagobert and that he is lying there still. This reference is to Dagobert II and therefore should not be confused with the burial place of Dagobert I.

Carrying on with the story, in 626 CE, Bishop Sulpitius (Sulpice) entered the scene as treasurer and close confidant of King Chlothar and continued to do so with Dagobert I. A church document called the *Vita Sulpicii Episcopi Biturgi* actually outlines the story that King Dagobert I ordered his representative, the merciless general Lollo (Lollonius), to reside at Bourges to bring the city more closely under the king's rule. The story goes that Sulpitius successfully intervened with King Dagobert I on behalf of the people of Bourges, who were predominantly Jewish at the time, after General Lollo demanded their allegiance to the king and the relatively new Roman Catholic faith. As a result of the gratitude shown by the people of Bourges, Sulpitius retired to a nearby monastery and died on January 17, 646, which rather conveniently is the same feast day of Saint Anthony the Hermit. The basilica in Bourges where Sulpitius is buried is called Navis because of the nearby port (the Latin root of the word is *navi,* meaning "to navigate") and remains to this day a place of pilgrimage along one of the many routes to Santiago de Compostela, the burial site of Saint James.[17]

In 632 the Merovingian nobles of Austrasia revolted under the mayor of the palace Pepin of Landen (Pepin II) against the authoratative rule of Dagobert I. The mayor, with the backing of the still fiercely independent people, demanded that Dagobert cede royal power in the easternmost of his realms. Dagobert relented to the rebellious nobles in 632 by putting his three-year-old son, Sigebert III, on the throne, somewhat appeasing them because Pepin believed that the boy's age was to his advantage. Dagobert's concession would indeed come back to haunt him in that Pepin II would ultimately be successful in overthrowing the last king of the Franks and succeed in instilling the Carolingian dynasty. The assumption of Saint Germain over Saint Vincent by Pepin III and Charlemagne in 754 signaled this transfer of power.

But this is not where the lingering story of the Merovingians' dominating power and descendancy from the union of Jesus and Mary Magdalene ends. The seventh century would prove to be one of infighting and political intrigue across all of Neustria and Austrasia. Dagobert I's son was named Sigebert III, and it was in 650 that, near Stenay in the Lorraine, the son of Sigebert III—Dagobert II—was born. However, fearing assassination by the then powerful mayors of the palace following the death of his father in 656, Dagobert II was packed off to an Irish monastery. Meanwhile the Austrasian throne was taken by Childebert the Adopted, son of Grimoald, the Austrasian mayor of the palace, whom the king had adopted before the birth of Dagobert II. After the downfall of Grimoald and Childebert, Dagobert's cousin Chlotar III, King of Neustria, secured the Austrasian throne (in 662) for Childeric II.[18]

This period of Merovingian domination was short-lived, because after Childeric was assassinated in 675, Dagobert II was found by Wilfrid, Bishop of York, and restored to the throne in 676. Unfortunately, Dagobert II was murdered only three years after he took the throne. This did lead to the unity of all the Frankish lands under Theodoric III, but it was nominal because of his weakness in spirit, which allowed the mayors of Austrasia to ultimately supplant the Merovingian dynasty. The key question remains, though, as to whether Dagobert II had produced a legitimate offspring prior to his assassination. There are recurring stories that Dagobert did not live the monk's life after his restoration to the throne. There are several records claiming that Dagobert II married a Visigothic princess in the village of Rennes-le-Château and that they had at least one child—a daughter, Adela—who would continue the Merovingian/Visogothic line.

Regardless, by 751 CE the Carolingians triumphed when Pepin the Short was crowned king of the Franks, and it is from him and the great Charlemagne that the current French monarchy derives. The Carolingians did hedge their bets though. The dynasty ensured familial loyalty across Europe by not only strategically intermarrying with the other major dynasty at the time, the Habsburgs, but also into several lines that claimed direct descendancy from the aforementioned Merovingian/Visogothic connection. The Carolingians could then also lay claim to the Holy Bloodline. And thanks in large part to the sheer will of Richelieu, the French monarchy became absolute following the Thirty Years' War. Richelieu's successor, Cardinal Mazarin, from the period following Richelieu's death in 1643 until his own death in 1661, would continue with machinations throughout both Old France and New France to ensure that the New World Rose Line sanctuaries remained safe.

THE CHILDREN OF SAINT VINCENT

One direct result of these machinations occurred in 1645, shortly after the death of Cardinal Richelieu, when Jean-Jacques Olier founded the Society of St. Sulpice, which in turn established seminaries throughout France that became known for their moral and academic teachings. During the period of the French civil wars—the Fronde—which reduced Paris to widespread misery and famine, Olier supported hundreds of Parisian families and provided many others with clothing and shelter. The poor were cared for according to methods of relief that had been inspired by the practical genius of Vincent de Paul, Olier's mentor. Hence, the Sulpicians would come to be known as "the children of Saint Vincent."[19]

The second great work of Olier was the establishment of the seminary of St. Sulpice. Through his parish, which he intended would serve as a model to the parochial clergy as well as to the members of his seminary, he quietly hoped to help give France a worthy secular priesthood, free from political and social influence. Within two years of its opening, the seminary, fulfilling the hopes of Olier, not only sent apostolic priests into all parts of France but also became the model according to which seminaries were founded throughout the kingdom.

The beginnings of the Sulpician movement were amid great poverty, which lasted many years, for Olier would never allow any revenues from the parish to be expended except on parish needs. From the start his intention was to make his seminary a national seminary; he did not want the Parish of St. Sulpice to be seen as being bound to any one geographic region. Thus the seminary depended directly on the Holy See, which uncharacteristically became, as time went on, more than pleased to provide almost unlimited funds to Olier.

The present Church of St. Sulpice that was featured in the movie *The Da Vinci Code* is the second building on the site; it was erected over a Romanesque church originally constructed during the thirteenth century. It is through the middle of the Church of St. Sulpice that the ancient Paris Meridian runs north to south. The new building was founded in 1646, with Anne of Austria (King Louis XIII's wife) laying the first stone. Anne is a perfect example of the strategic intermarriage that occurred in Europe between the eighth and seventeenth centuries. Anne was the eldest daughter of King Philip III (Habsburg) of Spain and his wife, Margaret (Habsburg) of Austria. Margaret's eldest brother was the Holy Roman Emperor Ferdinand II; her uncle was Archduke Leopold Wilhelm I.

Again, here is another of those strange stories that is puzzling, to say the least. Within two years of the formal establishment of the Society of St. Sulpice, Jean-Jacques Olier was able to transform it from a local secular movement based on charity to a national society that went on to gain favor with both church and state. Could it be that Olier had discovered something of prime importance relating to the earlier Merovingian dynasties and the claimed descendancy by the European royal families? Could it be that Olier had been able to interpret at least one layer of Poussin's painting, leading him to the conclusion that the

Holy Bloodline had been repositioned in New France? If so, Olier was playing a deadly game with not only the Vatican but also the most powerful dynastic families of Europe.

THE SULPICIANS IN MONTREAL

Apparently Olier also possessed a far-reaching global outlook. As noted previously, his zeal led to his helping to found the Societe de Notre-Dame de Montreal (Society of Our Lady of Montreal) pour la conversion des Sauvages de la Nouvelle-France (dedicated to the conversion of the Indians of New France). This was the society that would go on to organize the establishment of the colony of Fort Ville-Marie in New France.[20] After further consolidation of their influence in France, the Sulpicians undertook their first overseas mission in Montreal in 1657 and eventually were given complete control over much of the colony.

The Sulpicians quickly set to organizing Montreal. Official church records indicate that a cross was planted to designate the future placement of the church on June 29, 1672. The next day the first five stones were laid, which is rather odd in itself unless one realizes that the stones represented the four corners of the square, with the fifth signifying the fifth element. Or were they possibly meant to represent the five points of the star, Venus? Regardless, the first parish church of Notre-Dame would be built between 1672 and 1682.

Their seminary—Vieux Seminaire de Saint-Sulpice—was built from 1684 to 1687. The seminary has the honor of being the oldest structure standing in Montreal.[21] It is located in the historic district of Old Montreal, next to the present-day Notre-Dame Basilica—site of the original Church of Notre-Dame—facing the Place d'Armes Square. The seminary is positioned at the significant coordinates of 45°30'14"N and 73°33'25"W, denoting a significant latitude on the grid of Templar meridians.

Remember that the original cornerstone of the old Sulpician church of Notre-Dame constructed by the Sulpicians along the waterfront of Old Montreal contains the Master Mason marks of the Knights Templar (see figure 2.11 on p. 84). Montreal was officially founded in

Fig. 8.6. The official coat of arms of the Grand Seminarie du Saint-Sulpice of Montreal. Note the depiction of the stone tower and the guiding light of the five-pointed star (Venus?). Note also the diamond-shaped lozenges atop what could be two pillars. Also significant is the styled "M" of the monogram, which can also be read as IXXI. Compare this with the symbols found on the Masonic apron of Meriwether Lewis (see figure 8.8 on p. 266).

1632, yet it has been speculated that a Templar tower was built on the site around 1400 CE, as suggested by the rather intriguing stained-glass window found in the present-day Notre-Dame Basilica (see figure 1.5 on p. 36).

It certainly appears that the Sulpicians had the habit of building upon earlier foundations, both physically and spiritually. This habit continued in Montreal with the building of the current Notre-Dame Basilica, overseen by the St. Sulpician Jean-Jacques Lartigue, Vicar-General of Montreal. (Notre-Dame Basilica continues to this day to be the spiritual heart and soul of Montreal. Just recently, on January 22, 2016, a state funeral was held for Rene Angelil, late husband of the great

Québec singer Celine Dion.) On September 8, 1836, Montreal was made a bishopric, and Lartigue became the first bishop of Montreal, overseeing both Montreal's spiritual and administrative needs.[22] Succeeding Lartigue after his death in 1840 was Father Ignace Bourget, who would be responsible for consolidating the church's position throughout the entire Montreal archdiocese.

Bourget died on June 8, 1885, at a retreat attached to the Church of the Visitation in Sault-au-Recollet (Recollet Falls). Sault-au-Recollet is located on the edge of Ile de la Visitation, which is a small island in the center of the previously noted Rivière des Prairies. The Church of the Visitation at Sault-au-Recollet is the oldest remaining church in Montreal, built between 1749 and 1752 to commemorate the arrival of both Cartier and Champlain to New France.

When Bourget died in 1885, a funeral service for him was conducted by a Father Collin, the superior of the Sulpicians at the time. The funeral was at the Notre-Dame Basilica, and Bourget's body was buried alongside that of his predecessor, Jean-Jacques Lartigue, in a vault located under the southwest pillar of the dome of the then unfinished St. James Cathedral.

Once again there is a discrepancy in the story. Why would Bourget and Lartigue both be buried in a crypt in St. James Cathedral when the Notre-Dame Basilica had been built on the site of the original Sulpician Church of Notre-Dame? Could it have been the location of a second tower farther inland from the Old Montreal waterfront? Remember that the coat of arms of Lagarde shows two towers instead of just one.

The construction of St. James Cathedral had been ordered by Bourget to replace the former Saint-Jacques Cathedral, which had burned in 1852. Apparently his personal desire was to create a scale model of Saint Peter's Basilica in Rome, and it was ultimately reflected in the cathedral's design. The church, now known as Mary, Queen of the World Cathedral, is officially designated as a minor basilica in Montreal and is the current seat of the Roman Catholic archdiocese of Montreal.

Previously both the St. James Cathedral and the earlier Saint-Jacques Cathedral were dedicated to Saint James the Greater. James was the son of Zebedee and Salome and, along with his brother John, was one of the twelve apostles of Jesus. Saint James the Greater is the patron saint of Spain. Traditionally James was the first apostle to be martyred; his remains are held in Santiago de Compostela in Galicia (Spain). Of course, the traditional pilgrimage to the grave of the saint is known as the Way of St. James. Perhaps Bourget was signaling to the initiated that the site of St. James Cathedral in Montreal signified the arrival of earlier Holy Bloodline pilgrims to the New Jerusalem.

James was also one of only three apostles whom Jesus selected to bear witness to his Transfiguration, which his brother John wrote about in his gospels. John is generally credited as the author of the Gospel of John and four other books of the New Testament—the three Epistles of John and the Book of Revelation. Interestingly, there are claims that the Gospel according to John is based on the written testimony of the "Beloved Disciple"—the "disciple whom Jesus loved" (John 20:2 and John 21:24), who recently has been identified in some circles as Mary Magdalene, causing even greater controversy about the Holy Bloodline theory.

The location of the pillar and the vault of St. James Cathedral definitely harkens back to the details contained in the Royal Arch degree and even as far back as the Merovingian and Frank dynasties, if not further. In chapter 1 you might recall that the original 1845 letter concerning Thomas Lagarde dit St. Jean from Father Brunet to Monsignor Bourget, the bishop of Montreal at the time, had found its way into the archives of St. Sulpice at some later date. So what was the secret that Thomas Lagarde dit St. Jean conveyed to Father Brunet, who felt the need to convey the information to the bishop of Montreal in person?

Over a lifetime, Monsignor Bourget definitely exerted the Montreal archdiocese's authority to the fullest extent, both spiritually and physically. Again we come back to the notion that Montreal was identified as the center of a New Jerusalem. And again we continually come back to the idea that if something of immense significance was discovered in New France, which at one time extended over most of North America, then a direct line back to both the St. Sulpicians and the Knights Templar could be established.

BACK ON U.S. SOIL

The year 1845 was certainly an interesting year! That very spring the British launched the Franklin expedition, officially claiming that its goal was to discover a route across the Northwest Passage. But Sir John Franklin appears to have taken a wrong turn somewhere and headed south toward the mouth of the Albany River, which leads to Lake Winnipeg and eventually, via the Red River, to the Continental Divide and the Kensington Runestone.

That same year also saw the enormous preparations for the Mormon exodus, to be led by the newly elected leader Brigham Young. Following the murder of Joseph Smith in Nauvoo, Illinois, in 1844, it had become clear that peace was not possible between the Mormons and the locals. Consequently, Mormon leaders negotiated a truce so that the Latter-Day Saints could prepare to abandon the city and head west.

The year 1845 also saw the annexation of Texas by the United States in spite of the fact that Mexico still considered the territory to be theirs. This resulted in the Mexican-American War, which lasted from 1846 to 1848. With Americans as the victors, the territories of Alta, California; New Mexico; and Texas would be ceded to the government of the United States.

And 1845 was also the year that U.S. President James K. Polk announced to Congress that, based upon the concept of Manifest Destiny, the United States should aggressively expand into the West. At the time Manifest Destiny was the widely held belief that American settlers were destined to expand throughout the continent. Again, here is another of those rather synchronistic moments in time: President James K. Polk had been made a Master Mason in 1825. Polk's mentor and predecessor, Andrew Jackson, was a Mason as well, though his actual initiation date is lost. What *is* known is that in 1805 Jackson was deemed to be a Master Mason.

Did the U.S. government in 1845 somehow know that the last refuge of the Knights Templar in the New World was a Masonic lodge in the West (such as the Alamo Mission may have been or have been associated with) and that its related treasure lay in such a lodge also, guarded by one of the remaining, undefeated Native American nations? Or did the U.S. government just believe that it was the destiny of the American people to expand its territory, and thus that's why the Manifest Destiny mandate had been issued?

Sadly, Manifest Destiny had serious consequences for Native Americans of the southeastern United States, because it ultimately led to the ethnic cleansing of several groups of native people.

The concept of Manifest Destiny is generally believed to have started with an idea made possible by the Louisiana Purchase. Originally Thomas Jefferson believed that although North American Indians were the intellectual equals of whites, they had to live like the whites or inevitably be pushed aside by them. Jefferson's belief that whites and Native Americans would merge to create a single nation did not last his whole lifetime, though, and he began to believe that the natives should emigrate across the Mississippi River and maintain a separate society.

This type of thinking would first result in the Indian Removal Act of 1830, which over the next ten years would result in the forced relocation of several Native American nations from southeastern parts of the United States to what at that time would be designated as the Indian Territory. The oddest thing about this dark period in the history of the United States is that this Indian Territory was the only portion of the early United States west of the Mississippi River not yet claimed or allotted for settlement. Did the federal government preserve/designate this area for Indian resettlement for a specific underlying purpose? Rather curiously, even though the adjacent areas were all settled through government allotments, this area would go on to become the state of Oklahoma—the same area that earlier had been the subject of extensive Spanish exploration.

The Trail of Tears, as it has come to be known, was in fact a series of trails upon which waves of Native Americans, including the Choctaw (1831), Seminole (1832), Creek (1832), Chickasaw (1836), and Cherokee (1838), were forcefully driven from their homes by the U.S. military. For many the relocation to lands west of the Mississippi River was nothing more than a death march.

Fig. 8.7. Keystone of the main archway of the Alamo Mission, which displays the monogram found on the coat of arms of the Grand Seminary of St. Sulpice of Montreal. Photograph property of the author, William F. Mann.

The year 1836 marked the infamous Battle of the Alamo, where several Master Masons fought, including William Barrett Travis, James "Jim" Bowie, Davy Crockett, Almaron Dickinson, and James Butler Bonham. Officially there were only two Anglo survivors of the Battle of the Alamo—Susanna Wilkerson Dickinson, wife of Captain Dickinson, and their infant daughter. At least 182 other defenders were killed by the Mexican army, which was led by President General Antonio Lopez de Santa Anna, who was himself a Mason.

But there is another far more intriguing story relating to the deadly assault on the Alamo Mission near San Antonio de Bexar, which is located in modern-day San Antonio (Saint Anthony), Texas. This story claims that Davy Crockett somehow survived and lived out his years in relative obscurity. What I find to be the most fascinating aspect of

Fig. 8.8. Photo of Meriwether Lewis's Masonic apron, which is presently on display at the Grand Lodge of Montana Museum and Library in Helena, Montana. Note the apron's IXXI symbolism, which can also be found on the Templar cornerstone discovered in Montreal as well as on the Grand Semenarie du St. Sulpice of Montreal's coat of arms. Photograph property of the author, William F. Mann.

the Alamo story, however, is that the keystone above the main doorway of the mission displays the same St. Sulpician monogram as the coat of arms found on the Grand Seminary of St. Sulpice of Montreal. The Alamo Mission was founded in 1718 by Spanish Franciscans who had maintained a certain underlying loyalty to the St. Sulpicians.

Perhaps Lewis and Clark didn't discover the last Rose Line sanctuary, given that it may have been completely absorbed into the native culture at the time of their trek westward. Or maybe Meriwether Lewis remembered his Masonic vows as a Master Mason not to reveal the secrets to anyone other than to a fellow Mason, such as Thomas Jefferson. These questions lead to the larger question as to whether

Meriwether Lewis was murdered or committed suicide on his way to meet with Thomas Jefferson in Washington, D.C., in 1809? It certainly now appears as though somebody went to great trouble to prevent this national hero from revealing what he may have learned among the native lodges in the foothills of Montana.

9
The Last of the Bloodline Guardians

Fig. 9.1. Original illustration depicting the ancient symbol of the caduceus with the intertwining of two diamond-backed snakes, which in this case symbolize the DNA double helix of the Holy Bloodline. Illustration developed by the author, William F. Mann.

BLOOD-RED DIAMONDS

Whoever coined the phrase "What goes around comes around!" probably had no idea of how profound the saying would turn out to be. Throughout this book it's been proved time and time again that actions of epic proportion have had a ripple effect on so many levels that

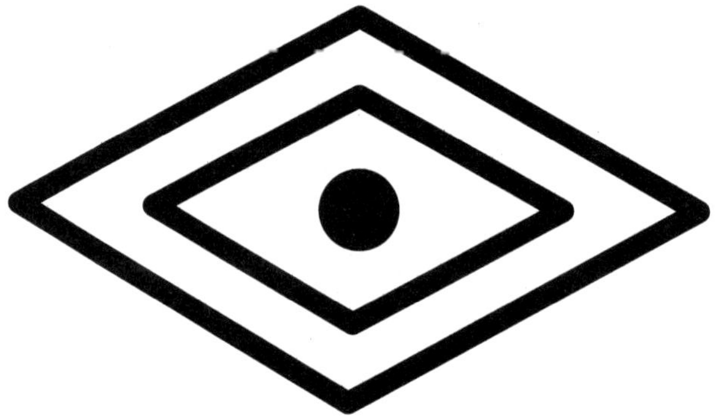

Fig. 9.2. Original Ilustration depicting the ancient native North American symbol of Wisdom, which again reflects the multigenerational descendancy of a familial bloodline. The dot is said to represent the Divine Being, the giver of life, the sun itself. Illustration developed by the author, William F. Mann.

eventually the effect is bound to come around and touch the original action in some manner. The Templars understood this only too well, for their very own existence ultimately hung in the balance. But the very purpose for existing was to maintain and protect not only the sacred treasure but also the secret knowledge associated with that treasure.

As a result the Templars never fully played their hand with either the Roman Catholic Church or the dynastic monarchies that at one time or another alternatively provided the Order with absolute autonomy and power or absolute disgrace and potential death. If the Templars truly possessed irrefutable proof of the Holy Bloodline and possessed relics of a nature that could be used to confirm future descendants, wisdom told them that the best way to leverage their "cards" to the maximum was not to fully expose them but to provide enough hints of their possession. The Templars knew that fear from the potential exposure of the truth would be more than the fear evoked by the truth itself.

In this light the Templars' enemies would have kept the Templars alive and, even better still, would try to turn them in their favor rather than kill them off and totally lose the secret of where the last refuge of the Knights Templar lay in the New World. The continued existence and influence of the Templars was thus guaranteed, as we have seen, to possess the hidden truth equated to sheer power for both church and state. As such it certainly now appears that the Masonic inner circle, which constituted most of the founding fathers of the United States, possessed at least some knowledge that the Templar treasure was hidden in North America. Over time many of those who had an inkling of where the treasure was hidden would have believed that the treasure was too powerful and therefore should be left where it lay; while others, who were not privy to the knowledge or understanding of the inner circle, foolishly went in search of it.

On the other hand there may be a double gambit playing itself out in this entire scenario even to this day. The Templars are known to be the creators of the international banking system and are known to have established themselves as the real power behind countries such as Switzerland. In this manner the Templars continue to have tremendous influence over world affairs, specifically within the European Union, through their monetary control of the world's finances.

Remember that Poussin not only portrayed Mary Magdalene leaning on the Knight Templar as her guardian but also hinted that the knight's real purpose was somehow hidden behind the truth of the Holy Bloodline. Maybe the inner circle of the Knights Templar order realized very early on that sheer force would not ensure an everlasting world peace. Maybe the Templars realized that whoever controlled the world's spiritual and physical purse strings would ultimately control the world.

It would be rather ironic, though, if the purported truth surrounding the Holy Bloodline turned out to be one big hoax. Funnier still, it would be even more ironic that the ultimate truth was guarded by the one race that still appears to be the very bane of both the United States and Canada, namely the First Nations. It's really quite evident for anyone with the eyes to see that ever since Samuel de Champlain arrived in Acadia there has been a steady effort by those in power to virtually annihilate the indigenous people of North America.

This was attempted by engaging them in warfare, mandating forced marches on them, and incarcerating them in residential schools. Or it was done through other more nefarious means such as introducing Old World diseases like smallpox and measles, to which they had no immunity. There is even documented proof in the nineteenth century that the U.S. government deliberately provided infectious blankets to the native population on a number of occasions. The result was and continues to be nothing less than a strategic genocide to eliminate the one group that stands in the way of an uncontested land claim on North America by Canada, the United States, and Mexico.

On June 22, 1763, it is recorded that Delaware and Shawnee war parties led by Chief Pontiac raided deep into Pennsylvanian settlements and laid siege to Fort Pitt in what is now the city of Pittsburgh. The siege was part of Pontiac's Rebellion, an effort by American Indians to drive the British out of the Ohio valley and back across the Appalachians. For the British general Jeffrey Amherst, the military situation over the ensuing summer became increasingly grim. The siege didn't let up until August 1, 1763, when most of the Indians broke off from Fort Pitt to intercept a body of five hundred British troops marching to the fort under Colonel Henry Bouquet. On August 5 these two forces met at the Battle of Bushy Run, where Bouquet and his men fought off the attack and relieved Fort Pitt on August 20. This is where the Indian effort to capture Fort Pitt ultimately failed. Following these events there is an insistence even to this day that the British commanding general ordered Bouquet to use smallpox as a biological weapon, transferring the disease using blankets that were handed out to the natives as a gesture of peace. This back and forth between the two parties took the form of correspondence that would come to be known as the Amherst-Bouquet letters.

Again coming full circle the question remains: What is the underlying reasoning behind the many intertwining power struggles that have occurred between various superpowers over the past two thousand years? The answer can't be as simple as a desire for world domination—as Doctor Evil, Austin Powers's archnemesis, would say! Perhaps it was recognized at least two thousand years ago that a particular blood type contained rather special powers when compared to other blood types. Perhaps the truth lies in the DNA makeup of those described as the "murdered magicians."*[1]

In a more modern context, on November 14, 2014, the *Toronto Star* carried the headline, "Jesus and Mary Magdalene Married, Researchers Say." After months of painstaking translation of an ancient text, which they call "the lost gospel," Professor Barrie Wilson of York University in Canada and Israeli Canadian writer Simcha Jacobivic claimed that Jesus had two children and that the original Virgin Mary was Jesus's wife, Mary Magdalene.† The ancient text, in the possession of the British Library since 1847, is called *The Ecclesiastical History of Zacharias Rhetor* and was written on animal skin in Syriac, a dialect of Aramaic, the language that Jesus spoke.[2]

Of course there have been other recent claims that Jesus was married, such as that contained in *The Gospel of Jesus' Wife* by Karen L. King. In 2012 she presented in her book the controversial claim that an ancient papyrus seemingly makes reference to Jesus having a wife, although her name is not mentioned. The author is certainly qualified to make such a claim in that she is a professor of divinity at Harvard Divinity School.

In response, as has happened on many similar occasions, an army of Christian scholars readily dismissed the validity or significance of King's claim, which once again resulted in the work and the credibility of the author virtually disappearing. As quickly as any claim comes forward concerning the potential marital union of Jesus and Mary Magdalene, it is dismissed by an army of righteous experts. For those

*The phrase "murdered magicians" was coined to describe the Templars by author Peter Partner in his 1987 book, *The Murdered Magicians, the Templars and Their Myth.* Partner's book essentially tries to analyze the origins of the beliefs that have grown up around the Templars, their wealth, and their supposed hidden knowledge and occult powers from the sixteenth to the twentieth centuries. Partner's conclusions are very similar to many other books of a similar vein: the Templars' real power developed out of centuries of cultural and familial breeding and intermarriage of the dynastic families of Europe.

†*The Toronto Star* November 13, 2014, news release and article were timed to coincide with the publication of Barrie Wilson and Simcha Jacobovici's *The Lost Gospel,* published by HarperCollins.

who thought that *The Da Vinci Code* was somehow going to change the world, think again. It's come and gone with barely a mention after its initial flurry, because it will be treated as fiction until physical evidence supporting the thesis behind the Holy Bloodline has finally been discovered and scientifically verified.

But let's just now suppose that the idea of a Holy Bloodline is indeed true and that hidden evidence supporting this thesis exists. And let's just suppose a portion of that hidden evidence can be found among the many intertwining strings of descendancy caused through what is basically centuries of interbreeding. Indeed, for centuries learned men have possessed knowledge about the inherent defects relating to interbreeding. The medical symbol, the caduceus with its intertwining strands of snakes representing the DNA double helix polymer of nucleic acids, was known to ancient Greek practitioners. In modern times the discovery was initially officially published in the journal *Nature* by James D. Watson and Francis Crick in 1953.

Watson and Crick reached their groundbreaking conclusion that the DNA molecule exists in the form of a three-dimensional double helix in 1953. However, without the scientific foundation provided by others in the late 1800s, this conclusion would never have occurred to them. It was the Swiss chemist Friedrich Miescher, who first identified DNA in the late 1860s. Then, in the decades following Miescher's discovery, other scientists such as Phoebus Levene and Erwin Chargaff carried out research that revealed additional details about the DNA molecule. Among other notable findings, these included DNA's primary chemical components and the ways in which they joined with one another. For any readers who are fans of the modern-day TV show *The Big Bang Theory,* a six-foot, double-helix DNA model takes center stage in Sheldon and Leonard's apartment.

The medieval Cistercians were another group that over the centuries had become well versed in animal husbandry. Hence it would now appear that the cloning in 1996 of "Dolly the sheep," which happened at the Roslin Institute of Scotland, located some five miles from Rosslyn Chapel, is no mere coincidence. It has also been reported that before his death Michael Jackson had actually paid millions of dollars to the very same laboratory in an attempt to have his DNA cloned. And in Rosslyn Chapel itself there stands the rather enigmatic Apprentice Pillar, which was carved in 1446 and also displays the DNA double helix.

Fig. 9.3. The so-called Apprentice Pillar, which is located in Rosslyn Chapel, displays the DNA double-helix polymer of nucleic acids. Photograph property of the author, William F. Mann.

In most native North American circles there is the belief that the blood is the body's central repository of all individual knowledge and memory stored from one's ancestral relations. The Old Mide'win—the Grand Medicine Society—in fact believes that this stored knowledge can be retrieved if the individual is well versed through initiation in traditional practices and ceremonies. The Mide'win shaman has become the symbol for this knowledge and understanding, possessing the archaic skills that allow him to call upon the ancestors for spiritual direction and guidance.

Like the Cistercian, the shaman was also trained in "animal husbandry," knowing when new blood had to be introduced to the tribe in order to keep the population healthy and strong. Tribal nations were known to systematically raid other nations with the express purpose of revitalizing the tribal bloodline through the enslaving of women and children.* The Apache especially were known to resort to such practices as their numbers dwindled over time due to a prolonged war with the U.S. government.

THE IMPORTANCE OF KEEPING THE BLOODLINE STRONG

In medieval Europe the instances of dynastic families petering out because of weakened stock and inbreeding was all too common. If the multigenerational inbred actually survived, mental disorders and rare blue-blood diseases such as hemophilia were all too prevalent. Probably the best known case of inbreeding concerns the tsesarevich Alexi, the hemophiliac son of Tsar Nicolas II and Tsarina Alexandra of Russia.

---

*Pre-European contact with native North Americans suggests that the earliest form of slavery was generally distinct from the form of African chattel slavery developed by Europeans in North America during the pre–Civil War period. Native tribes, specifically along the West Coast, made a habit of raiding other tribes to replace warriors who had died in battle. However, European influence greatly changed the slavery used by Native Americans. As trade with Europeans increased over the centuries, Plains Indians fell into destructive wars among themselves and raided other tribes to capture slaves for sale to Europeans.

Part of the related background to this case concerns the madness of King George III of England. King George was the third British monarch of the House of Hanover and was married to Princess Charlotte of the House of Mecklenburg-Strelitz. Both houses were among the longest ruling families of Europe and shared a common north German (Baltic) dynastic ancestry of west Slavic origin. The connection between the English and Russian families becomes more obvious when one realizes that Alix of Hesse-Darmstadt, a favorite grandchild of England's Queen Victoria, became the tsarina Alexandra. It was Alexandra who was a carrier of the gene for hemophilia, which she inherited from her maternal grandmother, Queen Victoria, whose own maternal grandmother, Princess Augusta Caroline Sophie Reuss of the German principality of Ebersdorf, was another carrier.[3]

Similar disorders and weaknesses must have developed through intermarriages in the Salian Frank and Merovingian dynasties and other lesser French dynasties that existed in the centuries subsequent to the marital union of Jesus and Mary Magdalene. This may have reached a point so as to cause alarm among their guardians and protectors—the Knights Templar—and their spiritual/bureaucratic arm, the Cistercians. Evidence of this weakened gene pool would certainly have become evident through the House of Stuart, given that it is speculated that the Holy Bloodline is intermingled with the blood of the self-proclaimed divine kings of Europe. For instance, James I, King of England (and IV of Scotland, the Stuart king), was described as having a tongue too big for his mouth and being so weak kneed that he couldn't walk on his own until he was seven years of age.[4]

If there was a need for new blood, the concept of developing strategic intermarriages between the strongest lines of native North Americans and the strongest lines of the Holy Bloodline are not as far-fetched as it first sounds. As noted previously, these strategic intermarriages would have occurred over centuries of secret transatlantic trade and interaction between the start of the twelfth century to the end of the sixteenth century. And, as also noted previously, it was believed that the Templars first established contact with the natives of North America somewhere around 1127, shortly after discovering

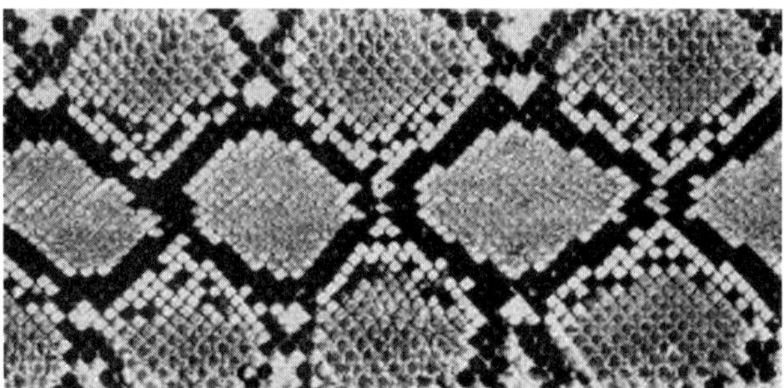

Fig. 9.4. Photograph of an eastern diamond-backed rattlesnake skin, from which the indigenous people of North America derived the symbolism that relates to their familial lines of descendency. Of course, if brother and sister were allowed to marry across multi-generations the bloodlline would be weakened and sickly. Only by marrying outside of the immediate family for several generations would a strong and healthy bloodline be maintained. Photograph property of the author, William F. Mann.

the ancient maps and other documents hidden under the ruins of the Temple of Solomon.*

Knowing this, the intertwined diamond-backed snakes of the modified caduceus take on another level of hidden meaning. The Old World symbolism behind the serpent of wisdom at one time or another became interchangeable with that of the dragon, which became associated with pre-Christian Druidic beliefs. The Celtic dragon and serpent were both ancient symbols of fertility, wisdom, and immortality. A hybrid horned dragon/snake figure was typically connected to the Celtic torque collar as a symbol of kingship and status.

In native North American (New World) lore the snake is symbolic of fertility and wisdom. In the Algonquin culture specifically, the snake symbolizes healing. Other traditions associate the snake with rebirth due to its ability to shed its skin. The intertwining of the two snakes of the caduceus—the DNA double helix—represents, as with the Celts,

*It is heavily speculated that upon discovering something of immense value under the Temple of Solomon, Hughes de Payens and the Knights Templar realized that it had to immediately be spirited away to the far ends of the Earth. Only then would it have been safe for Bernard of Clairvaux to petition the pope at the Council of Troyes to officially recognize the Order of the Knights Templar almost a decade later.

fertility, wisdom, immortality, healing, and rebirth. Many Renaissance paintings depicting the Crucifixion of Jesus demonstrate this same symbolism, showing the snake intertwined with Jesus himself, confirming his kingship and status.

In any event, the plotted strategic interactions would not only lead to physical intimacy between the two races but would obviously lead to a spiritual interaction on the highest level. Given the commonality of deep spiritual beliefs of the native North Americans and the medieval Knights Templar, it makes further sense that an exchange and blending of "inner secrets" would also occur over the centuries. This would most certainly occur as the two groups developed a special bond of peace, understanding, and trust through the open and honest exchange of their own unique knowledge with one another.

All of this has led to my own initiation in both the Masonic Knights Templar and the Old Mide'win, the Grand Medicine Society. However, given that I have made two solemn promises, I will not, in this book, expose the inner secrets or highly personal nature of the various rituals and ceremonies of those organizations. There's really no need to go into that much depth anyway. Instead, what I will reveal are several aspects of the two societies that I believe to be of prime importance to the argument that multigenerational interaction occurred across North America between the Knights Templar and various Algonquin Nations, interaction that allowed the Grail refugees to systematically occupy various Rose Line settlements until the establishment of their last refuge in the New World.

THE BEAR'S DEN

At this point hopefully the reader will accept that most of what has been conveyed is historically accurate and verifiable. The challenge now is to step into a different world of sorts, a netherworld—one of shadows, whispered passwords and signs, spiritual beliefs—one of transcendence. The reader will find comfort in the fact that the rituals and ceremonies of both the Mide'win and the Knights Templar have a common central belief in the Divine Being, whether it is seen to be God, the Creator, the Supreme Being, the Force of Nature, or Mother Earth. One other common theme is that through a belief in one true entity the initiate can be elevated to a position or state whereby they are able to *question,* to *understand,* and, eventually, to *share* in the Divine Being's wisdom.

One central realization through my various initiations is that the rituals and ceremonies of both the Mide'win and Knights Templar are virtual mirror images of each other. In fact, they share so many common signs, seals, tokens, mathematical elements, and moral allegorical interpretations that it is highly unlikely that they did not intermingle at some point. From the physical layout and requirements of the lodge to the spiritual rebirth of the candidate, it is strangely soothing to realize that regardless of the origins of either central belief, the two societies have evolved along parallel lines.

The modern-day equivalent of the medieval Knights Templar is considered to be the highest level of Christian Masonry that an initiate can obtain. Indeed, membership is open only to Royal Arch Freemasons who profess a belief in the Christian religion, specifically as it pertains to the Christian Mysteries. However, one does not necessarily have to believe that Jesus is the Divine Christ. The individual orders or degrees within Canada are the Knights of the Illustrious Red Cross, the Order of the Knights of Malta and of St. Paul (or Mediterranean Pass), and the final Order—the Knights of the Temple (Knights Templar).

Remember that to achieve the highest level of Knights Templar status in the York Rite arm of Freemasonry in Canada one must first go through the three basic degrees of Craft Masonry and the three degrees of the Royal Arch Chapter. When you add all of the degrees and orders together there are a total of nine levels.

Conversely, Old Mide'win—the Grand Medicine Society—is often wrongly described as being a secret religion of the Indians. Internally the spiritual tenets of the society are considered to be spiritual mysteries, or the Mystery of the Sacred Medicine. Mide practitioners, as we are sometimes known, are initiated and also ranked by degrees, or stages. Much like their mirror image presented through Christian Masonry, a member of the Grand Medicine Society cannot advance to the next higher degree until gaining full knowledge and understanding of that degree's requirements. Only after successful completion of the requirements of a degree may a candidate be considered for advancement into the next higher degree.

Similar to the basic principles of Freemasonry, everything taught in the Mide'win lodge—the wigwam—is by rote, by memory. The purpose of this is twofold. First of all, for centuries it's prevented the exposure of the sacred knowledge, and, second, it requires a high level of attention and proficiency from the apprentice initiate. I was surprised that there exists early accounts of the Mide'win from books written in the 1800s primarily by Jesuit missionaries that describe a group of elders who protected birchbark scrolls in hidden locations. One particular Jesuit by the name of Father W. J. Hoffman produced one of most comprehensive studies of the Mide'win traditions and ceremonies. This study, called *The Mide'wiwin or "Grand Medicine Society" of the Ojibwa,* was first published by the Smithsonian Institute in 1885–1886.[5]

By most accounts Mide'win is based on the Seven Fires prophecy with the first three degrees associated with the Three Fires. Within Freemasonry the Royal Arch, the fourth degree, was originally associated with the basic three degrees. Similarly, the Old Mide'win sometimes claim that the extended fourth degrees are only specialized forms of the fourth degree. Depending on the region, these extended fourth degrees can be comprised of the fourth to eighth degrees. A Mide'win initiate of the highest degree is often referred to as a 3 + 5. In comparison to the level achieved by the Knights of the Temple, the *Jiisakiwinini* is widely referred to by Old Mide'win elders as the highest degree of all the medicine practitioners in the Mide'win, but it must be remembered that it is a spiritual medicine that's achieved, not physical/plant-based medicine.

As noted previously, the Seven Fires prophecy kept by the Anishinabe/Algonquin is a prophecy originally taught among the Mide'win. In this case each fire represents a prophetical age marking phases or epochs in the life of the people of Turtle Island (North America). As noted, the Seven Fires prophecy represents key spiritual teachings for all of North America and suggests that the different colors and traditions of the human beings who reside there can come together on a basis of trust and respect. It is the Algonquin who are

Fig. 9.5. Rare birchbark scroll that depicts the layout of the initial Three Fires portion of the Mide'win lodge. Photograph property of the author, William F. Mann.

also the keepers of the Seven Fires prophecy wampum, which acts as a spiritual guidebook of sorts, defining protocol and the time lines relating to when each fire period is to be entered.

Associated with these time periods are traditions and ceremonies that are primarily designed to prepare one to enter the wigwam with an open heart and mind. And although these practices are meant to prepare one spiritually, they also have a practical aspect to them. In their original design they were tied to the changing four seasons and provided the ancient native an opportunity to gather, socialize, and reaffirm his or her family relations, which is of utmost importance to indigenous people.

Given that the Algonquin were a nomadic people who transferred their camps based on the movement and availability of their food supply, spring and fall ceremonial camps became the highlights of their existence. These camps also became places of learning for the young initiate to be further educated in the medicines of the Earth and the movement of the sun, stars, and moon.

Spring camp among the Algonquin became a time when the various tribal nations would leave their winter hunting territories and gather at strategic junctions such as major promontories or riverbanks to reap the spring fish run, to feast and celebrate their survival after a long and arduous winter, to trade winter crafts and furs, to reaffirm family ties and traditions, and to perform medicinal and spiritual ceremonies.

Spring camp was specifically centered around the need for fasting and sweating, which was required on so many levels. From a purely physical perspective fasting and sweating would cleanse/detox the body after a winter diet consisting of corn and grains, meat, and dried berries and fruit. But on a higher level the fasting ceremony was meant to allow the faster to travel to the netherworlds to dream, following which the tribal shaman would interpret the visions received.

Fall camp was similar in many ways, with the various tribal nations meeting at strategic spiritual points in the landscape among the lowest valleys and highest hills as they made their way to more protected areas where they would prepare for winter. As the colors turned and shadows grew longer, fall camp was a time of reaffirming ancestral ties, of connecting with the dead, and thanking the spirits for preparing them both spiritually and physically for the long and cold nights that were to come.

Fall was also the time of the retelling of the native history of life on Earth over the past six billion years. It was a time of native legend and lore when the young ones would learn valuable lessons, like being on the lookout for Raven, the trickster, who took great pleasure in creating fear and doubt.

For the past twenty years I have personally attended both spring and fall camps among my own Algonquin Nation. Over this time I have learned that the native way of life is embedded not only in spiritual teachings but in a sense of order and place. Similarly it was the Knights Templar who believed that out of chaos one could achieve a higher level of order. My trouble is that it has been very difficult to live in two worlds at once, especially when both are tugging at my heart. What I have especially learned is that I can't slip in and out of either world without having to decompress somewhat. If I don't allow for a period of adjustment when I return from a native camp, that's when my body starts to separate itself from my mind. These out-of-body experiences are especially difficult to control when one moves too quickly from a native communal world to a fast-paced, individually motivated, business environment.

In this light, about five years ago I fasted longer than twenty-four hours for the first time. I went five days and nights without food and water, after the proper native preparation, of course. Essentially what is required is that you personally construct beforehand what is considered to be a bear's den out in the woods and occupy it for five days, imitating the movement of the bear as she prepares to wake from her hibernation.

Fig. 9.6. Simulated bear's den constructed by the author where a five-day fasting ceremony was completed, thus allowing the author to convey his dreams to the tribal shaman and to gain spiritual insight into his future. Photograph property of the author, William F. Mann.

In much the same way as the rebirth or raising of the Master Mason, on the fifth day you emerge from the den into the light to celebrate the arrival of spring—the time when the mother bear has just given birth to her newborn.

ANTIENT RELATIONS

Variations of the old traditions and ceremonies still occur across the greater Algonquin Nation. However, the basic principles have remained the same for centuries, as have the principles of Freemasonry. In this manner, even though familial and fraternal ties may have been been broken on occasion, signs, seals, and tokens displayed upon recontact would have cemented the bond between the natives of North America and the Knights Templar during the pre-Columbian period when the Holy Bloodline and their guardians were moving forever westward.

Descendants of the original Grail refugees would have been guided from tribal nation to nation, all the while protected by their Knights Templar guardians and native protectors and guides. Ultimately the surviving generations would look nothing like the original group of Europeans who arrived on the shores in 1398 with Prince Henry Sinclair as their leader. By the seventeenth and eighteenth centuries the surviving families would have been mostly assimilated into the tribal nations with which they had strategically intermarried. They would also have assumed most of the local traditions and ceremonies, which were better suited to the local terrain and conditions.

However, they would not have forgotten the true purpose behind their existence and would also not have lost some of the physical European traits and characteristics that had been inbred in them over thousands of centuries. Hence, many of the eastern Mi'kmaq possess to this day the lighter skin, red-tinged hair, freckles, and blue eyes of the Norse Scots, much like that said to be possessed by the Mandan Indians.

The Mandan were said by many—including George Catlin, who spent several months among them in 1833—that because of their blue or gray eyes and lighter hair coloring they might possibly be descendants of the Welsh prince Madoc and his followers, who were said to have sailed to America from Wales in about 1170.[6] Catlin actually believed the Mandan were the "Welsh Indians" of North American folklore and legend. A later anthropologist named Hjalmar Holand even proposed that the Mandan characteristics were the result of interbreeding with Norse explorers, in part because of the Mandans' proximity to the Kensington Runestone.[7]

The only thing we know to be true is that the exact origins and early history of the Mandan remain unknown. Their oral history refers to them originally coming from an eastern location near a large body of water. Anthropologists and linguists who studied them have presented the theory that, like other Siouan-speaking people (including the Hidatsa), the Mandan originated in the area of the mid-Mississippi River Valley and the Ohio River Valley in present-day Ohio. Logically, then, the Mandan would have migrated northwest via the Missouri River. These same experts believe that this migration occurred possibly as late as the seventeenth century but probably occurred between 1000 CE and the thirteenth century, which corresponds nicely to the

Fig. 9.7. *Mandan Village,* 1833, by George Catlin. Note the round palisade village and the round permanent dwellings that evolved into a permanent agrarian settlement.

first wave of Norse explorers and Templars that are said to have arrived during that same period.

After their arrival on the banks of the Heart River, a tributary of the Missouri River located near present-day Mandan, North Dakota (46°49'46"N, 100°53'17"W), it's recorded that the Mandan constructed nine villages: two on the east side of the river and seven on the west side. At some point soon thereafter it is said that the Hidatsa people also moved into the region. Mandan tradition states that the Hidatsa were a nomadic tribe although they established amicable relations with the Mandan and constructed temporary villages north of them at the Knife River until such time that they moved farther west into the great northern plains.

The Mandan, Hidatsa, and Arikara (Sahnish) are known as the Three Affiliated Tribes of North Dakota. Their history tells how a large group of Hidatsa moved northwest in 1740–1742 and established a settlement adjacent to the Bow River near Cluny, Alberta, where the Blackfoot Crossing Historical Park is today. Curiously, in the area of the park, archaeologists have uncovered what appears to have been a fortified village constructed in a half circle and surrounded by a moat, similar to early Norse ring forts. The depression of the moat is still visible, as well as circular depressions of the earth lodges. The archaeological site is now known as the Cluny Earthlodge Village.[8] (Remember that the first Sulpicians originated from the Cluny Abbey in Burgundy during the twelfth century!)

Following this rather unique discovery, members of the Blackfoot Crossing Historical Park storyline committee traveled to North Dakota and met with some of the local Mandan elders. From them they learned that there is an oral history recounting that some groups of Mandan/Hidatsa once traveled north and later returned speaking another language. What's interesting about this story is that it coincides with an Old Mide'win story that speaks of an exodus of shamans from the upper Great Lakes area who apparently had banded together in 1740 and moved to the west, taking with them a large quantity of sealed boxes via packhorse and disappearing into the foothills of the Rocky Mountains.

Originally the Hidatsa were associated with the Crow, who also had migrated to the Great Plains and the western foothills of the Rocky Mountains in Montana. It was here that the Crow first shared a great deal of wild territory with the Shoshone and the Blackfoot. Over time the Blackfoot Confederacy ultimately became the dominant Indian nation of this vast area. Originally it (the Blackfoot Confederacy) consisted of three tribal nations that were united by commonalities of kinship and dialect. They all spoke the common language of the Blackfoot, which was one of the major Algonquin languages, as the Blackfoot Confederacy was the farthest western-ranging tribal consortium of the larger Algonquin Nation that spread from the foothills of the Rockies to the eastern seaboard.

The three tribal nations of the Blackfoot Confederacy were the Piegan, the Bloods (also called the Kaina), and the Siksika. The Blackfoot Confederacy became one of the great warrior nations, and at one time their combined territory stretched from the North Saskatchewan River to the Yellowstone River and from the Rocky Mountains to the South Saskatchewan. In the early eighteenth century, from the Shoshone they adopted the use of the horse, which gave them expanded range and mobility as well as advantages in hunting.

As time went on, though, the Blackfoot retreated to what is now southern Alberta and northwest Montana, including several remaining natural areas such as the Helena National Forest and the Beaverhead-Deerlodge National Forest. Surprisingly, in spite of their warrior reputation, it would be only the Blackfoot who refused to fight in both the Great Plains Indian Wars around 1870 and the Northwest/Louis Riel Rebellion of 1885. Could it be that the Blackfoot were protecting something of great value, so much so that they did not want to risk the attention of the Canadian and U.S. governments?

Ancient Blackfoot traditions are very complex and were kept a secret for centuries. Of course ceremonies were and still are very important to them, and this is one of the few times that all three subtribes would gather together. The ceremonies usually revolved around a dance—and their greatest tribal ceremony was the sun dance—which is still held every year during the summer.

The sun dance is a celebration of the sun, and rather curiously it is initiated by a virgin woman who pledges to take on the responsibilities of sponsoring the dance. The dance lasts four days, during which time the dancers undergo a fast. The ceremony ends with some of the strongest and bravest initiates having their chests pierced after which they are hung from poles of a tepee to prove their gratitude to their main deity, the sun. If any reader has seen the 1970 movie *A Man Called Horse,* starring Richard Harris, they will appreciate the individual spiritual conviction and courage that is required for the initiate to survive such a gruesome test.

Although their main Divine Being is the sun, the Blackfoot also believe in a supernatural being named Napi, which means "Old Man." Additionally, the Blackfoot tribe has complicated beliefs about supernatural powers in connection with nature and the forces found on Earth. They believe that animals have their own powers and that these animals can bestow these supernatural powers on someone in a dream. The dreams often revolve around the animal giving the dreamer a list of objects, songs, and rituals that the dreamer has to gather in order to use the power. When the dreamer awakes, he or she gathers those items together in a medicine bundle. (Medicine bundles are still often traded between individuals of the three aforementioned tribal nations.)

One other interesting belief of the Blackfoot revolves around water. The Blackfoot Nation believes that rivers and lakes hold special power due to the Underwater People who reside there; they are called the Suyitapis. Because of this belief to this day, traditional Blackfoot avoid eating fish or using canoes even though their territory is crossed by an extensive grid of streams and rivers.

There are many ways in which the history and culture of the Blackfoot overlap aspects of the story of Prince Henry Sinclair, the Knights Templar, and the Holy Bloodline as it moved westward to a final refuge. First of all the Blackfoot came from the east, and in this they are part of the larger Algonquin Nation, which includes the Mi'kmaq. As we have learned, it was the Mi'kmaq who first provided Sinclair and his followers with sanctuary. Second, the Blackfoot's main god is the sun, and their main ceremonial dance reflects the movement of the sun across the sky at various times of the year. Their ceremonial dance includes a virgin woman and the crucifixion of the initiate, even though these elements existed in Blackfoot culture long before the official arrival of the white man.

Then there is the Blackfoot belief that the animals—ranging from deer, elk, and beaver to snake, raven, and crow—all possess supernatural powers that can be bestowed on the individual. And in many ways the reference to Suyitapis and the Underwater People harkens right back to Bishop Sulpitius and the Merovingian practice of constructing vaults under rivers. There is also the concept of medicine bundles being created by dreams. Perhaps it is too far-fetched, but might the notion of these medicine bundles possessing special powers harken back to the bundles that were spirited away by the original Knights Templar close to a thousand years ago, virtually halfway around the world?

Saint Anthony and Saint Paul purportedly took to the wilderness to be closer to God. Closer to reality, it's been demonstrated that the painting by David Teniers the Younger incorporated what was known of early Spanish and French exploration across North America by a secretive Franciscan/Recollet fraternity in the first half of the seventeenth century.

It's also been demonstrated that the northwest area of the continent by that time still hadn't been officially explored or mapped, although inklings remained (judging by the number of "white Indian" settlements that were identified) that the upper Missouri River area was previously penetrated by at least the early Norse Christians. All Grail paths surely lead to the foothills of Montana and the land of the Blackfoot.

THE PILLARS OF FREEMASONRY

Meriwether Lewis must have suspected that something of immense value lay just beyond the Gates of the Mountains—the immense pillars of rock along the shores of the Missouri River—just south of Helena, the present-day capital of Montana. The presence of these pillars alone could have easily convinced Meriwether Lewis that he was entering the inner sanctuary of the temple.

Here are two of the more prominent "places & objects distinguished by such natural marks & characters of a durable kind, as that they may with certainty be recognized hereafter" that Jefferson had instructed Lewis to observe and to take coordinates of, as contained within the quote provided in chapter 6 (p. 291). As a Master Mason, the significance of the two pillars would surely not have been lost on him; they symbolized that he was about to enter a very sacred lodge.

In many cases the pillars of the lodge are portrayed in balance: one was shown as black and one being shown as white, much like the checkered pattern of the chessboard. The Gates of the Mountains are the result of glacial movement coming down from the Rocky Mountains, scouring out the soft white limestone that is present at the base of the foothills.

As noted earlier, before a candidate enters a Masonic lodge room for the first time he is required to stand before a closed door that leads

Fig. 9.8. Photograph of the Gates of the Mountains, Helena, Montana, which on one level could represent the two pillars leading to the inner sanctuary of the temple. Compare the layout and positioning of the two pillars to the landscape portrayed in the painting *St. Anthony and St. Paul Fed by Ravens* (see figure 4.2 on p. 122). Photograph property of the author, William F. Mann.

into the inner sanctum of the lodge. In many lodges he is prompted to quietly reflect on his life up to that moment, because the second the door opens it's anticipated that his life will change forever.

This is not to say, however, that all initiates are instantly elevated to a higher level of spiritual awareness. In fact some candidates go through the first of the three basic degrees of Craft Masonry before deciding that Masonry just isn't for them, which is perfectly fine. On the other hand there are those initiates who embrace Freemasonry almost too much, seeing hidden Masonic meaning throughout their everyday lives from then on. The trick is to maintain a balance and to apply a fair amount of skepticism to everything that one encounters.

Having said this, as related previously, the two famous pillars of the original Temple of Solomon are generally referred to as Joachim and Boaz. They are still known in some circles as lily columns, in that their tops, which are made of brass and forged at the foundry of the master builder Hiram, were adorned with artistic carvings of lilies. It bears repeating that a white water lily adorned the female column, Boaz, which represented the southern half of the Israeli kingdom; the male column, Joachim, was adorned by a blue water lily, which represented the northern half of the kingdom.

In Masonic circles, though, it is said that the pillars of the temple were built of stone and brick before the Great Flood to preserve the secrets of sacred geometry. Then after the Flood, Pythagoras found the two pillars and he, along with the great alchemist Hermes Trismegistus, conveyed these secret arts to the Greeks. The right-hand column was called Joachim and is associated with establishment and legality; the left-hand column was called Boaz and symbolizes strength. Hence the initiate may at some time achieve the same wisdom that Solomon himself possessed.

In many ways Saint Anthony and Saint Paul could also be seen to represent the two pillars of Freemasonry. Quite amazingly, David Teniers the Younger was clever enough to incorporate this symbolism into his painting. In his painting *St. Anthony and St. Paul Fed by Ravens* (see figure 9.10 on p. 294), hiding behind the two saints in the shadows is the rough portico, or doorway, which appears to be the entrance to a rather rustic lodge, or maybe even an old mine. (Remember, one of the

Fig. 9.9. *King Solomon.* An early eighteenth-century lithograph depicts King Solomon between the two pillars of the temple, which on one level denotes wisdom and beauty. The historical figure of King Solomon and his building of the temple has become the central focus to all that encompasses speculative Freemasonry. In this manner, King Solomon is viewed as the first worshipful master of the lodge or temple.

keys is to always look beyond.) The story of Saint Anthony tells us that he lived in an abandoned fortress; Saint Paul lived in an old cave, a den of sorts. Suspended from the two stone pillars adorning the entrance there hangs an elk horn and the carcass of a crow.

This is strange in that the theme of the painting revolves around Saint Anthony and Saint Paul's time in the desert whereby they were sustained by manna from heaven, delivered by ravens that had been sent to them by God. There is also the connected story of how ravens protected the martyred body of Saint Sulpice from vultures until it could be recovered and properly buried. (It is alleged that ravens still protect

Fig. 9.10. Enlarged detail of the painting of *St. Anthony and St. Paul Fed by Ravens,* which clearly shows the entrance to a rough dwelling, possibly a natural cave or animal den of some kind. Or perhaps it is suggestive of an old gold or silver mine—maybe a *lost* gold or silver mine? The key is to always look beyond what seems apparent.

the site today.) Again it appears that Teniers was well versed as to which tribal nation in the New World revered the raven.

In the Blackfoot culture ravens are believed to be a messenger of the spirit world and also are believed to be keepers of secrets. The symbolic lore of the Blackfoot describes the raven as a creature of metamorphosis, shape-shifting; in this it symbolizes change and transformation. Raven is also considered a trickster because of these attributes of transformation.

Foremost, though, Raven is the bearer of magic and a harbinger of messages from the cosmos. The Blackfoot shaman calls upon Raven in ritual so that visions can be clarified. Raven is also called upon in Blackfoot ritual for healing purposes. It is also believed that Raven may provide healing from a distance.

The Blackfoot are known for their astronomical knowledge, and this is evident by their many legends about the Sky Beings: Sun; (the wife) Moon; and (their son) Morning Star, and Venus. It is said that it is the songbird—Brings down the Sun—who tells the sky watcher of the habits of the Sky Beings. It is the songbird who tells the Blackfoot the names for the moons and how to read the signs in the skies. It is also the songbird that tells the Blackfoot the ancient star legends of the Seven Brothers (the Great Bear—the Big Dipper) and of the Lost Children (the Pleiades). In many Blackfoot legends it is the shape-shifter, Raven, who assumes the songbird's role.

GEOGRAPHICALLY SPEAKING . . .

All of this reinforces the notion that to specifically identify the exact location of the last refuge of the Knights Templar in the New World the learned initiate must follow the saintly clues back to their source. Only then, it is said, will the true location be revealed. So, geographically speaking, the origins of Saint Anthony and Saint Paul's beliefs definitely appear to be key to what lies beyond the Gates of the Mountains. The real challenge seems to be how to apply it to the Masonic symbolism found in the shadows of Teniers's painting of Saint Anthony and Saint Paul.

When one sails south through the Gates of the Mountains toward the source of the Missouri River the most immediate thing that appears is the small municipality of Townsend, Montana. Townsend was obviously named because of its location at the navigable end of the Missouri River. Townsend is located at 46°19'13"N, 111°31'4"W and was established in the late 1860s in response to the first settlers and gold miners who made their way into the area following Lewis and Clark's expedition.

Surveying the countryside around Townsend, which acts as a key intersection of meridians, what first strikes the viewer is the number of significant nearby mountain peaks. Two of these mountain peaks slyly hint at the bald saints as they are portrayed in Teniers's painting. To the southwest is Mount Baldy; to the northeast is Big Baldy Mountain. In the painting Saint Anthony is also sitting on his butt, all the while controlling the snake or monster. To the west is the community of Butte, Montana, and "atop" that is the small community of Anaconda, which happens to be close to the Snake River.

Immediately to the west of Townsend, along the border of Broadwater and Jefferson Counties, is a distinctive series of limestone outcrops known as Little Hogback. One of the stories attached to Saint Anthony is that he is the patron saint of the rather odd combination of pigs and skin diseases. As we have established earlier, in the Middle Ages ergotism, the rather gangrenous poisoning known as holy fire, or Saint Anthony's Fire, was named after monks of the Order of Saint Anthony who were particularly successful in treating this ailment with slabs of pork and lime. Hence the sly reference to Saint Anthony in naming the weathered limestone outcrops Little Hogback.

Etymologically speaking there is also a rather significant clue found in the name of the Piegan Blackfoot who still occupy this area in Montana. If the word is broken down to *Pi* (meaning "infinite") and the Celtic word *egan* (meaning "fire"), then there is the very interesting suggestion of a relationship to the infinite fire that can be expected if someone's feet are held to a fire to the point that they are blackened. Remember that the last grand master of the Knights Templar was tortured for seven years before finally being burned to death at the stake. It was said that the flesh on Jacques de Molay's feet had been virtually burned off by the inquisitor's hot poker long before his execution and that he had to be carried to his execution.

Just as significantly, directly west of Townsend are two very important mountain peaks. One is Elkhorn Peak, the other is Crow Peak. Remember that the pillars of the saints' rather crude entrance to their den—their "bear's den"—portrays an elk horn and a crow. Finally, by following the creeks that flow from the mountainside toward Townsend,

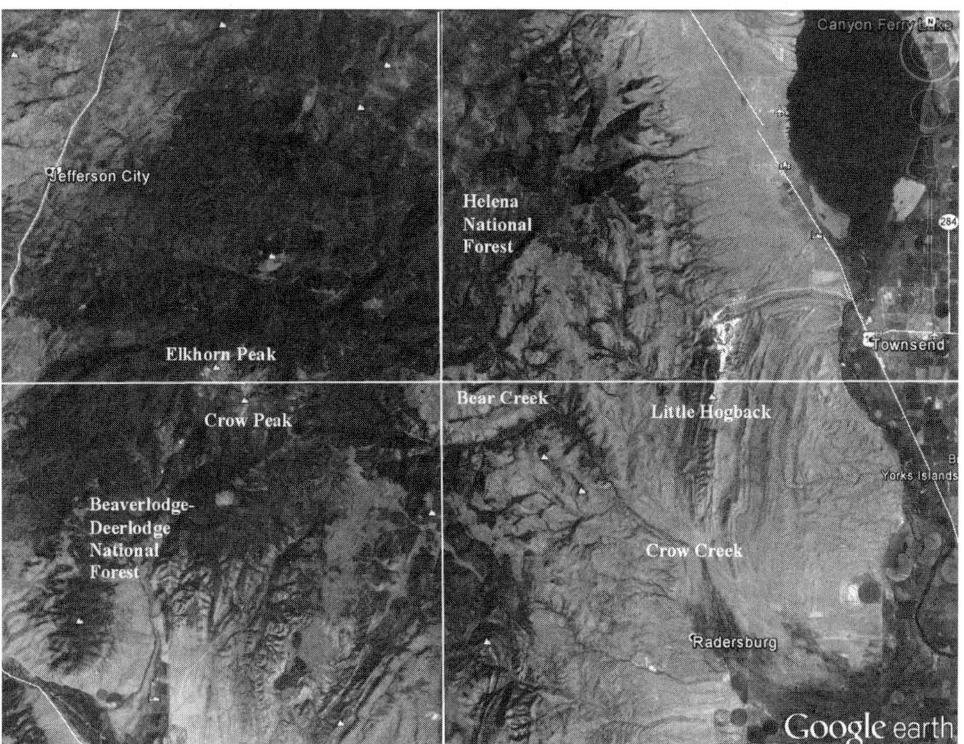

Fig. 9.11. A Google Earth image depicting the general location of the last refuge of the Knights Templar in the New World

the one true source can be determined. The major stream coming out of the mountains at this point is named Crow Creek. Rather significantly, one of its main tributaries is named Bear Creek, which runs to the west—straight as the crow flies. It is here, at the source of Bear Creek—at the source of life itself—that to this day Blackfoot legend says lies an immense treasure. It is here where there remains an undisturbed treasure trove in an ancient gold mine that once belonged to the Old Man of the Mountain—Prince Henry Sinclair himself. The trouble is that it is contained in a secret vault that is hidden underwater and protected by a series of sluice tunnels and watertraps, similar in scale and complexity to the system that was developed under Oak Island. To the would-be treasure hunter, beware of the mark of the old crow—the raven—for he is the blackfooted trickster!

10
X Marks the Spot

A PLAY ON WORDS

As the end of this book nears, after having unveiled the last refuge of the Knights Templar in the New World and the location of the remaining Templar treasure, the reader must be speculating on its potential recovery and rightful ownership. The reader must also be wondering about the true purpose behind my sharing this secret knowledge, other than the obligation to fulfill a four-hundred-year-old Native American prophecy.

The answer to these musings lies in my family ties. In many ways I've felt the need to share this knowledge ever since I first realized how my unique initiation into both the Knights Templar and Old Mide'win and the related strategic intermarriages between the natives and the Templars played into my overall story. What really sealed it was the information provided in the letter from Brunet to Bourget concerning my ancestor Thomas Lagarde dit St. Jean. Thomas Lagarde put his trust in Father Brunet as a fellow brother, as a fellow initiate. Hopefully that trust was returned, but we'll never know, given that there is no record of where, when, and how Thomas died.

One thing that this book has demonstrated is that for far too long now innocent and good people have been used as pawns by the historic superpowers that were both church and state. To think of the numbers who have suffered over the course of centuries just because of their religious beliefs or allegiances to their native country and that current

Fig. 10.1. Detail of the painting *St. Anthony and St. Paul Fed by Ravens* highlighting the area with Saint Paul and the crossed sticks. Note the faint X-shaped birthmark on top of Saint Paul's bald head. Could this be a faint reference to a physical location or a fainter reference to the male X chromosome that causes various traits such as male baldness?

world events are continuing these sufferings all in the name of God and Country is downright obscene. As well, the continuing oppression and abuse of women and children around the world has to stop, not only because it is the right thing to do but also for the sake of all mankind.

Some readers will probably not understand or want to understand the full extent of what is at stake here. North America is unique in that each of its three countries was founded upon individual but rather similar principles that appear to have been forgotten or were taken over by the religious right. The charters of the United States, Canada, and Mexico contain the principles of freedom from oppression and equality for all. What is also unique about these countries is that their indigenous peoples welcomed waves of New World explorers to their shores with peace and kindness, only to be repaid with discrimination and genocide.

If carved stone tablets, rune stones, or scrolls and writings are found among the treasure that speak to the earliest agreements between these early explorers and the native people it will be interesting to see if these "treaties" will be honored or ignored. It will also be most interesting to see who lays claim to being the rightful owner of the Templar treasure, including the many religious artifacts that surely remain part of it. Will these relics and religious objects be used for the good of mankind or used as justification for a new Holy Crusade? Given that the current world situation is becoming increasingly complex, perhaps it is most appropriate that the answer to this question is provided through a parable.

THE PARABLES OF JESUS

The teachings of Jesus have certainly become synonymous with the term *parable.* Indeed, the parables of Jesus have become some of the best known lessons in the world.[1] For two thousand years the very simplicity of the stories, when enriched by their own imagery, have allowed for central themes and archetypes to become standardized and accepted as an analogy of Jesus's own righteousness and divinity. Jesus's teachings, or parables, are therefore suitably described as spiritual lessons, or stepping-stones, to be learned as one reaches toward heaven.

For example, the parable of the prodigal son is probably one of the best known stories, dealing as it does with the central theme of loss and redemption. On the other hand, the parable of the hidden treasure is said to illustrate the great spiritual value of the kingdom of heaven and advise how to best avoid all physical trappings in order to reach it. This is a lesser-known parable of Jesus, appearing in only one of the canonical gospels of the New Testament. According to Matthew 13:44 the parable immediately precedes the parable of the pearl, which contains a similar theme of spiritual atonement and attainment.

Over the centuries individual parables have been interpreted on several different levels and attributed to several different physical locations. It's not in any way surprising then to believe that the parable of the hidden treasure would have a parallel meaning—a double entendre—to the inner circle of the Knights Templar, assuming that they were not only the guardians of the treasure of Solomon's Temple but also protectors of the Holy Bloodline.

The parable of the hidden treasure speaks to the discovery of a treasure in a field by someone other than the current owner of the field, who is totally unaware of its existence. The narrative relays that, unfortunately, the finder cannot extract the treasure, because he cannot afford to buy the field. Thus even though the discoverer has knowledge of the treasure he cannot attain it. The discoverer of the treasure becomes obsessed with the unattainable treasure while the kingdom of heaven remains readily attainable. Herein lies the moral dilemma contained in this parable.

Spiritually, from the church's perspective, it is said that the lesson to be learned from this parable is that the kingdom of heaven is the real treasure. An extension of that theme is that man should not be swayed by the trappings of physical treasure, for the spiritual kingdom of heaven is far more valuable. But it has also been said that the kingdom of heaven is the city of Jerusalem itself, which the Templars gained and lost and regained and lost over a series of crusades.

The 2005 Hollywood movie *The Kingdom of Heaven* starring Orlando Bloom and Eva Green played upon this very theme, in that Christian Jerusalem is defended against Saladin's army at all costs only to lose the city because of the sheer folly and arrogance of the leader of the Knights Templar, Guy of Lusignan. The point that most viewers will miss, though, is that the hidden Templar treasure had already been spirited away from Jerusalem and that the ill-fated Second Crusade was doomed from the start. By this time several factions of Christian orders were already fighting over what they considered to be the ultimate treasure—the city of Jerusalem—which turned out to be nothing more than a sun-drenched killing ground.

The movie *National Treasure,* although somewhat more lighthearted than *The Kingdom of Heaven,* presents essentially the same moral question toward the end of the movie as to what the main character—Benjamin Gates (played by Nicholas Cage)—will do following his discovery of the fictional Templar treasure found under Trinity Church in downtown Manhattan. In this case the central character makes the correct moral decision to turn the treasure over to the FBI with the assurance that it will be distributed among the great museums around the world to be enjoyed and studied by all mankind.

HONING IN ON THE TREASURE

Coming full circle once again, the moral debate between Saint Anthony and Saint Paul as depicted by Teniers in his painting *St. Anthony and St. Paul Fed by Ravens,* appears at first to be centered on the philosophical question of the very existence of God and the divinity of Jesus Christ. But as noted previously, there also appear to be several other hidden parallels that can be drawn from the painted rocks, artifacts, and books that surround the two saints.

In this light it appears that the saints are debating the question: What is the proper sequential application of geometric axioms required to unravel the mystery of where the holy treasure exactly lies? Another parallel debate between the two saints appears to be centered on the rather poignant question as to whether it is best to expose the secret knowledge that they've discovered or remain quiet and follow the tenets of the church.

What's interesting about Teniers's painting is that the two crossed sticks before Saint Paul suggest that X does indeed mark the spot. In one way this classic symbol can be seen to represent the Hooked X presented by Scott Wolter as being a hidden symbolic clue relating to the Holy Bloodline and the Sacred Feminine. Along a parallel line of thought, the X can actually be shown to be a physical marker of sorts in that the angle and composition of the X correspond to the physical landscape surrounding Townsend, Montana (see figure 10.2 on p. 305).

Figure 10.2 demonstrates that one slanted line of the X extends from the peak of Big Baldy Mountain in the northeast to the peak of Baldy Mountain in the southwest, nicely correlating to the positioning of the two bald saints—Saint Anthony and Saint Paul—in Teniers's painting. The other slanted line connects, through the Gates of the Mountains, the unincorporated areas of Craig in the northwest and Big Sky in the southeast. It is not surprising then to find within the background of the painting a stone crag, which is positioned immediately behind the two saints. The word "crag" is of Celtic origin, meaning "rock" or "precipice."

The location of Big Sky, Montana, is also quite interesting in relation to Teniers's painting in that a "blue book" (containing the known names and descendancy of the blue bloods?) is displayed at the southeast point of the slanted X. Just to the northwest of the present-day Big Sky Mountain Village resort, along the same northwest–southeast angled line of the X, is the aptly named Gallatin Peak, which reaches a staggering elevation of 3,357 meters, or 11,013 feet, above sea level.

Albert Gallatin is perhaps one of the least known heroes associated with the Lewis and Clark Corps of Discovery. Originally from Switzerland, he was a French Mason and secretary of the treasury of the U.S. government during Jefferson's tenure. Among his many personal triumphs, he engineered the financial details of the Louisiana Purchase and even helped plan the Lewis and Clark expedition.* In March of 1803 he asked mapmaker Nicholas King to prepare a new map of western North America incorporating the main features of nine of the most recent maps by other explorers, including George Vancouver, Alexander Mackenzie, and David Thompson. In essence, this little-known map provided Lewis and Clark with most of what they required to accomplish their stated objective and may also have provided them with other more secretive information.[2]

Rather incredibly, at the age of seventy Gallatin wrote a monumental treatise describing the characteristics, territories, and languages of

*Surprisingly, there is a continuous line in Albert Gallatin's life that has eluded significant inquiry from historians. He maintained a fairly extensive exchange of letters with Elizabeth Bonaparte. Elizabeth Patterson Bonaparte, known as Betsy, was the daughter of a merchant of Baltimore, Maryland, and was the first wife of Jerome Bonaparte and sister-in-law of Emperor Napoleon I of France. The correspondence includes, of all things, a certificate of divorce by Albert Gallatin.

all known Native American tribes, including those of Mexico. Then at eighty-one he founded the American Ethnological Society, and shortly before his death in 1849 he published several papers in the society's journal on the jargon or trade language that had emerged in the previous fifty years in the northwest area of America, including that of the Blackfoot.[3]

Not surprisingly, then, the nexus of Teniers's X that connects the four mountain peaks falls directly at the location of the bear's den—the Blackfoot lodge—that sits atop the distinctive white limestone outcrop known as Little Hogback. Remember that the name of the original settlement surrounding the San Antonio Mission in Texas was San Antonio de Bexar. In this case the X is deep in the heart of the black bear and not in Texas! Once again we find that dry sense of humor of the Templars shining through, suggesting that the heart of the Bear Goddess waits to be pierced once again.

The funniest thing about the analogies that surround the unveiling of the last refuge of the Knights Templar in the New World is the etymological application that has been applied on many levels. In other words, the "play on words" displayed by the Templars knows no bounds. What is truly amazing is how the two Renaissance painters—Poussin and Teniers—played right along, culminating in the extremely clever use of the symbolism of the crossed sticks.

On the simplest level the sticks appear to be nothing more than the walking sticks of two old men. On an entirely different level the sticks themselves resemble the ancient Celtic ell measurement, which is equal to thirty-seven inches. The suggestion here is that the saints—and by extension the Knights Templar—possessed an earlier Celtic knowledge that allowed them to accurately traverse North America using the traditional Celtic ell measurement. This means that the Templars understood and applied not only the lessons of the parables but on a more practical level, a "pair-of-ells."

THE CLUES KEEP COMING

But the clues don't stop here. It was through sheer genius that Teniers was able to relate his painting to the physical landscape of both the present-

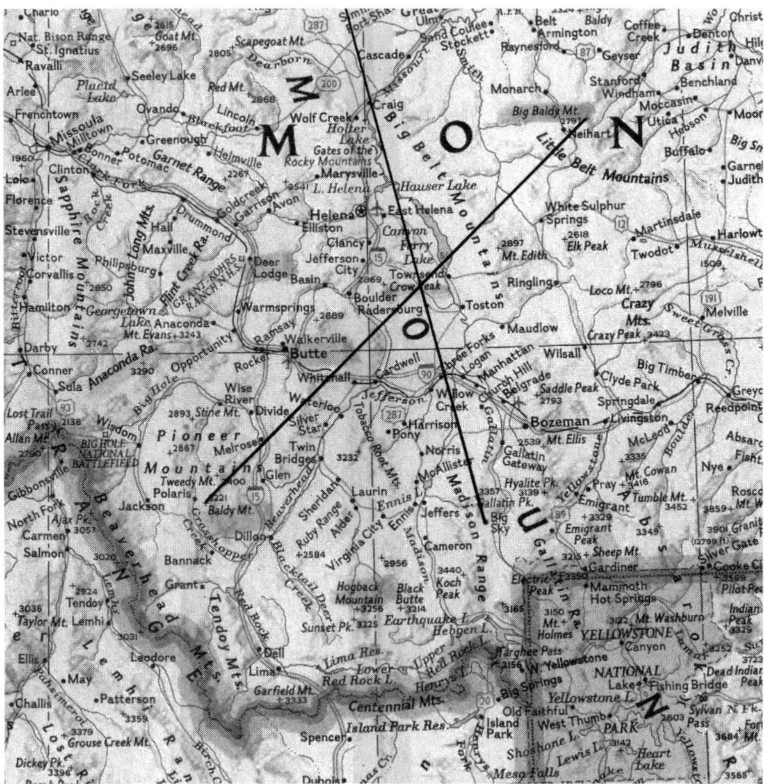

Fig. 10.2. Detailed map of Montana demonstrating how the X symbol found in David Teniers the Younger's painting *St. Anthony and St. Paul Fed by Ravens* corresponds to four distinctive mountain peaks or rock outcrops that surround the Townsend, Montana, area. The nexus of the X shows the location of "Mon taina"—"my refuge." Illustration copyright of the author, William F. Mann.

day northwestern and southwestern United States. Here once again is the notion of the inner circle and the outer circle, which acted in a manner to deflect the attention of the seeker. All the while Teniers rather amazingly presented in his themed painting evidence leading back to early pre-Christian Celtic exploration of the Americas. The only logical conclusion is that Teniers must have been provided with highly accurate maps and logs proving that the early Celts and other secret societies not only traveled all the way up the Missouri to present-day Montana but also surveyed and settled the area with remarkable skill and fortitude.

Fig. 10.3. Illustrated is a composite photograph of the Kensington Runestone, which is currently on permanent display at the Runestone Museum in Alexandria, Minnesota. The height-to-width dimensions of the stone are 2:1. The dimensions of the fountain found in figure 3.5 on p. 101 are too similar to be coincidental. Photograph property of the author, William F. Mann.

Teniers is telling us as much by depicting the many ancient texts lying around the ground and being examined by the saints. Here again are the ancient texts that the Templars discovered under the ruins of Solomon's Temple in Jerusalem, which eventually found their way into the secret collections of the seventeenth-century European chess masters—Cardinal Richelieu and Archduke Leopold Wilhelm I.

The Celts have been credited with exploring the New World by authors such as Barry Fell. Although he was a professor of invertebrate zoology at the Harvard Museum of Comparative Zoology, Fell is best known for his controversial work in New World epigraphy, which is the study of inscriptions. The Kensington Runestone is a perfect example of New World epigraphy—a Norse rune message carved on a stone marker. Through a vast array of highly detailed books, Fell argues that various inscriptions found across the Americas are best explained by extensive native North American contact with pre-Columbian Old World civilizations.

CASTING DISPERSIONS

Fell's central thesis is that a secret partnership existed between the pre-Christian Iberian Celts from Spain and Portugal and the daring Semitic seafarers who followed the waves of the Jewish Diaspora as early as 800 BCE. In part, Fell based his conclusions on the hundreds of inscriptions found across North America and the evidence provided by the hundreds of Celtic and Egyptian words found in the dialects of the northeastern Algonquin. As noted earlier, the relationship between the huge copper deposits of Isle Royale in Lake Superior and the headwaters of the Mississippi, Missouri, and other river systems across America were a mere hop, skip, and jump—the knight's chess move—away.

As noted previously, even though Barry Fell was an accomplished zoologist at Harvard University, he is best known for three books that claim that many centuries before Christopher Columbus reached America, Celts, Basques, Phoenicians, Egyptians, Carthaginians, and many others were making transatlantic journeys. Fell's interest in inscriptions began early in his career, but his most famous body of work started in 1976 with the publication of *America B.C.* It was at this point that Fell first proposed translations of specific inscriptions found on rock surfaces and artifacts in North and South America. Within the pages of *America B.C.*, Fell theorized that the carved inscriptions could no longer be attributed to the local indigineous people but instead were written in Old World scripts and languages. In spite of intense criticism from several prominent academics, his second and third books—*Saga America* (1980) and *Bronze Age America* (1982)—are just as compelling and just as commercially successful.

Unfortunately, Fell passed away without justly receiving the academic accolades that he so rightly deserved.

The intricate fabric of rivers of North America certainly provided the natural highways that allowed intrepid medieval explorers and settlers such as Prince Henry Sinclair and his inner circle of Knights Templar to easily seek out the many earlier settlements established by other New World travelers. As demonstrated, these inner sanctuaries corresponded to a secret grid pattern across America that was based on the earliest transatlantic traveler's astronomical skills, which enabled them to accurately establish both latitude and longitude.

Whether it was Iberian Celts or Semitic seafarers who followed in the wake of the Phoenicians, Carthaginians, Libyans, and Egyptians, or a partnership between these two groups that first established this grid pattern across North America, really doesn't matter. The point that can't be lost is that certain pre-Christian secret societies possessed the necessary antient skills to explore, map, and settle all of North America and that this and other secret knowledge ultimately came into the hands of the original Knights Templar.

THE JEWISH CONNECTION

Many of the original Templar families could actually claim Norse or Jewish origins, or a combination of both. The other point that can't be lost is that the period between 800 BCE and roughly 300 CE would certainly be witness to a series of dispersions in which the Jews in particular were driven out of the Middle East and Israel in periodic waves. In this light, perhaps the Semitic seafarers were actually looking to establish a New Jerusalem far away from their oppressors.

Of course there is another major event that took place prior to 800 BCE in the Middle East that involves the twelve tribes of Israel and their exodus from Egypt under Moses and Aaron, his brother. Unfortunately the exact date when the twelve tribes of Israel began to be known as "Israel" is not unanimously agreed upon by scholars and historians. However, it is an accepted fact that the transformation took place sometime before the thirteenth century BCE. This date is established because of the Israel Stele—a carved stone recording the event.* The Exodus record (Exodus 12:14) declares that the children of God spent 430 years in Egypt before settling in the chosen land![4]

It is further recorded that beginning with the conquering of the northern kingdom of Israel in 722 BCE by the Assyrians, the twelve lost tribes were either deported to Mesopotamia or scattered throughout the Middle East. Then in 568 BCE, after the overthrow of the kingdom of Judah by Nebuchadnezzar II of Babylon, a second wave of Jews was either sent into slavery in Babylon or made their way back to Mesopotamia (modern-day Iraq). This forced exodus followed the destruction of the first Temple of Solomon.

Next came what is known as the Hellenistic Diaspora in about 200 BCE. But the Jewish Diaspora during the Hellenistic period, unlike the earlier Babylonian Diaspora, did not occur because of forced expulsion. Most of the Jews expelled from Judea by the Babylonian king Nebuchadnezzar had by this time returned to the land of Zion.[5] The Hellenistic Diaspora was for the most part a voluntary movement of Jews into the Hellenistic kingdoms that created the Jewish presence outside Judea, especially in Ptolemaic Egypt. This diaspora was wedged between two worlds of thought: the Hellenistic values of the Greeks and the Mosaic Law.

Then around 66 CE, following a period of relative calm that led to the establishment of an independent Jewish kingdom under the Hasmonean dynasty, the Jews began to revolt against the Roman Empire. This was during the period known as the First Jewish-Roman War, which culminated in the destruction of Jerusalem and the second temple in 70 CE. Then, in 132 CE, the Jews rebelled again, this time against the Roman emperor Hadrian. During what is known as the Second Jewish-Roman War, Hadrian's army defeated the Jewish armies,

*The Israel Stele is also known as the Merneptah Stele. It has been interpreted as an inscription by the ancient Egyptian king Merneptah, who reigned between 1213 and 1203 BCE. It was discovered by Flinders Petrie in 1896 at Thebes and is now housed in the Egyptian Museum in Cairo.

and Jewish independence was lost. Jerusalem was turned into a pagan city called Aelia Capitolina, with the Jews being forbidden by Hadrian to live there. It was at this time that Hadrian changed the country's name from Judea to Syria Palaestina—Palestine—and it remained so named until Israel's declaration of independence in 1948.

Aelia Capitolina was originally intended to be Emporer Hadrian's gift to the Jewish people, with the hope of drawing them into the world empire of Rome. But soon after Hadrian left for the West a three-year rebellion led by Simon ben Kosiba erupted. This left the emperor furious with the Jews. When the revolt was eventually crushed, Hadrian wiped all of Judaea from the map. Privileges that the Jews had enjoyed from the time of Julius Caesar were revoked under the edicts of Hadrian. Except during the ninth of Av, the day of mourning, the Jews faced penalties for even laying eyes on the city.

Between 259 and 272 CE, with Rome in constant flux, the region fell under the rule of Odaenathus as king of the Palmyrene Empire. Following the victory of Emperor Constantine in the civil wars of the tetrarchy, the Christianization of the Roman Empire began in earnest. After the First Council of Nicaea in 325, Constantine's mother, Helena, visited Jerusalem in 326 and began the construction of churches and shrines. The immediate result was that Palestine became a center of Christianity, attracting numerous monks and religious scholars.

Reacting to this ever-increasing infiltration, the Samaritan Jews revolted in the fifth and sixth centuries in what is known as the Samaritan Revolts. These revolts, however, all but led to their near extinction. Then, in 614, Palestine was annexed by another Persian dynasty known as the Sassanids, until it returned to Byzantine control in 628. This made the Christians the only dominant group in the Palestine province for many decades onward.

Subsequently, during the Middle Ages, Jews divided into distinct regional groups that today are generally addressed according to two primary geographical groupings: the Ashkenazi Jews of northern and eastern Europe and the Sephardic Jews of Iberia, North Africa, and the Middle East. In part this division was due to the earlier geographical dispersion and resettlement of the Jews across all of the same areas. These groups have parallel histories, though, sharing many cultural similarities as well as a series of persecutions and massive population transfers, such as the expulsion from France in 1306 (by King Philippe the Fair, no less) and from Spain in 1492 (the year of Columbus's voyage).

Jews who lived in Christian Europe during the medieval period were often attacked by the local population and forced to convert to Christianity. However, many Jews, known as Anusim (meaning the "forced ones"), continued practicing Judaism in secret while living outwardly as Christians. The best known Anusim communities were the Jews of Iberia, although they existed throughout Europe.[6]

In much the same way the early Holy Bloodline families of France and Spain quietly converted to Catholicism from Judaism. These noble families had descended directly from the Jewish lines of David and Aaron, which had escaped from Jerusalem shortly before or possibly just after the fall of the Second Temple in 70 CE. It is said that for close to a thousand years they passed down the knowledge of the relics and artifacts concealed beneath the ruins of Solomon's Temple to a chosen son of each family until they were able to recover the treasure in the wake of the First Crusade.

By the start of the First Crusade in 1096 the members of these Jewish families had most certainly become fully Christianized and thus were supported by the pope at that time—Pope Urban II. Secretly these families would have considered themselves "super families," descendants of the very first followers of Christianity and guardians and protectors of the true Holy Grail. Hence many of the families would come to be known as the Rex Deus families, otherwise known as the God-Kings of Europe.*

Several modern researchers and authors, including author and

---

*As far as I can determine, the term "God-Kings of Europe" was first coined in modern terms by the author (and professor) Hugh Montgomery.

university professor Hugh Montgomery, have identified some of the sons of the Jewish/Christian families who made up the original Knights Templar. These individuals were officially recognized in 1120, including their first grand master—Hughes de Payens. They are Geoffrey de Saint Omer, Payen de Montdidier, Archambaud de Saint Agnan, Andre de Montbard, Geoffrey Bisol, and two knights recorded only by their Christian names of Rossal and Gondemar. The ninth member remains unknown.

What *is* known is that vast familial networks encompassing all of France and then Scotland and England were borne out of strategic marriages among the super families. In France specifically, these super families first occupied Burgundy, Champagne, and the Languedoc. From there they extended into the imperial county of Flanders, Picardy, Provence, Gascony, Limousin, and Auvergne and across the Pyrenees into the county of Barcelona and the kingdom of Aragon.

As previously highlighted, this was also the time of rapid Cistercian expansion throughout the regions, an expansion that was largely fed by benefactions and recruitment from the same super families. These Cistercians became the main scribes, clerks, and notaries for the Templar order. Indeed, some Cistercian abbeys had the facilities to produce, multiply, and store important marriage contracts, land deeds, and charters. Of course, this information has proved invaluable in tracking the Holy Bloodline from its origins in the Middle East and its intermixing with the Vikings and the Normans, through to France, England, and Scotland, and ultimately to the New World.

ALL IN THE FAMILY

Starting some twenty years ago, as I began to intently explore my own family genealogy, I became very adept at predicting when a family line would make its move, so to speak. Delving back through medieval times it became all too clear that an invisible (Cistercian?) hand was at work. It was as though there was a built-in multigenerational clock in the various familial lines that would signal when a new strain of blood was required to strengthen the bloodlines. On many of these occasions,

Fig. 10.4. Photograph of a modern-day decorative clay bowl produced by Turtle Clan Pottery of the Six Nations, which is located just outside of Brantford, Ontario, Canada. Brantford is named after the Mohawk chief Joseph Brant, who led the Iroquois Five Nations into Upper Canada following the American Revolution. Brant was a well-known Freemason. Note the repetitive diamond-shaped lozenge pattern. Photograph property of the author, William F. Mann.

when deemed appropriate, two siblings of one family would marry two siblings of another.

Of course some of this could be attributed to geographical familiarity and level of station, but there was something more. As I delved more into the various family lines it became obvious that a pattern had been established—a pattern that over time could be likened to the diamond strand of the snake. The pattern repeatedly showed that from any one notable strategic marriage the lines would branch out for at least four generations before being allowed to come back together after another four generations, thus producing an infinite pattern based on the number 8, which itself represents infinity.

The appendices to this book contain lineages that are pertinent to our narrative. Appendix 1 displays my own descendancy from Rollo Rognvaldsson through Ethelred de Wessex to William F. Mann.

Appendix 2 illustrates my descendancy from Rollo Ragnvaldsson through William the Conqueror. Appendix 3 displays my wife's descendancy from Rollo Rognvaldsson through Prince Henry Sinclair to Sharon Marie (MacKinnon) Mann, and Appendix 4 illustrates my wife's descendancy from Rollo Ragnvaldsson through William the Conqueror. It must be noted that I've only displayed, out of hundreds of different family lines, four outline descendant reports to prove a very specific point as it relates the overall theme contained in this book. At first glance the outline descendant reports may appear to be the same, but upon closer examination it becomes evident that the theory of the diamond-lozenge approach worked very well, keeping to the strict rules of strategic intermarriage.

These four outline descendant reports can be carried back through the God-Kings of Europe; England; and Outremer (the Holy Land), as described by Hugh Montgomery; through the Salian Franks and Merovingians; the Romans; the Celts; the Goths; the various royal houses of Europe; the Baltic and Scandinavian kings and queens; the Carolingians; the Normans; William the Conqueror; the kings of Scotland, Ireland, and Wales; the Scottish and French Knights Templar; the Ashkenazim and Sephardim; the high priests of the temple; and the Houses of David and Bethany. All in all, the MacKinnon-Mann family GEDCOM (Genealogical Data Communication) that I've compiled contains close to twenty thousand names.

These descendant reports are not presented in any way to try to impress the reader but only to demonstrate the practice of strategic intermarriage throughout the ages. For example, it was customary for the governor of a New France fur-trading community to forge a lasting relationship by marrying off one of his sons to the daughter of the local Algonquin chief. In this case, an "unknown" Algonquin princess married the son of Mathieu Le Neuf du Herrisson—governor of Trois-Rivières, Lower Canada. Le Neuf du Herrisson was a favorite of the first governor of New France—Samuel de Champlain—who would surely have given his blessing to such a strategic union if it guaranteed safe passage up the Ottawa River and then the French River to Lakes Huron, Michigan, and Superior.

Mathieu Le Neuf du Herrisson himself even managed to marry into a more distinctive family line than his own. Jeanne Le Marchand de La Celloniere et La Rocque (or La Roche) belonged to one of the most illustrious Norman families at the time. Both Mathieu and Jeanne arrived in New France in 1636 with their two sons, Michel and Jacques Le Neuf. Their 1599 marriage contract from the Huguenot temple in Saint Thury-Harcourt, Caen, Normandy, France, shows Jeanne's parents as being Lieutenant Gervais Le Marchand, Sieur de la Celloniere et la Rocque and Stevonotte de St. Germain.

Mathieu Le Neuf du Herrisson was considered to be a Dandonneau—a Huguenot fur-trading merchant—and was also considered to be a provincial nobleman, given that he was a member of the lesser nobility of Normandy. It appears that he was sent to New France to establish the feudal aristocracy in the name of French king Louis XIII, which is again one of those curious happenings, because, by 1636, Cardinal Richelieu was at the height of his power after having defeated the Huguenot uprising in 1629 at their stronghold, the port of La Rochelle. This was the same port from which the Templar treasure purportedly disappeared on that fateful night—October 13, 1307.

It is said that the Le Neuf family was the first noble family to settle permanently in New France (recall that Champlain was not noble by birth). The Le Neuf's eldest son, Michel, became the sieur du Herrisson and a judge, marrying a young Algonquin princess whose name is not known. The younger son, Jacques, was made sieur de la Potterie and eventually governor of Trois-Rivières. The Le Neuf family prospered through the fur trade (much like the Templars had two hundred years earlier), thanks in part to Michel's in-laws, and became fabulously wealthy by seventeenth-century standards.

Michel's daughter Anne appears to have sealed the deal by marrying Antoine Desrosiers II. At this time, because of her mother's matriarchal lineage, Anne would have been considered to be a full-blooded Algonquin and any offspring that were produced after this would also have been considered to be full-blooded, thus initiating her descendants into the Algonquin Nation. This allowed them to be fully absorbed into the native North American culture as well as into the Canadian wilderness.

THE ST. CLAIR SINCLAIR DNA PROJECT

A good friend of mine, Steve St. Clair, has been doing a tremendous amount of work in relation to DNA matching and genealogical research along his own family lines. The group that he oversees can be found through the St. Clair Sinclair DNA Project's website (www.stclairresearch.com). For anyone interested in exploring the most recent research relating to DNA and what it can and cannot prove, I highly recommend that the information in this website be thoroughly read, explored, and pondered.

From the research group's very beginning in 2004, Steve has doggedly pursued the relationships between various St. Clair/Sinclair/Sinkler/de Clare family lines, topping more than 180 related DNA tests by various family members around the world. The DNA research, when augmented by historic genealogical records, is producing fascinating results. Steve is extremely likeable yet tenacious as a bulldog and definitely demonstrates most of the St. Clair traits, including an affinity for baldness.

After testing a relatively small number of St. Clair/Sinclair/Sinkler/de Clare family members worldwide, Steve noticed that there were several displayed Haplogroups that didn't seem to share a common ancestor until quite far back in ancient time, to at least 30,000 BCE. Very simply, a Haplogroup is derived from a specific group of genetic markers known as SNPs (Single Nucleotide Polymorphism), which identify a common ancestral origin—a clan or tribe of sorts. The common analogy is that a modern family is like a majestic oak tree that is made up of many branches, which accumulate in the past at the trunk and ultimately its deepest roots.

Steve's developed hypothesis is that because the St. Clair/Sinclair/Sinkler/de Clare name is adopted from land in western Europe, some of the family's ancestors with wildly differing Haplogroups some five hundred to one thousand years ago might have found themselves living on the land at a time when surnames were being adopted. Or this anamoly may prove that the reigning Scottish laird/earl at the time not only collected the rents when he made his tenured rounds but also made sure that during his visit the man of the house was absent!

All joking aside, if Steve's theory proves correct for even two of the family lineages, then the study will prove that the St. Clair/Sinclair/Sinkler/de Clare family origins are far more complex than traditional genealogical documents can resolve. In other terms, the branches of the family tree may extend in all directions, including the intermixing of northern and southern European blood with Middle Eastern and native North American strands before they come back together to one deeply rooted ancestor.

This is where my bloodline really starts to flow. As has been demonstrated through more extensive genealogical research and tracking, there appears to be quite a significant intermixing of St. Clair/Sinclair/de Clare blood among my ancestors approximately a thousand years ago. This was around the time of the earlier Norse/Norman conquest of France, then England, and leading up to the First Crusade. In support of this theory I had my DNA tested through the St. Clair Sinclair DNA Project, using Family Tree DNA (FTDNA), which is a commercial genetic testing company based in Houston, Texas.

Needless to say, the results have proved to be quite startling to both Steve and myself. Whereas the St. Clair Sinclair DNA Project primarily falls in the R1b Haplogroup, along with some E1b and I1, and with various sub-clades and mutations, my Haplogroup surprisingly turns out to be the deeply rooted J-Z467, with a large number of very unique SNPs. To date, Family Tree DNA has not been able to show any exact matches to my Haplogroup and the unique array of SNPs to which I have proved positive.

In the simplest of terms, R1b members' most ancient ancestors were Haplogroup N in Africa. The very ancient ancestors of R1b came out of Africa in the second wave to leave the continent as Haplogroup B about sixty thousand years ago, gathering specific Germanic and Barbaric ancestral traits as it first went north. This B Haplogroup eventually became the R Haplogroup that eventually became R1b and R1a. The St. Clair Research members who have been tested are almost all R1b1c.

On the other hand, as one drills down, Haplogroup J-Z467 is a more defined Haplogroup following Haplogroup J-M172. Using the analogy of the majestic oak tree, J-Z467 are its deep roots, J-M172 is its trunk, and Haplogroup J is the jumping-off point where the various tree branches start to grow. The Haplogroup J is widely believed to be associated with the spread of agriculture from Mesopotamia (formerly Sumeria and Akkadia) and the Fertile Crescent, which began about 10,000 years ago. This area is said to be the cradle of civilization in that the earliest pottery, writing, and development of the wagon wheel all came from here. Its distribution is centered in western Asia and southeastern Europe in association with the presence of Neolithic archaeological artifacts, with evidence that J-M172 belonged to the Neolithic agricultural innovators who followed the rainfall. There is a preponderance of both Sephardic Jews and Ashkenazi Jews in the J-M172 Haplotype, along with a small percentage of Cohenim—the patrilineal priestly line of descent in Judaism—which followed the diaspora waves.

The ancestor of the Cohenim is Aaron, brother of Moses. Many believe that descent from Aaron is verifiable with a Y-DNA test. Indeed, the first published study in genealogical Y chromosome DNA testing found that a significant percentage of Cohens had distinctively similar DNA. These Cohens tended to belong to Haplogroup J, with Y-SNP values clustered unusually closely around a haplotype of six markers known as the Cohen Modal Haplotype (CMH). Most researchers indicate that this could be consistent with a shared common ancestor, or with the hereditary priesthood having originally been founded from members of a single closely related clan. Both of my sons and I share the first five out of six markers of the Cohen Modal Haplotype, which at this point really doesn't confirm or deny anything.

Haplogroup J-M172 is linked to the earliest indigenous populations of Anatolia and the Aegean, along with the Iberian Peninsula. J-M172 has been shown to have specifically expanded west of the Euphrates Valley, with moderate distribution in Anatolia, Caucasus, the eastern Mediterranean, and the ancient Greek world long before being linked with the farthest extent of the Roman Empire and waves of Jewish Diaspora.

One interesting aspect of Steve St. Clair's research focuses on the previously mentioned tentacle concerning the small group of Norman super families who, through strategic marriage alliances, moved into the southeast of England (Norfolk, Sussex, Essex) following William the Conqueror. Once these families had established their landed titles they set about establishing a series of associated abbeys and priories. One such group consisted of the families of de Vere, Bigod, de Clare, de Mortimer, and de Mandeville. As such, Outline Descendant Report No. 1, as found in appendix 1, demonstrates how descendants of Rollo strategically intermarried with the de Vere/Bigod/de Mortimer/de Clare/de Mandeville super family during and following their transision from Normandy to England.

Could this movement of long-converted families into southeastern England in the eleventh century signal secret advance preparations to receive the Templar treasure from its hiding place in France? Remember that following the Battle of Hastings (October 24, 1066) the victor, William the Conqueror, consolidated his position and future holdings in England. Movement of this nature would have presented the perfect cover for all sorts of things being shipped across the English Channel from Normandy.

Although the formation of the original Knights Templar did not formally happen until the early twelfth century, planning for the recovery, transport, and movement from one hiding place to another really started the day after the treasure was hidden by the temple priests and then abandoned during the sacking of Jerusalem in 70 CE. Eventually the real "inner" treasure of the Temple of Solomon could have made its way to Rosslyn via France and then England. This means that the Templar treasure that purportedly left the port of La Rochelle in 1307 on Templar ships, going directly to Scotland, could have been the perfect ruse of all time.

Prior to my doing this research on the Mann family name, it (the Mann family) was always rather naively thought to have its deep ancestral roots in Norfolk, England, and nowhere else. In as much, this is still true, but I now realize that the roots extend well beyond. For example, Outline Descendant Report No. 1 shows Julianna Bigod marrying a Jordon Bourne in the twelfth century. Julianna was the daughter of Hugh Bigod of Belvoir Castle, Leicestershire, England, and Juliana de Vere of Essex, England. Hugh Bigod, who is buried in Thetford Abbey,

Norfolk, was the son of Roger Bigod and Adeliza de Tosni. Juliana de Vere was the daughter of Aubrey de Vere and Adeliza de Clare, both of Essex. Adeliza de Clare is buried in St. Osthys Priory, Essex, England.

Julianna's grandfather, Roger Bigod, was the first earl of Norfolk and East Anglia and sherriff of Norfolk and Suffolk. The father of Roger Bigod was Robert Bigod, who was born in 1035 in St. Sauveur, Normandy, France. St. Sauveur is a very interesting name, but it also appears to have been the starting point of this particular branch of this super family.

Connecting another important conceptual dot, the historic little village of St. Sauveur is part of Les Andelys, which just happens to be the birthplace of Nicolas Poussin. And quite close to the small present-day community of St. Sauveur is the farming village of Manneville. Although the population of the village is around five hundred individuals there remains a rather noteworthy Church of Saint Sulpice, which dates from the eleventh century.

Roger Bigod was the first of this great family to settle in England following the Battle of Hastings, affirming his undying allegiance to the Norman king. In William the Conqueror's time, Bigod possessed 6 lordships in Essex and 117 in Suffolk, besides diverse manors in Norfolk. Roger Bigod's first task upon arriving in England was to fortify Norwich Castle and the countryside around Norwich. Following the accession of Henry I, he obtained Framlingham in Suffolk as a gift from the crown.

Then in 1103 he founded the Cluniac Abbey of Thetford, in Norfolk, one of the most important East Anglian monasteries and dedicated it to Our Lady. From this time on other members of this super family quietly established abbeys and priories throughout East Anglia, perhaps as potential sanctuaries for other members of the Holy Bloodline making their way out of mainland Europe.

THE BIG Y

The Old Mide'win have a very interesting saying that never fails to gain a chuckle among the initiates: "Never ask why, just ask how!" As such, a lot of background information has been provided in this book, which demonstrates how a number of seemingly disparate world events could have more than one common thread. In this case the common thread among numerous bloodlines leads to the last refuge of the Knights Templar in the New World.

Blood genetics, along with DNA and genome jargon alone, is very hard to understand. I certainly am not an expert in this field. Very simply, each person normally has one pair of sex chromosomes in each cell. The Y chromosome is present in males, who have one X and one Y chromosome; females have two X chromosomes. The Y chromosome is passed only from father to son; thus, the analysis of Y chromosome DNA can be used in genealogical research. The Y chromosome spans close to sixty million building blocks of DNA (base pairs) and represents close to 2 percent of the total DNA in cells.

Even though the study of DNA and X and Y chromosomes has only occurred over the past fifty years, secret symbolism relating to the DNA's double strands has existed for centuries. Does this prove that the medieval Templars and Cistercians knew about genomes and genetic mutations? As noted previously, it's hard to think so, but what they surely understood and witnessed were the effects of interbreeding through their practice and experience of animal husbandry. This still doesn't explain, though, the X painted on Saint Paul's bald head, or the IXXI carved on the Templar cornerstone of Notre-Dame Bascilica in Montreal, or the double helix of the Apprentice Pillar.

Coming back to the modern era, FTDNA and other DNA testing labs now offer what they have coined as the "Big Y." The Big Y product is billed as a direct paternal lineage test designed to explore deep ancestral links of our common paternal tree. It is described as a test of thousands of known branch markers and millions of places where there may be new branch markers. In layman's terms, the Big Y promises to study your whole paternal tree, not just one branch.

It was Steve St. Clair who, during a recent telephone conversation with Scott Wolter and me, insisted that I take the Big Y test. I had a distinct inclination to ask "Why?" but caught myself and refrained, instead just asking how to go about it.

As Steve has repeatedly noted, the St. Clair Research Group is attempting to build a lasting legacy for the worldwide St. Clair family. The last thing that the group needs is for someone to use the results to make rash and breathless pronouncements. I wholeheartedly agree and have only acknowledged the results of my own testing to date in order to stimulate further sober and scientific discussion. I present no absolute conclusions. It's up to the reader to decide if they so wish, but I caution against any rash assumptions or conclusions at this point. As I've indicated throughout this book, only when verifiable relics have been found, tested, and compared will the true answer be known.

THE ONE OUTSTANDING QUESTION

Meanwhile there remains one outstanding question that can be answered at this time: Coming full circle for the very last time, what information did Thomas Lagarde dit St. Jean convey to Father Brunet on June 23, 1845? The answer to this question is as intriguing and perplexing as any of the information that has been presented thus far in this book.

In speaking further with my fellow Knight Templar and bonded friend from Montreal, who provided me with a copy of the original letter from Father Brunet to Bishop Bourget, I questioned him at length as to whether he had further evidence with respect to the secret information that Lagarde had conveyed to Brunet. Through a faint smile he indicated that he did but couldn't provide a copy of it for fear that it might be stolen from him or something far more sinister might befall him. Of course this caused me to pause, which allowed him to catch his own breath and explain his dilemma. Certainly it must be noted at this critical point that I have not been able to substantiate my friend's claim that the letter in fact existed.

It is recorded by the Church of Jesus Christ of Latter-Day Saints that by October of 1830 converts to the church were teaching the gospel to family and friends in Canadian cities and towns less than two hundred miles from Palmyra, New York. During the period between 1830 and 1845, Mormon missionaries traveled throughout Upper Canada (now Ontario) and the more easterly Maritime provinces of British

North America. As a result, it was recorded that some twenty-five hundred Canadians joined the church in Kingston, Earnestown, Toronto, Brantford, Mount Pleasant, North and South Crosby, and elsewhere. Yet many of these Canadian converts migrated to the U.S. centers of the church or fell away. Indeed, the 1861 Upper Canada census counted only seventy-four Mormons in all of Upper Canada.

It is also proudly noted by the Church of Jesus Christ of Latter-Day Saints that some of its well-known pioneers such as Brigham Young, Parley P. Pratt, Orson Pratt, John E. Page, and even the prophet Joseph Smith himself visited and preached in Upper Canada. Brigham Young specifically traveled to Upper Canada as a missionary between April and August of 1832, just shortly after formally joining the church, traveling the entire distance by foot.

As noted, Lower Canada (Québec) was then largely impervious to competing religious influences because of the iron will of the bishop of the vast Montreal archdiocese at the time: Bishop Ignace Bourget. The Roman Catholic Church officially believed and still believes that Mormonism teaches that human beings may, by practicing the tenets of its faith, become gods and goddesses themselves, with their own planets full of people worshipping them.

So what was it about Upper Canada that attracted the interest of most of the men who would go on to comprise the original Quorum of the Twelve Apostles? The reference provided by the LDS Church itself identifying both Brantford and Mount Pleasant as areas of visitation are extremely interesting, because directly adjacent to these two communities lies one of the largest Iroquoi settlements in Canada.

The Six Nations had fought alongside the British during the American Revolution, led by their stoic chief, Joseph Brant, and in return received from the British Crown in 1793 the vast land grant known as the Simcoe Patent. After the revolution, Brant led his people into Upper Canada, and the city of Brantford actually got its name from the famous crossing of the Grand River, hence Brant's Ford became Brantford. The Six Nations' territory was to run six miles on either side of the Grand River from its source to its outlet in Lake Erie, covering some 675,000 acres. (The Six Nations now occupies a reserve of approximately 50,000 acres, having had the land sold, leased, or farmed by squatters.)

Joseph Brant went on to lead an esteemed life, becoming actively involved in both the Anglican Church and Freemasonry. In 1776 he was initiated in Cliftonian Lodge No. 47 on a visit to England, where he had the distinction of having his Masonic apron given to him by King George III. Then in 1798 he became a founding master of Brantford Lodge No. 11 and was affiliated as well with Barton Lodge No. 10 in Hamilton, Ontario.

Interestingly, the first five presidents of the Church of Jesus Christ of Latter-Day Saints—Joseph Smith, Brigham Young, John Taylor, Wilford Woodruff, and Lorenzo Snow—were all initiated into Freemasonry at the Nauvoo Lodge in Illinois. On April 6, 1840, the Grand Lodge of Illinois was formed by the Mormon patriarch Judge James Adams. The first grand master—Abraham Jonas—issued a dispensation and instituted the lodge at Nauvoo on March 15, 1842. Not surprisingly then, Joseph Smith was made a Freemason "at sight" by Grand Master Abraham Jonas, then formally initiated in the first degree on the same night and passed through the second degree and raised in the third degree during the next evening.

The strange thing is that Brigham Young petitioned for membership on December 30, 1841, prior to Joseph Smith. On March 17, 1842—the day following Joseph Smith's raising in the third degree—Nauvoo Lodge accepted Young's petition for membership. It appears that Joseph Smith had to be initiated first, even though in Masonry all men are considered equal. In any event, Brigham Young was initiated on April 7, 1842, passed on April 8, and raised on April 9. Rather conspicuously, Young was known to have worn a Masonic tie tack at various times for the rest of his life—at least two extant photographs attest to this (see figure 10.5).

To make a long story short, my friend and Knights Templar colleague indicated that there is a handwritten letter from Brother Brigham Young, dated sometime in 1844, to Brother Thomas Lagarde dit St. Jean indicating that they both, as Masons, shared a common bond in seeing that all of God's children regained their promised land.

Fig. 10.5. Undated photograph of the Mormon leader Brigham Young sporting a Masonic tie tack, which clearly shows the compass and the square.

Apparently Young then went on to say that he had met a Mohawk in Brantford in 1832 who not only claimed to somehow be related to Lagarde but also claimed that Lagarde possessed invaluable knowledge relating to a system of latitudinal and longitudinal grids across North America.

Young supposedly then went on to explain that Lagarde and his family would be more than welcome to travel with the Mormons to escape the British persecution that Lagarde faced. The Mormons were preparing to leave Nauvoo to go west in search of a New Jerusalem and would be willing to have Lagarde's company in exchange for the information about the secret meridians that Lagarde possessed. Of course, if true, information of this nature would have been pure gold to Bishop Bourget.

An upshot of this is that not only would Bourget have gained invaluable information concerning the Mormons' intentions—information that he could trade between the British occupiers of Lower Canada and the U.S. government—but he also finally had it confirmed that indeed there existed an antient knowledge that could lead to the last Templar sanctuary. As to what he did with this information is a mystery unto itself, assuming that the letter did exist. Under the assumption that it did exist, did Thomas Lagarde dit St. Jean also convey this information to the Mormons?

Thomas Lagarde must certainly have felt conflicted about who he could trust. After all, he was condemned to death by the British of Montreal and on the run. On the other hand, it now appears that he was the rightful guardian and protector of an invaluable treasure. The shame of it all is that it's apparent that Thomas Lagarde died, like many initiates before him, protecting the secret. As the Anishinabe/Algonquin prophecies predicted more than four hundred years ago, it's now time for the truth to be exposed, because for too long the guardians and protectors of the Holy Grail have made too great a sacrifice!

Epilogue
A Higher Level

Fig. E.1. Classic square and compass enclosed by the circle and carved in stone. Note the diamond-shaped lozenge found in the inner circle and the relative 2:1 width-to-height ratio of the stone itself, when compared to the relative dimensions of the Kensington Runestone. Photograph property of the author, William F. Mann.

WHAT'S BRED IN THE BONE

Remember the significance of the number 11? In numerology the first level is represented by the numbers 1 to 10; 11 signifies the initiate's movement to the next level. This book has been structured in much the same way. Chapters 1 to 10 have gradually given those reading through the first level an all-increasing understanding and knowledge in relation to the immense wealth of historic and esoteric material that's required to move on through the epilogue to a higher level of illumination. Hopefully the reader now understands the complexity of the many layers of teachings that are required to reach this level of wisdom. Do not despair if you don't totally understand what's been presented. Many initiates can go a lifetime without fully comprehending what has been put before them.

One person who understood this completely was the great Canadian author Robertson Davies. Among his many award-winning novels he penned the classic *What's Bred in the Bone,* which so perfectly captures one of the main themes in *this* book. Through a subtle and layered use of archetypes, Davies impressed upon the reader the special spiritual bond that can form between the master and his initiate, between the old man and the newborn child, between grandfather and grandson, between husband and wife.

The same type of bond is what led me in the first place to pursue my involvement in both Freemasonry and the Old Mide'win. From a Masonic perspective my great-uncle was my surrogate grandfather, because his brother had died before I was born. What I didn't realize until after my great-uncle's death was that Frederic George Mann had achieved the highest level of Masonry by becoming the supreme grand master of the Knights Templar of Canada, a quasi-military Christian Masonic order.

I shouldn't have been surprised, though. The Mann family has always been a military family. My grandfather and great-uncles all fought in the First World War for England, while my grandmother drove an ambulance just behind the front lines. During the Second World War my father and his four brothers all fought for the Canadian Armed Forces. One brother, my uncle Vic, was killed in Holland and earning the Silver Star.

The irony about this episode is that for the first two years of the war my uncle's regiment, the Argyll and Sutherland Highlanders of Canada (Princess Louise's), enjoyed one of the softest assignments of the war. They guarded Edward VIII and Wallis Simpson, the Duke and Duchess of Windsor, while the couple stayed in the Bahamas. After this the regiment was shipped to Europe where on October 29, 1944, Sargent Victor John Mann was killed instantly while saving the lives of several fellow soldiers.

Fig. E.2. Photograph showing Edward VIII and his wife, Wallis Simpson—the Duke and Duchess of Windsor—which was taken in the Bahamas in 1942. Surrounding the duke and duchess are members of the Argyle and Sutherland Highlanders of the Canada Regiment of Hamilton, Ontario, Canada. To the left of Wallis Simpson is Sargent Victor John Mann, the uncle I never knew, and to the right of Edward VIII is the commander of the regiment—Lieutenant Colonel Ian Sinclair. Photograph property of the author, William F. Mann.

Throughout the ages there have been millions of similar stories concerning the young brave warriors who go off to war and fight valiantly yet in most cases not quite knowing what they are fighting for. The story of Prince Henry Sinclair and his Knights Templar is no different. Prince Henry and his inner circle must have totally understood the immense responsibility that they carried while sailing to North America. But for the foot soldier and those family members who accompanied them, things would have been different. They would have to have put their entire faith and trust in their leaders.

Meanwhile, across Europe, Knights Templar of every rank would provide the perfect blind to what was occurring halfway around the world. Unfortunately in most cases this resulted in the ultimate sacrifice by those Templars who appear to have intentionally stayed behind to be arrested.

From an Old Mide'win perspective, the irony surrounding my mother's family is rather different, but the results are essentially the same. It always appeared as though she carried a burden of guilt her whole life. Although I'm sure that she understood all too well her hidden heritage, she always claimed that her side of the family was "Black French." To admit during her generation that she was Indian would have resulted in a lifetime of ridicule and scorn.

The ironic thing was that the more she dismissed it the more obvious it became because of family traits in her children that were hard to disguise. From the time of our birth my sisters and I were constantly being asked whether we were Indians because of our skin color and facial characteristics. The high cheekbones and straight, dominant nose is hard enough to disguise, but the intangibles, especially on my part, were just as hard to explain.

Ever since I can remember I've had an inexplicable, special bond with the wilderness, animals, Earth, and anything spiritual in nature. Needless to say, I am just as comfortable in the native wigwam as I am in the Masonic lodge room or the corporate world. Unfortunately, it was only after my mother died that my sisters and I were able to delve into our family background, discovering as we had suspected an entirely different way of life and about two thousand new cousins. To say that we have embraced this side of our family is now an understatement.

To be so comfortable and accepted in the inner circles of Masonic Templarism and Old Mide'win has certainly been rewarding from a spiritual perspective, but to come away with the realization that a bond existed between the two secret societies in pre-Columbian times has been extra special. As noted previously, the similarities between the various rituals and orders is uncanny, to say the least. And then to be able to apply what has been learned to ultimately discover the many hidden layers of esoteric application in the paintings of Teniers and Poussin has been no less than mesmerizing. The sheer genius it took for those artists to develop the hidden messages contained in their paintings is staggering.

To be able to discover a four-hundred-year-old treasure map leading to the last refuge of the Knights Templar in the New World is absolute icing on the cake. As to what the actual treasure yields, that remains to be seen. With regard to whom takes possession of it and where it ultimately ends up, that also remains to be seen. Hopefully its contents will be used to renew peace and prosperity around the world and also, for once and for all, reaffirm the Sacred Feminine.

But I must warn the would-be treasure hunter to think twice if you're considering traveling to Montana to try to penetrate the final refuge and recover the Templar treasure for your own purposes. As any fan of the *Indiana Jones* movies will tell you, the treasure is always guarded by elaborate booby traps and demons. In this case, the Templars and their native brothers ensured that only a learned initiate of both societies will recognize the inner door to the lodge—the bear's den—and what lies just beyond that door.

Remember one thing: Let He Who Has the Understanding Use It with Wisdom.

Appendices

Outline Descendant Reports

When the dates have been excluded it means that a definitive date could not be determined.

Appendix I

Outline Descendant Report from Rollo Rognvaldsson (860–932) through Ethelred de Wessex (?–1016) to William F. Mann (1954–present)

1. **Rollo Rognvaldsson, first duke of Normandy (860–932)** b: 860 in Maer, Nord-Trondelag, Norway, d: 932 in Notre Dame, Rouen, Normandy, France

    + **Poppa de Valois (872–938)** b: 872 in Bayeux, Calvados, Basse-Normandie, France, d: 938 in Neustria, Normandy, France

2. **William I. Longsword Normandy (893–942)** b: July 30, 893 in Rouen, Seine-Maritime, Haute-Normandie, France, d: Dec. 17, 942, in Island Picquigny, Somme River, Normandy, France

    + **Sprote de Bretagne (911–940)** b: Aug. 28, 911, in Normandy, France, d: 940 in Normandy, France

3. **Richard I, "the Fearless," Duke of Normandy (933–1027)** b: Aug. 28, 933, in Fecamp, Seine-Maritime, Haute-Normandie, France, d: Aug. 23, 1027, in Fecamp, Seine-Inferieure, France

    + **Gonnor de Crepon, Duchess of Normandy (936–1031)** b: Nov. 21, 936, in Arques la Bataille, Seine-Inferieure, Normandy, France, d: 1031 in Neustria, Normandy, France

4. **Emma de Normandy (?–1052)** b: in Normandy, France, d: March 6, 1052, in Winchester, Hampshire, England

    + **Ethelred "the Unready" de Wessex (?–1016)** b: in Wessex, England, d: April 23, 1016, in London, Middlesex, England

5. **Emma de England (1003–1068)** b: 1003 in London, Middlesex, England, d: 1068 in Bourne, Lincolnshire, England

    + **Hereward de Bourne (1025–1077)** b: 1025 in Bourne, Lincolnshire, England, d: 1077 in Bourne, Lincolnshire, England

6. **Eustace de Bourne (1044–1119)** b: 1044 in Bourne, Lincolnshire, England, d: 1119 in Wittenham, Surrey, England

    + **Elizabeth de Clare (1074–1117)** b: 1074 in Clare, Suffolk, England, d: 1117 in London, England

7. **Eustace Bourne (1101–1198)** b: 1101 in Wittenham, Surrey, England, d: 1198 in London, Middlesex, England

    + **Lucy de Taillebois (1101–1191)** b: 1101 in Hertford, Hertfordshire, England, d: 1191 in London, England

8. **Richard Bourne (1121–1203)** b: 1121 in London, Middlesex, England, d: 1203 in Wittenham, Surrey, England

    + **Lettia Scotland (1119–1178)** b: 1119 in Edinburgh, Fife, Scotland, d: 1178 in Wittenham, Surrey, England

9. **Jordon Bourne (1142–1219)** b: 1142 in London, Middlesex, England, d: 1219 in London, Middlesex, England

    + **Julianna Bigod (1142–1198)** b: 1142 in Norfolk, England, d: 1198 in London, England

10. **William Bourne (1163–1239)** b: 1163 in London, Middlesex, England, d: 1239 in London, Middlesex, England

    + **Lady Johanna de Percy (1169–1245)** b: 1169 in Scarborough, Yorkshire, England, m: 1189 in London, England, d: 1245 in London, Middlesex, England

11. **Thomas Bourne de Loch (1198–1272)** b: 1198 in London, Middlesex, England, d: 1272 in London, Middlesex, England

    + **Isabel de Vere (1186–1263)** b: 1186 in Broad Oaks, Essex, England, d: Dec. 23, 1263, in London, England

12. **Lord Richardus Locke (1217–1299)** b: 1217 in Middlesex, England, d: 1299 in Oxford, Oxfordshire, England

    + **Lady Lucy de Quincy (1218–1265)** b: 1218 in Lincoln, Lincolnshire, England, d: March 6, 1265, in Clerkenwell, London, England

13. **Lord William "Lok" Locke (1241–1303)** b: 1241 in Oxford, Oxfordshire, England, d: 1303 in Oxford, Oxfordshire, England

    + **Lady Emma Clifford (1241–1267)** b: 1241 in Herefordshire, England, d: 1267 in Oxford, Oxfordshire, England

14. **Lord Thomas Locke (1260–1345)** b: 1260 in Oxford, Oxfordshire, England, d: 1345 in Lenn, Wiltshire, England

    + **Lady Elizabeth de Holland (1260–1328)** b: 1260 in Holland, Lancashire, England, d: 1328 in Lenn, Wiltshire, England

15. **Lord Robert Locke (1304–1379)** b: 1304 in Merton Abbey, Surrey, England, d: 1379 in Lenn, Wiltshire, England

    + **Lady Alice FitzAlan (1314–1376)** b: 1314 in Arundel, Sussex, England, d: Jan. 24, 1376, in Lenn, Wiltshire, England

16. **Lord William Locke (1351–1423)** b: 1351 in Lenn, Wiltshire, England, d: 1423 in Lenn, Wiltshire, England

    + **Lady Joan de Mortimer (1372–1405)** b: 1372 in Usk, Monmouthshire, Wales, d: Oct. 8, 1405, in Lenn, Wiltshire, England

17. **Lord John (sheriff of London) Locke (1400–1492)** b: 1400 in Lenn, Wiltshire, England, d: 1492 in St. Mary Le Bow, London, England

    + **Eleanor Neville (1407–1472)** b: 1407 in Durham, Durham, England, d: 1472 in St. Albans, Hertfordshire, England

18. **Lord Thomas Locke (1434–1507)** b: 1434 in Lenn, Wiltshire, England, d: 1507 in London, Middlesex, England

    + **Lady Joan Wilcockes (1455–1512)** b: 1455 in Rotherham, Yorkshire, England, d: 1512 in London, Middlesex, England

19. **Thomas Locke (1494–1561)** b: 1494 in Brockhampton, Dorset, England, d: 1561 in Stallbridge, Dorset, England

    + **Unknown**

20. **Nicholas Locke (1517–1580)** b: 1517 in Brockhampton, Dorset, England, d: 1558 in Plush, Dorset, England

    + **Eleasar (1550–1605)** b: 1550 in London, Middlesex, England, d: March 30, 1605, in Higher Colscombe, Slapton, Gloucestershire, England

21. **Nicholas Locke (1574–1648)** b: 1574 in Brockhampton, Dorset, England, d: 1648 in Dorset, England

    + **Frances Lansden (1578–1612)** b: 1578 in Somerset, England, d: April 28, 1612, in Publow, Somerset, England

22. **Thomas Locke (1611–1660)** b: Feb. 10, 1611 in Somersetshire, England, d: 1660 in England

    + **Sarah Homewood (1620–1659)** b: June 18, 1620, d: 1659

23. **Thomas Locke (1659–1693)** b: Oct. 23, 1659, in East Grinstead, Sussex, England, d: 1693

    + **Ann (1673–1693)** b: circa 1673, d: 1693

24. **William Lock (1693–1715)** b: Nov. 23, 1693, in Worth, Sussex, England, d: 1715

    + **Sarah Wheeler (1694–1714)** b: circa 1694, d: 1714

25. **Mary Lock (1714–1763)** b: Sept. 2, 1714, in Stoughton, Sussex, England, d: 1763

    + **William Cousens (1718–1746)** b: 1718 in Barnham, Sussex, d: 1746

26. **James Cousens (1754–?)** b: May 15, 1754, in Barnham, Sussex

    + **Elizabeth Cowdrey (1740–?)** b: 1740 in Yapton, Sussex, m: Nov. 10, 1782, in Yapton, Sussex, England

27. **Mary Cousens (1769–?)** b: 1769 in Yarmouth, Norfolk, England

    + **Edmund Jubey (1773–?)** b: 1773 in Yarmouth, Norfolk, England

28. **James Cousens Jubey (1793–?)** b: Sept. 23, 1793, in Yarmouth, Norfolk, England

    + **Mary Cousens (1786–1864)** b: 1786 in Hastings, Sussex, England, d: 1864 in Hastings, Sussex, England

29. **Ann Cousens Jubey (1813–?)** b: 1813 in Yarmouth, Norfolk, England

    + **Henry James Mann (1809–1860)** b: 1809 in Norwich, Norfolk, England, d: 1860 in Norwich, Norfolk, England

30. **Henry Mann (1841–1890)** b: March 31, 1841, in Norwich, Norfolk, England, d: 1890 in Norwich, Norfolk, England

    + **Elizabeth Cooke Dales (1835–?)** b: 1835 in Alford, Lincolnshire, England, m: Feb. 28, 1864, in Alford, Lincolnshire, England

31. **Frederick Arthur Mann (1867–1949)** b: 1867 in Alford, Lincolnshire, England, d: 1949 in Norwich, Norfolk, England

    + **Sarah Ann Baker (1867–1965)** b: May 14, 1867, in Southrepps, Norfolk, England, d: June 30, 1965

32. **Raymond Harry Mann (1897–1955)** b: Nov. 2, 1897, in Norwich, Norfolk, England, d: April 3, 1955, in Brantford, Ontario, Canada

    + **Elsie May Hankins (1897–1978)** b: May 14, 1897, in Royston, Yorkshire, England, d: June 23, 1978, in Brantford, Ontario, Canada

33. **William Frank Mann I (1920–1993)** b: March 13, 1920, in Brantford, Ontario, Canada, d: 1993 in Brantford, Ontario, Canada

    + **Edna Dorine Demers (1924–1993)** b: March 9, 1924, in Pembroke, Ontario, Canada, d: 1993 in Brantford, Ontario, Canada

34. **William Frank Mann II (1954–present)** b: 1954 in Brantford, Ontario, Canada

    + **Sharon Marie MacKinnon (1954–present)** b: 1954 in Little Bras D'Or, Cape Breton, Canada

Appendix 2

Outline Descendant Report from Rollo Ragnvaldsson (860–932) through William the Conqueror (1024–1087) to William F. Mann (1954–present)

1. **Rollo Rognvaldsson, first duke of Normandy (860–932)** b: 860 in Maer, Nord-Trondelag, Norway, d: 932 in Notre Dame, Rouen, Normandy, France

    \+ **Poppa de Valois (872–938)** b: 872 in Bayeux, Calvados, Basse-Normandie, France, d: 938 in Neustria, Normandy, France

2. **William I. Longsword Normandy (893–942)** b: July 30, 893, in Rouen, Seine-Maritime, Haute-Normandie, France, d: Aug. 23, 1027, in Fecamp, Seine-Inferieure, France

    \+ **Sprote de Bretagne (911–940)** b: 911 in Bretagne, France, d: 940 in Normandy, France

3. **Richard I, Duke of Normandy (933–996)** b: Aug. 28, 933, in Fecamp, Seine-Maritime, Haute-Normandy, France, d: Nov. 20, 996, in Fecamp, Seine-Inferieure, France

    \+ **Gonnor de Crepon (936–1031)** b: 936 in Normandy, France, d: 1031 in Neustria, Normandy, France

4. **Richard II, "Le Bon," Duke of Normandy (963–1027)** b: 963 in Normandy, France, d: Aug. 28, 1027, in Fecamp, Seine-Inferieure, France

+ **Judith de Bretagne (982–1017)** b: 982 in Bretagne, France, d: June 16, 1017, in Normandy, France

5. **Robert I, Duke of Normandy (999–1035)** b: 999 in Normandy, France, d: July 2, 1035, in Nicea, Bithynia, Turkey

+ **Harlette de Falaise (1003–1050)** b: 1003 in Falaise, Clavados, France, d: 1050 in Mortain, Normandy, France

6. **William I, the Conqueror (1024–1087)** b: Oct. 14, 1024, in Falaise, Normandy, France, m: 1040, d: Sept. 9, 1087, in Hermentruville, Rouen, Seine-Maritime, France

+ **Maud de Flandren (1032–1083)** b: 1032 in Flanders, France, m: 1040, d: Nov. 3, 1083, in Caen, Calvados, France

7. **Henry I Beauclerc (1068–1135)** b: 1068 in Selby, Yorkshire, England, d: Dec. 1, 1135, in St. Denis, Seine-St. Denis, France

+ **Sibyl Corbet (1075–1157)** b: 1075 in Alcester, Warwickshire, England, d: 1157 in Pontesbury Woodcote, Shropshire, England

8. **Robert de Caen (1088–1147)** b: 1088, d: 1147

+ **Amicici Fitzhamen de Meullent (1090–1157)** b: 1090, d: 1157

9. **Richard Fitzrobert (1124–1184)** b: 1124 in Bristol, Gloucestershire, England, d: 1184

+ **Mathilde de St. Clair (1135–?)** b: 1135

10. **(Unknown first name)** de Creully (1143–?) b: 1143

+ **Enguerrand Seigneur de La Lande Patry (1140–1196)** b: 1140, d: 1196

11. **Mathilde Patry (1162–1215)** b: 1162, d: 1215

+ **Raoul V. Tesson (1159–1213)** b: 1159 in Normandy, France, d: 1213

12. **Petronille Tesson (1197–1230)** b: 1197, d: April 26, 1230

+ **William Paynel (1195–1253)** b: 1195, d: Dec. 20, 1253

13. **Raoul Paynet dit Tesson (1218–1270)** b: 1218, d: 1270

+ **Petronille de Montfort (1221–?)** b: 1221 in France

14. **Jean Ler Tesson (1235–?)** b: 1235 in France

+ **Unknown**

15. **Jean II Tesson (1250–?)** b: 1250 in France

+ **Thomasse Inconnue (1262–?)** b: 1262 in France

16. **Isabelle Tesson (1280–?)** b: 1280 in France

+ **Roland III de Vassy (1275–?)** b: 1275 in France

17. **Jeanne de Vassy (1313–?)** b: 1313 in France

+ **Robert Rousee (1310–?)** b: 1310 in France

18. **Perette Rousee (1330–?)** b: 1330 in France

+ **Jean de La Poterie (1320–?)** b: 1320 in France

19. **Almaric de La Poterie (1362–?)** b: 1362 in France

+ **Philipotte de Lignon (1365–?)** b: 1365 in France

20. **Jean de La Poterie (1395–?)** b: 1395 in France

+ **Perette de Roussel (1400–?)** b: 1400 in France

21. **Jeanne de La Poterie (1425–1459)** b: 1425 in France, d: 1459 in France

+ **Jean de Saint-Germain (1425–1459)** b: 1425, d: 1459 in Normandy, France

22. **Olivier de Saint-Germain (1445–1505)** b: 1445, d: 1505 in Normandy, France

+ **Jeanne de Rouelle (1450–?)** b: 1450 in France

23. **François de Saint-Germain (1480–?)** b: 1480 in France

+ **Helene de Corday (1485–?)** b: 1485 in France

24. **Olivier de Saint-Germain (1515–1587)** b: 1515, d: 1587 in France

    + **Françoise de Breul (1525–1599)** b: 1525 in France, d: 1599 in France

25. **Stevenotte de St. Germain (1550–1599)** b: 1550 in Normandy, Calvados, Basse-Normandie, France, d: Nov. 28, 1599, in Normandy, Calvados, Basse-Normandie, France

    + **Gervais Le Marchand (1545–1599)** b: 1545 in Caen, Lixieux, Normandy, France, d: Nov. 28, 1599, in Caen, Lixieux, Normandy, France

26. **Jeanne Marchand (1574–1647)** b: 1574 in Normandy, Calvados, Basse-Normandie, France, d: April 1647 in St. Sauveur, Bayeux, Normandie, France

    + **Mathieu Le Neuf (1575–1622)** b: 1575 in Caen, Normandy, France, d: Nov. 24, 1622, in Caen, Normandy, France

27. **Michel Le Neuf (1601–1642)** b: 1601 in Thurly Harcourt, Caen, Lisieux, Normandy, d: 1642 in Québec, New France

    + **Unknown Algonquin:** Trois-Rivières, Québec

28. **Anne Le Neuf Du Herisson (1632–1711)** b: 1632 in Trois-Rivières, St. Maurice, New France, m: Nov. 24, 1647, in Trois-Rivières, St. Maurice, New France, d: Oct. 16, 1711, in Champlain, New France

    + **Antoine Desrosiers II (1617–1691)** b: April 14, 1617, m: Nov. 24, 1647, in Trois- Rivières, St. Maurice, New France, d: Aug. 8, 1691, in Champlain, New France

29. **Antoine Desrosiers III (1650–1722)** b: June 16, 1650, in Trois-Riviéres, New France, d: Nov. 28, 1722, in Champlain, New France

    + **Marie René Lepelle (1678–1721)** b: 1678, d: 1721

30. **Pierre Derosiers-Lafreniere (1719–1782)** b: Aug. 4, 1719, in Baptiste Sorel, New France, d: May 27, 1782, in Ste. Genevieve, Berthier, New France

    + **Marie Madeleine Boucher (1733–1811)** b: March 16, 1733, in

Berthier, Berthierville, Québec, Canada, d: May 23, 1811, in Berthier, Berthierville, Lower Canada

31. **Jean Baptiste Françoise Desrosiers-Lafreniere (1759–1832)** b: Dec. 23, 1759, in Berthier, Lower Canada, m: Aug. 6, 1787, in St. Cuthbert, Lower Canada, d: Aug. 10, 1832, in Berthierville, Lower Canada

    + **Marie Therese Fontaine-Latourelle (1770–1793)** b: May 30, 1770, in Berthierville, Lower Canada, m: Aug. 6, 1787, in St. Cuthbert, Lower Canada, d: Oct. 14, 1793, in Berthierville, Lower Canada

32. **Marguerite Desrochiers (1793–1822)** b: July 21, 1793, d: Dec 11, 1822

    + **Joseph Turcotte (1788–1848)** b: 1788, d: Oct. 5, 1848, in Lower Canada

33. **Francis Xavier Turcotte (1814–1900)** b: 1814 in Lower Canada, m: Oct. 5, 1849, on Ile du Grand Calumet, Lower Canada, d: Jan. 9, 1900, in Petawawa, Ontario, Canada

    + **Sophie Lagarde dit St. Jean (1832–1917)** b: April 25, 1832, in St. Eustache, Québec, Canada, m: Oct. 5, 1849, on Ile Du Grand Calumet, Québec, Canada, d: Dec. 24, 1917, in Pembroke, Renfrew, Ontario, Canada

34. **Lizzie Elizabeth Turcotte (1863–?)** b: Jan. 1863 on Black River, Pontiac, Québec, Canada, m: July 7, 1879, in Pembroke, Renfrew, Québec, Canada,

    + **Michel Chartrand (1851–?)** b: Aug. 15, 1851, on Allumette Island, Pontiac, Québec, Canada, m: July 7, 1879, in Pembroke, Renfrew, Québec, Canada

35. **Albertine Chartrand (1892–1967)** b: April 30, 1892, in Petawawa, Renfrew, Ontario Canada, d: 1967, Camrose, Alberta, Canada

    + **Benjamin Demers (1898–1964)** b: 1898 on Allumette Island, Pontiac, Québec, Canada, d: 1964 in Dinsmore, Saskatchewan, Canada

36. **Edna Dorine Demers (1924–1993)** b: March 9, 1924, in Pembroke, Ontario, Canada, d: 1993 in Brantford, Ontario, Canada

    + **William Frank Mann I (1920–1993)** b: March 13, 1920, in Brantford, Ontario, Canada, d: 1993 in Brantford, Ontario, Canada

37. **William Frank Mann II (1954–present)** b: 1954 in Brantford, Ontario, Canada

    + **Sharon Marie MacKinnon (1954–present)** b: 1954 in Little Bras D'Or, Cape Breton, Canada

Appendix 3

Outline Descendant Report from Rollo Rognvaldsson (860–932) through Prince Henry Sinclair (1355–?) to Sharon Marie (MacKinnon) Mann (1954–present)

1. **Rollo Rognvaldsson, first duke of Normandy (860–932)** b: 860 in Maer, Nord-Trondelag, Norway, d: 932 in Notre Dame, Rouen, Normandy, France

   + **Poppa deValois (872–938)** b: 872 in Bayeux, Calvados, Basse-Normandie, France, d: 938 in Neustria, Normandy, France

2. **William I. Longsword Normandy (893–942)** b: 893 in Rouen, Seine-Maritime, Haute-Normandie, France, d: Dec. 17, 942, in Island Picquigny, Somme River, Normandy, France

   + **Sprote de Bretagne (911–940)** b: Aug. 28, 911, in Normandy, France, d: 940 in Normandy, France

3. **Richard I, "the Fearless," Duke of Normandy (933–1027)** b: Aug. 28, 933 in Fecamp, Seine-Maritime, Haute-Normandie, France, d: Aug. 23, 1027, in Fecamp, Seine-Inferieure, France

   + **Gonnor DeCrepon, Duchess of Normandy (936–1031)** b: Nov. 21, 936, in Arques la Bataille, Seine-Inferieure, Normandy, France, d: 1031 in Neustria, Normandy, France

4. **Richard II, "Le Bon," Duke of Normandy (958–1027)** b: Aug. 23, 958, in Falaise, Calvados, Normandy, France, d: Aug. 28, 1027, in Fecamp, Seine-Maritime, Haute-Normandie, France

+ **Poppa de Envermeu (?–1078)** b: Normandy, France, d: Jan. 8, 1078, in Monastaere de L'Ordre de St. Benoist, Missines, France

5. **Mauger "the Young" of Normandy, Count de St. Clair and Corbeil (986–1040)** b: 986 in Rouen, Seine-Maritime, Haute-Normandie, France, d: 1040 in Champagne, Dordogne, Aquitaine, France

    + **Germaine of Corbeil (?–1012)** b: Champagne, Dordogne, Aquitaine, France, d: 1012 in Corbeil, Marne, Champagne-Ardenne, France

6. **Waldron de St. Clare (1006–1054)** b: 1006 in St. Clair sur Elle, Manche, Basse-Normandie, France, d: 1054 in Barnstable, Devonshire, England

    + **Margaret Helen of Normandy (1017–1070)** b: 1017 in Fecamp, Seine-Maritime, Haute-Normandie, France, d: 1070 in France

7. **William "the Seemly" de St. Clair, first baron of Roslin (1038–1090)** b: 1038 in Rosslyn, Orkney, Scotland, d: 1090 in Rosslyn Castle, Midlothian, Scotland

    + **Dorothy Doratha of Raby Dunbar (?–1097)** b: Raby, Scotland, d: 1097

8. **Henri "the Crusader" de St. Clair, second baron of Roslin (1089–1140)** b: 1089 in Roslin, Midlothian, Scotland, d: 1140 in Roslin, Midlothian, Scotland

    + **Rosabel Forteith of Strathearn (1089–1180)** b: 1089, d: 1180

9. **Henri "the Councellor" de St. Clair, third baron of Roslin (1131–1180)** b: 1131 in Rosslyn Castle, Midlothian, Scotland, d: 1180 in Rosslyn, Orkney, Scotland

    + **Margaret Grathaway (1140–)** b: 1140, d: Scotland

10. **William de St. Clair, fourth baron of Roslin (1162–1214)** b: 1162 in Rosslyn, Midlothian, Scotland, d: 1214 in Roslin, Midlothian, Scotland

    + **Agnes of March de Dunbar (1160–1180)** b: 1160 in Dunbar, East Lothian, Scotland, d: 1180 in Rosslyn Castle, Midlothian, Scotland

11. **Henri de St. Clair, Baron of Roslin (1192–1222)** b: 1192 in Rosslyn Castle, Midlothian, Scotland, d: circa 1222 in Roslin, Midlothian, Scotland

    + **Katherine of Strathearn (1195–?)** b: 1195 in Strathearn, Scotland, d: Rosslyn Castle, Midlothian, Scotland

12. **Henri William de St. Clair, fifth earl of Orkney, fifth baron of Rosslyn (1214–1270)** b: 1214 in Rosslyn Castle, Roslin, Midlothian, Scotland, d: 1270 in Rosslyn Castle, Roslin, Midlothian, Scotland

    + **Margaret Mar (1210–?)** b: 1220 in Mar, Aberdeenshire, Scotland, m: 1235 in Rosslyn Castle, Midlothian, Scotland, d: Rosslyn Castle, Midlothian, Scotland

13. **William St. Clair, sixth earl of Orkney, sixth baron of Rosslyn (1230–1297)** b: 1230 in Rosslyn Castle, Midlothian, Scotland, d: 1297 as prisoner in Tower of London, Middlesex, England

    + **Matilda Nisbit (1255–?)** b: 1255 in the Islands, Orkney, Scotland, m: 1267, d: England

14. **Henry Sinclair, seventh baron of Roslin, commander of Knights Templar at Bannockburn (1283–1335)** b: 1283 in Rosslyn Castle, Midlothian, Scotland, d: Jan. 28, 1335, in Roslin, Midlothian, Scotland

    + **Alice de Fenton (1260–1336)** b: 1260 in Clan Fenton, East Lothian, Scotland, d: 1336 in Rosslyn

15. **William St. Clair (1313–1330)** b: 1313 in Rosslyn Castle, Mid-Lothian, Scotland, d: Aug. 25, 1330, in Teba, Malaga, Andaluc, Spain

    + **Rosabell Rosabelle (1285–?)** b: 1285 in Roslin, Midlothian, Scotland, d: Dec. in Rosslyn Castle, Midlothian, Scotland

16. **William St. Clair (1328–1358)** b: 1328 in Rosslyn Castle, Edinburgh, Midlothian, Scotland, d: 1358 in Orkney Islands, Scotland

    + **Isabella Strathern (1338–?)** b: 1338 in Strathearn, Perth, Scotland, d: Roslin, Scotland

17. **Henry Sinclair (Prince) (1355–?)** b: 1355 in Orkney Islands, Scotland

+ **Jean Haliburton (1355–1400)** b: 1355 in Dirleton, Eastlothian, Scotland, d: 1400 in Roslin, Midlothian, Scotland

18. **Henry Sinclair (1389–1422)** b: 1389 in Orkney Islands, Scotland, d: 1422 in Roslin, Midlothian, Scotland

+ **Egidia Douglas (1391–1438)** b: 1391 in Nithsdale, Dumfries-Shire, Scotland, d: 1438 in the Orkney Islands, Scotland

19. **William Sinclair (1408–1480)** b: 1408 in Caithness, Scotland, d: 1480 in Kirkcaldy, Fife, Scotland

+ **Marjory Sutherland (1416–1480)** b: 1416 in Dunbeath, Caithness, Scotland, m: Nov. 15, 1456, in Ravenscraig, Fife, Scotland, d: circa 1480 in Dunbeath Castle, Caithness, Scotland

20. **William Sinclair (1430–1513)** b: 1430 in Caithnessshire, Scotland, d: Sept. 9, 1513, in Offlodden, Branxton, Northumberland, England

+ **Christian Leslie (1432–1501)** b: 1432 in Caithnessshire, Scotland, d: March 16, 1501, in Caithness, Scotland

21. **Henry Sinclair (1459–1513)** b: 1459 in Caithnessshire, Scotland, d: Sept. 9, 1513, in Branxton, Northumberland, England

+ **Margaret Hepburn (1456–1542)** b: 1456 in Bothwell, Lanarkshire, Scotland, d: Nov. 8, 1542, in Bothwell, Lanarkshire, Scotland

22. **Lady Sinclair (1490–1505)** b: 1490 in Edinburgh, Midlothian, Scotland, d: 1505

+ **William Knox (1486–1513)** b: 1486 in Edinburgh, Midlothian, Scotland, d: 1513 in Flodden, Scotland

23. **John Knox (1505–1572)** b: 1505 in Edinburgh, Midlothian, Scotland, d: Nov. 24, 1572, in Edinburgh, Midlothian, Scotland

+ **Margaret Stewart (1540–1612)** b: 1540 in Ayrshire, Scotland, d: 1612 in Edinburgh, Midlothian, Scotland

24. **Elizabeth Knox (1570–1625)** b: 1570 in Irongray, Ayrshire, Scotland, d: 1625 in Glasgow, Lanarkshire, Scotland

+ **John Welch (1569–1622)** b: 1569 in Irongray, Ayrshire, Scotland, d: 1622 in London, England

25. **Lucy Welch (1613–1650)** b: May 20, 1613, in Jonsac, France, d: 1650 in Glasgow, Lanarkshire, Scotland

+ **James Alexander Witherspoon (1610–1649)** b: 1610 in Brighouse, Scotland, d: 1649 in Brighouse, Scotland

26. **James Witherspoon II (1640–1691)** b: 1640 in Brighouse, Scotland, d: 1691 in Scotland

+ **Helen Welch (1644–1702)** b: 1644 in Brighouse, Scotland, m: Oct. 25, 1685, in West Lothian, Scotland, d: 1702 in Newburg, Preston, West Virginia, New England

27. **Janet Witherspoon (1670–1734)** b: 1670 in Dumfries, Dumfries-shire, Scotland, d: Sept. 30, 1734, on the ship the *Good Intent* between Ireland and South Carolina,

+ **John Witherspoon (1670–1737)** b: 1670 in Begardie, Glasgow, Scotland, d: 1737 in Boggy Swamp, Williamsburg, South Carolina

28. **Janet Witherspoon (1695–1761)** b: 1695 in Begardie, Glasgow, Scotland, d: 1761 in Williamsburg, South Carolina

+ **John Fleming (1685–1750)** b: 1685 in Scotland, d: 1750 in Kingstree, Williamsburg, South Carolina

29. **Janet Fleming (1729–1770)** b: 1729 in Kilmarnock, Ayrshire, Scotland, d: 1770 in South Carolina

+ **Andrew Boyd (1725–1795)** b: 1725 in Kilmarnock, Ayrshire, Scotland, m: March 1750, d: 1795 in Jefferson, Georgia, United States

30. **John Boyd (1750–?)** b: July 29, 1750, in Kilmarnock, Ayrshire, Scotland

+ **Unknown**

31. **Hugh Boyd (1780–?)** b: 1780 in Scotland

+ **Mary MacFarlane (1780–?)** b: 1780 in Glenfinnan, Moidart,

Scotland, m: 1801 in Scotland, d: Dofdougald Macfarlane Margar, Scotland

32. **Mary Catherine Boyd (1810–1877)** b: 1810 in Nova Scotia, Canada, d: Oct. 8, 1877, New Campbellton, Cape Breton, Nova Scotia, Canada

    + **Angus McLellan (1823–1907)** b: 1823 in Inverness, Scotland, d: Sept. 22, 1907, in New Campbellton, Cape Breton, Nova Scotia, Canada

33. **Catherine McLellan (1861–1942)** b: 1861 in New Campbellton, Cape Breton, Nova Scotia, Canada, d: Dec. 15, 1942

    + **William Robert McKinnon (1855–1932)** b: 1855, d: Jan. 26, 1932

34. **William "Red" McKinnon (1892–1970)** b: Aug. 15, 1892, d: May 3, 1970, in New Campbellton, Cape Breton, Nova Scotia, Canada

    + **Elizabeth Beatrice Serroul (1895–1958)** b: 1895, d: 1958 in Little Bras D'Or, Cape Breton, Nova Scotia, Canada

35. **William David MacKinnon (1920–1955)** b: 1920, d: 1955 in Little Bras D'Or, Cape Breton, Nova Scotia, Canada

    + **Mary Penderghast (1927–2004)** b: 1927 on Boularderie Island, Cape Breton, Nova Scotia, Canada, d: 2004 in Little Bras D'Or, Cape Breton, Nova Scotia, Canada

36. **Sharon Marie MacKinnon (1954–present)** b: 1954 in Little Bras D'Or, Cape Breton, Canada

    + **William Frank Mann II (1954–present)** b: 1954 in Brantford, Ontario, Canada

Appendix 4

Outline Descendant Report from Rollo Ragnvaldsson (860–932) through William the Conqueror (1024–1087) to Sharon Marie (MacKinnon) Mann (1954–present)

1. **Rollo Rognvaldsson, first duke of Normandy (860–932)** b: 860 in Maer, Nord-Trondelag, Norway, d: 932 in Notre Dame, Rouen, Normandy, France

   + **Poppa de Valois (872–938)** b: 872 in Bayeux, Calvados, Basse-Normandie, France, d: 938 in Neustria, Normandy, France

2. **William I. Longsword Normandy (893–942)** b: July 30, 893, in Rouen, Seine-Maritime, Haute-Normandie, France, d: Dec. 17, 942, in Island Picquigny, Somme River, Normandy, France

   + **Sprote de Bretagne (911–940)** b: Aug. 28, 911 in Bretagne, France, d: 940 in Normandy, France

3. **Richard I, "the Fearless," Duke of Normandy (933–1027)** b: Aug. 28, 933, in Fecamp, Seine-Maritime, Haute-Normandie, France, d: Aug. 23, 1027, in Fecamp, Seine-Inferieure, France

   + **Gonnor de Crepon (936–1031)** b: 936 in Normandy, France, d: 1031 in Neustria, Normandy, France

4. **Richard II, "Le Bon," Duke of Normandy (963–1027)** b: 963 in Normandy, France, d: Aug. 28, 1027, in Fecamp, Seine-Inferieure, France

+ **Judith de Bretagne (982–1017)** b: 982 in Bretagne, France, d: June 16, 1017, in Normandy, France

5. **Robert I, Duke of Normandy (999–1035)** b: 999 in Normandy, France, d: July 2, 1035, in Nicea, Bithynia, Turkey

   + **Harlette de Falaise (1003–1050)** b: 1003 in Falaise, Clavados, France, d: 1050 in Mortain, Normandy, France

6. **William I, the Conqueror (1024–1087)** b: Oct. 14, 1024, in Falaise, Normandy, France, m: 1040, d: Sept. 9, 1087, in Hermentruville, Rouen, Seine-Maritime, France

   + **Maud de Flandren (1032–1083)** b: 1032 in Flanders, France, m: 1040, d: Nov. 3, 1083, in Caen, Calvados, France

7. **Adelaide of England (1062–1138)** b: 1062 in Normandy, France, d: March 8, 1138, in Marsilly, Aquitaine, France

   + **Stephen de Blois (1045–1102)** b: 1045 in Blois, Loir-et-Cher, France, d: May 19, 1102, in Ramula, Holy Land

8. **Theobald de Blois (1088–1152)** b: 1088 in Blois, Loir-et-Cher, France, d: Jan. 8, 1152, in Lagny Sur Marne, Seine et Marne, Ile de France, France

   + **Maud de Carinthia (1097–1160)** b: 1097 in Karnten, Austria, d: Dec. 13, 1160, in Fontevrault Abbey, Anjou, France

9. **Theobald de Blois (1127–1191)** b: 1127 in Blois, Loir et Cher, Orleanais Centre, France, d: 1191 in Acre, Palestine

   + **Alix Capet (1150–1195)** d: 1150 in Paris, Ile de France, France, d: 1195 in France

10. **Marguerite de Blois (1170–1231)** b: 1170 in Blois, Loir-et-Cher, France, d: May 7, 1231, in France

    + **Gautier II, Seigneur de Avesnes (1181–1245)** b: 1181 in Avesnes, Pas-de-Calais, Nord-Pas-de-Calais, France, d: June 1245 in Guise, Aisne, France

11. **Marie D. Avesnes (1200–1241)** b: 1200 in Blois, Loir et Cher, Orleanais Centre, France, d: 1241 in France

    + **Hugues Ier de Chaitillon Sur Marne (1193–1264)** b: 1193, d: 1264

12. **Jean Ier de Coligny (1239–1279)** d: 1269 in Coligny, Ain, France, d: 1279

    + **Jeanne de La Roche de Vaneau (1259–1369)** b: 1259 in Vaneau, Dsur, France, d: 1369

13. **Étienne de Coligny (1279–?)** b: 1279 in Montheiul, France

    + **Elenore de Thoire Villars (1309–?)** b: 1309 in France

14. **Jean de Coligny (1335–1397)** b: 1335 in Coligny, Ain, France, d: 1397

    + **Marie de Kerge (1335–1397)** b: 1335 in Fouvent, Haute Saine, France, d: Aug. 18, 1397

15. **Jacques de Coligny (1369–1413)** b: 1369 in Coligny, Ain, France, d: 1413 in Bresse, Italy

    + **Hugnette de La Baume (1369–1437)** b: 1369 in Coligny, Ain, France, d: 1437

16. **Guillaume de Coligny (1412–1457)** b: 1412 in Bresse, Italy, d: Aug. 24, 1457, in Chatillion-sur-Loing, France

    + **Catherine Lourdin de Saligny (1420–1449)** b: 1420 in Chatillon-sur-Loing, France, d: Aug. 21, 1449, in France

17. **Jean de Coligny (1440–1481)** b: 1440 in Chatillon-sur-Loing, France, d: 1481 in Chatillon-sur-Loing, France

    + **Eleonore de Courcelles (1447–1510)** b: 1447 in Chatillon-sur-Loing, France, d: 1510 in Chatillion-sur-Loing, France

18. **Gaspard de Coligny (1470–1522)** b: 1470 in Châtillon, Allier, Auvergne, France, d: Aug. 4, 1522, in Châtillon, Allier, Auvergne, France

    + **Marie Louise de Montmorency (1483–1541)** b: 1483 in Paris, France, d: June 12, 1541, in Chatillion-sur-Loing, France

19. **Gaspard II Dentremont de Coligny (1518–1572)** b: Feb. 16, 1518, in Chatillon-sur-Loing, France, d: Aug. 24, 1572, in Paris, France

    \+ **Jacqueline D'Entremont de Montbel (1531–1600)** b: 1531 in Isere, Savoie, Rhone-Alpes, France, d: July 6, 1600, in Milan, Milano, Lombardia, Italy

20. **Countess Beatrice D'Entremont-De Coligny (1572–1671)** b: Dec. 1572 in Champagne, Dordogne, Aquitaine, France, d: 1671 in Savoie, Rhone-Alpes, France

    \+ **Baron Claude Antoine de Mevillon Mius D'Entremont (1565–1602)** b: 1565 in Flanders, Normandy, France, m: June 17, 1600, in Savoy, France, d: 1602 in Savoyeux, Haute-Saone, Franche-Comte, France

21. **Philippe Mius D'Entremont D'Azit (1601–1700)** b: Nov. 14, 1601, in Cherbourg, Manche, Basse-Normandie, France, d: 1700 in Grand Pre, Acadia

    \+ **Madeleine Helie du Tillet (1626–1679)** b: 1626 in Cherbourg, Manche, Normandy, France, d: 1679 in Pobomcoup, Cape Sable, Acadia

22. **Phillippe Mius D'Azy (1660–1708)** b: 1660 in Pobomcoup, Cape Sable, Acadia, d: 1708 in Lehave, Acadia

    \+ **Marie Amerindienne (Mi'kmaq)** (1670–) b: circa 1670 in Acadia

23. **Madeleine Mius dit D'Azy (1712–?)** b: circa 1712 in Acadia

    \+ **Jean Baptiste Guedry (1694–1726)** b: 1694 in Port Royal, Annapolis Valley, Acadia, d: Nov. 13, 1726, in Boston, Mass. (hung for piracy)

24. **Marie Guedry (1724–1800)** b: 1724 in Port Royal, Acadia, d: 1800 in Port Royal, Annapolis Valley, Acadia

    \+ **Germain LeJeune dit Briard (1693–1735)** b: 1693 in La Have, Acadia, d: 1735 in Port Royal, Annapolis, Acadia

25. **Christopher Chrysostome LeJeune (1740–1818)** b: 1740 in Pisiquit, Acadia, d: 1818

    + **Louise Marguerite Hache Gallant (1737–1772)** b: March 3, 1737, in Rivière du Nord-Est, Ile St. Jean, Acadia m: Aug. 26, 1771, in Petit Bras d'or, Acadia d: 1772

26. **Margaret Briard Young (Mi'kmaq) (1775–1847)** b: circa 1775 in Port Royal, Annapolis Valley, Acadia, d: Jun 19, 1847, in Petit Bras d'or, Acadia

    + **François Young Lejeune (Mi'kmaq) (1772–1838)** b: 1772 in Bras d'or, Cape Breton, Nova Scotia, m: 1793, d: March 28, 1838, in Bras d'or, Cape Breton, Nova Scotia

27. **Mary Ann Young (Mi'kmaq) (1811–?)** b: Nov. 30, 1811, in Cape Breton, Nova Scotia

    + **Patrick Penderghast (1796–?)** b: 1796 in Ireland

28. **William Penderghast (1842–?)** b: Nov. 14, 1842, in Cape Breton, Nova Scotia

    + **Mary Margaret Mahan (1845–?)** b: 1845 in Nova Scotia

29. **Patrick Penderghast (1887–?)** b: Aug. 30, 1887, in Cape Breton, Nova Scotia, Canada

    + **Florence McIntyre (1893–1994)** b: 1893 on Boularderie Island, Cape Breton, Nova Scotia, d: 1994 in Cape Breton, Nova Scotia, Canada

30. **Mary Penderghast (1927–2004)** b: 1927 in Cape Breton, Nova Scotia, Canada d: 2004 in Little Bras d'or, Cape Breton, Nova Scotia, Canada

    + **William David MacKinnon (1920–1955)** b: 1920, d: 1955 in Little Bras d'or, Cape Breton, Nova Scotia, Canada

31. **Sharon Marie McKinnon (1954–present)** b: 1954 in Little Bras d'or, Cape Breton, Nova Scotia, Canada

    + **William Frank Mann II (1954–present)** b: 1954 in Brantford, Ontario, Canada

Notes

INTRODUCTION. A TIMELY TRILOGY

1. Pohl, *Prince Henry Sinclair,* 54–55.
2. Bradley, *Holy Grail Across the Atlantic,* 9–12.
3. Baigent, Leigh, and Lincoln, *Holy Blood, Holy Grail,* 117–28.
4. Sinclair, in *The Sword and the Grail,* 15–24.
5. Ibid., 28–32.
6. Hannon, *The Discoverers,* 36–40.
7. Butler and Wolter, *America,* 1–10.
8. Baigent and Leigh, *The Temple and the Lodge,* 30–33.

CHAPTER 1. D'ARTT OF THE ANTIENTS

1. MacNulty, *Freemasonry,* 26; Rutherford, *Celtic Lore,* 146.
2. Baigent, Leigh, and Lincoln, *Holy Blood, Holy Grail,* 60–93. But also see Barber, *The Trial of the Templars;* and Upton-Ward, *The Rule of the Templars,* 73–84, for more detail concerning the beliefs and philosophy behind the Order before and after their bitter downfall in 1307 and subsequent return from the shadows in 1314.
3. MacKenzie, *The Royal Masonic Cyclopaedia,* 374–79, 715.
4. Frazer, *The Golden Bough,* 161–67.
5. MacKenzie, *The Royal Masonic Cyclopedia,* 193–95.
6. Butler, *Butler's Lives of the Saints,* 15–16.
7. Trento, *The Search for Lost America,* 190–93.
8. Wilson, *The Columbus Myth,* 16–19.

9. Pohl, *Prince Henry Sinclair,* 178–79. Most of the background story concerning Prince Henry Sinclair originates from Pohl's book, although some references to Glooscap have been independently checked using later sources such as Bradley's *Holy Grail Across the Atlantic;* Kay Hill's *Glooscap and His Magic;* and Andrew Sinclair's *The Sword and the Grail.*
10. Charroux, *Treasures of the World,* 31–42.
11. Bradley, *Holy Grail Across the Atlantic,* 45–79.

CHAPTER 2.
A GOD FOR ALL SEASONS

1. Baigent, Leigh, and Lincoln, *Holy Blood, Holy Grail,* 250.
2. Ashe, *Mythology of the British Isles,* 244–49.
3. Frazer, *The Golden Bough,* 161–67.
4. Sinclair, *The Sword and the Grail,* 119–27. But also see Pohl, *Prince Henry Sinclair,* 7–25.
5. Gimbutas, *The Language of the Goddess,* 265–70.
6. Chadwick, *The Celts,* 17–27.
7. Baigent, Leigh, and Lincoln, *Holy Blood, Holy Grail,* 455–70.
8. Charroux, *Treasures of the World,* 23–24.

CHAPTER 3.
OUT OF THE WILDERNESS

1. Fanthorpe and Fanthorpe, *Rennes-le-Château,* 17, 40–41.
2. Baigent, Leigh, and Lincoln, *Holy Blood, Holy Grail,* 250–51.
3. Cantor and Rabinowitz, *The Encyclopaedia of the Middle Ages,* 87.
4. Baigent, Leigh, and Lincoln, *Holy Blood, Holy Grail,* 209–44.
5. Deveau and Ross, *The Acadians of Nova Scotia,* 62–63; Bradley, *Holy Grail Across the Atlantic,* 144–46.
6. Birch, *History of Scottish Seals,* 17.
7. Baigent, Lincoln, and Leigh, *Holy Blood, Holy Grail,* 133, 285–89.
8. Butler, *Butler's Lives of the Saints,* 15–16.
9. Mann, *The Knights Templar in the New World,* 93–96.
10. Fanthorpe and Fanthorpe, *Rennes-le-Château,* 92–96.

CHAPTER 4. OLD HABITS NEVER DIE

1. Chilvers, "David Teniers the Younger," *The Oxford Dictionary of Art and Artists,* 316–24.
2. Liedtke, *Flemish Paintings in the Metropolitan Museum of Art,* 17–42.
3. Van der Kiste, *Emperor Francis Joseph,* 2–4.
4. Michael Sussman, *Der Dom zu Magdeburg,* 23–40.
5. Wallace-Hadrill, *The Long-Haired Kings,* 47–55.
6. Butler, *Butler's Lives of the Saints,* 115–17.
7. Ibid., 118.
8. Ibid., 236–39.
9. Lincoln, *The Holy Place,* 54, 71; along with Gardner, *Bloodline of the Holy Grail,* 287–302.
10. Mann, *The Lives of the Popes in the Early Middle Ages,* vol. 4, *The Popes in the Days of Feudal Anarchy,* 891–999.
11. Turner, "Anicius Manlius Severinus Boethius," *The Catholic Encyclopedia,* vol. 2, 873–905.
12. Patai, *The Jewish Alchemists,* 60–91.
13. Smith, *The Business of Alchemy,* 25–57.

CHAPTER 5. CASTLES IN THE SKY

1. Baigent, Leigh, and Lincoln, *Holy Blood, Holy Grail,* 113–14.
2. Henry Lincoln, *The Holy Place,* 16–22.
3. Baigent, Leigh, and Lincoln, *Holy Blood, Holy Grail,* 2.
4. Ibid., 4.
5. Ibid., 30–31.
6. Butler, *Butler's Lives of the Saints,* 37.
7. Ibid., 35.
8. Ibid., 272–73.
9. Ibid., 274.
10 Ibid., 45–53.
11. Sinclair, *The Sword and the Grail,* 89–107.
12. Hapgood, *Maps of the Ancient Sea Kings,* 1–5.
13. Miller, *The Golden Thread of Time,* 76–86.
14. MacNulty, *Freemasonry,* 16.

CHAPTER 6.
HAPPY TRAILS TO YOU

1. Thomas, *Rivers of Gold,* 15–27.
2. Kamen, *Empire,* 56–60.
3. Thomas, *Rivers of Gold,* 105–17.
4. Cutright, *A History of the Lewis and Clark Expedition,* 58.
5. Kamen, *Empire,* 80–82.
6. Thomas, *Rivers of Gold,* 143–45.
7. Arrington, *Brigham Young,* 1–35.
8. Bradley, *Swords at Sunset,* 72–77.
9. Arrington, *Brigham Young,* 44–45.
10. Forsberg, *Equal Rites,* 17–18.
11. Ibid., 27–30.
12. Buerger, *The Mysteries of Godliness,* 201–3.
13. Arrington, *Brigham Young,* 158.
14. Buerger, *The Mysteries of Godliness,* 48–50.

CHAPTER 7.
NORTH BY NORTHWEST

1. David Bates, *William the Conqueror,* 173–84.
2. Pulsiano and Wolf, *Medieval Scandinavia: An Encyclopedia,* 205–8.
3. Taken from Donald Wiedman's website: https://lavalhallalujah.wordpress.com.
4. Anderson, *The Orkneyinga Saga.*
5. Phillips, *The Crusades: An Encyclopaedia,* 207–15.
6. Wolter, *The Hooked X,* 1–15.
7. Eisler, *The Red Man's Bones,* 16–22.
8. Ibid., 27–28.
9. Flandreau, *The Vérendrye Overland Quest of the Pacific,* 145–50.

CHAPTER 8.
THE ENTRANCE TO THE LODGE

1. MacNulty, *Freemasonry,* 17.
2. MacKenzie, *The Royal Masonic Cyclopedia,* 84–85.

3. MacNulty, *Freemasonry,* 5.
4. Blanchard, *Eminence,* 86–94.
5. Ibid., 6.
6. Farquhar, *A Treasure of Royal Scandals,* 89.
7. Stevenson, *The Origins of Freemasonry,* 38–44.
8. Farquhar, *A Treasure of Royal Scandals,* 140–48.
9. Longford, *Wellington,* 45
10. Glozier, *Scottish Soldiers in France in the Reign of the Sun King,* 234–37.
11. Robertson, *The Life of Sir Robert Moray,* 8–14.
12. Ibid., 22–24.
13. Ibid., 76–80.
14. Purcell, *Saint Anthony and His Times,* 44–45.
15. Ibid., 116–17.
16. Duby, *France in the Middle Ages 987–1460,* 134–39.
17. Butler, *Butler's Lives of the Saints,* 67–71.
18. Purcell, *Saint Anthony and His Times,* 121–22.
19. Kauffman, "The Sulpician Presence," 677–95.
20. Ibid., 642–43.
21. Ibid., 624–23.
22. Ibid., 584–89.

CHAPTER 9. THE LAST OF THE BLOODLINE GUARDIANS

1. Partner, *The Murdered Magicians, the Templars and Their Myth,* 3–4.
2. The *Toronto Star,* November 13, 2014.
3. Vorres, *The Last Grand Duchess,* 115–20.
4. Solomon, *King James VI and I Political Writings,* 452–53.
5. Hoffmann, *The Mide'wiwin or "Grand Medicine Society" of the Ojibwa,* 143–65.
6. Pritzker, *A Native American Encyclopedia,* 324–28.
7. Holand, *An English Scientist in America 130 Years before Columbus,* 205–19.
8. Parks Canada, *A Directory of Designations of National Historic Significance of Canada,* 111–22.

CHAPTER 10. X MARKS THE SPOT

1. Pentecost, *The Parables of Jesus,* 10.
2. Walters, *Albert Gallatin,* 320–24.
3. Ibid., 74–85.
4. Hasel, "Israel in the Merneptah Stele," 54–56.
5. Gaston, *Historical Issues in the Book of Daniel,* 103–7.
6. Baer, *A History of the Jews in Christian Spain,* 34–57.

Bibliography

Adams, Dickinson, ed. *The Papers of Thomas Jefferson: Jefferson's Extracts from the Gospels.* Princeton, N.J.: Princeton University Press, 1983.

Addison, Charles G. *The History of the Knights Templar.* Kempton, Ill.: Adventures Unlimited Press, 1997. First published in London, 1842.

Aitchison, Leslie. *A History of Metals,* 2 vols. New York: John Wiley & Sons, 1960.

Allen, John Logan. *Passage through the Garden: Lewis and Clark and the Image of the American Northwest.* Urbana: University of Illinois Press, 1975.

Allmand, Christopher. *The Hundred Years' War, England & France at War c. 1300–1450.* Cambridge, UK: Cambridge University Press, 1988.

Alofsin, Anthony. *Frank Lloyd Wright: The Lost Years, 1910–1922: A Study of Influence.* Chicago: University of Chicago Press, 1993.

Ambrose, Stephen E. *Lewis & Clark: Voyage of Discovery.* Washington, D.C.: National Geographic Society, 1998.

Andersen, Hans Christian. *The Complete Fairy Tales and Stories.* Translated by E. C. Haugaard. New York: Anchor Press/Doubleday, 1974.

Anderson, Joseph, ed. *The Orkneyinga Saga.* Translated by Jon A. Hjaltalin and Gilbert Goudie. Edinburgh: Edmonston and Douglas, 1873.

Anderson, Rasmus, ed. *The Norse Discovery of America.* London: Norruena Society, 1906.

Andrews, Richard, and Paul Schellenberger. *The Tomb of God: The Body of Jesus and the Solution to a 2,000-Year-Old Mystery.* London: Little, Brown and Co., 1996.

Arrington, Leonard J. *Brigham Young: American Moses.* New York: Alfred A. Knopf, 1985.

Ashe, Geoffrey. *King Arthur's Avalon.* Revised edition. London: Collins, 1966.

———, ed. *The Quest for Arthur's Britain.* London: Granada Publishing Limited, 1968.

———, ed. *The Quest for America.* New York: Praeger Publishers, 1971.

———. *Kings and Queens of Early Britain.* London: Methuen, 1982.

———. *Avalonian Quest.* London: Methuen, 1986.

———. *Land to the West.* London: Methuen, 1986.

———. *Mythology of the British Isles.* London: Methuen, 1990.

Authwaite, Leonard. *Unrolling the Map.* New York: Reynal and Hitchcock, 1935.

Baer, Yitzhak. *A History of the Jews in Christian Spain.* Philadelphia: Jewish Publication Society, 1993.

Baigent, Michael, Richard Leigh, and Henry Lincoln. *The Holy Blood and the Holy Grail.* London: Jonathan Cape, 1982. Published in the United States under the title *Holy Blood, Holy Grail.* New York: Random House, 2004.

———. *The Messianic Legacy.* London: Jonathan Cape, 1986.

Baigent Michael, and Richard Leigh. *The Temple and the Lodge.* London: Jonathan Cape, 1989.

———. *The Dead Sea Scrolls Deception.* London: Corgi Books, 1991.

———. *The Elixir and the Stone.* London: Viking, 1997.

Baker, Daniel B., ed. *Explorers and Discoverers of the World.* Washington, D.C.: Gale Research, Inc., 1993.

Ball, Martin J., and James Fife, eds. *The Celtic Languages.* London: Routledge, 2002.

Barber, Malcolm. *The Trial of the Templars.* Cambridge, UK: Cambridge University Press, 1991.

Barbour, Philip. *The Three Worlds of Captain John Smith.* Boston: Houghton Mifflin Company, 1964.

Bates, David. *William the Conqueror.* Stroud, UK: Tempus, 2004.

Bayley, Harold. *The Lost Language of Symbolism.* Totowa, N.J.: Rowman and Littlefield, 1974. First published by William and Norgate, 1912.

Begg, Ean C. M. *The Cult of the Black Virgin.* London: Arkana, 1985.

Bennett, John G. *Gurdjieff, the Making of a New World.* London: Turnstone Books, 1973.

Bergin, Joseph. *Cardinal Richelieu: Power and the Pursuit of Wealth.* New Haven, Conn.: Yale University Press, 1985.

Bernard of Clairvaux. *On the Song of Songs.* Translated by Kilian Walsh, OCSO. Kalamazoo, Mich.: Cistercian Publications, Inc., 1983.

Bernier, Francine. *The Templars' Legacy in Montreal, the New Jerusalem.* Amsterdam: Frontier Publishing, 2001.

Billon, Frederick L. *Annals of St. Louis: The French and Spanish Period.* St. Louis, Mo.: Nixon-Jones Printing Co., 1886.

Birch, Walter de Gray. *History of Scottish Seals from the Eleventh to the Seventeenth Century.* London: Nabu Press, 2011.

Bird, Will R. *Off-Trail in Nova Scotia.* Toronto: The Ryerson Press, 1956.

Birks, Walter, and Robert A. Gilbert. *The Treasure of Montsegur.* London: Thorsons Publishing Group, London, 1987.

Blake, Peter. *The Master Builders: Le Corbusier, Mies Van Der Rohe, Frank Lloyd Wright.* New York: Alfred A. Knopf, 1960.

Blanchard, Jean-Vincent. *Eminence: Cardinal Richelieu and the Rise of France.* New York: Walker Books, 2013.

Bohlander, Richard E., ed. *World Explorers and Discoverers.* New York: Macmillan Publishing Company, 1992.

Bolon, Carol R., Robert S. Nelson, and Linda Seidel. *The Nature of Frank Lloyd Wright.* Chicago: University of Chicago Press, 1988.

Bord, Janet, and Colin Bord. *Mysterious Britain.* London: Granada Publishing Limited, 1974.

Bowra, Cecile Maurice. *From Virgil to Milton.* New York: St. Martin's Press, 1962.

Boudet, Henri. *La vraie langue celtique et le cromleck de Rennes-les-Bains.* Nice, France: Belisane, 1984. Facsimile of 1886 original.

Bowen, Catherine Drinker. *Francis Bacon: The Temper of a Man.* Boston: Little, Brown and Company, 1963.

Boyajian, James C. *Portuguese Trade in Asia under the Habsburgs, 1580–1640.* Baltimore, Md.: John Hopkins University Press, 1993.

Bradley, Michael. *Holy Grail Across the Atlantic.* Toronto: Hounslow Press, 1988.

———. *The Columbus Conspiracy.* Toronto: Hounslow Press, 1991.

———. *Grail Knights of North America.* Toronto: Hounslow Press, 1998.

———. *Swords at Sunset.* Toronto: Manor House Publishing, Inc., 2015.

Brooks, H. Allen. *The Prairie School: Frank Lloyd Wright and His Midwest Contemporaries.* Toronto: University of Toronto Press, 1972.

Brown, Dan. *Angels & Demons.* New York: Atria, 2000.

———. *The Da Vinci Code.* New York: Doubleday, 2003.

Brydon, Robert. *A History of the Guilds, the Masons, and the Rosy Cross.* Roslin, Midlothian, Scotland: Rosslyn Chapel Trust, Rosslyn Chapel, 1994.

Budge, E. A. Wallis. *The Egyptian Book of the Dead.* New York: Dover Publications, 1967.

———. *The Gods of the Egyptians,* vols. 1 and 2. New York: Dover Publications, 1969.

———. *Osiris and the Egyptian Resurrection,* vols. 1 and 2. New York: Dover Publications, 1973.

———. *An Egyptian Hieroglyphic Dictionary,* vols. 1 and 2. New York: Dover Publications, 1978.

Buerger, David John. *The Mysteries of Godliness: A History of Mormon Temple Worship.* Salt Lake City, Utah: Signature Books, 2002.

Burstein, Dan, ed. *Secrets of the Code: The Unauthorized Guide to the Mysteries behind the Da Vinci Code.* New York: CDS Books, 2004.

Butler, Alan, *The Goddess, the Grail & the Lodge.* Winchester, UK: O-Books, 2004.

Butler, Alan, and Stephen Dafoe. *The Templar Continuum.* Belleville, Canada: Templar Books, 1999.

Butler, Alan, and Janet Wolter. *America: Nation of the Goddess.* Rochester, Vt.: Destiny Books, 2015.

Butler, Alban. *Butler's Lives of the Saints.* Edited by Michael Walsh. San Francisco: HarperCollins, 1991.

Camille, Michael. *Gothic Art: Glorious Visions.* New York: Harry N. Abrams, 1996.

Campbell, Joseph. *Myths to Live By.* New York: Arkana, 1971.

Canada Department of Mines and Resources. *Geology and Economic Minerals of Canada.* Ottawa, 1947.

Canada Department of Tourism and Culture. *Nova Scotia Travel Guide.* Halifax, NS, 1993.

Cantor, Norman F., and Harold Rabinowitz, eds. *The Encyclopaedia of the Middle Ages.* New York: Viking Press, 1999.

Carlson, Suzanne. "Loose threads in a Tapestry of Stone: The Architecture of the Newport Tower." *NEARA Journal* 35, no. 1 (summer 2001).

Cary, Max, and Eric Herbert Warmington. *The Ancient Explorers.* London: Methuen and Company, 1929.

Catholic Bible Press. *The Holy Bible Containing the Old and New Testaments, New Revised Standard Version* (Catholic edition). Wichita, Kansas, 1993.

Catlin, George. *Letters and Notes on the Manners, Customs, and Conditions of North American Indians,* 2 vols. London: self-published, 1844. Reprint: Dover Publications, 1973.

Cavendish, Richard, ed. *Encyclopedia of the Unexplained.* London: Arkana, 1989.

Chabert, Joseph Bernard Marquis de. *Carte Reduite des Costes de l'Acadie, de l'Isle Royale, et de la Partie Meridionale de l'Isle de Terre-Neuve. Dressee sur les Observations faites par Ordre du Roi en 1750 et 1751. Paris: Voyage fait par ordre du Roi en 1750 et 1751, dans L'Amerique Septentrionale.* Paris: Del'Imprinerie Royale, 1753.

Chadwick, Nora. *The Celts.* Harmondsworth, UK: Pelican Books, 1971.

Chandler, David G. *The Campaigns of Napoleon.* New York: Macmillan, 1966.

Champlain, Samuel de. *The Works of Samuel de Champlain,* 6 vols. & folio. Edited by H. P. Biggar. Toronto: University of Toronto Press, 1971.

Chaplin, Dorothea. *Mythological Bonds between East and West.* Copenhagen: Einar Munksgaard, 1938.

Charpentier, Louis. *The Mysteries of the Chartres Cathedral.* Translated by Ronald Fraser and Janette Jackson. Northhamptonshire, UK: Thorsons Publishers Ltd., 1972.

Charroux, Robert. *Treasures of the World.* London: Frederick Muller Limited, 1966.

Chatelaine, Maurice. *Our Ancestors Came from Outer Space.* London: Pan Books, 1980.

Chilvers, Ian, ed. "David Teniers the Younger." *The Oxford Dictionary of Art and Artists.* Oxford: Oxford University Press, 2009.

Choyce, Leslie. *Nova Scotia: Shaped by the Sea.* New York: Viking/Penguin, 1996.

Churton, Tobias. *The Golden Builders: Alchemists, Rosicrucians and the First Free Masons.* Lichfield, UK: Signal Publishing, 2002.

Clark, Andrew Hill. *Acadia: The Geography of Early Nova Scotia to 1760.* Madison: The University of Wisconsin Press, 1968.

Clark, Kenneth. *Leonardo Da Vinci.* London: Penguin Books, 1959.

Clarke, George Frederick. *Expulsion of the Acadians: The True Story.* Fredericton, N.B.: Brunswick Press, 1980.

Clayton, Peter A. *Chronicle of the Pharaohs.* London: Thames & Hudson, 1994.

Clinton, William Jefferson. *My Life.* New York: Random House, 2004.

Coldstream, Nicola. *Medieval Architecture.* Oxford, UK: Oxford University Press, 2002.

Collins, Andrew. *Gateway to Atlantis: The Search for the Source of a Lost Civilization.* London: Headline Book Publishing, 2000.

Coppens, Philip. *The Stone Puzzle of Rosslyn Chapel.* Amsterdam: Frontiers Publishing and Adventures Unlimited Press, 2004.

Costain, Thomas B. *The White and the Gold: The French Regime in Canada.* New York: Doubleday & Co., 1954.

Creighton, Helen. *Bluenose Ghosts.* Toronto: McGraw-Hill Ryerson, 1957.

———. *Bluenose Magic.* Toronto: McGraw-Hill Ryerson, 1968.

———. *Folklore of Lunenburg County, Nova Scotia.* Toronto: McGraw-Hill Ryerson, 1976.

Crooker, William S. *The Oak Island Quest.* Windsor, NS: Lancelot Press, 1978.

———. *Oak Island Gold.* Halifax, NS: Nimbus Publishing, 1993.

Dabney, Virginius. *Virginia: The New Dominion.* Garden City, New York: Doubleday & Sons, 1971.

Cutright, Paul Russell. *A History of the Lewis and Clark Expedition.* Norman: University of Oklahoma Press, 2000.

Daraul, Arkon. *Secret Societies, Yesterday and Today.* London: Frederick Muller Limited, 1961.

Davidson, Robert. *The Old Testament.* London: Hodder & Stoughton, 1964.

Delaney, Frank. *The Celts.* London: Grafton Books, 1989.

Delpar, Helen, ed. *The Discoverers: An Encyclopedia of Explorers and Exploration.* New York: McGraw-Hill Company, 1980.

Deveau, Alphonse, and Sally Ross. *The Acadians of Nova Scotia, Past and Present.* Halifax, NS: Nimbus Publishing, 1992.

Devoto, Bernard. ed. *The Journals of Lewis & Clark.* Boston: Mariner Books, 1997.

Dingledine, Raymond C., Lena Barksdale, and Marion Belt Nesbitt. *Virginia's History.* New York: Scribner's, 1956.

Diefendorf, Barbara B. *Beneath the Cross. Catholics and Huguenots in Sixteenth-Century Paris.* Oxford: Oxford University Press, 1991.

Dobbs, Betty J. T. *The Foundations of Newton's Alchemy.* Cambridge, UK: Cambridge University Press, 1975.

Dodge, Stephen C. *Christopher Columbus and the First Voyages to the New World.* New York: Chelsea House Publishers, 1991.

Dor-Ner, Zvi, and William Scheller. *Columbus and the Age of Discovery.* New York: William Morrow and Company, Inc., 1991.

Doyle, Sir Arthur Conan. *Sherlock Holmes: The Complete Novels and Stories,* vols. I and II. Toronto and New York: Bantam Books, 1986.

Drosnin, Michael. *The Bible Code.* New York: Simon and Schuster, 1997.

Duby, Georges. *France in the Middle Ages 987–1460: From Hugh Capet to Joan of Arc.* Oxford, UK: Wiley-Blackwell, 1993.

Duncan, Dayton and Ken Burns. *Lewis & Clark: The Journey of the Corps of Discovery.* New York: Alfred A. Knopf, 1997.

Duriez, Colin. *The C. S. Lewis Handbook.* Essex, UK: Monarch Publishers, 1990.

Eco, Umberto. *Foucault's Pendulum.* London: Picador, 1990.

———. *The Name of the Rose.* London: Picador, 1984.

Eisler, Benita. *The Red Man's Bones: George Catlin, Artist and Showman.* New York: W. W. Norton, 2013.

Erdeswick, Sampson. *A Survey of Staffordshire.* London: J. B. Nichols, 1984.

Eschenbach, Wolfram von. *Parzival.* Translated by Helen M. Mustard and Charles E. Passage. New York: Vintage, 1961.

Etlin, Richard A. *Frank Lloyd Wright and Le Corbusier: The Romantic Legacy.* Manchester, England: Manchester University Press, 1994.

Elting, John R. *Amateurs, To Arms! A Military History of the War of 1812.* Chapel Hill, N.C.: Algonquin, 1991.

Evans, James. *The History & Practice of Ancient Astronomy.* Oxford, UK: Oxford University Press, 1998.

Everett, Felicity, and Struan Reed. *The USBORNE Book of Explorers, From Columbus to Armstrong.* London: USBORNE Publishing, 1991.

Fabricius, Johannes. *Alchemy.* Northamshire, UK: The Aquarian Press, 1976.

Fairbairn, James. *Crests of the Families of Great Britain and Ireland.* Revised by Laurence Butters. Rutland, Vt.: Charles E. Tuttle Co., 1968.

Fanthorpe, Patricia, and Lionel Fanthorpe. *The Holy Grail Revealed: The Mysterious Treasure of Rennes-le-Château.* North Hollywood, Calif.: Newcastle Press, 1982.

———. *The Oak Island Mystery: The Secret of the World's Greatest Treasure Hunt.* Toronto: Hounslow Press, 1995.

———. *Rennes-le-Château.* Middlesex, UK: Bellevue Books, 1991.

Farmer, David H. *The Oxford Dictionary of Saints.* Oxford, UK: Oxford University Press, 1982.

Farquhar, Michael. *A Treasury of Royal Scandals.* New York: Penguin Books, 2001.

Fath, Edward Arthur. *The Elements of Astronomy.* New York: McGraw-Hill, 1934.

Faust, Patricia L., ed. *Historical Times Illustrated Encyclopedia of the Civil War.* New York: Harper & Row, 1986.

Fell, Barry, *America B.C.* New York: Pocket Books, 1979.

———. *Bronze Age America.* Toronto: Little, Brown, 1982.

Feugere, Pierre, Louis Saint Maxent, and Gaston de Koker. *Le Serpent Rouge.* SRES Vérités Anciennes, 1981.

Finnan, Mark. *The First Nova Scotian.* Halifax, NS: Formac, 1997.

Flandreau, Grace. *The Vérendrye Overland Quest of the Pacific.* Seattle, Wash.: Shorey Bookstore, 1971.

Fleming, Thomas J. *The Louisiana Purchase.* Hoboken, N.J.: John Wiley and Sons, 2003.

Foote, Henry Wilder. *Thomas Jefferson: Champion of Religious Freedom, Advocate of Christian Morals.* Boston: Beacon Press, 1947.

Ford, Paul., ed. *The Works of Thomas Jefferson,* vol. 10. New York: G. P. Putnam's Sons, 1905.

Forsberg, Clyde R. *Equal Rites: The Book of Mormon, Masonry, Gender, and American Culture.* New York: Columbia University Press, 2003.

Franklyn, Julian, and John Tanner. *An Encyclopaedic Dictionary of Heraldry.* Oxford, UK: Pergamon, 1969.

Fraser, Mary L. *Folklore of Nova Scotia.* Antigonish, NS: Formac, 1928.

Frazer, James G. *The Golden Bough.* New York: Macmillan, 1923.

———. *Magic and Religion.* London: Watts, 1944.

Frith, Henry. *The Romance of Navigation: A Brief Record of Maritime Discovery.* London: Ward, Lock, and Bowden, 1893.

Furneaux, Rupert. *The Money Pit Mystery.* New York: Fontana/Collins, 1976.

Ganong, William Francis. *Crucial Maps.* Toronto: University of Toronto Press, 1964.

Gardner, Lawrence. *Bloodline of the Holy Grail: The Hidden Lineage of Jesus Revealed.* Shaftesbury, UK: Element, 1996.

———. *Genesis of the Grail Kings.* London: Bantam, 1999.

———. *Lost Secrets of the Scared Ark.* London: Element, 2003.

Gaston, Thomas E. *Historical Issues in the Book of Daniel.* Oxford, UK: Taanath Shiloh, 2009.

Gaustad, Edwin. *Sworn on the Altar of God: A Religious Biography of Thomas Jefferson.* Grand Rapids, Mich.: William B. Eerdman's Publishing Co., 1996

Geoffrey of Monmouth. *History of the Kings of Britain.* Edited and translated by Lewis Thorpe. Harmondsworth, UK: Penguin, 1966.

Gilbert, Adrian. *The New Jerusalem.* New York: Bantam, 2002.

Gill, Brendan. *Many Masks: A Life of Frank Lloyd Wright.* New York: Putnam, 1987.

Gimbutas, Maria A. *The Language of the Goddess.* San Francisco: HarperSanFrancisco, 1991.

Giraud, Victor. *Bibliographie de Taine.* Paris: Picard 1902.

Glozier, Matthew. *Scottish Soldiers in France in the Reign of the Sun King.* Leiden, Holland: Brill Academic Publishing, 2004.

Goode, J. Paul. *Goode's World Atlas.* New York: Rand McNally & Co., 1991.

Goodrich, Norma Lorre. *King Arthur.* Danbury, Conn.: Franklin Watts, 1986.

Gordon, Cyrus L. *Before Columbus.* New York: Crown Publishers, 1971.

Goss, John. *The Mapping of North America.* Secancus, N.J.: The Wellfleet Press, 1990.

Gould, Robert F. *Gould's History of Freemasonry.* London: Caxton, 1933.

Grant, Michael. *Myths of the Greeks and Romans.* New York: New American Library, 1962.

Graves, Robert. *The White Goddess: A Historical Grammar of Poetic Myth.* New York: Farnar, Straus and Giroux. 1948.

———. *The White Goddess.* London: Faber and Faber, 1961.

Graves, Robert, and Raphael Patai. *Hebrew Myths: The Book of Genesis.* Garden City, N.J.: Doubleday and Co. Inc. 1964.

Greenberg, Joseph H. *Indo-European and Its Closest Relatives: The Eurasiatic Family,* vol. 2, Lexicon. Stanford, Calif.: Stanford University Press, 2002.

Grigsby, John. *Warriors of the Wasteland.* London: Watkins Publishing, 2002.

Guirdham, Arthur. *Catharism: The Medieval Resurgence of Primitive Christianity.* Paris: St. Helier, 1969.

———. *The Cathars and Reincarnation.* London: Neville Spearman, 1976.

Gurney, Gene. *Kingdoms of Europe.* New York: Crown Publishers, 1982.

Haagensen, Erling, and Henry Lincoln. *The Templars' Secret Island: The Knights, the Priest and the Treasure.* Gloucestershire, UK: The Windrush Press, 2000.

Haliburton, Thomas Chandler. *History of Nova Scotia,* 2 vols. Halifax, NS: Joseph Howe, 1829.

Hall, Manly P. *The Lost Keys of Freemasonry.* Richmond, Va.: Macoy Publishing and Masonic Supply, 1976.

Hancock, Graham. *The Sign and the Seal: The Quest for the Lost Ark of the Covenant.* Toronto: Doubleday Canada, 1992.

Hannon, Leslie F. *The Discoverers.* Toronto: McClelland & Stewart, 1971.

Harden, Donald. *The Phoenicians: Ancient People and Places.* London: Thames & Hudson, 1963.

Hart, Gerald E. *Fall of New France: 1755–1760.* Montreal: W. Drysdale, 1888.

Hanna, Leslie F. *The Discoverers.* New York: Random House, 1983.

Hannay, James. *The History of Acadia (1605–1763).* St. John, NB: J. & A. McMillan, 1879.

Hapgood, Charles. *Maps of the Ancient Sea Kings.* Philadelphia: Chilton Books, 1968.

Harris, Reginald V. *The Oak Island Mystery.* Toronto: The Ryerson Press, 1967.

Hasel, Michael G. "Israel in the Merneptah Stele." *Bulletin of the American Schools of Oriental Research,* 296 (1994): 54–56.

Hawkins, Gerald S. *Stonehenge Decoded.* New York: Doubleday, 1965.

Heindenreich, Conrad E. *Cartographica: Explorations and Mapping of Samuel de Champlain, 1603–1632.* Toronto: University of Toronto Press, 1976.

Heinlein, Robert. *Beyond this Horizon.* 1942. New York: Baen Books, 2001.

Hickey, Donald. *The War of 1812: A Forgotten Conflict.* Urbana, Ill.: University of Chicago Press, 1989.

Higenbottam, Frank. *Codes and Ciphers.* London: English Universities Press, 1973.

Hill, Kay. *Glooscap and His Magic: Legends of the Wabanaki Indians.* Toronto: McClelland and Stewart, 1963.

———. *More Glooscap Stories: Legends of the Wabanaki Indians.* Toronto: McClelland and Stewart, 1988.

Hitchcock, Henry Russell. *In the Nature of Materials: The Buildings of Frank Lloyd Wright: 1887–1941.* New York: Da Capo Press, 1975.

Hitsman, J. Mackay. *The Incredible War of 1812.* Toronto: University of Toronto Press, 1973.

Hodges, Henry. *Technology in the Ancient World.* London: Penguin, 1970.

Hoffmann, Walter James. *The Mide'wiwin or "Grand Medicine Society" of the Ojibwa.* Whitefish, Mont.: Kessinger Publishing, 2010.

Holand, Hjalmar R. *An English Scientist in America 130 Years before Columbus.* Ephraim, Wisc.: Self-published, 1932.

Holroyd, Stuart, and Neil Powell. *Mysteries of Magic.* London: Bloomsbury Books, 1991.

Holt, Elizabeth Gilmore, ed. *Literary Sources of Art History: An Anthology of Texts from Theophilus to Goethe.* Princeton, N.J.: Princeton University Press, 1947.

Hope, Joan. *A Castle in Nova Scotia.* Kitchener, Canada: Kitchener Printing, 1997.

Horne, Alex. *King Solomon's Temple in the Masonic Tradition.* London: Aquarian Press, 1971.

Horsman, Reginald. *The Causes of the War of 1812.* New York: A. S. Barnes, 1962.

Hutchinson, William. *The Spirit of Masonry.* New York: The Antiquarian Press, 1987.

Hyde, William. *Encyclopedia of the History of St. Louis,* 4 vols. New York: Howard Conard, 1899.

Israel, Gerald, and Jacques Lebar. *When Jerusalem Burned.* New York: William Morrow, 1973.

Izzo, Alberto, and Camillo Gubitosi. *Frank Lloyd Wright: Three-quarters of a Century of Drawings.* New York: Horizon Press, 1981.

Jackson, Donald, ed. *Letters of the Lewis and Clark Expedition with Related Documents,* 2 vols. Urbana: University of Illinois Press, 1978.

Jackson, Kenneth. *Language and History in Early Britain: A Chronological Survey of the Brittonic Languages, 1st to 12th century A.D.* Edinburgh: University Press, 1971.

"Jesus, Mary Magdalene Married, Researchers Say." *Toronto Star,* November 13, 2014.

Josephus, Flavius. *The Complete Works.* Translated by William Whiston. New York: Thomas Nelson Publishers, 1999.

Jung, Carl G. *Collected Works.* London: Routledge; Princeton, N.J.: Princeton University Press. Volumes include *Archetypes and the Collective Unconscious,* 1959; *The Interpretation of Nature and the Psyche,* 1955; *Mysterium*

Coniunctionis, 1963; *Psychology and Alchemy,* 1953; *The Structure and Dynamics of the Psyche,* 1969.

———. *Memories, Dreams, Reflections.* London: Fontana, 1972.

———. *Synchronicity.* London: Routledge, 1972.

Kamen, Henry. *Empire: How Spain Became a World Power, 1492–1763.* New York: Harper Perennial, 2004.

Kauffman, Christopher J. "The Sulpician Presence." *The Catholic Historical Review,* vol. 75, no. 4 (October, 1989): 677–95.

Kerr, Donald Gordon Grady. *Historical Atlas of Canada,* 3rd revised. Toronto: Thomas Nelson & Sons Limited, 1975.

Kostof, Spiro. *A History of Architecture.* New York: Oxford University Press, 1995.

Kukla, Jon. *A Wilderness So Immense: The Louisiana Purchase and the Destiny of America.* New York: Alfred A. Knopf, 2003.

Knight, Christopher, and Robert Lomas. *Uriel's Machine: The Prehistoric Technology that survived the Flood.* London: Century, 1999.

———. *The Book of Hiram: Freemasonry, Venus and the Secret Key to the Life of Jesus.* London: Century, 2003.

Knight, Gareth. *The Secret Tradition in Arthurian Legend.* Wellingborough, UK: Aquarian Press, 1983.

Krupp, Edwin C., ed. *In Search of Ancient Astronomies.* New York: Penguin Books, 1984.

Laidler, Keith. *The Head of God: The Lost Treasure of the Templars.* London: Weidenfeld & Nicolson, 1998.

Laseau, Paul, and James Tice. *Frank Lloyd Wright: Between Principle and Form.* New York: Van Nostrand Reinhold, 1992.

Law, Vivien. *The History of Linguistics in Europe: From Plato to 1600.* Cambridge, UK: Cambridge University Press, 2002.

Lescarbot, Marc. *History of New France,* vol. 2. Translated by W. L. Grant. Toronto: The Champlain Society, 1911.

Lethbridge, Thomas Charles. *Herdsmen and Hermits: Celtic Seafarers in the Northern Seas.* Cambridge, UK: Bowes and Bowes, 1950.

Levi, Eliphas. *Transcendental Magic: Its Doctrine and Ritual.* London: Rider, 1964.

———. *History of Magic.* London: Rider, 1968 reprint; New York: Weiser, 1969.

———. *The Key of the Mysteries.* London: Rider, 1968 reprint; Hackensack, N.J.: Weiser; and New York: Weiser, 1970, paperback.

Liedtke, Walter A. *Flemish Paintings in the Metropolitan Museum of Art.* New Haven, Conn.: Yale University Press, 1984.

Lincoln, Henry. *The Holy Place.* London: Jonathan Cape, 1991.

Linklater, Eric. *The Royal House of Scotland.* London: Macmillan Books, 1970.

Lomas, Robert. *The Invisible College.* London: Headline Book Publishing, 2002.

Longfellow, Henry Wadsworth. *Evangeline.* New York: Pelican, 1999.

Longford, Elizabeth. *Wellington: The Years of the Sword.* London: Weidenfeld and Nicolson, 1969.

Loomis, Roger Sherman. *Celtic Myth and Arthurian Romance.* New York: Haskell House, 1967.

———. *Studies in Medieval Literature: A Memorial Collection of Essays.* New York: B. Franklin, 1970.

———. *The Grail: From Celtic Myth to Christian Symbol.* Princeton, N.J.: Princeton University Press, 1991.

MacCulloch, John Arnold. *The Religion of the Ancient Celts.* Edinburgh: T. & T. Clark, 1911.

Mackey, Albert G. *An Encyclopedia of Freemasonry and Its Kindred Sciences.* Chicago, Ill.: The Masonic History Company, 1921.

———. *The Symbolism of Freemasonry.* Chicago, Ill.: The Masonic History Company, 1926.

Mackey, James P., ed. *An Introduction to Celtic Christianity.* Edinburgh: T. & T Clark, 1989.

MacKenzie, Kenneth. *The Royal Masonic Cyclopaedia.* Wellingborough, UK: The Aquarian Press, 1987.

MacNulty, W. Kirk. *Freemasonry: A Journey through Ritual and Symbol.* London: Thames & Hudson, 1991.

Mallery, Arlington. *Lost America.* Washington, D.C.: Overlook, 1951.

Mallery, Arlington, and Mary Harrison. *The Rediscovery of Lost America.* New York: E. P. Dutton, 1979.

Mann, Horace K. *The Lives of the Popes in the Early Middle Ages: The Popes in the Days of Feudal Anarchy,* vol. 4. New York: Robert Appleton Company, 1910.

Mann, William F. *The Knights Templar in the New World: How Prince Henry Sinclair Brought the Grail to Acadia.* Rochester, Vt.: Destiny Books, 2004.

Markale, Jean. *The Templar Treasure at Gisors.* Rochester, Vt.: Inner Traditions, 2003.

———. *The Church of Mary Magdalene.* Rochester, Vt.: Inner Traditions, 2004.

Mathers, Samuel Liddell MacGregor. *The Key of Solomon the King.* London: George Redway, 1888.

———. *The Kabbalah Unveiled.* New York: Weiser, 1970.

Mathews, John. *The Household of the Grail.* Wellingborough, UK: The Aquarian Press, 1990.

Matthews, Caitlin. *The Elements of the Celtic Tradition.* Shaftesbury, UK: Element Books, 1989.

Maunder, Edward Walter. *The Astronomy of the Bible.* London: Hodder and Stoughton, 1909.

McClusky, Stephen C. *Astronomies and Cultures in Early Medieval Europe.* Cambridge, UK: Cambridge University Press, 1998.

McFarlane, Peter, and Wayne Haimila. *Ancient Land, Ancient Sky.* Toronto: Alfred A. Knopf, 1999.

McGhee, Robert. *Canada Rediscovered.* Ottawa: Canadian Museum of Civilization, 1991.

Meiss, Millard. *French Painting in the Time of Jean de Berry: The Limbourgs and Their Contemporaries.* New York: George Braziller, 1974.

Melanson, Margaret C. *The Melanson Story: Acadian Family, Acadian Times.* Moncton, NB: Self-published, 2003.

Menzies, Gavin. *1421: The Year China Discovered America.* London: Bantam Press, 2002.

Merot, Alain. *Nicolas Poussin.* New York: Abbeville Press Publishers, 1990.

Miller, Crichton E. M. *The Golden Thread of Time.* Warwickshire, UK: Pendulum, 2001.

Milton, John. *Paradise Lost.* Edited by John Leonard. New York: Penguin Classic Series, 2003.

Moncrieffe, Iain. *The Highland Clans.* New York: Clarkson N. Potter, 1967.

Morrison, N. Brysson. *Mary Queen of Scots.* New York: Vanguard Press, 1960.

Morison, Samuel Eliot. *The Great Explorers: The European Discovery of America.* New York: Oxford University Press, 1978.

Moscati, Sabatino, ed. *The Phoenicians.* New York: Abbeville Press, 1988.

Moulton, Gary E., ed. *The Journals of the Lewis & Clark Expedition.* Lincoln: University of Nebraska Press, 1988.

———. ed. *The Journals of the Lewis & Clark Expedition,* 13 vols. Lincoln: University of Nebraska Press, 2002.

Mouni, Sadhu. *The Tarot.* London: Allen & Unwin, 1962. Hackensack, N.J.: Wehman, 1962.

Mowat, Farley. *West Viking.* Toronto: McClelland and Stewart Limited, 1965.

Munro, Robert William. *Highland Clans and Tartans.* London: Peerage Books, 1987.

Murray, Margaret A. *The Divine King in England.* London: Faber, 1954.

Nutt, Alfred Trubner. *Studies on the Legend of the Holy Grail.* New York: Cooper Square Publishers, 1965.

O'Connor, D'Arcy. *The Money Pit.* New York: Coward, McCann & Geoghegan, 1976.

———. *The Big Dig.* New York: Ballantyne, 1988.

Ondantjie, Christopher. *The Prime Ministers of Canada.* Toronto: The Pagunin Corporation Ltd., 1985.

Ovason, David. *The Secret Architecture of Our Nation's Capital: The Masons and the Building of Washington, D.C.* New York: HarperCollins, 2000.

Parkman, Francis. *Pioneers of France in the New World.* New York: Library of America, 1983. First published in 1885.

Parks Canada. *A Directory of Designations of National Historic Significance of Canada: Earthlodge Village National Historic Site of Canada.* www.pc.gc.ca (accessed January 29. 2016).

Partner, Peter. *The Murdered Magicians, the Templars and Their Myths.* Oxford, UK: Oxford University Press, 1982.

Parton, James. *Life and Times of Benjamin Franklin,* 2 vols. Boston: Houghton Mifflin Co., 1897.

Patai, Raphael. *The Jewish Alchemists: A History and Source Book.* Princeton, N.J.: Princeton University Press, 1994.

Penhallow, William S. "Astronomical Alignments in the Newport Tower." *NEARA,* March 21, 2004.

Pentecost, J. Dwight. *The Parables of Jesus: Lessons in Life from the Master Teacher.* Grand Rapids, Mich.: Kregel Publications, 1998.

Philip, James A. *Pythagoras and Early Pythagoreanism.* Toronto: University of Toronto Press, 1966.

Phillips, Graham. *The Templars and the Ark of the Covenant.* Rochester, Vt.: Bear & Company, 2004.

Phillips, Jonathan. *The Crusades: An Encyclopaedia.* Santa Barbara, Calif.: ABC-Clio, 2006.

Picknett, Lynn. *Mary Magdalene.* New York: Carroll & Graf, 2003.

Picknett, Lynn, and Clive Prince. *The Templar Revelation.* New York: Touchstone, 1997.

Platt, Colin. *The Atlas of Medieval Man.* London: Peerage Books, 1979.

Poe, Edgar Allan. *The Complete Tales and Poems of Edgar Allan Poe.* Toronto: Vintage, 1975.

Pohl, Frederick J. *The Lost Discovery.* New York: W. W. Norton, 1952.

———. *Prince Henry Sinclair: His Expedition to the New World in 1398.* New York: Clarkson N. Potter, 1974.

———. *Americus Vespucci, Pilot Major.* New York: Octagon Books, 1996.

Pope, Marvin H. *Song of Songs.* Anchor Bible Series. Garden City, New York: Doubleday & Co., Inc., 1983.

Pritzker, Barry M. *A Native American Encyclopedia: History, Culture, and Peoples.* Oxford, UK: Oxford University Press, 2000.

Pulsiano, Phillip, and Kirsten Wolf. *Medieval Scandinavia: An Encyclopedia.* New York: Garland, 1993.

Purcell, Mary. *Saint Anthony and His Times.* Dublin: M. H. Gill & Son, Ltd., 1960.

Quarrell, Charles. *Buried Treasure.* London: MacDonald & Evans Ltd., 1955.

Ralls, Karen, and Ian Robertson. *The Quest for the Celtic Key.* Edinburgh: Luath Press, 2002.

Ramsay, Raymond H. *No Longer on the Map.* New York: The Viking Press, 1972.

Rand, Silas Tertius. *Legends of the Micmacs.* New York: Longmans, Green & Co., 1894.

Regardie, Israel. *The Golden Dawn,* 3rd ed. St. Paul, Minn.: Llewellyn, 1970.

———. *Roll Away the Stone.* St. Paul, Minn.: Llewellyn, 1968.

———. *The Tree of Life,* 2nd ed. New York: Weiser, 1969.

Reuter, Timothy, ed. *New Cambridge Medieval History,* vols. I–III. Cambridge, UK: Cambridge University Press, 1999.

Rhonda, James P. *Lewis and Clark among the Indians.* Lincoln: University of Nebraska Press, 1988

Rhys, John. *Celtic Folklore: Welsh and Manx,* 2 vols. Oxford, UK: Clarendon Press, 1901.

Robertson, Alexander. *The Life of Sir Robert Moray.* Whitefish, Mont.: Kessinger Publishing, LLC, 2010.

Robertson, John Ross. *History of Freemasonry in Canada,* 2 vols. Toronto: Grand Lodge Masonic Archives, 1899.

Robinson, John J. *Born in Blood.* New York: M. Evans and Company, 1989.

Roche, O. I. A., ed. *The Jeffersonian Bible.* New York: Clarkson N. Potter, Inc., 1964.

Ross, Anne. *The Pagan Celts.* Totowa, N.J.: Barnes & Noble, 1986.

Rutherford, Ward. *Celtic Lore.* London: The Aquarian Press, 1993.

Ryan, Peter. *Time Detectives: Explorers and Mapmakers.* London: Belitha Press, 1989.

Sadler, Henry. *Masonic Facts and Fictions, Aquarian Press.* Wellingborough, UK: The Aquarian Press, 1985.

Sanford, Charles B. *The Religious Life of Thomas Jefferson.* Charlottesville: University Press of Virginia, 1984.

Schick, Edwin A. *Revelation, the Last Book of the Bible.* Philadelphia: Fortress Press, 1977.

Schwartz, Lilian. "Leonardo's Mona Lisa." *Art and Antiques.* January 1987.

Scott, Martin. *Medieval Europe.* London: Longmans, Green and Co. Ltd., 1967.

Secrest, Meryle. *Frank Lloyd Wright: A Biography.* Chicago: University of Chicago Press, 1998.

Sède, Gérard de. *L'Or de Rennes.* Paris: J'ai Lu, 1967.

Sedgwick, Henry D. *The House of Guise.* Indianapolis, Ind.: Bobbs-Merrill Co., 1938.

Silberer, Herbert. *Hidden Symbolism of Alchemy and the Occult Arts.* New York: Moffat, Yard & Co., 1917.

Sinclair, Andrew. *The Sword and the Grail.* New York: Crown, 1992.

———. *The Discovery of the Grail.* London: Century, 1998.

———. *The Secret Scroll.* London: Birlinn, 2002.

Smith, John. *A Map of Virginia. With a Description of the Countrey, the Commodities, People, Government and Religion.* Oxford, UK: Joseph Barnes, drawn in 1608, originally published 1612.

———. *The Complete Works of Captain John Smith.* Edited by Philip Barbour. Chapel Hill: University of North Carolina Press, 1986.

Smith, Pamela H. *The Business of Alchemy: Science and Culture in the Holy Roman Empire.* Princeton, N.J.: Princeton University Press, 1994.

Smollett, Tobias, ed. *The Works of Voltaire, a Contemporary Version.* Translated by William F. Fleming. New York: E. R. DuMont, 1901.

Smyth, Albert Henry, ed. *The Writings of Benjamin Franklin,* 10 vols. New York: The Macmillan Co., 1905–6.

Solomon, H. S. *King James VI and I Political Writings.* Cambridge, England: Cambridge University Press, 1995.

Sora, Steven. *Secret Societies of America's Elite.* Rochester, Vt.: Destiny Books, 2003.

———. *The Lost Colony of the Templars.* Rochester, Vt.: Destiny Books, 2004.

Stearns, Peter N., ed. *The Encyclopedia of World History; Ancient, Medieval, and Modern, Chronologically Arranged,* sixth edition. Boston: Houghton Miffilin Company, 2001.

Spicer, Stanley T. *Glooscap Legends.* Hantsport, NS: Lancelot, 1991.

Starbird, Margaret. *The Women with the Alabaster Jar.* Santa Fe, N. Mex.: Bear & Company, 1993.

Starkey, Dinah. *Scholastic Atlas of Exploration.* New York: HarperCollins Publishers Ltd., 1993.

Steiner, Rudolph J. *Mysticism at the Dawn of the Modern Age.* New York: Steinerbooks, 1960.

Stevenson, David. *The Origins of Freemasonry.* Cambridge, UK: Cambridge University Press, 1990.

Stoddard, Whitney S. *Art and Architecture in Medieval France: Medieval Architecture, Sculpture, Stained Glass, Manuscripts: The Art of the Church Treasuries.* Boulder, Colo.: Westview Press, 1966.

Stokstad, Marilyn. *Medieval Art.* Boulder, Colo.: Westview Press, 1986.

Sugden, John. *Tecumseh: A Life.* New York: Holt, 1997.

Sumption, Johathan. *The Albigensian Crusade.* London: Faber and Faber, 1978.

Sussman, Michael. *Der Dom zu Magdeburg.* Munich, Germany: DKV Kunstführer Nr. 415/2, 1997.

Tafel, Edgar. *Years with Frank Lloyd Wright.* Gloucester, Mass.: Peter Smith Inc., 1985.

Taylor, F. S. *The Alchemists.* New York: Schuman, 1949.

Temple, Robert, K. G. *The Sirius Mystery.* London: Futura, 1976.

Tennyson, Lord Alfred. *The Holy Grail and Other Poems.* London: Stanan and Co., 1870.

———. *Idylls of the Kings.* London: Penguin, 1961.

The Hours of Jeanne d'Evreux: Queen of France at the Cloisters. New York: The Metropolitan Museum of Art, 1957.

Thiering, Barbara. *Jesus & the Riddle of the Dead Sea Scrolls.* Toronto: Doubleday, 1992.

Thomas, Charles. *Celtic Britain: Ancient Peoples and Places.* London: Thames and Hudson, 1986.

Thomas, Hugh. *Rivers of Gold: The Rise of the Spanish Empire, from Columbus to Magellan.* New York: Random House, 2005.

Thomas, Lowell. *The Untold Story of Exploration.* New York: Dodd, Mead and Company, 1935.

Thomas, Marcel. *The Golden Age: Manuscript Painting at the Time of Jean, Duke of Berry.* New York: George Braziller, 1979.

Thwaites, Reuben Gold, ed. *The Jesuit Relations and Allied Documents,* vols. 1–71. Cleveland, Ohio: The Burrows Brothers Company, 18.

Tompkins, Peter. *Secrets of the Great Pyramids.* New York: Harper & Row, 1971.

Trefethen, Joseph M. *Geology for Engineers.* Princeton, N.J.: D. Van Nostrand, 1949.

Trento, Salvatore Michael. *The Search for Lost America.* Chicago: Contemporary Books, 1978.

Turner, William. "Anicius Manlius Severinus Boethius." *The Catholic Encyclopedia,* vol. 2. Rome, Italy: Vatican Press, 1913.

Upton-Ward, J. M. *The Rule of the Templars.* Woodbridge, UK: Boydell Press, 1997.

Van der Kiste, John. *Emperor Francis Joseph: Life, Death and the Fall of the Habsburg Empire.* Gloucester, UK: Sutton Publishers, 2005.

Vérendrye, Pierre Gaultier de Varennes de La. *Journal and Letters of Pierre Gaultier de Varennes de La Vérendrye and His Sons.* Edited by Lawrence J. Burpee. Toronto: The Champlain Society, 1927.

Vermaseren, Maarten Jozef. *Mithras, the Secret God.* London: Chatto, 1959; New York: Barnes & Noble, 1963.

Vermes, Geza. *The Dead Sea Scrolls in English.* Harmondsworth, UK: Pelican Books, 1962.

Verne, Jules. *Journey to the Centre of the Earth.* London: Penguin, 1965.

Voragine, Jacobus de. *The Golden Legend: Readings on the Saints,* vols. 1 and 2. Translated by William Granger Ryan. Princeton, N.J.: University of Princeton Press, 1993.

Vorres, Ian. *The Last Grand Duchess.* Toronto: Key Porter Books, 2001.

Waite, Arthur E. *The Hidden Church of the Holy Grail.* London: Rebman Limited, 1909.

———. *The New Encyclopaedia of Freemasonry.* New York: Weathervane Books, 1970.

Waldener, Carl. *Encyclopedia of Native American Tribes.* New York: Facts on File Publishing, 1988.

Wallace-Hadrill, J. M. *The Long-Haired Kings and Other Studies in Frankish History.* London: Methuen and Co., Ltd., 1962.

Wallace-Murphy, Tim. *Rex Deus.* Shaftesbury, UK: Element, 2000.

Wallace-Murphy, Tim, and Marilyn Hopkins. *Rosslyn, Guardian of the Secrets of the Holy Grail.* Shaftesbury, UK: Element, 1999.

———. *Templars in America.* York Beach, Maine: Weiser, 2004.

Walters, Raymond. *Albert Gallatin: Jeffersonian Financier and Diplomat.* Pittsburg, Penn.: University of Pittsburg Press, 1957.

Ward, John Sebastian Marlow. *Freemasonry and the Ancient Gods.* London: Baskerville, 1926.

Ward, Adolphus William, and Alfred Rayney Waller, eds. *The Cambridge History of English and American Literature,* 18 vols. Cambridge, UK: Cambridge University Press, 1907–21.

Warhart, Sidney, ed. *Francis Bacon: A Selection of His Works.* Toronto: MacMillan of Canada, 1965.

West, John Anthony. *Serpent in the Sky.* Wheaton, Ill.: Theosophical Publishing House, 1983.

Williamson, Hugh Ross. *The Arrow and the Sword.* London: Faber, 1947; New York: Fernhill, 1955.

Williamson, John. *The Oak King, the Holly King, and the Unicorn.* New York: Harper & Row, 1986.

Willis, Peter. *Dom Paul Bellot: Architect and Monk.* Newcastle upon Tyne, UK: Elysium Press Publishers, 1996.

Wilson, Colin. *The Occult.* London: Hodder, 1971; New York: Random House, 1971.

Wilson, Ian. *The Columbus Myth.* Toronto: Simon and Schuster, 1991.

Wilson, John A. *The Culture of Ancient Egypt.* Chicago: The University of Chicago Press, 1951.

Wind, Edgar. *Pagan Mysteries in the Renaissance.* London: Peregrine, 1967.

Wolff, Hans, ed. *America. Early Maps of the New World.* Munich: Prestel, 1992.

Wolkstein, Diane. *Inanna: Queen of Heaven and Earth, Her Stories and Hymns from Sumer.* New York: Harper and Row. 1983.

Wolter, Scott. *The Hooked X: The Key to the Secret History of North America.* St. Cloud, Minn.: North Star Press of St. Cloud, 2009.

Wood, David. *Genisis.* Turnbridge Wells, UK: The Baton Press, 1985.

Wright, Frank Lloyd. *Frank Lloyd Wright: An Autobiography.* London: Quartet Books, 1943.

Wolf, John B. *Louis XIV.* New York: Norton, 1968.

Wroth, Lawrence C. ed., *The Voyages of Giovanni da Verrazzano, 1524–1528.* New Haven, Conn.: Yale University Press, 1970.

Yates, Frances Amelia. *Giordano Bruno and the Hermetic Tradition.* London: Routledge, 1964; Chicago: University of Chicago Press, 1964: New York: Random House, 1969.

———. *The Art of Memory.* London: Routledge, 1966.

———. *The Rosicrucian Enlightenment.* London: Routledge, 1972.

Young, George. *Ancient Peoples and Modern Ghosts.* Queensland, NS: Self-published, 1980.

Index

Page numbers in *italics* indicate illustrations.

About the Author

William F. Mann has a long and distinguished Masonic career, due in part to his family's multigenerational involvement in Freemasonry. He is currently a member of Oakville Lodge #400, Ancient Free & Accepted Masons of Canada, White Oaks Chapter No. 104, Royal Arch Masons of Canada, Salem Council #9, Royal and Select Master Masons of Ontario, Macassa Bay Lodge No. 9 of Royal Ark Mariners, and Sir William York Rite College #57. He is also a 32nd-degree Scottish Rite Mason, being a member of Murton Lodge of Perfection, Hamilton Sovereign Chapter of Rose Croix, and Moore Sovereign Consistory, Hamilton, Ontario, Canada. William is also a Past Preceptor of Godfrey de Bouillon Preceptory #3, Hamilton District No 2, of the United Religious and Military Orders of St. John's of Jerusalem, Palestine, Rhodes and Malta, of the Order of the Temple Knights Templar of Canada. Right Eminent Knight William F. Mann is also a Grand Council Officer of the Sovereign Great Priory of Canada. William was recently presented with the further honor of being appointed Grand Archivist and Grand Historian for the Knights Templar of Canada. And, finally, William has most recently been distinguished as a member of Harington Conclave, No. 16 of the Masonic and Military Order of Knights of the Red Cross of Constantine, K.H.S. and St. John the Evangelist.

He is the author of three controversial books, all of which have been published by Destiny Books, a division of Inner Traditions • Bear & Company: *The Knights Templar in the New World: How Henry Sinclair Brought the Grail to Acadia*; *The Templar Meridians: The Secret*

Mapping of the New World; and now his third book in the trilogy, *Templar Sanctuaries in North America: Sacred Bloodlines and Secret Treasures.* The author has appeared on several radio programs, including Whitley Streiber's *Dreamland* and *Red Ice Radio, Sweden,* and on a number of television documentaries. Most recently he appeared on the hit H2 series *America Unearthed* alongside his friend and host, Scott Wolter.

A registered professional planner, forester, landscape architect, and environmental management consultant, William has more than thirty-five years of combined public/private experience in the fields of municipal governance and is a member of the Algonquins of Greater Golden Lake, which is one of thirteen nations constituting the Algonquins of Ontario. This group is presently engaged in a major land claims settlement with the Province of Ontario and the Government of Canada that encompasses Canada's capital city, Ottawa, extending throughout the Ottawa River valley and Algonquin Park. William has also been initiated into the Old Mide'win—the Grand Medicine Society—and is a highly respected elder within the First Nations. He lives in Milton, Ontario, Canada, with his wife, Sharon Marie, and their two sons, Will and Thomas. In what little spare time that he has, William is an award-winning artist, specializing in watercolors and acrylics, relying heavily on a lifelong love for art and art history.

BOOKS OF RELATED INTEREST

The Knights Templar in the New World
How Henry Sinclair Brought the Grail to Acadia
by William F. Mann

The Templar Meridians
The Secret Mapping of the New World
by William F. Mann

The Secrets of Masonic Washington
A Guidebook to Signs, Symbols, and
Ceremonies at the Origin of America's Capital
by James Wasserman

The Templars and the Assassins
The Militia of Heaven
by James Wasserman

An Illustrated History of the Knights Templar
by James Wasserman

The Lost Treasure of the Knights Templar
Solving the Oak Island Mystery
by Steven Sora

America: Nation of the Goddess
The Venus Families and the Founding of the United States
by Alan Butler and Janet Wolter
Foreword by Scott F. Wolter

Founding Fathers, Secret Societies
Freemasons, Illuminati, Rosicrucians, and
the Decoding of the Great Seal
by Robert Hieronimus, Ph.D.
with Laura Cortner